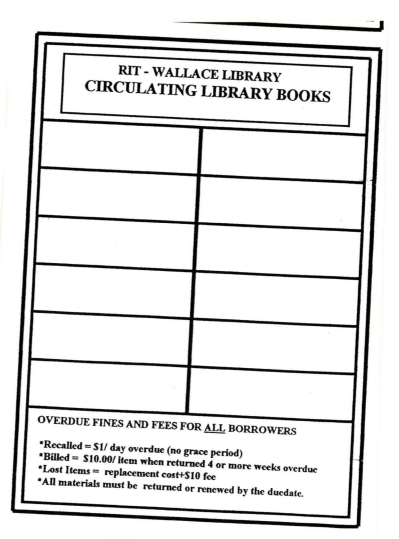

RIT - WALLACE LIBRARY
CIRCULATING LIBRARY BOOKS

OVERDUE FINES AND FEES FOR <u>ALL</u> BORROWERS

*Recalled = $1/ day overdue (no grace period)
*Billed = $10.00/ item when returned 4 or more weeks overdue
*Lost Items = replacement cost+$10 fee
*All materials must be returned or renewed by the duedate.

JOHN STUART MILL

ON LIBERTY AND CONTROL

JOHN STUART MILL
ON LIBERTY AND CONTROL

JOSEPH HAMBURGER

PRINCETON UNIVERSITY PRESS

PRINCETON, NEW JERSEY

Library of Congress Cataloging-in-Publication Data

Hamburger, Joseph, 1922—

John Stuart Mill on liberty and control / Joseph Hamburger.

p. cm.

Includes index.

ISBN 0-691-00717-9 (hardcover : alk. paper)

1. Mill, John Stuart, 1806–1873 On liberty. 2. Liberty.

I. Title. JC223.M75H35 1999

323.44—dc21   99-13520   CIP

This book has been composed in Sabon

The paper used in this publication meets the minimum requirements
of ANSI / NISO Z39.48-1992 (R 1997) (*Permanence of Paper*)

http://pup.princeton.edu

Printed in the United States of America

1   3   5   7   9   10   8   6   4   2

For LH, AH, JH, PH, & BZ

CONTENTS

EDITOR'S NOTE

LATE in the afternoon of Thursday, August 21, 1997, my father, Joseph Hamburger, told his secretary, Mrs. Ruth Muessig, that during the following week he would bring her the final revisions for this book. He was in good spirits and seemed as vigorous as ever. Shortly thereafter, he went to Lighthouse Point, where he had often gone with my mother, Lotte, to walk near the entrance to the harbor. Although he completed his walk, he did not return to finish the last revisions for this book or to pursue his other, numerous projects.

Reluctant to modify arguments or to resolve issues my father had left for further consideration, I have altered his manuscript only where clearly guided by his notes or by necessity. Fortunately, he left a manuscript that was almost ready for publication, and therefore his book can now be published in all substantial detail as he had planned it.

—P.A.H.

PREFACE

IT is commonly believed that Mill unequivocally favored individual liberty. In *On Liberty* he eloquently proclaimed the value of complete liberty of speech and, with few limitations, conduct; and with passion and sensitivity he upheld individuality as an ideal character. All this is commonplace, and it would seem to be absurd to challenge it. Yet it is my purpose to do just that. While Mill did value liberty and individuality, there is evidence—a great deal of it, I believe—that he also advocated placing quite a few limitations on liberty and many encroachments on individuality. It will be shown that, far from being libertarian and permissive, Mill advocated the introduction of inhibitions, moral restraints, and social pressures. He therefore can be seen as having argued for a combination of liberty and control. In providing for both, he was not self-contradictory. On the contrary, it will be shown that the coexistence of liberty and control reflected a coherent strategy for moral reform that occupied him when *On Liberty* was written and during the last decades of his life.

To suggest that Mill advocated both liberty and control is to go against the current of opinion that dominates Mill scholarship. There is a tradition of interpretation—what Mill would have called "received opinion"—that emphasizes Mill's unequivocal advocacy of liberty and his wish to expand it almost without limit. The title of his book encourages this view, and even more, his fine rhetoric and passionate conviction silence questions that might arise from examination of all the arguments he actually puts forward. The consensus about Mill's advocacy of liberty is not confined to the scholarly literature, for his views have become part of our intellectual culture, and as such they are regarded as particularly significant for being linked to the defense of such core values in the modern ethos as liberty, privacy, and individuality. In support of these values Mill is cited as an authority by editorial writers, publicists, and even judges.

In the interpretation offered here it is assumed that *On Liberty* should be read in light of Mill's overarching purpose of bringing about moral reform, or, as he called it, moral regeneration. It will be shown that all the arguments in *On Liberty*, including those that appear to contradict one another, are part of a coherent perspective that reflects his strategy for reaching this goal. To establish the connections between *On Liberty* and Mill's broader strategy, it will be necessary to consider, along with the text of *On Liberty*, Mill's intentions in writing the essay, insofar as he revealed them; his other, mainly contemporary, writings, in which he addressed issues that also arise in the essay; and the intellectual and broadly social context of Mill's work, which in part he reflected but mainly criticized and sought to alter.

In contrast to this approach, in much of the commentary, *On Liberty* is analyzed as if Mill's only purpose in writing it was to establish a principle of liberty that specifies the many circumstances in which free choice is permitted and the few in which it might be limited. Those adopting this approach search the essay for Mill's rationale for liberty, and they evaluate the soundness of his arguments for it. They isolate the text from its historical context and often from most of Mill's other writings, and analyze it as if Mill wrote to develop a rationale for individual liberty that would contribute to the development of twentieth-century liberalism. Thus they search his essay for indications that he had a conception of an autonomous individual existing in a realm of privacy which should be protected from intrusions by government and especially by society. Eager to appropriate Mill's authority for their own views, these authors seek to reconcile Mill's arguments with their own. To do this, they interpret and reinterpret Mill's words and arguments to find in them a coherent defense of the conception of liberty these commentators wish to uphold. Mill's varied and ambiguous uses of such words as coercion, interest, and harm are tortuously interpreted to make Mill's position compatible with twentieth-century conceptions of liberty, and Mill's arguments are recast so they are congenial to twentieth-century theories. An example of this is the assumption that Mill used the category "other-regarding," in spite of the fact (as pointed out by Richard Wollheim) that Mill never used this phrase.[1] One could compile a long bibliography of books and articles that explain what Mill meant by "other-regarding" actions. Another, even more egregious example is the presentation of Mill's position, not as put forth by him, but "reconstructed" and "improved," so that Mill is shown as one who would have agreed with the defense of liberty formulated by the commentators.[2] Those who interpret Mill in these ways ignore Mill's

---

[1] Richard Wollheim, "John Stuart Mill and Isaiah Berlin: The Ends of Life and the Preliminaries of Morality," in *The Idea of Freedom: Essays in Honor of Isaiah Berlin*, ed. Alan Ryan (Oxford: Oxford University Press, 1979), 268.

[2] Fred R. Berger, *Happiness, Justice, and Freedom: The Moral and Political Philosophy of John Stuart Mill* (Berkeley: University of California Press, 1984), 63, 296, passim. Recognizing that " 'autonomy' is not a term [Mill] employs himself," Gray candidly acknowledges that he uses "terms and distinctions that would have seemed foreign to Mill." Gray states that it is "inevitable that my interpretation must be in the nature of a frankly conjectural reconstruction." John Gray, "Mill's Conception of Happiness and the Theory of Individuality," in *J. S. Mill's On Liberty in Focus*, ed. John Gray and G. W. Smith (London: Routledge, 1991), 191. Similarly Waldron acknowledges that he is engaged in a "reconstruction" of *On Liberty*. J. Waldron, "Mill and the Value of Moral Distress," *Political Studies* (1987): 421. Arneson acknowledges that the term "autonomy" does not appear in *On Liberty*, yet constructs an argument that Mill "flirts with the concept and that it is autonomy he values most highly—that Mill really meant, not freedom, but autonomy." R. J. Arneson, "Mill

intentions and the connections, as he explained them, between *On Liberty* and his proposals for reform of society and its morality.

The same authors not only attribute to Mill words and arguments he did not use, they also turn a blind eye to arguments he did use which are incompatible with their preconceptions. They hold that for conduct which did not harm others, Mill forbade the use of opinion as a source of pressure on an individual; and that Mill defended the liberty of such an individual to do as he wished without taking into account the opinions of others. Yet there is evidence—in *On Liberty* as well as in contemporary writings—that Mill allowed the very opposite and even recommended directing social pressure and shaming against those who were selfish or in other ways morally unworthy.

The interpretation introduced here has implications for Mill's position as a leading representative of liberal thought. The protection of a private sphere against intrusion from government and society is usually regarded as an essential ingredient of liberalism, and it is often assumed that Mill, in distinguishing between self-regarding conduct and other kinds, was using the public-private distinction without labeling it as such. It will be argued, however, that this explanation of Mill's distinction is not viable, as he allows encroachments, intrusions, and penalties for conduct on both sides of it; and that, therefore, in his conception of self-regarding conduct, there are not the protections provided to a private sphere in liberal thought. In fact, Mill allowed and even recommended directing social pressure and shaming against those exhibiting disapproved conduct, and thus the frequently made claim that Mill's conception of self-regarding conduct represented a realm of inviolable privacy must be questioned.

Liberalism is often associated with moral neutrality, but Mill did not seek such neutrality. The intrusions he welcomed in the private sphere reflected a theory of morals that allowed him to justify penalties for a wide range of conduct. Accordingly, it is impossible to attribute to him either the moral neutrality or the moral pluralism often associated with liberalism.

Another hallmark of liberalism—individual rights—is explicitly disclaimed by Mill, and while it might be argued that in his account of individuality claims are made which are tantamount to the assertion of an inherent right, it will be shown that since he urged penalties for many

---

versus Paternalism," *Ethics* 90 (1979-80): 476, 478, and passim. Wollheim imaginatively extends Mill's argument "in the general direction in which he was facing." He offers a "line of argument that I have attributed to Mill. . . . An element of this is speculation, and it all goes beyond what Mill asserts." But "on reflection, Mill would have accepted it." Richard Wollheim, "John Stuart Mill and the Limits of State Action," *Social Research* 40 (1973): 20–21. Dworkin attributes to Mill notions difficult to locate in his writings, eg., liberty as independence and thus dignity. Ronald Dworkin, *Taking Rights Seriously* (London: Duck-

kinds of self-expression, his claim on behalf of individuality was anything but absolute. Indeed, Mill's regime was so censorious, and the range of conduct that was discouraged and forbidden was so great, it must be considered whether Mill was as great an enthusiast for liberty and toleration as generally believed.

Mill's uncertain status as a spokesman for liberalism is further indicated by his mixed relationship to the Enlightenment. As empiricist, Benthamite, religious skeptic, opponent of church and aristocracy, Mill found Enlightenment thought congenial. This was evident in his eagerness to further the erosion of existing customs, mores, and religion, and this part of his outlook was reflected in his telling us that he modeled himself on the *philosophes*.[3] Yet he also shared certain goals of the counter-Enlightenment—the establishment of moral authority, discipline, stability, and social cohesion. This was reflected in his admiration for critics of the Enlightenment, notably Coleridge, who was portrayed by Mill as representing a nineteenth-century reaction to the previous century and as one who understood moral and social needs to which Bentham, representing the eighteenth century, was blind. Mill's sympathy with the counter-Enlightenment was also evident in his attraction to Comte's ideas, many of which he retained even after he criticized some of them and quarreled with Comte. With Comte, he continued to believe that ideas and goals associated with the Enlightenment and the French Revolution were useful but insufficient. While these were important for undermining existing customs, beliefs, and institutions, including Christianity and the church, an additional step had to be taken to establish substitutes for what suffered destruction. New institutions, moral beliefs, and authorities were to be introduced, for such things were necessary for wholesome individuals and a wholesome regime. The view that Mill was a spokesman for liberalism relies on half this outlook—the part that includes his Benthamism, his opposition to Christianity, and his belief that custom is despotic; but it ignores the other part, which called for moral authority, individual restraint, and social control. His belief in the importance of these things has serious implications for his status as a spokesman for liberalism.

Criticisms of recent liberal thought have raised questions about its conception of individual liberty in relation to law, custom, mores, opinions, and religious belief, that is, to ways some liberty may be reduced in order to accommodate these other aspects of social life. These issues are also addressed in Mill's work—both in *On Liberty* and in other writings. But there is more than one way of interpreting how Mill thought of such

---

worth, 1977), 263.
  [3] *Autobiography, Collected Works of John Stuart Mill*, ed. John M. Robson (Toronto: University of Toronto Press, 1963–1991) [hereafter *CW*], *1*, 111.

relationships. Most commentators hold that Mill consistently sought to diminish custom, opinion, and religion so that the realm of liberty could be enhanced. In this book I argue that, while Mill expected temporary, tactical advantage from dismantling the particular social controls that existed in his time, he regarded social controls of some kind as necessary and desirable even though they allowed for less than full and expansive liberty. As a consequence, far from being compatible with modern liberal thought, *On Liberty* should be regarded as being implicitly critical of it. My purpose is to elucidate Mill's perspective—in *On Liberty* and generally—and to show that a careful reading of *On Liberty* and consideration of his other writings on related subjects do not support arguments about liberty made by many who enlist Mill in their cause.

Questioning Mill's credentials as a liberal is made difficult, for it runs counter to what is widely believed. Mill ruminated about this problem generally in his diary where he took note of the obstacles to "altering an opinion already formed," especially when the opinion was "deep seated" and part of the permanent furniture of the mind.[4] The conviction that Mill unequivocally advocated individual liberty is such an opinion, it being an example of what he called "reigning opinions." This difficulty is all the greater because Mill has become, ironically, in light of his opinions about religion, something of a sacred figure—"the saint of rationalism," Gladstone called him. Indeed, alarms go off if the orthodoxy of which he is a part is questioned. One critic, a contemporary of Mill's, the logician and economist W. Stanley Jevons, discovered this. "I fear it is impossible to criticize Mr. Mill's writings without the danger of rousing animosity."[5] More recently hostile reaction was again elicited when Maurice Cowling published *Mill and Liberalism* (1963), in which he argued that for Mill liberty was not an ultimate value and that the arguments in *On Liberty*, and in all of Mill's works, were designed to bring into existence a society that would be quite oppressive. Reviewers, while finding flaws in Cowling's argument, also emphatically expressed moral indignation against his "daring assault on Mill's standing as the apostle of liberty."[6]

The reaction to Cowling's book was as harsh and extreme as Cowling's analysis of Mill. Many reviewers sensed that Mill was less the focus of Cowling's critique than modern liberalism, which Mill was presumed to represent. In fact, he was called its godfather. As Cowling subsequently explained, *Mill and Liberalism* was meant to be "a contribution to Con-

---

[4] Diary, 2 February [1854] *CW*, 27, 649.

[5] Jevons to W. Summers, 16 Dec 1874, *Letters and Journals of W. Stanley Jevons* (London, 1886), 329.

[6] John C. Rees, "The Reaction to Cowling on Mill," *Mill Newsletter* 1, no. 2 (spring 1996): 9.

servative belief."[7] Thus Cowling's book was often discussed in ideological terms, reviewers being especially provoked by the accusation that Mill was guilty of "more than a touch of something resembling moral totalitarianism." To liberals, these were fighting words, especially as Mill had contributed substantially to shaping the liberal perspective, and thus it is not surprising that there was so much outrage. Amidst the heat and anger, however, some of Cowling's insights were neglected, especially his recognition that Mill was fundamentally hostile to Christianity and eager to substitute a secular religion of humanity for outmoded Christian belief. Cowling made himself vulnerable, however, by exaggerating Mill's position, portraying him as dogmatic and as seeking to establish an "oppressive consensus" with "binding authority" and as advocating "moral indoctrination," and therefore downplaying Mill's genuine belief in the value of liberty.[8] Far from being tainted with moral totalitarianism, Mill will be presented here, as he presented himself, as advocating both social controls *and* liberty. This makes his position far different from the near-libertarianism often attributed to him, but it also distances him from the oppressive and despotic posture that he is made to adopt in Cowling's book.[9]

[7] Maurice Cowling, *Mill and Liberalism*, 2nd ed. (Cambridge: Cambridge University Press, 1989), xliii.

[8] Cowling, *Mill and Liberalism* (Cambridge: Cambridge University Press, 1963), xii, 28, 104, 117.

[9] My account of Mill radically differs from what is generally found in the literature and what I have been teaching for many decades. As will be seen, Mill's attitudes about religion and his theory of history are important for my understanding of Mill, and this book is in some respects a study of Mill on religion. G. W. Smith points to my concern about limits on liberty, although he does not introduce the religion of humanity. Recognizing Mill's link between virtue and freedom, Smith notes "a highly authoritarian outcome which only Mill's reluctance (or inability) to carry his theory of freedom to its logical conclusion prevents." G. W. Smith, "J. S. Mill on Freedom," in *Conceptions of Liberty in Political Philosophy*, ed. Z. Pelczynski and J. Gray (London: Athlone Press, 1984), 199. See also ibid. at 200, 201–2 and 209–11. Although he does not introduce the religion of humanity, Smith clearly sees an authoritarian and illiberal side of Mill. Ibid, 211; *Utilitas* 1 (5/1989): 113–34, passim, esp. 115 and end; G. W. Smith, "The Logic of J. S. Mill on Freedom," *Political Studies* (1987): 243.

Mill has often been regarded as an ecclectic thinker whose arguments lacked coherence. Especially in *On Liberty*, which it was argued, included claims to the principle of utility and at the same time the assertion that liberty was inherently valuable and therefore valuable independent of its utility. According to this traditional interpretation, espoused by Isaiah Berlin, Gertrude Himmelfarb, and C. L. Ten, there is an irreconcilable conflict between liberty and utility, and Mill is contradictory and incoherent. Others, revisionists, have held that Mill was coherent and systematic—specifically, that *On Liberty* was coherent and compatible with other writings, including *Utilitarianism*, and that the arguments of *On Liberty* can be subsumed under *a* utilitarian rubric—*On Liberty* being interpreted as maximizing individual liberty. In this book I take neither of these positions: I reject the first, for I hold that *On Liberty* is coherent within itself and as part of a wider program which had a defined purpose—indeed, given Mill's assumptions about human nature and history, was entirely coherent. However, I go on to argue that the coherence it enjoyed was not based on the

Although my analysis differs from both Jevons's and Cowling's, my conclusions, like theirs, may be regarded as heretical, and therefore I appeal to Mill—to his conviction that inquiry requires openness to all opinions—and to the evidence, much of which, I believe, has been left out of consideration. Mill did not present his perspective or agenda systematically in one place, and therefore, as already suggested, it is necessary to piece it together from many sources. This is partly because Mill's perspective developed over time, but more because of rhetorical considerations.[10] Thus his agenda was reflected in *On Liberty* but was not fully presented there. Accordingly, this book will focus on *On Liberty* but will in addition draw on a large body of Mill's other writings, particularly those from 1831 onward, including his revealing diary of 1854 and his letters, especially those that seem more candid than others, such as the ones written to Harriet Taylor Mill, Alexander Bain, and Auguste Comte. If I quote from these sources more than seems suitable to some readers, I do this to demonstrate that the views I attribute to Mill were in fact held by him. It will be argued that these sources reflect a coherent perspective and strategy and that many reflect and are part of a program he conceived as consistent parts of a larger whole.[11]

It will become evident throughout, and explicit in chapter nine, that I interpret Mill as making an esoteric argument in *On Liberty* and elsewhere, and no doubt some will suggest this is inappropriate, especially in regard to the author of *On Liberty*, who urged openness, candor, and absolutely free discussion as the path to truth. This is indeed paradoxical, but my response to such suggestions is that my attribution of esotericism to Mill does not arise from any theory or predisposition on my part but from acknowledgments by Mill himself.

---

definition of utilitarianism put forward by revisionists such as Pym, Rees, and Gray. Rather it was based on his plan for the moral regeneration of character and society, which included his proposals for reforming human nature and society. These plans, moreover, had implications for individual liberty far different from the libertarianism attributed to him by revisionists. Thus, although I am a revisionist in holding *On Liberty* consistent with *Utilitarianism*, I differ from revisionists in my understanding of *On Liberty*; Mill was systematic and coherent, but with less liberty than revisionists have sought to sustain.

[10] These will be laid out in chapter nine.

[11] Mill's acknowledgments will be examined later, but an early example may be useful already here. In 1833, Mill wrote: "Whoever . . . wishes to produce much immediate effect upon the English public, must . . . take pains to conceal that [his idea] is connected with any ulterior views. If his readers or his audience suspected that it was part of a *system*, they would conclude that his support even of the specific proposition, was not founded on any opinion he had that it was good in itself, but solely on its being connected with Utopian schemes, or at any rate with principles which they are 'not prepared' (a truly English expression) to give their assent to. . . . In writing to persuade the English, one must tell them only of the next step they have to take, keeping back all mention of any subsequent step. Whatever we may have to propose, we must contract our reasoning into the most confined limits; we must place the expediency of the particular measure upon the narrowest grounds on

Only a sampling of the evidence showing that Mill approved control as well as liberty is introduced in chapter one—enough, I hope, to show that, prima facie, there is a problem for the widely held view that in promoting liberty he also sought to minimize control. In chapter two there is an account of his redefinition of the goals of reform—his turning from narrowly political to moral reform, from changing institutions to transforming character. This shift provided the context and justification for his approval of restrictions on liberty. Mill's views about religion, which were closely connected with his speculations about politics, society, morals, and liberty, occupy the next four chapters. His program for de-Christianizing Western culture and bringing about a fully secular society, which formed part of his plan for moral reform, is described in chapters three, four, and five. And his proposal of a substitute, secular religion, which would socialize all persons with a sense of social responsibility, is presented in chapter six. In chapter seven Mill's familiar conception of individuality is shown to be not only an ideal of character but also a constellation of personal qualities that would be instrumental for implementing his plan for moral reform. The way he proposed to implement this plan and its consequences for individual liberty are explored in chapters eight and nine. The implications of this interpretation for Mill's relationship to liberalism are considered in the epilogue.

---

which it can rest; and endeavour to let out no more of general truth, than exactly as much as is absolutely indispensable to make out our particular conclusion." "Comparison of the Tendencies of French and English Intellect" (1833), CW, 23, 445–46.

ACKNOWLEDGMENTS

I WELCOME this opportunity to express my gratitude for the award of a fellowship by the Woodrow Wilson International Center for Scholars, where the writing of this book began in 1992; and for the fellowships in support of the research for the book from the Earhart Foundation and the National Endowment for the Humanities.

I have greatly benefited from comments and criticisms made by friends and colleagues. I especially appreciate informative and stimulating conversations about particular aspects of the book with Frank Turner, Steven Smith, and Victor Gourevitch. I am also grateful to Geoffrey W. Smith for carefully reading the entire manuscript and making many helpful suggestions. In addition, I am glad to acknowledge the always generous help, including illuminating observations, from Ann and Jack Robson. Among others who have been helpful are the necessarily anonymous readers whose reports to publishers included welcome encouragement and useful criticism. I have also greatly benefited from critical comments and stimulating discussion by colleagues in the Political Theory Workshop at Yale University and by participants in a colloquium on Mill's *On Liberty* held at Aspen in 1989 and sponsored by Liberty Fund. Of course, none of these persons is responsible for any errors of fact or judgment, nor do they necessarily agree with my conclusions.

I especially wish to thank Mrs. Ruth Muessig for once again mediating between me and the word processor and for displaying superhuman patience and tolerance in face of what must have seemed my endless alterations.

I also record my gratitude to the following institutions for permission to quote from manuscripts in their collections: the British Library; the British Library of Political and Economic Science at the London School of Economics; the College Archives, Imperial College of Science, Technology and Medicine, London; Jagiellonian University Library; the National Library of Scotland; the Pierpont Morgan Library; the Public Record Office; Statni Oblastni Archiv Litomerice; the Masters and Fellows of Trinity College Cambridge; University of Birmingham Library; University College London; and University of London.

Early formulations of some of the argument of this book appeared in "Religion and *On Liberty*," in *A Cultivated Mind: Essays on J. S. Mill Presented to John M. Robson*, ed. Michael Laine (Toronto: University of Toronto Press, 1991); "How Liberal Was John Stuart Mill?" (Austin: Harry Ransom Humanities Research Center, 1991), reprinted in *Adventures with Britannia: Personalities, Politics and Culture in Britain*, ed.

William Roger Louis (London: Tauris, 1995); and "Individuality and Moral Reform: The Rhetoric of Liberty and the Reality of Restraint in Mill's *On Liberty,*" *Political Science Reviewer* XXIV (1995), reprinted in *J. S. Mill's Social and Political Philosophy: Critical Texts*, ed. G. W. Smith (London: Routledge, 1998), vol. 2.

JOHN STUART MILL

ON LIBERTY AND CONTROL

Chapter One

LIBERTY *AND* CONTROL

> Liberty is often granted where it should be withheld,
> as well as withheld where it should be granted.
> (*John Stuart Mill*)

IN 1854 when planning *On Liberty* Mill told his longstanding friend George Grote that he "was cogitating an essay to point out what things society forbade that it ought not, and what things it left alone that it ought to control."[1] This statement put as much emphasis on control as on liberty, which is just how Grote understood it, for he told another friend, Alexander Bain, "It is all very well for John Mill to stand up for the removal of social restraints, but as to imposing new ones, I feel the greatest apprehensions."[2]

What Mill told Grote indicates that he intended *On Liberty* to be a defense of both liberty *and* control, and also an explanation of the circumstances that called for one or the other. And knowing about this intention, announced in the mid-1850s, makes it necessary that we at least examine the text of *On Liberty*, published in 1859, to determine if it reflects what the author intended when it was first planned. This is called for all the more by the inclusion in *On Liberty* of a passage similar to the explanation of his purpose in the conversation with Grote: "liberty is often granted where it should be withheld, as well as withheld where it should be granted" (301; citations in parentheses are to *On Liberty*).[3]

The report of what Mill told Grote was published in 1882 in the well-known first biography of Mill written by his friend Alexander Bain. Yet Mill's statement of his plan for *On Liberty* is almost never discussed in any of the vast array of articles and books offering interpretations of *On Liberty*. Nor is the possibility, suggested by the conversation with Grote, that Mill advocated substantial controls as well as liberty, ever seriously considered. Instead, most all commentators have regarded Mill as wishing to expand the realm of individual freedom to the greatest possible extent and as reluctantly providing minimal constraints on each individual to

---

[1] Alexander Bain, *John Stuart Mill: A Criticism with Personal Recollections* (London, 1882), 103. According to Bain, Mill had for Grote "an almost filial affection, and generally gave him the earliest intimation of his own plans." Ibid., 83.

[2] Ibid., 104.

[3] Citations in parentheses are to *On Liberty*, CW, 18, 216.

prevent harm to others. The most prominent spokesman for this widely shared view, Isaiah Berlin, thus tells us, "the definition of negative liberty as the ability to do as one wishes . . . is, in effect, the definition adopted by Mill." As one of the "fathers of liberalism," Mill wanted "a maximum degree of non-interference compatible with the minimum demands of social life."[4]

There is, then, broad agreement, that Mill sought an expansive liberty and minimal restraint. The vast majority of commentators hold that, while he places some limits on individual liberty, these limits fall very short of anything resembling control; and that for Mill, interference, denial of choice, coercion, and encroachments on individuality are abhorrent. In the words of one of the most prominent recent interpreters of Mill, "If anyone has given classic expression to the case for liberty it is surely Mill. Such is the dominant view. . . . [He] emerges by common consent as the most eminent advocate of individual freedom."[5]

Accompanying this general agreement, it is true, there are differences in interpretation, notably between those who regard Mill's position as incoherent—because he defended liberty as having intrinsic value while also claiming to ground his argument on utilitarianism—and those who deny any contradiction. Isaiah Berlin is the most prominent spokesman for the first of these positions.[6] In opposition to this view, a variety of attempts have been made to show that Mill's defense of liberty is compatible with his utilitarianism. Those taking this position differ in various ways, but they all seek to discover parallel or compatible arguments in *On Liberty* and other works, especially *Utilitarianism* and *System of Logic*, and in several cases they redefine or reformulate Mill's arguments to achieve their goal. John C. Rees and Alan Ryan are among the leading contributors to this position.[7]

---

[4] Isaiah Berlin, "Two Concepts of Liberty," in *Four Essays on Liberty* (Oxford: Oxford University Press, 1969), 139, 161. John Gray calls Mill "a true liberal," a "paradigmatic liberal," and "an unqualified liberal." *Mill on Liberty: A Defence* (London: Routledge, 1983), 119. And for C. L. Ten, *On Liberty* is "the most eloquent expression of the liberal theory of the open society." *Mill on Liberty* (Oxford: Clarendon, 1980), 1.

[5] John C. Rees, *John Stuart Mill's* On Liberty, ed. G. L. Williams (Oxford: Clarendon, 1985), 125.

[6] Isaiah Berlin, "John Stuart Mill and the Ends of Life," in *Four Essays on Liberty*, 192 and passim. See also C. L. Ten, "Mill's Defence of Liberty," in *Traditions of Liberalism*, ed. Knud Haakonssen (Sydney: Centre for Independent Studies, 1988), 145–46 and passim. This position has also been attributed to James Fitzjames Stephen and Gertrude Himmelfarb: John Gray and G. W. Smith, Introduction, *J. S. Mill's On Liberty in Focus*, ed. John Gray and G. W. Smith (London: Routledge, 1991), 2–3.

[7] This position has been labeled 'revisionist' in contrast to the interpretation of Berlin, *et al.*, which has been called 'traditionalist': Gray and Smith, ibid., 1–19; and by John Gray, *Mill on Liberty: A Defence* (London: Routledge & Kegan Paul, 1983), 131, n. 17. Revisionists include Rees, Ryan, Gray, Richard Wollheim, and Fred Berger. Recently Gray has greatly

This is not the only dispute to be found in the recent literature on Mill's *On Liberty*. There are different opinions about his definition of harm, his views on the enforcement of morality, the ideas and persons (including Harriet Taylor Mill) that influenced his arguments, and his intentions (was he voicing complaints against the confining customs of Victorian England or was he making claims with more enduring significance?). And there are a few who disapprove of the libertarian, even licentious conception of liberty that they find in his book. Most, however, whether they approve or disapprove, whether they welcome him to the ranks of those defending liberty or blame him for encouraging moral laxity and permissiveness, and whatever their views about the relation of his defense of liberty to his utilitarianism, share the belief that *On Liberty* includes proposals for no more than minimal restraint or control.

There have been dissenters from the consensus view. In a few cases it has been suggested that Mill rejected negative liberty and, without using the phrase, moved toward or even adopted a conception of positive liberty.[8] In this interpretation, it is held that Mill looked to the cultivation of virtue that would be a source of self-restraint. With one exception, those who take this position do not suggest, however, that individual liberty would be very much diminished, nor do they suggest that Mill approved social controls of the kind or of the scope that will be attributed to him in the chapters below.[9]

A few others have radically dissented from the consensus view, most notably Maurice Cowling.[10] Although some reviews of Cowling's book

---

altered his defense of Mill as both a liberal and as a utilitarian. *Mill on Liberty: A Defence*, 2d ed. (London: Routledge, 1996), 130–58.

[8] H. S. Jones, "John Stuart Mill as Moralist," *Journal of the History of Ideas* 53 (April–June 1992): 287–308; Bernard Semmel, *John Stuart Mill and the Pursuit of Virtue* (New Haven: Yale University Press, 1983), passim; James P. Scanlon, "J. S. Mill and the Definition of Freedom," *Ethics* 78 (1957–58): 201, 203–6. This view is implicit in the account by Nicholas Capaldi, "John Stuart Mill's Defense of Liberal Culture," *Political Science Reviewer (PSR)* 24 (1995): 210–11, 226. Also G. W. Smith: see note 9 below.

[9] The exception is G. W. Smith, who suggests "that the question of the status of *On Liberty* as a paradigmatically liberal document is perhaps due . . . for reconsideration," "Enlightenment Psychology and Individuality: The Roots of J. S. Mill's Conception of the Self," *Enlightenment and Dissent* (1992): 86; and, Mill's "theory of freedom seems irresistibly to entail extensive intervention by society," "J. S. Mill on Freedom," in *Conceptions of Liberty in Political Philosophy*, ed. Zbigniew Pelczynski and John Gray (New York: St. Martins, 1984), 210; see also 199–200, 211.

[10] On Cowling, see Preface, above, at notes 7–10. See also H. J. McCloskey, "Mill's Liberalism," *Philosophical Quarterly* 13 (April 1963): 143–56; Richard Vernon: see chapter 6, n. 78. Janice Carlisle discerns an authoritarian theme in *On Liberty*, relying, however, on the flavor of his language and not on the substance of his arguments. She points to his panoptic imagery, which is traced back to Bentham, and his use of the inspection principle, especially as it is internalized to provide self-restraint and self-control: *John Stuart Mill and the Writing of Character* (Athens: University of Georgia Press, 1991), 197–204.

expressed agreement with his thesis, neither he nor any of the moderate dissenters from the consensus view have generated substantial questioning of the widely shared opinion that in *On Liberty* Mill sought to maximize individual liberty and sought to reduce the power and authority of governments, society, and public opinion to restrict it.[11]

This dominant interpretation gains strong support from Mill's prominent and emphatic arguments for an expansive liberty—for half of the agenda as he described it to Grote, which focused on "what things society forbade that it ought not." Early in his first chapter, in keeping with the book's title, Mill identifies an oppressive society as the greatest threat to individual liberty. There is a threat of tyranny, not only from government, but from society itself, and it is heightened in democratic societies, which (using Tocqueville's famous phrase) are the source of a "tyranny of the majority."

> When society is itself the tyrant—society collectively, over the separate individuals who compose it—its means of tyrranizing are not restricted to the acts which it may do by the hands of its political functionaries. Society can and does execute its own mandates: and if it issues wrong mandates instead of right, or any mandates at all in things with which it ought not to meddle, it practices a social tyranny more formidable than many kinds of political oppression, since though not usually upheld by such extreme penalties, it leaves fewer means of escape, penetrating much more deeply into the details of life, and enslaving the soul itself. (219–20)

Protection was necessary, Mill concluded, not only against the magistrate but "against the tyranny of the prevailing opinion and feeling." (220)

Having identified the threat to individual liberty, Mill went on to establish a barrier to protect it. In the most famous passage in the book he proclaimed "one very simple principle, as entitled to govern absolutely the dealings of society with the individual in the way of compulsion and control." (223)

> That principle is, that the sole end for which mankind are warranted, individually or collectively, in interfering with the liberty of action of any of their number, is self-protection. That the only purpose for which power can be rightfully exercised over any member of a civilized community, against his will, is to prevent harm to others. His own good, either physical or moral, is not a sufficient warrant. He cannot rightfully be compelled to do or forbear. . . . To justify that, the conduct from which it is desired to deter him, must be calculated to produce evil to some one else. The only part of the conduct of any one, for which he is

[11] John C. Rees, "The Reaction to Cowling on Mill," *Mill Newsletter* 1, no. 2 (spring 1966): 2–11.

amenable to society, is that which concerns others. In the part which merely concerns himself, his independence is, of right, absolute. Over himself, over his own body and mind, the individual is sovereign. (223–24)

Mill went on to describe "the appropriate region of human liberty." It consisted of liberty of conscience, including liberty of opinion and sentiment and publication; liberty of tastes and pursuits, including the framing of a plan of life to suit one's own character; and the liberty of combination (225–26).

While *On Liberty* most obviously is an eloquent and elaborately argued plea for considerable individual liberty (ranging from liberty of thought, discussion, and publication to liberty of action), the question raised here is whether in the book Mill also establishes grounds for control and restraint—not modest restraints occasioned by the application of the harm principle, which all commentators recognize—but more considerable restraints that would be put in place frequently as a result of implementing the other part of the agenda described to Grote, which concerned "things [society] left alone that it ought to control."

———

There are indications that a positive answer should be given to this question. Mill did endorse certain controls, and one of these seems to contradict his argument in chapter one about a part of conduct that concerned the individual actor and did not harm others: with respect to such conduct, Mill said, the individual was absolutely independent and sovereign.[12] This is what he called self-regarding conduct, and it was one side of his distinction between such conduct and other kinds that harmed other individuals or the public (282). This distinction is widely believed to be the foundation of his defense of liberty, and most of those subscribing to the consensus view, whatever side they take in the various disputes about Mill's position, assume that this definition defined the large area of inviolable freedom. John C. Rees, for example, concludes that, "according to the doctrine of *On Liberty* encroachments [on individuality] constitute an improper interference with 'self-regarding' conduct: the individual is being held accountable for actions that cause no harm to others."[13] And

---

[12] According to Rees's widely accepted reformulation, harm is understood to be harm to the *interests* of others: *Mill's On Liberty*, 142–46.

[13] John C. Rees, *John Stuart Mill's* On Liberty (Oxford: Oxford University Press, 1985), 46. See also Berlin, *Four Essays*, 190; R. J. Haliday, "Some Recent Interpretations of John Stuart Mill," *Philosophy* 43 (January 1968): 1. Apparently the concept 'self-regarding' was adopted from Bentham: see "Bentham" (1838), *CW*, 10, 94, and "Nature" (1874), *CW*, 10, 394.

according to C. L. Ten, Mill claimed "that individual liberty in the area of self-regarding actions should be absolute."[14]

Yet these interpretations of Mill's position are not compatible with the following statement in chapter four of *On Liberty*: "*A person may suffer very severe penalties at the hands of others, for faults which directly concern only himself*" (278; emphasis added).[15] To take another example in which this statement is ignored, Marshall Cohen, in an introduction to a widely used edition of Mill's writings, asserts that it is "Mill's principle that self-regarding actions are inviolable" and that for Mill "the only justification for interfering with the liberty of a member of a civilized community 'is to prevent harm to others.' "[16] In yet another example, we are told by John Gray, "A man failed to be a free man in Mill's view, if he was subject to force or coercion in the self-regarding area."[17] The contrast between these statements by representatives of one variant or another of the consensus view and Mill's statement that very severe penalties may be suffered even for self-regarding conduct invites further inquiry. Can Mill's statement be reconciled with any of the variants of the consensus interpretation? Or, does the statement in chapter four point to circumstances that justified the control mentioned in Mill's conversation with Grote?

Mill went on to describe both the kind of conduct that would suffer very severe penalties and the character of those penalties. The objectionable conduct, Mill explained in chapter four, reflected the "lowness or depravation of taste" of "inferior" persons (278). And there can be no doubt that it was self-regarding, for Mill clearly said such persons were "doing no wrong to any one" (278). The consequences they faced also were clear: they would become "necessarily and *properly* a subject of distaste, or, in extreme cases, even of contempt" (278; emphasis added).[18] Distaste and contempt are instruments of control, and the persons exposed to them would find their liberty threatened and reduced. Such expo-

---

[14] C. L. Ten, *Mill on Liberty*, 40. "The central argument of the essay *On Liberty* hinges upon the strategic distinction between that part of individual conduct which has consequences for the welfare of others . . . and that part which, comprising the inward domain of consciousness . . . is the appropriate region for the most absolute human freedom": Albert William Levy, "The Value of Freedom: Mill's Liberty (1859–1959)," in *Limits of Liberty: Studies of Mill's* On Liberty, ed. Peter Radcliff (Belmont, Calif.: Wadsworth, 1966), 14.

[15] This crucial passage will be discussed below in chapter 8, text at note 11.

[16] *The Philosophy of John Stuart Mill*, ed. Marshall Cohen (New York: Modern Library, 1961), xxix, xxxi. "The view for which Mill is celebrated is that it is never right to interfere with purely self-regarding actions, but only with harmful other- regarding ones, and then not always.": H. J. McCloskey, *John Stuart Mill: A Critical Study* (London, 1971), 104.

[17] John Gray, *Mill On Liberty: A Defence* (London: Routledge, 1983), 78.

[18] The words 'distaste' and 'contempt' are repeated at 282. See below, chapter 8, text at notes 44ff, for a fuller discussion.

sure was one of the consequences that might attend self-regarding conduct, and distaste and contempt were among the "very severe penalties" for self-regarding faults that Mill, inconspicuously but certainly, introduced as part of his argument.

Most spokesmen for the consensus interpretation have ignored Mill's approval of expressions of distaste and contempt and have argued that Mill would have allowed full liberty to those whose conduct was low and depraved, a position that follows from the assumption that Mill would not allow interference with self-regarding conduct. Thus C. L. Ten holds that

> Mill readily concedes that self-regarding conduct has certain adverse effects on others. His argument is that a principled defence of individual liberty will lead us to discount these effects on others. For example, other people may be affected by my conduct because they dislike it, *find it disgusting*, or regard it as immoral. These effects, taken in themselves, are never good reasons for interfering with my conduct. (Emphasis added)[19]

And elsewhere Ten asserts, "Mill would not regard the revulsion or disgust as a relevant reason for interfering with self-regarding conduct."[20] Here we are told that even disgust and revulsion do not justify our interfering with another person's liberty, whereas in fact Mill tells us that low and depraved conduct will and should elicit distaste and contempt, which surely are ways of interfering. Mill's words—distaste and contempt—clearly have great affinity with what Ten calls disgust and revulsion. Since those exposed to distaste and contempt are likely to regard such judgments as censorious and as attempts to direct social pressure against them, it is necessary to consider whether Mill's advocacy of distaste and contempt is an example of the kind of control mentioned in his conversation with Grote.[21]

————————

Another indication that Mill advocates control as well as liberty appears in his discussions of the harm principle where he reveals that he defines harm quite broadly. This is surprising in light of the emphasis he placed on the individual's absolute claim to independence in matters that concern himself and his assurance that, "Over himself, over his own body and mind, the individual is sovereign" (224). Statements such as this strongly suggest that the individual would not be "amenable to society" (224)

[19] Ten, *Mill*, 6.

[20] Ibid., 29; see also 4, 41.

[21] A few have not ignored Mill's view on distaste and contempt but have distorted his meaning to make his usage compatible with the consensus interpretation.

for much of his conduct. This impression is reenforced by the way he distinguished harmful conduct from that which is self-regarding—by characterizing it as conduct of a person who "is led to violate a distinct and assignable obligation to any other person" (281). This suggests that harm was narrowly defined and that the individual, though not immune from society's harsh judgments, at least would not be subject to them very often. This impression is reenforced by much recent commentary. Rees, for example, interprets the harm principle as not being applicable to most of the wide range of conduct that affects others but rather only to that which adversely affects the interests of others. And some have held that conduct which only causes offense or moral distress (morality dependent harm, so-called) is not the kind of harm Mill had in mind. Both these interpretations have the effect of narrowly defining the kind of harm that justifies interference.[22]

Mill's examples of how the harm principle would be applied, however, point to a rather different conclusion, for they show that he was prepared to locate harm and punish those responsible for it in situations he thought would occur frequently. One of his examples was primary education. Parents had a sacred duty to educate their children. Not to provide instruction and training for a child's mind, like denying it food for its body, was "a moral crime, both against the unfortunate offspring and against society" (302). Mill proposed examinations to begin at an early age, first to determine whether a child could read, and later for an expanding range of subjects. The goal was to make acquisition and retention of a certain minimum knowledge "virtually compulsory" (303). Failure on the examinations would lead to a moderate fine to the father, to be paid, if necessary, by his labor.[23]

Mill went further and insisted that the moral responsibilities and obligations associated with parenting and marriage also be enforced.

> The fact itself, of causing the existence of a human being, is one of the most responsible actions in the range of human life. To undertake this responsibility—to bestow a life which may be either a curse or a blessing—unless the being on whom it is to be bestowed will have at least the ordinary chances of a desirable existence, is a crime against that being. (304)

The consequence, Mill argued, extended beyond the child—and here his Malthusianism was evident. With overpopulation already a problem,

---

[22] Richard Wollheim, "John Stuart Mill and the Limits of State Action," *Social Research* 40 (1973): 9, 15–17; Jeremy Waldron, "Mill and the Value of Moral Distress,"*Liberal Rights* (Cambridge: Cambridge University Press, 1993), 117–20.

[23] A question about the child's liberty did not arise, for his doctrine of liberty applied to those in the maturity of their faculties (224). Thus it was not an interference with liberty to forcibly place prostitutes who were still minors in industrial homes: "I think the objection to the interference with personal liberty begins when the age of education, properly called, ceases." "The Contagious Diseases Act" (1871), *CW*, *21*, 368.

adding to the workforce increased competition and reduced wages, and this was "a serious offence against all who live by the remuneration of their labour" (304). Mill concluded that laws such as existed in some Continental countries, which forbade marriage unless the parties could demonstrate they could support a family, "do not exceed the legitimate power of the State." Since such laws prohibited an act injurious to others, violation "ought to be subject to reprobation, and social stigma, even when it is not deemed expedient to superadd legal punishment" (304).[24] Elaborating on this, he held that, "What is wanted is, not that the good should abstain in order that the selfish may indulge, but such a state of opinion as may deter the selfish from this kind of intemperance by stamping it as disgraceful."[25] His defense of penalties—enforced by law or imposed by opinion—that would restrict marriage and childbearing is another example of his broad definition of harm, and is the occasion for his criticism of "current ideas of liberty, which . . . would repel the attempt to put any restraint upon [a person's] inclinations when the consequence of their indulgence is a life or lives of wretchedness and depravity to the offspring" (304).[26] Elsewhere he called having a large family that one could not maintain a "species of incontinence" and one of "the diseases of society."[27]

Obligations within a family—to spouse or children—Mill also considered in his few discussions of divorce. Here too he was concerned to prevent harm, and consequently he did not approve of liberty to dissolve the marriage contract, in spite of his wish to consider the happiness of both husband and wife. In *On Liberty* he equivocates and resists endorsing divorce on two grounds: if children are called into existence during the marriage, their claims supersede the wishes of either spouse; and even if

[24] Commenting on these passages, he added, "I have however expressly guarded myself against being understood to mean that legal restrictions on marriage are *expedient*. That is altogether a different question, to which I conceive no universal and peremptory answer can be given": Mill to Dr. Henry MacCormac, 4 December 1865, CW, 16, 1124.

[25] "Newman's Political Economy" (1851), CW, 5, 449. "All persons . . . should abdicate the right of propagating the species at their own discretion and without limit. . . . But before this solution of the problem can cease to be visionary, an almost complete renovation must take place in some of the most rooted opinions and feelings of the present race of mankind." "Vindication of the French Revolution of February 1848," CW, 20, 350. See also, Diary, 26 March [1854], CW, 27, 664: "If children are the result [of sexual relations], then indeed commences a set of important duties towards the children, which society should enforce upon the parents much more strictly than it now does."

[26] Commenting on this part of Mill's position, Frederic Harrison called it "a Chinese tyranny of an ominous kind." Explaining, he said, "The vehement language against the 'mischievous act' of poor persons in breeding sounds strangely in the mouth of an apostle of freedom." *Tennyson, Ruskin, Mill; and Other Literary Estimates* (New York: Macmillan, 1900), 283–84. G. W. Smith recognizes that Mill favored "extensive interference in an aspect of personal life which he found distasteful and antisocial": "J. S. Mill on Freedom," in *Conceptions of Liberty in Political Philosophy*, ed. Zbigniew Pelczynski and John Gray, 210–11.

[27] *Political Economy*, CW, 2, 368.

a marriage is childless, each spouse has obligations to the other, which arise from the long-term expectations that are formed when marriage is promised or initiated. Consequently he disagreed with Humboldt, who proposed that marriages might be dissolved on the initiative of either partner (300–301). Bain confirmed that Mill never advocated divorce.[28] Mill did not explain how he would enforce laws that made it difficult and in some circumstances impossible to divorce, but punishments of some sort would be required, and presumably in scope and severity they would be consistent with his proposed punishments for other aspects of family relations.

His examples of family obligations were among those he had in mind when proclaiming, "liberty is often granted where it should be withheld" (301). To allow parents to neglect the education of their children or to have children they might not care for were among the "misplaced notions of liberty [which] prevent moral obligations on the part of parents from being recognized" (304). Since such misplaced liberty was widely permitted, he could observe that interference by government "is, with about equal frequency, improperly invoked and improperly condemned" (223).

His expansive conception of harm is not fully revealed by these examples concerning education, parenting, and marriage, for in explaining his notion of injury to others, he defined some types of injury that greatly enlarged his conception of harm. Thus he included as injurious acts, falsehood or duplicity in dealing with others and unfair or ungenerous use of advantages over others. Each of these are "injurious to others" and are "fit objects of moral reprobation, and, in grave cases, of moral retribution and punishment" (279). Both would be difficult to prove; and the latter justified punishment for the conduct of ambitious persons engaged in competition. But he explained, "As much compression as is necessary to

---

[28] Bain, *Mill*, 130, 165n. His hesitations about divorce were confirmed in conversation during his last years with John Morley: *Fortnightly Review* 21 (1 January 1874): 13. In *Political Economy* he classified marriage as a contract binding in perpetuity. Since he would not allow the parties themselves to revoke their engagements, he suggested they might be released on a sufficient case being made out before an impartial authority: *CW, 3*, 953–54. He was more accepting of divorce in an early essay on marriage written (probably in 1832–33) at Harriet Taylor's request not long after they first met: "On Marriage," *CW, 21*, 45–49. For her views on the same subject, see "On Marriage," *CW, 21*, 376–77. In correspondence over the years his opinions varied, but late in life he tended to avoid stating an opinion, saying that he was reluctant to decide until women had the political rights that would allow them to take part in deciding the issues and until there was greater experience of marriage between equals. Meanwhile, however, he was for allowing divorce only in extreme cases: Mill to John Nichol, 18 August 1869, *CW, 17*, 1634. On disappointment of expectations as a punishable violation of justice, see *Utilitarianism, CW, 10*, 256. There was one situation in which Mill unequivocally advocated divorce: if a man communicated venereal disease to his wife: "Contagious Diseases Acts," *CW, 21*, 354–55.

prevent the stronger specimens of human nature from encroaching on the rights of others, cannot be dispensed with" (266).[29]

The expansion of Mill's conception of harm did not stop here, however, for he added, "not only these acts, but the *dispositions* which lead to them, are properly immoral, and fit subjects of disapprobation which may rise to abhorrence" (279; emphasis added). He then offered a long list of such *punishable* dispositions:

> Cruelty of disposition; malice and ill-nature; that most anti-social and odious of all passions, envy; dissimulation and insincerity; irascibility on insufficient cause, and resentment disproportioned to the provocation; the love of domineering over others; the desire to engross more than one's share of advantages ... the pride which derives gratification from the abasement of others; the egotism which thinks self and its concerns more important than everything else, and decides all doubtful questions in its own favour. (279)

"These are," Mill added, "moral vices, and constitute a bad and odious moral character" (279). Thus he was prepared to punish not only conduct but faults of character, and this was not likely to enlarge the realm of liberty. Yet it is difficult to find discussion of what Mill says about punishing dispositions in the vast literature on *On Liberty.*[30]

His observations about punishments, in *On Liberty* and elsewhere, suggest that Mill was not uncomfortable with severity. The punishments he recommended for those violating family obligations were rather draconian. He discerned in the beating of a horse a disposition to tyrannize over the helpless and therefore the probability that women and children would be victimized. This was an example of the "cruelty of disposition; malice and ill-nature," which were among the faults of character for which he would welcome punishments (279). In the newspaper article describing this case he advocated more severe punishment than the law then allowed, and he urged "putting down strongly ... the brutal vices of the worst part of the populace."[31] And in an analysis of the kind of person who is "cruel by character, or, as the phrase is, naturally cruel," he argued that "this is not one of the natural inclinations which it would

---

[29] These are akin to what he elsewhere called the most marked cases of injustice—wrongful aggression or wrongful exercise of power over another person: *Utilitarianism, CW, 10,* 256. He agreed with Comte that personal hygiene was obligatory—not a matter of prudence but of duty: *Auguste Comte and Positivism, CW, 10,* 340.

[30] Elsewhere he offered a definition of "a good or a bad habitual *disposition*—a bent of character from which useful, or from which hurtful actions are likely to arise": *Utilitarianism, CW, 10,* 220n.

[31] Harriet Taylor and John Stuart Mill, "The Case of William Burn" (17 November 1846), *CW, 24,* 953–54.

be wrong to suppress. The only question would be whether it is not a duty to suppress the man himself along with it."[32]

Not only the worst part of the populace, but children also were to feel severity, for if education is to be effective, they must experience "rigid discipline and known liability to punishment."[33] Mill's own education reflected his father's application of this principle. Francis Place described the discipline Mill faced at age eleven. "No fault, however trivial, escapes his [James Mill's] notice; none goes without reprehension or punishment of some sort." A brother and sister were denied dinner at the usual hour of 1:00, as punishment for not reading lessons well. John shared in this punishment, as he was lenient on them. Consequently they were still at their books at 3:00 and would not get dinner until six. "The fault today is a *mistake in one word*."[34] Following such experience, Mill's conclusion is not surprising: "I do not believe that fear, as an element in education, can be dispensed with," though when he wrote this, he softened sufficiently to add, "but I am sure it ought not be the predominant element."[35] He continued to recognize, however, the utility of harshness and severity, even when not associated with failure or wrongdoing, and thus he valued "ascetic discipline. . . . We do not doubt that children and young persons will one day be again systematically disciplined in self-mortification; that they will be taught, as in antiquity, to control their appetites, to brave dangers, and submit voluntarily to pain, as simple exercises in education."[36] This disposition was reflected in his views of moral psychology, for he held that moral responsibility rested on the feeling that failure made one liable for punishment. "Responsibility means punishment. When we are said to have the feeling of being morally responsible for our actions, the idea of being punished for them is uppermost in the speaker's mind."[37] If a person harmed others, moreover, society not only "must inflict pain on him for the express purpose of punishment" but also "must take care that it be sufficiently severe" (280). He felt outrage about the "humanity-

---

[32] 32 "Nature," *CW*, *10*, 398.

[33] Early Draft of Autobiography, *CW*, *1*, 52. The Early Draft, rather than *Autobiography*, will be cited, as it is often different from *Autobiography*; also, it provides a more accurate reflection of Mill's state of mind and beliefs at about the time *On Liberty* was planned. Early Draft was composed in late 1853 and early 1854. *On Liberty* was planned in 1854 and completed in late 1857.

[34] Quoted in Stillinger, "John Mill's Education: Fact, Fiction, and Myth," in *A Cultivated Mind: Essays on J. S. Mill Presented to John M. Robson*, ed. Michael Laine (Toronto: University of Toronto Press, 1991), 26–27.

[35] Early Draft, *CW*, *1*, 54.

[36] *Auguste Comte and Positivism*, *CW*, *10*, 339.

[37] *An Examination of Sir William Hamilton's Philosophy* (1865), *C*, *9*, 454; see also 458–59n. Also, "No case can be pointed out in which we consider anything as a duty, and any act or omission as immoral or wrong, without regarding the person who commits the wrong and violates the duty as a fit object of punishment": Mill's note, in James Mill, *Analysis of the Phenomena of the Human Mind* (1829), ed. John Stuart Mill (London, 1869), 2, 325.

mongering" of juries that were too lenient with criminals.[38] Bain, familiar with his belief in severity, spoke about his "revengeful sentiment."[39]

There are pervasive indications that the society Mill approved would be a rather censorious place. While the response to harmful conduct might be legal punishment, Mill held out another possibility for less egregious cases and instances in which legal enforcement was inexpedient. In these circumstances we "make amends . . . by bringing a strong expression of our own and the public disapprobation to bear on the offender."[40] This he called "the moral coercion of public opinion" (223). He referred to this kind of punishment quite frequently.

Some rules of conduct . . . must be imposed by law in the first place, and *by opinion* on many things which are not fit subjects for the operation of law. (220; emphasis added)

If any one does an act hurtful to others, there is a . . . case for punishing him, by law, or, where legal penalties are not safely applicable, *by general disapprobation*. (224; emphasis added)

The offender may . . . be justly punished *by opinion*, though not by law. (276; emphasis added)

[One who violates an obligation] is deservedly *reprobated*, and might be justly punished. (281; emphasis added)

[F]or such actions as are prejudicial to the interests of others, the individual is accountable, and may be subjected either to *social* or to legal punishment. (292; emphasis added)

Acts injurious to others. . . . are fit objects of *moral reprobation*, and, in grave cases, of moral retribution and punishment. (279; emphasis added)

An act injurious to others . . . ought to be a subject of *reprobation, and social stigma*, even when it is not deemed expedient to superadd legal punishment. (304; emphasis added)

Disapprobation, moral reprobation, and social stigma—these are manifestations of social pressure, and they were intended to reduce individual liberty, as Mill showed by describing such things as "enforcement of restraints" (220) and "moral coercion"(223).[41] Moreover, the application

---

[38] Harriet Taylor and John Stuart Mill, "The Acquittal of Captain Johnstone" (10 February 1846), *CW*, 24, 865. Johnstone had brutally murdered three seamen under his command but was found not guilty because of temporary insanity.

[39] Bain, *Mill*, 151.

[40] *Utilitarianism*, *CW*, 10, 246.

[41] Also, "We think that the general good requires that [a wrongdoer] should be punished, if not by the law, by the displeasure and ill offices of his fellow-creatures"; there will be a

of such punishments would not be accompanied by any of the procedural safeguards that are available in the judicial institutions responsible for deciding upon legal punishments. Nowhere does Mill precisely define the offenses that would receive extra legal punishments, nor does he discuss how such punishments could be measured to fit the offense. Yet they are one of the social controls that could legitimately restrict individual liberty.

The full extent of the censoriousness unleashed by Mill is revealed when recalling that the moral coercion of public opinion which he endorsed for harmful conduct, including dispositions to such conduct, would coexist with the expressions of distaste and contempt and other pressures of opinion he sanctioned for certain self-regarding actions. There is a problem here for anyone wishing to portray Mill as a friend to an ample individual liberty.

———————

Suggesting that Mill advocated controls does not mean that his proposals for individual liberty were not the most prominent part of his overall position in *On Liberty*. No more than a reminder of his famous phrases and arguments need be mentioned. He opposed all censorship and advocated full and complete freedom of discussion and publication: "If all mankind minus one, were of one opinion, and only one person were of the contrary opinion, mankind would be no more justified in silencing that one person, than he, if he had the power, would be justified in silencing mankind" (229). His liberal sentiments are also evident in his complaint about the "yoke of opinion" (223) and the "despotism of custom" (272). Mill's liberal inclinations are also fully displayed in his celebration of individuality. Persons possessing it are free in conduct as well as in opinion. They "act upon their opinions—to carry these out in their lives, without hindrance, either physical or moral, from their fellowmen." They engage in "experiments in living" (261), are spontaneous (261), and are uninhibited by fear of being called eccentric (269). Their behavior is so useful and so conducive to true happiness that "free scope should be given to varieties of character" (261) and "individuality should assert itself" (261).

What we have, therefore, is advocacy of both liberty *and* control, and an explanation of Mill's overarching argument in *On Liberty* must explain the coexistence of these apparently opposite positions. This is made necessary because the provisions for controls were not small exceptions to a general presumption that in most circumstances an expansive liberty

---

"feeling of indignation, or resentment." Mill's note, in James Mill, *Analysis*, 2, 325. Cowling suggests that "Mill was one of the most censorious of nineteenth-century moralists":

ought to prevail. Such an explanation for restrictions would be acceptable if Mill limited liberty only to restrain a few imprudent persons whose occasional excess caused harm to others. But the range of cases in which he would punish, his approval of punishments for mere dispositions toward conduct that might injure others, and above all, his explanation of his purposes to George Grote indicate that his rationale for liberty in combination with control requires a different explanation. It is also necessary to explain how, for Mill, the provisions for both control and liberty were not contradictory, but in fact were compatible means of implementing a coherent plan of moral reform. Not least, it is necessary to explain why proposals for control as well as liberty were included in an essay with a title that suggested the presence of only one.

Mill and Liberalism, 143.

Chapter Two

CULTURAL REFORM

> An almost complete renovation must take place in
> some of the most rooted opinions and feelings of the
> present race of mankind.
> *(John Stuart Mill)*

PROVISION for control as well as liberty in *On Liberty* can be
traced to Mill's greatly increased wish for cultural and moral reform during the 1840s and 1850s. Of course, he had never been
indifferent toward this kind of reform, but at an earlier stage his goal as
a reformer was limited to fundamentally changing institutions rather than
to altering character or human nature. He believed that well designed
institutions would discourage or deter actions that were economically irrational or politically corrupt. He was, after all, a child of Benthamism,
which was primarily concerned with institutional reform—whether in the
political, legal, administrative, or economic realms. While still quite
young, Mill discovered in Bentham's writings "what might truly be called
an object in life; to be a reformer of the world," and he thought of reform
as Bentham thought of it.[1] Rules were to be made and situations created
to deter the kind of conduct that prevented the achievement of the greatest
happiness by the greatest number. Democratic reforms, for example, were
expected to frustrate the satisfaction of sinister, that is, separate, interests
and to allow the more widely shared interests of all people to be reflected
in the making of public policy, and this would be achieved without altering the self-seeking character of human nature. Mill made the same assumption during the 1830s when he tried to organize and animate the
Philosophic Radicals in Parliament; he urged them to seek constitutional
changes—an extended suffrage, more frequent Parliaments, and a secret
ballot—which would redistribute political power so that public policy
would promote the interests of the majority.

Mill's approach gradually changed and by the 1850s he was no longer
confident that institutional change would bring about genuine improvement. By this time he witnessed a vast change in public opinion, which
had been mobilized in support of many constitutional, economic, and

---

[1] Early Draft, *CW, 1,* 136. He also described how when reading the *Traité de Legislation,*
Bentham's doctrine "burst on one with all the force of novelty. . . . The feeling rushed upon

administrative changes. Many reforms had been put in place, including some that he and other Benthamites had advocated. The Reform Act was passed in 1832 and the Poor Law Amendment Act in 1834. Public pressure for free trade developed during the 1830s and led to the abolition of the corn laws in 1846. Of course, Mill was not equally pleased by all the changes that had been made, but he acknowledged the many improvements in both institutions and policies.

Yet, in spite of all this, by mid-century he was disappointed.

> I have seen, in the last twenty years [this was written in late 1853 or early 1854], many of the opinions of my youth obtain general recognition, and many of the reforms in institutions, for which I had through life contended, either effected or in course of being so. But these changes have been attended with much less benefit to human well being than I should formerly have anticipated, because they have produced very little improvement in that on which depends all real amelioration in the lot of mankind, their intellectual and moral state.[2]

This disappointment led to doubts about the importance of institutional reform in the immediate future. "For almost a century now," he told Comte, "all theoretical and practical attempts at reshaping the condition of mankind simply by institutional reform alone have actually been found ineffective." This, he explained, was "a fact enlightened minds consider ever more evident." Therefore an emphasis on "moral progress and intellectual culture for the popular masses" was called for.[3] He noted (in what obviously was a self-description) "a growing skepticism, even among ardent supporters of popular institutions, as to their being, after all, the *panacea* they were supposed to be for the evils that beset our social system. Sincere Democrats are beginning to doubt whether the *desideratum* is so much an increased influence of popular opinion, as a more enlightened use of the power which it already possesses."[4]

Turning away from organic reform, he shifted focus and began redefining his goal as a reformer. "At present [he said in 1850] I expect very little from any plans which aim at improving even the economical state of the people by purely economical or political means. We have come, I think, to a period, when progress, even of a political kind, is coming to a halt, by reason of the low intellectual and moral state of all classes: of the rich as much as of the poorer classes."[5] His friend John Sterling observed this

---

me that all previous moralists were superseded, and that here indeed was the commencement of a new era in thought" (66).

[2] Ibid., 244.

[3] Mill to Comte, 23 October 1842, *The Correspondence of John Stuart Mill and Auguste Comte*, ed. Oscar A. Haac (New Brunswick, Transaction, 1995), 110.

[4] "Duveyrier's Political Views of French Affairs" (1846), CW, 20, 300.

[5] Mill to Edward Herford, 22 January 1850, CW, 14, 45.

shift: Mill "was brought up in the belief that Politics and Social Institutions were everything, but he has been gradually delivered from this outwardness, and feels now clearly that individual reform must be the groundwork of social progress."[6]

Having located the obstacle to improvement in morals and motives more than in institutions, Mill's reformism became more ambitious and more radical, while the achievement of its goals was projected further into the future. "I am now [1853–54] convinced that no great improvements in the lot of mankind are possible until a change takes place in the fundamental constitution of their modes of thought."[7] He now aspired to alter not opinions so much as the values, underlying attitudes, and beliefs that were reflected in, and perhaps formative of, opinions. Mill is often regarded as an advocate for improved education, which of course he was; but the term 'education,' associated with cognition and schooling, fails to capture his deeper and more important goal—to shape moral feelings and beliefs. Thus he aimed to bring about "a renovation . . . in the bases of belief."[8] To promote true opinions about really important matters, he now sought nothing less than "the reconstruction of the human intellect ab imo [from the bottom up]."[9]

Mill's focus on values and motivations was sometimes expressed as a concern about character. Whereas earlier he and other Benthamites thought reform could be achieved not by appealing to unselfish benevolence but by the "enlightening [of] the selfish feelings" without, however, eliminating them, now he believed that improvement could be brought about only by greatly reducing selfishness itself.[10] Describing his "ideal of future improvement" during this period, he explained that "to render any such social transformation practicable an equivalent change of character must take place both in the uncultivated herd who now compose the labouring masses, and in the immense majority of their employers."[11] Since he was seeking fundamental change in those basic springs of action which formed character, it is not surprising that Mill, with increased frequency,

---

[6] Reported by Caroline Fox, 9 March 1843: Caroline Fox, *Memories of Old Friends*, ed. Horace N. Pym (London, 1882), 2, 8–9.

[7] Early Draft, *CW*, *1*, 244.

[8] Ibid., 246.

[9] Diary, 18 February [1854], *CW*, *27*, 655. His young friend John Morley observed his wish for "a fundamental re-constitution of accepted modes of thought" and for a "fundamental renovation of conviction," which he called Mill's "crisis of middle age." "Mr. Mill's Autobiography," *Fortnightly Review* 21 (1 January 1874): 15, 16, 19.

[10] Early Draft *CW*, *1*, 112. Collini has taken note of Mill's interest in character, though he associates it with a widely shared concern among late-century intellectual figures, whereas here it is related to the development of a political perspective that distinguished Mill from most contemporaries. Stefan Collini, *Public Moralists: Political Thought and Intellectual Life in Britain 1850–1930* (Oxford: Clarendon, 1991), 121–69.

[11] Ibid., 238.

now used such terms as 'regeneration' and 'renovation' to describe the changes that had to be made. Thus, "an almost complete *renovation* must take place in some of the most rooted opinions and feelings of the present race of mankind" (emphasis added).[12] And he confessed that public affairs "do not occupy so much of my thoughts as they once did; it is becoming more and more clearly evident to me that the mental *regeneration* of Europe must precede its social regeneration" (emphasis added).[13]

The magnitude of change which Mill sought was such that it can be said without exaggeration that he wished to bring about a cultural revolution. The full extent of the changes, it is true, were usually projected into the distant future, but he also would have welcomed a sudden transformation, for he thought that "changes effected rapidly and by force are often the only ones which in given circumstances would be permanent."[14] Looking back at an earlier period, he criticized what had been his willingness to be content with "superficial improvement" and his having been "indulgent to the common opinions of society." Now he identified with those who sought really radical change—"freethinkers, socialists, and visionary reformers of the world."[15] Drastically expanding the targets of what he would change, now more than ever he praised heretical opinions. They were "almost the only ones the assertion of which tends in any way to regenerate society." He claimed that at this period "our opinions [his and Harriet's] were now far *more* heretical than mine had been in the days of my most extreme Benthamism."[16] He went far beyond Christian Socialists: in addition to changing the relation between masters and workmen, he also looked for "changes fully as great in existing opinions and institutions on religious moral and domestic subjects."[17] He was unworried by the consequences of such changes on social stability: "I look upon this expression of loosening the foundations of society . . . as a mere bugbear to frighten imbeciles with." Thus he was untroubled by vast cultural upheavals, even if they were to be as world shaking as had been the introduction of Christianity or the Reformation.[18] While acknowledging that

[12] "Vindication of the French Revolution of February 1848" (1849), *CW, 20*, 350. For other examples of Mill's use of the term 'renovation,' see Early Draft, *CW, 1*, 246; *CW, 13*, 739; *On Liberty, CW 18*, 237; "Chapters on Socialism," *CW, 5*, 749; "Grote's History of Greece [5], " *CW, 25*, 1164.

[13] Mill to Robert Barclay Fox, 19 December 1842, *CW, 13*, 563. For other examples of Mill's use of the term 'regeneration,' see Early Draft, *CW, 1*, 112, 114, 238; *13, 553; 14*, 239; *17*, 1535; Diary, 27 January [1854], *27*, 647; *On Liberty, 18*, 128, 138, 146, 291; *Subjection of Women* (1869), *21*, 266, 336.

[14] Mill to John Chapman, 9 June 1851, *CW, 14*, 68.

[15] "Grote's Plato" (1866), *CW, 11*, 387.

[16] Early Draft, *CW, 1*, 236, 238.

[17] Mill to unidentified correspondent, 9 June 1851, *CW, 14*, 70.

[18] "Stability of Society" (1850), *CW, 25*, 1181.

things were not as bad in his time as they had been in the fifteenth century, he confessed "often . . . wishing for the age of Savonarola."[19]

The move away from conventional politics to a concern with morals and character in both individuals and in the culture was most pronounced during the 1840s and 1850s, but there had been anticipations of this development. Mill recalled that his mental crisis when he was twenty had led to a playing down of the importance of "the ordering of outward circumstances" and a corresponding emphasis on "the internal culture of the individual."[20] His attention again focused on this soon after his mental crisis when Mill was torn by a public dispute that had enduring consequences; it arose from the critique of his father's essay "Government" by Macaulay, not yet famous as Member of Parliament or historian but already well known as a rising star of the *Edinburgh Review*. Macaulay had criticized James Mill's well-known essay for using the *a priori* method; the syllogisms Mill constructed, Macaulay argued, failed to capture the rich cultural variety that made it ridiculous to draw inferences about humans generally. He noted, for example, that morally sensitive Englishmen educated to believe in constitutional values did not usually conduct themselves in the selfish, corrupt, exploitative manner that James Mill predicated for all rulers. Moral and cultural considerations, in other words, made a difference.

Mill was troubled by Macaulay's argument and in the end he altered his own views to take Macaulay's into account. This accommodation was slow to develop, for Mill had difficulty facing the unraveling of his father's—and his own—beliefs. Moreover, his dislike of Macaulay, both personally and for his Whig politics, was another obstacle to recognizing the force of Macaulay's views. Mill's initial way of resolving his difficulty was the decision "that both Macaulay and my father were wrong."[21] This even-handed condemnation was perpetuated in Mill's *Logic* where the method of each (the "geometric method" of James Mill and the "chemical method" of Macaulay) were rejected. This rejection was nominal however, a fig leaf to cover his capitulation to Macaulay's position. Having denied that the actions of rulers were determined by their personal interests (the view of his father and Bentham), he went on to "insist only on what is true of all rulers, viz., that the character and course of their actions is largely influenced (independently of personal calculation) by the habitual sentiments and feelings . . . which prevail throughout the community

---

[19] Mill to William Maccall, 11 November 1849, *CW*, *14*, 38. He regarded certain violent upheavals in the past as having been justifiable, and in his own time he was prepared to consider violence as a way of reaching morally justified goals: Geraint Williams, "J. S. Mill and Political Violence," *Utilitas* 1 (May 1989): 102–11.

[20] Early Draft, *CW*, *1*, 146.

[21] Ibid., 166.

of which they are members."[22] He accepted Macaulay's criticism of his father, which opened his eyes to the importance of individual character as shaped by the underlying beliefs and values instilled by culture. Much later Mill acknowledged that as a result of Macaulay's critique, "a foundation was thus laid in my thoughts for the principal chapters of what I afterwards published on the 'Logic of the Moral Sciences' [Book VI of *A System of Logic*]."[23] This was the part of *Logic* in which Mill set out his ideas about the science of ethology, "which corresponds to the art of education; in the widest sense of the term, including the formation of national or collective character as well as individual."[24] This part of the *Logic* provided the epistemological rationale for Mill's move to cultural politics during the 1840s and 1850s.

There were other experiences that anticipated and influenced his emphasis on cultural politics. The impact of St. Simonism, which coincided with Macaulay's critique of his father, was great. In "Spirit of the Age" (1831), which reflected this influence, he focused on the underlying moral and social perspectives which affected politics but originated in the larger culture. Thus he was concerned with "modes of thinking," opinions, the "sources of moral influence," the foundations of intellectual and moral authority, and changes in "the human mind, and in the whole constitution of human society."[25] Coleridge, whose breakfasts he attended in Highgate in 1832, also directed Mill's attention to these considerations, and this influence was reflected in his essay on Coleridge, who, in contrast to Bentham, was portrayed as one who understood the importance of having a "philosophy of society" and a "philosophy of human culture."[26]

Mill's turn from conventional to cultural politics was sparked and perhaps shaped by Harriet Taylor. His grievances against existing society and his definition of his remedies took shape in cooperation with her. They had been intellectually intimate since the early 1830s and especially after their marriage in 1851. This intimacy was increased by their isolation, born of their disdain for general society, which Mill called "so thoroughly insipid an affair," to be avoided by anyone with serious intellectual inter-

[22] *A System of Logic Ratiocinative and Inductive. Being a Connected View of the Principles of Evidence and the Methods of Scientific Investigation* (1843), *CW*, 8, 891.
[23] Early Draft, *CW*, 1, 168.
[24] *Logic*, 8, 869. On the consequences of Macaulay's critique for Mill's philosophical assumptions and understanding of the practical limits to political activity, see G. W. Smith, "Freedom and Virtue in Politics: Some Aspects of Character, Circumstances and Utility from Helvetius to J. S. Mill," *Utilitas* 1 (May 1989): 122–24, 130. One consequence was "to raise the prospect of reforming human nature out of egoism and low hedonism" (130).
[25] "The Spirit of the Age" (1831), *CW*, 22, 228–29, 231, 312.
[26] "Coleridge" (1840), *CW*, 10, 139.

ests.[27] To Mazzini Mill expressed their shared preference: "We, like you, *feel* that those who would either make their lives useful to noble ends, or maintain any elevation of character within themselves, must in these days have little to do with what is called society."[28] They were thrown together even more closely by their suspicion that Mill's old friends disapproved of their closeness while Harriet was still the wife of John Taylor. After the marriage, only rarely was he available for late afternoon walks and could only be seen by visiting him at the India House for fifteen minutes or so. He never went into any society, Bain tells us, except the monthly meetings of the Political Economy Club.[29] As he and Harriet became increasingly isolated his intellectual explorations were made almost exclusively in her company.

Harriet Taylor had strong radical inclinations and beliefs before her meeting with Mill. She had been part of a freethinking, socially radical circle in which the Unitarian minister William Johnson Fox figured prominently. Admirers of the writings of Mary Wollstonecraft and Shelley, and critical of the society that bridled them, especially on matters of divorce and expression of opinion about marriage and the status of women, the few members of this circle found in it mutual approval for their unorthodox arrangements, including Fox's *ménage de trois* and Harriet's unconventional relations with both Mill and her husband, which, however, appear to have been, with both, asexual.[30] Fox, unhappily married, became mentor to Eliza and Sarah, daughters of his friend Benjamin Flower, the radical editor and publicist. With Eliza a romantic attachment developed, which led to separation from his wife and difficulties with his congregation, though Mineka supports the view of their friends who "never doubted the innocence of their relationship."[31] When Fox introduced Mill to Harriet in 1830 she, like others close to Fox, already was a severe critic of existing society, including most of its conventions and practices. Mill came to share the social life of these hypercritical, somewhat marginal

---

[27] Early Draft, *CW*, *1*, 234.

[28] Mill to Giuseppe Mazzini, 21 February 1858, *CW*, *15*, 548.

[29] Bain, *Mill*, 93.

[30] On the probable asexual character of Mill's relationship with Mrs. Taylor, see Francis E. Mineka, *The Dissidence of Dissent: The Monthly Repository 1806–1838* (Chapel Hill: University of North Carolina Press, 1944), 273. The coterie also included W. J. Linton, Dr. Southwood Smith, Thomas Wade, Richard Henry Horne, William Bridges Adams, Margaret and Mary Gillies, and Eliza and Sarah Flower. F. B. Smith, *Radical Artisan: William James Linton 1812–97* (Manchester: University of Manchester Press, 1973), 9–17. Mineka's conclusion is in keeping with Mill's claim that the relationship "was one of strong affection and confidential intimacy only" and that they were without "impulses of that lower character": Early Draft, *CW*, *1*, 236.

[31] Mineka, *Dissidence of Dissent*, 195; see also 182–83, 188–95; Mill to W. J. Fox, [14 July 1834], *CW*, *12*, 228–29; Harriet Martineau to W. J. Fox, 1 March [1838], in Harriet Martineau, *Selected Letters*, ed. V. Sanders (Oxford: Clarendon, 1990), 52–53.

and disaffected literary intellectuals, and he found them congenial and shared many of their opinions. "All [in this circle] had more or less of alliance with her in sentiments and opinions," he explained; "Into this circle I had the good fortune to be admitted."[32]

Harriet Taylor's radicalism notably included a critique of romantic love and marriage. "The progress of the race *waits* for the emancipation of women from their present degraded slavery to the *necessity* of marriage, or to modes of earning their living which (with the sole exception of artists) consist only of poorly paid and hardly [sic] worked occupations, all the professions, mercantile clerical legal and medical, as well as all government posts being monopolized by men." Dependent as they were on marriage, "the great practical ability of women . . . is now wasted on worthless trifles or sunk in the stupidities called *love*."[33]

Harriet's radicalism was not confined to issues relating only to women. She rejected Christianity, advocated "equalizing among all the individuals comprising the community," and spoke favorably though loosely about the attractions of socialism and communism.[34] These views were accompanied and perhaps fueled by resentments about social class from which even Mill's friends were not immune. Writing in 1849 after the revolutionary events in Paris, she directed her anger onto them.

> Grote always paints his fine acquaintances couleur de rose. That they [the upper classes] dislike and condemn the French proceedings I have no doubt. . . . Tocqueville is a notable specimen of the class which includes all such people as the Sterlings Romillys Carlyles Austins—the gentility class—weak in moral[s] narrow in intellect timid, infinitely conceited, and gossiping. There are very few men in this country who can seem other than more or less respectable puppets to us.[35]

Mill was not wrong in attributing to her "an earnest protest . . . against society as at present constituted," but his moderate words failed to capture Harriet's anger in her fervid criticisms.[36] "Society like all tyrants . . .

[32] Early Draft, *CW, 1*, 194. A few years later Carlyle reported that Mill "restricts himself I fancy to the Fox-Taylor circle of Socinian Radicalism (a lamed cause at this time)": Thomas Carlyle to John A. Carlyle, 27 July 1838. *Collected Letters of Thomas and Jane Welsh Carlyle*, ed. Charles Richard Sanders *et al.* (Durham: Duke University Press, 1985), 10, 137. See also F. A. Hayek, *John Stuart Mill and Harriet Taylor: Their Friendship and Subsequent Marriage* (London: Routledge, 1951), 23–26.

[33] Ibid., 122–23. Harriet Taylor's views on the status of women were shared by others in the Fox circle, notably by William Bridges Adams and by Fox: Mineka, *Dissidence of Dissent*, 284–96.

[34] Hayek, *Mill and Harriet Taylor*, 123.

[35] Harriet Taylor to Mill, 9 July 1849, Mill-Taylor Collection, vol. 50, pp. 96–97, British Library of Political and Economic Science.

[36] As with her views on the position of women, her perspective was shared in the Fox circle, especially with William Bridges Adams, whose "wholesale indictment of English so-

bullies all who submit to be its subjects."[37] This and other themes that showed up in *On Liberty* issued from her pen as early as 1832:

> The root of all intolerance, the spirit of conformity, remains; and not until that is destroyed, will envy hatred and all uncharitableness, with their attendant hypocricies, be destroyed too. Whether it would be religious conformity or social conformity, no matter which the species, the spirit is the same: all kinds agree in this one point, of hostility to individual character, and individual character if it exists at all, can rarely declare itself openly while there is, on all topics of importance a standard of conformity raised by the indolent minded many and guarded by a [word in mansucript indecipherable] of opinion which, though composed individually of the weakest twigs, yet makes up collectively a mass which is not to be resisted with impunity.[38]

She touched on yet other themes that surfaced in *On Liberty*—a defense of eccentricity and a complaint about "a propriety-ridden people"—as she cried out on behalf of the lonely, oppressed individual facing a despotic society.[39]

The broad sweep of her condemnation of society, including its mores and customs, is most sharply revealed in a surviving memorandum headed "Popular Fallacies." She pointed to widely held but false beliefs.

> That the great object of women's life is love.

> That the chief objects and enjoyments in life of mankind are and should be the legalized propagation of the species and the education of their young.

> That what is useful and beautiful in the religious feeling is necessarily connected with any tradition on the subject—either Jewish or Christian or any other. . . .

> That the exercise of the sexual functions is in any degree a necessity. (It is a matter of education)

> That the non exercise of them is necessarily a deprivation.

> That the Bible is Holy.[40]

Harriet's contempt for existing institutions was also reflected in the adjectives she frequently used to describe those who benefited most from their

---

cial and moral standards [was] expressed in uncompromising and vigorous language": Mineka, *Dissidence of Dissent*, 291.

[37] Harriet Taylor, "The Usages of Society," n.d., British Library of Political and Economic Science.

[38] Harriet Taylor, "An Early Essay" [*c.* 1832], in Hayek, *Mill and Harriet Taylor*, 275.

[39] Ibid, 276.

[40] Harriet Taylor, "Popular Fallacies," n.d., Mill-Taylor Collection, British Library of Political and Economic Science.

perpetuation. Her letters and notes were peppered with descriptions of such persons as low, deadening, disgusting, vulgar, degrading.[41]

Many have denied that Harriet made a substantial contribution to Mill's thought. They have read the extravagant eulogies in his dedications to *On Liberty* and *Principles of Political Economy*, and the comparison in the *Autobiography* of Harriet with Shelley, which included the statement that "in thought and intellect Shelley, so far as his powers were developed in his short life, was but a child to her."[42] Such effusions led Alexander Bain to say that Mill's statements "will be treated as pure hyperbole, proving, indeed, the strength of his feelings, but not the reality of the case."[43] Bain even refers to "his extraordinary hallucination as to the personal qualities of his wife." Many others have come to the same conclusion.[44]

Analysis of Mill's eulogies, however, will show that he did not exaggerate her contribution to his new understanding of the goals for reform. For all his effusive language, his praise emphasized her moral outlook, which included criticisms of existing society and a vision of human perfectibility.

Since Mill regarded Harriet as one who enlarged and ennobled his moral feelings and his conception of the proper goals for society, his praise for her did not mean that he had a diminished view of his own talents and achievements. He distinguished between his own talents and hers; she possessed qualities which, he thought, he lacked, but this did not mean he was without qualities different from hers and also important. His eulogies of Harriet can be clarified in light of the division of intellectual labor set forth in the *Logic* where he distinguished between art and science. Both were important, and though art involved more elevated activity, the two functions were complementary and both were necessary to achieve moral improvement. Art defined the end, while science devised the means to reach that end. Morality or ethics was in the realm of art, and the area of scientific knowledge parallel to it consisted of the sciences of human nature and society.[45] Thus art "asserts that the attainment of the given

[41] Harriet Taylor to W. J. Fox, 10 May 1848, Mill-Taylor Collection, British Library of Political and Economic Science.

[42] Early Draft, *CW, 1*, 194.

[43] Alexander Bain to Helen Taylor, 6 September 1873, Mill-Taylor Collection, British Library of Political and Economic Science.

[44] Bain, *Mill*, 171. Mineka also is skeptical, as is Pappé: *Dissidence of Dissent*, 274; H. O. Pappé, *John Stuart Mill and the Harriet Taylor Myth* (Melbourne: Melbourne University Press, 1960,), *passim*.

[45] Logic, *CW, 8*, 942; see also 949: In addition. to morality, art also included policy and aesthetics. For a similar statement of this perspective on Mill's evaluation of Harriet Taylor Mill's contribution, see John M. Robson, ed., Mill, *A Selection of His Works*, xvi–xviii. See also Susan Mendus, "The Marriage of True Minds: The Ideal of Marriage in the Philosophy of John Stuart Mill," in *Sexuality and Subordination: Interdisciplinary Studies of Gender in the Nineteenth Century*, ed. Susan Mendus and Jane Rendall (London: Routledge, 1989), 184–85.

end is desirable," specifying the "first principles of Conduct." Science, on the other hand, seeks knowledge and identifies the means for achieving moral ends.[46]

Mill probably had Harriet in mind when he made this distinction. When he described her to others—in letters, dedications of his books, and the *Autobiography*—he cast her in the role of artist as defined in the *Logic*. She worked in "the region of ultimate aims" and therefore "in the highest regions of philosophy."[47] Her moral perspective, moreover, was less a product of her intellect than her moral sense: her moral ideas were derived from the heart much more than from the head. Soon after she died, he said her "entire faith in the ultimate possibilities of human nature was drawn from her own glorious character."[48] He extolled "her great and loving heart," her "noble soul," and her having been "the companion of all my feelings."[49] Thus in the dedication of *On Liberty*, the emphasis was on her "exalted sense of truth and right" and her "great thoughts and noble feelings," that is, on moral rather than specifically intellectual qualities.

His own role, in contrast, was in the realm of science rather than morality, and it required intellectual qualities more than those of the heart. In his later writings, he explained, "What was abstract and purely scientific was generally mine: the properly human element came from her."[50] This and other descriptions of what each contributed to his writings corresponded to the division of labor laid out in the *Logic*. "My own strength lay wholly in . . . theory, or moral and political science," whereas she defined the moral ends served by his scientific endeavors. The function of the scientific observer or reasoner "is only to show that certain consequences follow from certain causes, and that to obtain certain ends, certain means are the most effectual. Whether the ends themselves are such as ought to be pursued . . . is no part of his business."[51] With this understanding of his distinctive function, there was nothing self-depreciatory in his high praise for his wife. All the praise—for her moral vision, her character, her noble soul— recognized qualities that complemented but which were not in competition with his own. Regarding the subjects he wrote about most extensively (logic, political economy, government) he did not claim she was the source of his ideas.

[46] *Logic*, CW, *8*, 944, 949, 951.
[47] Early Draft, CW, 1, 194
[48] Mill to Louis Blanc, 4 March 1859, CW, *15*, 601.
[49] Hayek, *Mill and Harriet Taylor*, 267; Mill to William Thomas Thornton, 9 November 1858, CW, *15*, 574.
[50] Early Draft, CW, *1*, 256.
[51] *Logic*, CW, *8*, 950.

Mill's view that Harriet was engaged in the art of morality is made plausible by recalling her actual moral judgments—her severe, angry condemnation of her own society, especially its family, sexual, and religious arrangements, and its oppressiveness, which stunted its many victims. Her moral disgust was not concealed, nor was her belief that the source of corruption was endemic, and this nourished Mill's conviction in 1854 that a "reconstruction of the human intellect *ab imo*" was necessary. The idea of reconstruction implies a remedy that was anything but small in scale or incremental; it is implicitly utopian, and Harriet's allusions to the future, although rarely concrete, showed that she had a vision of a society characterized by freedom, equality, and justice, in which selfishness would be abolished and altruism would prevail.

Mill shared these hopes, and he suggested that she was the source of them. In the suppressed dedication of the *Principles of Political Economy* she was described as "the most eminently qualified of all persons known to the author either to originate or to appreciate speculations on social improvement." The inscription on her tomb referred to her contribution to the future happiness of mankind: "Her influence has been felt in many of the greatest improvements of the age and will be in those still to come. Were there but a few hearts and intellects like hers this earth would already become the hoped-for heaven."[52] In these statements Mill alluded to Harriet's substantial contribution to the shift in his outlook during the 1840s and 1850s—the shift to concern with morals and motives and their sources in the culture, and therefore the change from conventional politics to cultural-intellectual politics, which were concerned with moral education and religion. Of course, Mill was not indifferent to these matters earlier in his life, and one can find allusions to them in writings that probably were immune from Harriet's influence, but in light of what we know about her great concern with these matters, which was much greater than Mill's during the first decades of their friendship (1830–50), there is no reason to reject Mill's attributions of influence to her, especially as in doing so he was not renouncing his own claims as the man of science who was responsible for most of the *Logic* and *Political Economy*, to say nothing of *Representative Government* and the multitude of substantial essays on economics and philosophy.

This conclusion is borne out by several of the acknowledgments he made of her influence, notably in the *Autobiography*, where he makes it clear that she was the main source of his belief that the transformation of morality and culture was necessary. The *Political Economy*, due to her encouragement, "never treats the mere arrangements of modern society as final," and this led him to visualize greatly altered social arrangements,

---

[52] Hayek, *Mill and Harriet Taylor*, 122, 267.

making possible new understandings about private property and allowing him to "contemplate possibilities, as to the springs of human action in economical matters, which had only been affirmed by Socialists and in general fiercely denied by political economists."[53] Similar testimony was given elsewhere. In 1854 he claimed to have experienced "the continual elevation of my standing point and change of my bearings towards all the great subjects of thought. But the explanation is that I owe the enlargement of my ideas and feelings to *her* influence."[54] She was "the source of a great part of all that I have attempted to do, or hope to effect hereafter for human improvement."[55]

These statements were not vague testimonials; he was referring to the shift in his outlook that took place during the 1840s and 1850s. He was aware that a great change was occurring. Writing in the 1850s, and referring specifically to the period since the completion of *Logic*, he said his writings were "largely and in their most important features the direct product of her own mind. . . . In the great advance which I have since made in opinion I was wholly her pupil. Her bolder and more powerful mind arrived before mine at every conclusion which was derived from a more thorough comprehension of the present and insight into the future."[56] He also said, without her influence, "all I possessed before is of little value,"[57] and, "Whenever I look back at any of my own writings of two or three years previous, they seem to me like the writings of some stranger whom I have seen and known long ago."[58] His sense of indebtedness for the redirection of his thought was reflected in a conversation of 1865, when, with tears in his eyes, he claimed, "she was above everyone and inspired everyone."[59]

––––––––––

Mill thought of his hoped-for cultural revolution in light of his understanding of historical change. Looking at the broad sweep of history, he focused on ideas and beliefs as defining characteristics of an age and as levers of change. Looking back, one could observe the decline of some beliefs and the emergence of others—Christianity followed paganism, Protestantism (in northern Europe) succeeded Catholicism, the Enlightenment challenged Christianity. An era was often defined by the beliefs that

[53] Early Draft, *CW*, *1*, 254, 256.
[54] Diary, 20 February [1854], *CW*, *27*, 655–56.
[55] Early Draft, *CW*, *1*, 192.
[56] Early Draft, *CW*, *1*, 234 n.
[57] Early Draft, *CW*, *1*, 196.
[58] Diary, 20 February [1854], *CW*, *27*, 655.
[59] Kate Amberley's diary, 20 Feb. 1865, *The Amberley Papers. The Letters and Diaries of Lord and Lady Amberley*, eds. Bertrand & Patricia Russell (London, Hogarth, 1932), *1* 372. Harriet Taylor Mill's influence on Mill was first emphasized by Hayek in *Mill and Harriet Taylor*.

were most widely accepted, and since Mill was especially interested in morality and conduct, he focused on moral and religious beliefs. Of course, the process was untidy—old beliefs, though no longer dominant, survived, and new beliefs were accepted by some but not all. Such a situation was what he called a transitional state of society, a conception taken from Comte and the St. Simonians.

It implied that disagreements resulting in a mixture of old and new beliefs were temporary and abnormal, and that typically there would be general agreement about the beliefs that were worthy and true. These typical, presumably more normal, times were called organic eras by the St. Simonians. Transitional eras were characterized by disagreement among the elites, popular rejection of the elite's claim to moral authority, and a condition of intellectual disagreement that was somewhat anarchic; in contrast, during organic eras there was harmony, as the elites all shared the same beliefs, and the populace accepted their authority and deferred to it. Mill's adoption of these views was most evident in his early essays, "The Spirit of the Age" (1831), but for the remainder of his life he used these St. Simonian categories in his thinking about history and social change, though in later years he did not often use the St. Simonian terminology.[60]

In this perspective, long-term, fundamental change was driven by ideas and beliefs and not by legislation or economic forces. Those whose ideas prevailed determined the future development of society. "It is what men think, that determines how they act."[61] The goal was to get possession of "the intellects and dispositions of the public," whereas impatient reformers (as he had been during the 1820s and 1830s) only aimed to gain possession of the government.[62] Because ideas and beliefs were the keys to long-term, substantial change, the clash of opinions had the greatest political importance, for without it new ideas would be denied an opportunity to gain acceptance. This consideration gave liberty to discuss and publish one's opinions its significance, for it made possible what Mill called "revolutions of opinion" (252). Out of this process, "the united authority of the instructed" would emerge, and because the beliefs of the average man would be shaped by this authority, those who stood for the most compelling ideas were in a position to gain great power.[63] Thus by attaching so

[60] See below, chapter 6, note 47, for citations to places where he referred to transitional states of society.

[61] *Considerations on Representative Government* (1861), *CW*, *19*, 382.

[62] *Political Economy*, *CW*, *3*, 799, The assumption that one could shape the future by forming motives and beliefs and therefore the culture was also evident in Mill's occasional use of the terms 'spiritual' and 'temporal,' which he took from Comte, who persuaded him that work in the spiritual (intellectual, philosophic) realm was superior to work in the temporal (active, political) realm. See Comte to Mill, 17 January 1842; Mill to Comte, 25 February 1842, 23 October 1842: *Correspondence of Mill and Comte*, 45–46, 51, 110.

[63] *Representative Government*, *CW*, *19*, 382.

much importance to ideas and beliefs, he was also elevating the intellectual and, by comparison, diminishing the importance of the party or Parliamentary politician. This was not a retreat from politics so much as a recognition of the political significance of ideas and beliefs. Cultural politics came to the fore as the intellectual, in addition to being a man of letters, became a politician.

The way in which the intellectual might shape the future was described in the *Logic*, and especially in the chapter added in 1862, after Mill concentrated his attention on cultural politics. To attribute great influence to the intellectual, Mill had to revise his views on historical causation. Earlier he held that progress almost certainly would take place: the "general tendency is, and will continue to be, saving occasional and temporary exceptions, one of improvement; a tendency towards a better and happier state." Moreover, he also believed "the proximate cause of every state of society is the state of society immediately preceding it." Each great change in society influenced the previous stage; and the mode of thinking at any given stage (for example, Polytheism, Christianity, or the critical philosophy of modern Europe) was "a primary agent in making society what it was at each successive period . . . each of them . . . being mainly an emanation . . . from the previous state of belief and thought." This understanding did not allow much scope for the initiative of speculative thinkers seeking to alter the course of history, and it was tied to his assumption that one might discover laws "according to which social states generate one another as society advances."[64]

Mill in 1862 revised these opinions and made the speculative thinker more of an innovator with vast influence in the long term if not in the immediate future. Now such persons were freed from the constraints imposed by the laws of history.

> Eminent men do not merely see the coming light from the hill-top, they mount on the hilltop and evoke it; and if no one had ever ascended thither, the light, in many cases, might never have risen upon the plain at all. Philosophy and religion are abundantly amenable to general causes; yet few will doubt, that had there been no Socrates, no Plato, and no Aristotle, there would have been no philosophy for the next two thousand years, nor in all probability then; and that if there had been no Christ, and no St. Paul, there would have been no Christianity.[65]

Describing the role he hoped to play, he explained that the work of great intellectual figures would germinate and produce tremendous effects in the distant future.

---

[64] *Logic, CW, 8*, 912–14, 924, 927.
[65] Ibid., 938.

It must not be concluded that [their] influence . . . is small, because they cannot bestow what the general circumstances of society, and the course of its previous history, have not prepared it to receive. . . . Great men, and great actions, are seldom wasted: they send forth a thousand unseen influences. . . . Even the men who for want of sufficiently favourable circumstances left no impress at all upon their own age, have often been of the greatest value to posterity.[66]

The "greatest speculative thinker," in this revised view, became a formative influence in history.[67]

To play such a part, the intellectual had to address issues large enough to define an era, for example, democracy, enlightenment, or Christianity. In an earlier age when speculative thinkers did this, "The writers of reputation and influence were those who took a side, in a very decided manner, on the great questions, religious, moral, metaphysical, and political; who were downright infidels or downright Christians, thorough Tories or thorough democrats, and in that were considered, and were, extreme in their opinions."[68] This style of thinking had been depreciated throughout Mill's lifetime. His father had been branded an advocate of "utopian democracy" by Macaulay.[69] The Philosophic Radicals, including Mill as their intellectual leader, had been criticized for being extreme, dogmatic, and uncompromising. The practice of compromise and conciliation had been elevated to a national virtue by Burke and in that part of the Whig tradition for which Macaulay spoke in Parliament and which he celebrated in his *History of England*. All this was an obstacle to Mill's grand strategy for reform, and in his 1854 diary he announced his determination to counter this current. "The time is now come, or coming, for a change the reverse way."[70]

Most mid-nineteenth-century intellectuals responded to the extremism of earlier times by promoting moderation and splitting differences—by compromise. This, after all, was the English way. England, Mill said rather disdainfully, was "the native country of compromise."[71] The English "take something from both sides of the great controversies, and make out that neither extreme is right, nor wholly wrong. . . . this is done by way of mere compromise."[72] For this tendency Mill condemned Macaulay as well as the entire ethos.[73] The shrinking away from extremes,

---

[66] Ibid., 939–40.

[67] Ibid., 938. This was foreshadowed in "Bentham" (1838), *CW, 10,* 77.

[68] Diary, 18 January [1854], *CW, 27,* 644.

[69] Thomas Babington Macaulay, "Mill on Government" (March 1829), *Miscellaneous Writings of Lord Macaulay* (London, 1860), *1,* 301.

[70] Diary, 18 January [1854], *CW, 27,* 644.

[71] "Coleridge" (1840), *CW, 10,* 131.

[72] Diary, 18 January [1854], *CW 27,* 644.

[73] Macaulay "in some degree ministers to English conceit— only in some degree, for he never 'goes the whole' in anything. He is very characteristic and so is his book [*History of*

both in speculation and in practice, came more from "an instinct of caution than a result of insight," and thus the English mind was "too ready to satisfy itself with any medium, merely because it is a medium, and to acquiesce in a union of the disadvantages of both extremes instead of their advantages." As a consequence, intellectual life was flabby and superficial. "The age seemed smitten with an incapacity of producing deep or strong feeling. . . . An age like this, an age without earnestness, was the natural era of compromises and half-convictions."[74] Rejecting this, Mill favored immoderate bold assertion. "I know that compromises are often inevitable in practice, but I think they should be left to the enemy to propose—reformers should assert principles and only *accept* compromises."[75] In contrast to Macaulay and the entire tenor of the time, there were only a few who met Mill's standards. To his wife, he wrote,

> I can think only of two (now that Carlyle has written himself out, and become a mere commentator on himself) who seem to draw what they say from a source within themselves: and to the practical doctrines and tendencies of both of these, there are the gravest objections. Comte, on the Continent; in England (ourselves excepted) I can think only of Ruskin.[76]

This perspective was evident in *On Liberty* where Mill complained, "That which would strengthen and enlarge men's minds, free and daring speculation on the highest subjects, is abandoned" (242). Instead, he believed that "bold free expansion in all directions is demanded by the needs of modern life."[77]

In rejecting compromise, Mill advocated its opposite with an unusual twist, for he was opposed to moving to a single extreme, and instead, he sought to combine what was best from all bold, radical ideas without diluting any of them. He wished to discover "a deeper doctrine underlying both the contrary opinions."[78] This was repeated in *On Liberty*: "Truth, in the great practical concerns of life, is so much a question of the reconcil-

---

England (1849), vols. 1, 2], of the English people and of his time." Mill to Harriet Taylor, 27 January [1849], *CW*, *14*, 6.

[74] "Coleridge" (1840), *CW*, *10*, 141–42. Also: "It is easy to be practical, in a society all practical: there is a practicalness which comes by nature, to those who know little and aspire to nothing; exactly this is the sort which the vulgar form of the English mind exemplifies. . . . " Mill, "Armand Carrel," *CW*, *20*, 173.

[75] Mill to William Johnson Fox, [end of 1849], *CW*, *14*, 39.

[76] Diary, 21 January [1854], *CW*, *27*, 645.

[77] Diary, 6 February [1854], *CW*, *27*, 651.

[78] Diary, 18 January [1854], *CW*, *27*, 644. The same theme underlay his proposal for the constitution: "A better doctrine [than any that had emerged in recent debate between the two parties] must be possible; not a mere compromise, by splitting the difference between the two, but something wider than either, which, in virtue of its superior comprehensiveness, might be adopted by either Liberal or Conservative without renouncing anything which he really feels to be valuable in his own creed": *Representative Government*, *CW*, *19*, 373.

ing and combining of opposites" (254). This combination was not to be a dilution of the extremes but rather a selection of the best they contained. For example, as Mill considered the negative philosophy of the previous three centuries and the reaction to it in Comte's conception of a regenerated society, he decided that each side, Comte and the liberals, had about half the truth, and "each sees what the other does not see."[79]

The attempt to select and combine, of course, was to be Mill's task. This was evident in his wish to find a synthesis of the best from what appeared to be polar opposites, for example, from Bentham and Coleridge; and it was evident in his wish to combine order with progress, enlightened leadership with democratic control, competition with a just distribution of rewards, and, it will be argued, control with liberty. In *On Liberty* Mill argued for free discussion of other "standing antagonisms of practical life"—democracy and aristocracy, property and equality, cooperation and competition, luxury and abstinence, and significantly, sociality and individuality, as well as liberty and discipline (254).[80]

Mill thought of his own role in relation to these themes. He was to be the bold, radical thinker, out of step with his own time, whose speculations would serve to bring into existence a new moral and social order in the distant future. He was not alone in this project, for Harriet also had the rare qualities of the "great speculative thinker" described in the Logic.[81] Incorporating her ideas, his writings were to be the works of theory that would prove useful in the distant future when society would be prepared to receive them. "It is as a preparation for that time that my speculations . . . may be valuable."[82] Although Mill was not actively engaged in conventional politics, his speculation about future morality and society had great relevance to politics in the largest sense. Thus he regarded writing as a mode of action, bearing not so much on the outward world as "upon the spiritual world of thought and feeling, the action of the artist, the preacher, and the philosopher."[83] Of course, it was difficult to discern all the features of "the impending transformation of society," but Mill's speculations had this distant end in sight.[84] Although he could not expect to see the building completed, at least, with Harriet's help, he could serve as its architect.

[79] *Auguste Comte and Positivism* (1865), CW, *10*, 313.

[80] It was a commonplace in politics that a party of order or stability and a party of progress or reform are both necessary, "until the one or the other shall have so enlarged its mental grasp as to be a party equally of order and of progress, knowing and distinguishing what is fit to be preserved from what ought to be swept away." *On Liberty*, CW, *18*, 253.

[81] *Logic*, CW, *8*, 938.

[82] Mill to Henry Taylor, 5 July 1861, CW, *15*, 731.

[83] "Armand Carrel," CW, *20*, 194–95.

[84] Mill to Pasquale Villari, 28 February 1872, CW, *17*, 1873.

These thoughts reveal the vast expanse of his ambition. Of course, political ambition was not new to him. Even before reaching manhood he had "juvenile aspirations to the character of a democratic champion."[85] And during the 1830s he offered intellectual leadership to the Philosophic Radicals and even wished to be in Parliament with them.[86] Throughout his life Parliament never lost its fascination for him, and of course he even served briefly as a Member (1865–68), but in the 1840s and 1850s his ambition was turned away from conventional politics and directed to nothing less than the reshaping of moral ideas and beliefs.

Mill's aspirations were revealed in his identification of his project with Plato's. From boyhood he had felt "reverential admiration for the lives and character of heroic persons; especially the heroes of philosophy," and now in his middle years he described Plato's project in the same terms that he used to explain his plan for moral reform.[87] Plato, he said, judged the Sophists from the

> superior elevation of a great moral and social reformer: from that height he looked down contemptuously enough, not on them alone, but on statesmen, orators, artists—on the whole practical life of the period, and all its institutions, popular, oligarchical, or despotic; *demanding a reconstitution of society from its foundations, and a complete renovation of the human mind.* (emphasis added)[88]

Mill was convinced that there was a parallel with his own time: "It is most certain that Plato, if he returned to life, would be to the full as contemptuous of our statesmen, lawyers, clergy, professors, authors, and all others among us who lay claim to mental superiority, as he ever was of the corresponding class at Athens."[89] And, we might add, as Mill was in London.

There were obstacles, however, to accomplishing a project like Plato's. People were too complacent, custom was too much respected, received opinion was not sufficiently questioned for a plan of moral reform and renovation, such as Mill's, to succeed. Consequently, the work of Socra-

---

[85] Early Draft, *CW*, *1*, 164, 166.

[86] Bain, *Mill*, 124.

[87] Early Draft, *CW*, *1*, 114. F. E. Sparshott labels Mill "very deeply a Platonist. . . . The very detail and texture of his thought reflects that of Plato": Introduction, *Essays on Philosophy and the Classics*, *CW*, *11*, xxxiii; however, on defects in Mill's understanding of Plato, see xl–xli. In the introduction to one of the Dialogues he translated and published, Mill complained that at that time there were in Britain only 100 persons who had read Plato and only 20 who do read him: ibid., 40. For testimony about how Mill was inspired by Plato, see ibid., 150.

[88] "Grote's History of Greece [5]" (1850), *CW*, *25*, 1162. See also "Grote's History of Greece [II]" (1853), *CW*, *11*, 329.

[89] "Grote's Plato," *CW*, *11*, 387. Mill alluded to another parallel between himself and Plato in saying, with regard to the religion of the country, Plato "probably rejected it altogether": "Grote's History of Greece [II]," *CW*, *11*, 332.

tes, who of course prepared the way for Plato's thought, "requires to be done again, as the indispensable condition of that intellectual renovation, without which the grand moral and social improvements, to which mankind are now beginning to aspire, will be for ever unattainable.[90] The work of Socrates was to question, to generate skepticism, to undermine the foundations of the established order. Socrates was valued for his *elenchus*, which was necessary before a new order could be constructed on the ruins of the old. "The common notions of the present time on moral and mental subjects," Mill explained, "are as incapable of supporting the Socratic cross-examination as those of his own age." Thus Socrates, "as the direct antagonist of such unsifted general notions and impressions on moral subjects,"[91] was the model for the part of Mill's plan for moral reform that called for weakening the foundations of the old order that still survived during the present transitional period. Thus Socrates was a kind of man "at all times needful, and seldom more needed than now."[92] Mill often tried to perform this Socratic function, but he also provided for it by promoting free discussion and criticism of established ideas and customs in *On Liberty*, all to set the stage for reconstruction and renovation. The ambition, radicalism, and utopian goal of Mill's thought as it developed in mid-life could not have been revealed more clearly.

Since so much of history was determined by the fall of one set of beliefs and the rise of another, Mill evaluated ideas as they were related to this process. They were either old or new and belonged, respectively, to "the stationary part of mankind" or "the progressive part."[93] There were also those in advance of their age (Mill transparently used this language to refer to his own ideas)[94] and those which he depreciated by calling them "received opinion."[95] Philosophies and doctrines were labeled as they played a part in the struggle of ideas. Some were destructive, others constructive.[96] The contrasting but complementary philosophies of Bentham and Coleridge were characterized with these labels. Bentham's philosophy was negative, critical; it helped destroy old traditions and beliefs, but it

---

[90] "Grote's History of Greece [5]," CW, 25, 1164.

[91] "Grote's History of Greece [5]," CW, 25, 1163–64. Since Plato was the recorder or creator of Socrates, Mill also attributed the Socratic function to Plato, making the elenctic as well as the dogmatic Plato: "Grote's Plato," CW, 11, 413. In this Mill follows Grote: see George Grote, *Plato and the Other Companions of Sokrates*, 1, 270–71. One might add that while Mill would have rejected the notion that there were two Mills, he subscribed to a "two Platos" doctrine: "two complete Platos in Plato—the Sokratist and the Dogmatist": CW, 11, 415.

[92] "Grote's History of Greece [II]," CW, 11, 309.

[93] "Spirit of the Age" (1831), CW, 22, 245. The categories 'stationary' and 'progressive' were also applied to the development of society in Greece. "Grote's History of Greece [II]," CW, 11, 313.

[94] For example, Mill to William E. Hickson, 14 April 1851, CW, 14, 61; Mill to John Chapman, 20 June 1851, ibid., 72.

[95] "Spirit of the Age," CW, 22, 290.

[96] Mill to Henry Samuel Chapman, 28 May 1849, CW, 14, 34.

was incomplete. What it neglected, however, might be supplied by Coleridge's, which was constructive.

Fashioning his own political role in relation to these antinomies, Mill brought his pen to bear on two intellectual fronts—he tried to undermine much that was old and established while also proposing new ideas that might fill the gap left by the success of destructive criticism. These dual functions were called for by his living, as he believed, in a transitional era, when old ideas, though no longer sustainable, survived, and new ideas, though entertained by a few advanced thinkers, were not yet established. "The old opinions in religion, morals, and politics, are so much discredited in the more intellectual minds as to have lost the greater part of their efficacy for good, while they have still vitality enough left to be an effectual obstacle to the rising up of better opinions on the same subjects."[97] Therefore, the negative, destructive, Socratic, Benthamite critique of the old had to be continued to remove the vestiges of old opinions about religion and morality. "The period of decomposition . . . is not yet terminated," and therefore to bring down the "shell of the old edifice," it had to be subjected to continuous criticism.[98] "The principle itself of dogmatic religion, dogmatic morality, dogmatic philosophy is what requires to be rooted out."[99] To bring about this result was one of the functions of the ample freedom proposed in the chapter on liberty of thought and discussion in *On Liberty*. There Mill defended "negative logic," which pointed out weaknesses in established theories without, however, establishing new truths (251).

Mill's task did not end there, however. "Negative criticism would indeed be poor enough as an ultimate result." It was only a first stage which was to be followed by the attaining of "positive knowledge or conviction" (251–52). This will happen only

> when a renovation has been effected in the bases of belief, leading to the evolution of another faith, whether religious or not, which they [the philosophic minds] can believe. Therefore I hold that all thinking or writing, which does not directly tend towards this renovation, is at present of very little value beyond the moment.[100]

While the negative, destructive tactics required the promotion of individual liberty, the positive role that tended toward renovation would have, it will be seen, highly problematic consequences for liberty.

---

[97] Early Draft, *CW, 1*, 244. 246.

[98] *Auguste Comte and Positivism, CW, 10*, 325.

[99] "Civilization," *CW, 18*, 144.

[100] Early Draft, *CW 1*, 246. "The new synthesis is barely begun, nor is even the preparatory analysis completely finished," and it was necessary to proceed with this, for "the old edifice will remain standing until there is another ready to replace it": *Auguste Comte and Positivism, CW, 10*, 325–26. Since he wished to undermine what was established while also

The contributions Mill wished to make to the politics of ideas and beliefs—on both the negative and positive sides—were revealed in his writings of the 1850s and early 1860s. The rapid composition of his many essays on a variety of subjects written during the decade or so beginning in 1853 was a consequence of the ill health he and Harriet experienced at that time. Coughing fits and spitting of blood convinced Mill that he was suffering from tuberculosis, the disease from which his father died, and that he would die in the very near future. Both he and Harriet sought more benign climates—Harriet in the south of France and Mill, after a few months with her in France, in Italy, Sicily, and Greece (late 1854 until mid-1855)—and it is only because they did not travel together that we have Mill's long letters to her and his diary of 1854, also written for her, which reveal his expectations of imminent death and its effect on his intellectual activities.[101]

Experiencing frightening symptoms just as he developed strong conviction about the great significance of his new ideas about moral reform, Mill suddenly felt a sense of urgency. "Those who have thoughts and feelings to impress on the world have a great deal of hard work to do, and very little time to do it in," he wrote in his diary. "The regeneration of the world in its present stage is a matter of business." Also, "I feel bitterly how I have procrastinated in the sacred duty of fixing in writing, so that it may not die with me, everything that I have in my mind which is capable of assisting the destruction of error and prejudice and the growth of just feelings and true opinions."[102] And to Harriet he wrote, "I now feel so strongly the necessity of giving the little time we are sure of to writing things which nobody could write but ourselves, that I do not like turning aside to anything else."[103] Since there was not time for long treatises, he decided on essays, which, in any case, were more suitable for a large audience. These essays were to contain "concentrated thought—a sort of mental pemican, which thinkers, when there are any after us, may nourish themselves with and then dilute for other people."[104] The focus, then, was on the distant future. Not many conversions among his contemporaries were expected, but he was consoled by looking ahead. "We *must* be satisfied with keeping alive the sacred fire in a few minds when we are unable to do more."[105] He hoped that in the future there

---

promoting renovation, his friend John Morley discerned both criticism and belief in his thought and called the combination a "double way of viewing": "Mr. Mill's Autobiography," *Fortnightly Review* 21 (1 January 1874): 5.

[101] Diary, 19, 24, 25, 26, 28, 30, 31 March; 1, 3, 12 April [1854], CW, 27, 663–67.

[102] Diary, 19, 27 January [1854], CW, 27, 644, 647.

[103] Mill to Harriet Taylor Mill, 30 June [1854], CW, 14, 222.

[104] Mill to Harriet Taylor Mill, 29 January [1854], CW, 14, 141–42. On pemican, see Gertrude Himmelfarb, *On Liberty and Liberalism: The Case of John Stuart Mill* (New York: Knopf, 1974), 243, 253.

[105] Mill to Alexander Bain, 6 August 1859, CW, 15, 631.

would be a new generation of intellectual leaders that would be "capable of taking up the thread of thought and continuing it."[106] This hope—or plan—allowed Mill to say, "Books are a real magic, or rather necromancy—a person speaking from the dead, and speaking his most earnest feelings and gravest and most recondite thoughts."[107]

At first he had in mind one or two posthumous volumes of essays: "my heart is set on having these in a state fit for publication quelconque, if we live so long, by Christmas 1855."[108] When a little less gloomy he hoped to publish a volume "almost annually for the next few years if I live as long."[109] With his wife, a list of subjects was composed: differences of character (nation, race, age, sex, temperament), love, education of tastes, the religion of the future, Plato, slander, foundation of morals, utility of religion, socialism, liberty, doctrine that causation is will, nature, justice, ballot, family, convention. He asked if this agenda will be "a tolerable two years work"![110] He regarded his autobiography as part of the mental pemican, as it included opinions "which we have not written anywhere else, and which will make it as valuable in that respect . . . as the best thing we have published."[111]

In referring to the things "we" published of course he included Harriet Taylor Mill. The substance of the essays of this period he represented as hers as well as his own. He wielded the pen but authorship was joint. "I regard the whole of what I am writing or shall write as mere raw material, in what manner and into what to be worked up to be decided between us."[112] Their close cooperation in the planning and preparation of these essays has a direct bearing on how one judges Harriet Mill's contribution to works published under Mill's name alone. He wished to have both their names on the title page of the prospective volume of essays.[113] And in the dedication of *On Liberty* he said, "Like all that I have written for many years, it belongs as much to her as to me" (216). Later, in the *Autobiography*, he called *On Liberty* a "joint production" and said, "The whole mode of thinking of which the book was the expression, was emphatically hers," and he acknowledged her influence more pointedly by adding, "I also was so thoroughly imbued with it that the same thoughts naturally occurred to us both."[114] He gave her even greater credit in a part

[106] Mill to Harriet Taylor Mill, 29 January [1854], *CW, 14*, 141–42.
[107] Diary, 6 April [1854], *CW, 27, 666.*
[108] Mill to Harriet Taylor Mill, 29 January [1854], *CW, 14*, 142.
[109] Mill to Harriet Taylor Mill, 25February [1855], *CW, 14*, 348.
[110] Diary, 7 March [1854], *CW, 27, 659.* Mill to Harriet Taylor Mill, [30] August 1853; 7 February [1854]; 24 June [1854]; 30 June [1854]; *CW, 14*, 111, 152, 218, 221–22.
[111] Mill to Harriet Taylor Mill, 10 February [1854], *CW, 14*, 154.
[112] Mill to Harriet Taylor Mill, 20 March [1854], *CW 14*, 190.
[113] Mill to Harriet Taylor Mill, [30] August 1853, *CW, 14*, 112.
[114] *Autobiography, CW, 1*, 257, 259.

of the early draft to his autobiography that subsequently was deleted. In it he distinguished between publications that preceded *Political Economy* and those that followed (up to 1853–54 when this passage was composed). The latter belonged to a period "characterized by the predominating influence of my wife's intellect and character." Those from the earlier period, if published after they became intellectually intimate, benefited from her revisions and suggestions, but they "were not, like the subsequent ones, largely and in their most important features the direct product of her own mind . . . . in the great advance which I have since made in opinion I was wholly her pupil."[115]

Not all the subjects in their list became the occasion for an essay, but several did—the foundation of morals (in *Utilitarianism* [1861]), utility of religion, socialism, nature, and of course liberty. Some subjects were discussed in more than one completed essay, for example, the religion of the future was included in "Utility of Religion," *Utilitarianism*, and *Auguste Comte and Positivism*; and love and family were briefly discussed in *On Liberty* before being taken up in *Subjection of Women*. And a few, notably "differences of character," which would have been part of his work on ethology, were never completed and perhaps were not even begun.[116] He described the essays eventually completed as dealing with "some of the fundamental questions of human and social life."[117]

That Mill wished to include these many subjects in his mental pemican indicates that he regarded all of them as contributing to his plan for moral and cultural reform that was to bring about regeneration and the reconstruction of the human intellect. And since he aimed to perform both destructive and constructive functions with regard to opinion and belief, we should assume that both were included in the body of work produced during the 1850s and 1860s and that perhaps both purposes were served in single works, including the essay on liberty.

---

[115] Early Draft, *CW*, *1*, 234 n.
[116] Mill to Alexander Bain, 14 November 1859, *CW*, *15*, 645.
[117] *Autobiography*, *CW*, *1*, 245.

Chapter Three

MILL AND CHRISTIANITY

> I was brought up from the first without any religious belief,
> in the ordinary meaning of the term. . . . I am thus one of the
> very few examples, in this country, of one who has, not
> thrown off religious belief, but never had it.
>
> (*John Stuart Mill*)

REGENERATION was to be preceded by destruction. Beliefs surviving from the past that were obstacles to the emergence of a new moral order were to be eliminated. Progress required hastening this demise of the old morality, which, beyond the circles of the most advanced and emancipated thinkers, still enjoyed the support of most people. "The old opinions in religion, morals, and politics are so much discredited in the more intellectual minds"; however, "they have still life enough in them to be a powerful obstacle to the growing up of any better opinions on those subjects."[1] Mill therefore mounted an attack on these old opinions, especially those about religion and custom. He carried out the negative, destructive part of his strategy for moral reform by seeking to cast doubt on these two pillars of existing moral opinion and belief, and *On Liberty* was an important instrument for the achievement of this goal.

The distinguishing feature of the old morality, according to Mill, was selfishness. Criticisms of it and egotism became a recurring theme in his thinking during the early 1850s. It appeared in his diary as disapproval of vanity for being "a moral defect; a form of selfishness; a dwelling on, and caring about, self and what belongs to it, beyond the just measure."[2] It was reflected in the softening of his criticisms of socialism in the third edition (1852) of his *Political Economy*, and especially in the chapters greatly influenced by Harriet, "Of the Stationary State" and "On the Probable Futurity of the Labouring Classes." In the first of these he implicitly condemned self-seeking by criticizing "the ideal of life held out by those who think that the normal state of human beings is that of struggling to get on; that the trampling, crushing, elbowing, and treading on each other's heels, which form the existing type of social life, are the most desirable lot of human kind"; and in describing the northern and middle

---

[1] *Autobiography, CW, 1,* 245, 247.
[2] Diary, 25 January [1854], *CW, 27,* 646.

states in America as places where "the life of the whole of one sex is devoted to dollar-hunting, and of the other to breeding dollar-hunters." In the other of these two chapters he criticized paternalistic theories for ignoring the fact that all privileged and powerful classes, whether of rich in relation to poor, kings in relation to subjects, or men in relation to women, while presenting themselves as protectors, in fact "have used their power in the interest of their own selfishness."[3] The same harsh judgment was clearly implied in his favorable accounts of society following a moral transformation, when the prevailing motivation would be concern for others rather than for oneself.

For Mill to condemn selfishness required a considerable shifting of intellectual ground, for he had been taught to assume that in some form or other self-seeking was unalterably a part of human nature. Of course this did not mean its consequences were always approved, but it was assumed that it could be channeled or directed to useful ends by well-arranged institutions. This view underlay political economy and Bentham's utilitarianism, and the radical changes in Mill's views about these two fields of inquiry reflected his determination to reconstruct their psychological foundations in ways that made them compatible with his new conviction that motivations could be altruistic rather than selfish. This was part of his project for moral regeneration and for "the reconstruction of human intellect."

Some of his harshest criticisms of selfishness linked it to Christianity. The real task of religion was to direct emotions and desires away from low objects and to be "paramount over all selfish objects of desire." Moreover, it ought to make us disinterested: "It carries the thoughts and feelings out of self, and fixes them on an unselfish object, loved and pursued as an end for its own sake." Christianity, however, in Mill's view, did anything but this:

> The religions which deal in promises and threats regarding a future life, do exactly the contrary: they fasten down the thoughts to the person's own posthumous interests; they tempt him to regard the performance of his duties to others mainly as a means to his personal salvation; and are one of the most serious obstacles to the great purpose of moral culture, the strengthening of the unselfish and the weakening of the selfish element in our nature.[4]

This analysis Mill repeated quite often. Although Christianity was a spiritual religion, "we are instructed to obey from selfish motives."[5] Far from elevating one's thoughts, it became "a personal affair between an individual and his Maker, in which the issue at stake is but his private salvation.

---

[3] *Principles of Political Economy,* CW, 2, xciii; 3, 754, 754n., 760.
[4] "Utility of Religion," CW, 10, 422; see also 426.
[5] "Coleridge," CW, 10, 145.

Religion in this shape is quite consistent with the most selfish and con-tracted egoism, and identifies the votary as little in feeling with the rest of his kind as sensuality itself."[6]

Christianity, therefore, far from being a tool for criticizing existing cul-ture, actually was congenial to that culture, a support, and worse, an obstacle to changing it.

> There is a very real evil consequent on ascribing a supernatural origin to the received maxims of morality. That origin consecrates the whole of them, and protects them from being discussed or criticized. So that if among the moral doctrines received as part of religion, there be any which are imperfect—which were either erroneous from the first, or not properly limited and guarded in the expression, or which unexceptionable once, are no longer suited to the changes that have taken place in human relations (and it is my firm belief that in so-called Christian morality, instances of all these kinds are to be found), these doctrines are considered equally binding on the conscience with the noblest, most permanent and most universal precepts of Christ.[7]

For this reason Mill sought to undermine the assumption that morality was linked to supernatural religion, and this became one of the arguments of his essay "Utility of Religion," which was written during the mid-1850s, though not published until after his death.

These themes—the immorality of selfishness, its link to Christianity, and the consequence that Christian belief, because it insulated morality from scrutiny and criticism, was an obstacle to reform—are reflected in the argument of *On Liberty* though they are anything but explicit or prominent in that book. During the decade before *On Liberty* was pub-lished, however, these arguments were developed in other writings where Mill assembled weapons for the campaign to de-Christianize moral phi-losophy and, as a long-term goal, popular belief. Since he regarded the tie between morality and supernatural religion pernicious, he sought to sever it. And since he regarded the divine ingredient in moral thinking a "poi-sonous root," he undertook to extirpate it.[8]

This part of his strategy for moral reform was readily adopted, for he had been educated to it, and he could assume it would have had his father's and Bentham's approval. James Mill, though brought up a Presbyterian, was led by his own reflections to reject religious belief, whether based on

---

[6] *Considerations on Representative Government*, CW, *19*, 401.
[7] "Utility of Religion," CW, *10*, 417. Upholding the precepts of Christ, for Mill, was not incompatible with rejecting Christianity.
[8] Diary, 25 February [1854], CW, *27*, 656–57.

revelation or natural religion. Moreover, he rejected it on moral more than intellectual grounds, looking on religion "as the greatest enemy of morality," a view which in later years his son shared. The father personally directed the son's education and kept him away from schools and universities to avoid his being contaminated by their religious and other false teaching. Thus Mill was brought up, as he explained, "without any religious belief, in the ordinary meaning of the term."[9] He told Comte about his "rare fate of never having believed in God";[10] and Carlyle, "I have *never* believed Christianity as a religion."[11] In this respect he thought himself almost unique, for he had "not thrown off religious belief, but never had it." Consequently, he felt distanced from it, regarding the beliefs of his contemporaries much as he did Greek religion as he had read about it in Herodotus. He recognized that such beliefs were held fervently, but he could not possibly feel empathy with those who held them.[12]

Although, like his siblings, he was baptized and as a child was occasionally taken to church, he did not take part in religious services during the remainder of his life.[13] During the early 1830s, as part of William Johnson Fox's circle of friends, he heard Fox preach at the Unitarian South Place Chapel, and, according to his wife's son Algernon, he went to Roman Catholic churches to listen to the music, but such casual exposure hardly indicates religious belief.[14]

Even though Mill was exposed to arguments, evidence and various opinions about the "impenetrable problems" regarding religion, and to works on ecclesiastical history, especially of the Reformation, he was not permitted to disagree with his father, nor, probably, was he inclined to. "It would have been totally inconsistent with my father's idea of duty to allow me to imbibe notions contrary to his convictions and feelings respecting religion." Nor, apparently, was he exposed to many theological works, even those by earlier skeptics.[15]

Most of Mill's criticisms of Christianity can be traced back to his father. These included the argument that the Biblical account of creation was utterly implausible. James Mill also had pointed to the incoherence of theological views, asking, as his son did later, why a beneficent God would make a hell for which a majority of mankind was destined.[16] The father's

[9] Early Draft, CW, 1, 40, 42; see also, 108. *Autobiography*, CW, 1, 41.

[10] Mill to Auguste Comte, 15 December 1842, *Correspondence Mill and Comte*, 118.

[11] Mill to Thomas Carlyle, 5 October 1833, CW, 12, 182.

[12] Early Draft, CW, 1, 44.

[13] Alexander Bain, *James Mill: A Biography* (London, 1882), 90–91; at age eight he attended the parish church at Thornecomb, Somerset: Bain, *Mill*, 5, 139. Also: "John Stuart Mill, the Saint of Rationalism," *Westminster Review*, 11 (Jan. 1905).

[14] Algernon Taylor, *Memories of a Student* (2nd ed.; London, 1895), 24.

[15] Early Draft, CW, 1, 44; Bain, *Mill*, 139.

[16] Early Draft, CW, 1, 42; Bain, *James Mill*, 295–308.

war against intuitionism was also carried on by the son; both regarded it as a claim of epistemological authority for supernatural religion.

James Mill's shaping of his son's opinions was reinforced by Jeremy Bentham, who had an immense impact on the youthful Mill, whose education was "in great measure, a course of Benthamism."[17] One part of Bentham's teaching was the necessity of eliminating religion from moral and political deliberations, for he regarded religion as "an enemy to human happiness" and religious motivation as an obstacle to the rational pursuit of self-interest. Consequently Bentham had "the declared aim of extirpating religious beliefs, even the idea of religion itself, from the minds of men."[18] The *Analysis of the Influence of Natural Religion on the Temporal Happiness of Mankind* (1822), which Grote composed from Bentham's large collection of notes, was read in manuscript by Mill, who made a marginal analysis of it. This work, which, Mill tells us, "made a great impression on me," was critical of natural religion as well as of beliefs about futurity and heaven and hell. Bentham (and Grote) argued that religious sanctions were ineffective, that religion was pernicious, and that only good would follow from its complete disappearance.[19] More than thirty years later, in "Utility of Religion," Mill traced many of his ideas about religion back to the *Analysis*.[20]

Although Mill did not enlarge much on Bentham's and his father's arguments against Christianity, his disbelief was different, as he explained late in life, in a conversation reported by John Morley.

> Made remarks on the difference in the feeling of modern refusers of Christianity as compared with that of men like his father, impassioned deniers who believed that if only you broke up the power of the priests and checked superstition, all would go well—a dream from which they were partially awakened by seeing that the French revolution, which overthrew the Church, still did not bring the millennium.[21]

[17] Early Draft, *CW*, *1*, 66.

[18] James E. Crimmins, "Bentham on Religion: Atheism and the Secular Society," *Journal of the History of Ideas* 47 (January–March 1986): 94, 105. Crimmins also refers to Bentham's "zealous atheism" during his later years, when Mill knew him: "Bentham's Religious Writings: A Bibliographic Chronology," *The Bentham Newsletter*, no. 9 (June 1985): 30. James E. Crimmins, *Secular Utilitarianism: Social Science and the Critique of Religion in the Thought of Jeremy Bentham* (Oxford: Clarendon, 1990), 15, 19, 234, 253, 282.

[19] Early Draft, *CW*, *1*, 72; Crimmins, *Secular Utilitarianism*, 225.

[20] "Utility of Religion," *CW*, *10*, 406. Mill's depreciation of Paul and Paulism can also be traced to Bentham; it was the main theme of Bentham's *Not Paul But Jesus* (1823), which, though not mentioned in the *Autobiography*, Mill must have read. See Crimmins, *Secular Utilitarianism*, 233–41, esp. 235, 237.

[21] John Morley, *Recollections* (London: Macmillan, 1921), *1*, 61. James Mill regarded dogmatic atheism as absurd. Yet he rejected Deism, and concluded that about the origin of the world, nothing could be known. *Autobiography*, *CW*, *1*, 41.

His elders assumed that the goal of reform would be readily achieved once religion and the superstition and sinister interests with which it was combined were eliminated. But for Mill, the extirpation of religious belief, along with the customs and morality with which it was intertwined, was only the first step. It was part of the process of wiping clean the cultural slate as a prelude to moral regeneration. Since both parts of the process had to take place, Mill insisted on the necessity not only for "negative logic" but also for "positive truths" (251), in other words, for other beliefs which would define the goals and provide the motivation for individual conduct. Thus in his writings of the 1850s the attack on Christianity was combined with his proposals for ways to establish substitutes for the morality and religious beliefs that were to expire.

Mill tried to undermine Christian theology in published writing only indirectly—by criticizing the doctrine of innate ideas, or, as he also called it, intuitionism. His critique appeared in *Logic* (1843), *Examination of Sir William Hamilton's Philosophy* (1865), and more briefly in "Coleridge" (1840), "Whewell on Moral Philosophy" (1852), and in the *Autobiography*.[22] Although this critique was directed against the epistemological position which held "that truths external to the mind may be known by intuition or consciousness, independently of observation and experiment," Mill's real target was Christianity and the established institutions and moral beliefs with which it was allied.

> Thus intuitionism was the great intellectual support for false doctrines and bad institutions. By the aid of this philosophy every inveterate belief and every strong feeling . . . is dispensed from the obligation of justifying itself by evidence or reason, and is erected into its own sufficient justification. There never was such an instrument devised for consecrating all deep-seated prejudices. It is the main doctrinal pillar of all the errors which impede human improvement.[23]

He acknowledged the same to Comte. His attack on intuitionism in *Logic* "was the most important thing to do, since this school alone is essentially theological and since its philosophy here presents itself as the national support of the old social order, and not only in terms of Christian, but even of Anglican ideas."[24] Or, as he told Theodor Gomperz in 1854, it was "the greatest speculative hindrance to the regeneration so urgently required, of man and society."[25]

[22] Early Draft, *CW*, *1*, 270; "Coleridge," *CW*, *10*, 127.
[23] Early Draft, *CW*, *1*, 232.
[24] Mill to Auguste Comte, 11 July 1842, *Correspondence Mill and Comte*, 83.
[25] Mill to Theodor Gomperz, 19 August 1854, *CW*, *14*, 239. Alan Ryan, Introduction to *Examination of Sir William Hamilton's Philosophy*, *CW*, *9*, ix, xi, xxxv.

Although in published writings Mill concentrated on the intuitionist position, in unpublished writings he made it clear that he subscribed to most of the arguments that had been put forth by others who radically criticized Christianity. For one, he questioned the coherence of theistic arguments, arguing that such incompatible attributes as complete beneficence and unlimited power were often attributed to the deity.

> Not even on the most distorted and contracted theory of good which ever was framed by religious or philosophical fanaticism, can the government of nature be made to resemble the work of a being at once good and omnipotent.[26]

Facing this problem, Mill concluded, involves one "in moral perplexities without end."[27]

This was not an end to his criticisms. As already suggested, Mill asked how one can worship a being who could make a Hell and create generations of persons destined to be consigned to it. The precious gift of salvation was bestowed on so few, while countless millions have lived and died, sinned and suffered. "It would have cost the Divine Giver as little to have vouchsafed [it] to all, as to have bestowed [it] by special grace upon a favoured minority."[28]

Mill also cast doubt on the credibility of the theistic claims.

> The divine message, assuming it to be such, has been authenticated by credentials so insufficient, that they fail to convince a large proportion of the strongest and most cultivated minds, and the tendency to disbelieve them appears to grow with the growth of scientific knowledge and critical discrimination.[29]

Mill's skepticism was such that he thought religious faith could only survive in persons "with a torpid and inactive state of the speculative faculties."[30] Mill could hardly believe that his friend John Sterling was "able . . . still to believe Christianity without doing violence to his understanding."[31] But Sterling was exceptional. For most with an "exercised intellect," there was no way to sustain faith, "save by sophistication and perversion, either of the understanding or of the conscience."[32] In On Liberty he also described the person with "deep conscientiousness, and subtle and refined understanding, who spends a life in sophisticating with an intellect he cannot silence, and exhausts the resources of ingenuity in attempting to reconcile the promptings of his conscience and reason with

---

[26] "Nature," CW, 10, 389.
[27] "Utility of Religion," CW, 10, 423. Similar arguments were made in letters and in his diary: CW, 14, 53; 15, 540, 709; 27, 659.
[28] "Utility of Religion," CW, 10, 424.
[29] Ibid., 424–25.
[30] Ibid., 425.
[31] Mill to Thomas Carlyle, 28 April 1834, CW, 12, 225.
[32] "Utility of Religion," CW, 10, 425.

orthodoxy" (242). This led Mill to lament the waste of talent that went into Christian theology, which he wished "to blot entirely out."[33] The intellectual grounds of religious belief, he concluded, "require[d] to be backed by moral bribery or subornation of the understanding."[34]

Even though he thought Christian theology rationally indefensible, this did not put an end to his argumentation, for there remained the position of natural religion. He had in mind "those who reject revelation . . . [and] take refuge in an optimistic deism, a worship of the order of Nature or of Providence at least as full of contradictions, and as perverting to the moral sentiments, as any of the received forms of Christianity."[35] Consideration of this kind of theology was especially important, as "the Christianity of our day has borrowed a considerable part of its colour and flavour from sentimental deism."[36] Thus he directed his attention to the phenomena of nature to undermine deistical arguments which appealed to its marvels as evidence of a deity having been the creator of the natural order. Far from regarding the order of nature with awe, he was struck by the recklessness of Nature which issued in such things as hurricanes, pestilence, disease, famine, and flood, which were evidence of nature's anarchy, chaos, destruction, cruelty, and injustice. Writers on natural theology had "exhausted the resources of sophistry," but without success.[37] What kind of God, he asked, would have created a natural order which included such things.

> The adoration of such a being cannot be with the whole heart, unless the heart is first considerably sophisticated. The worship must either be greatly overclouded by doubt, and occasionally quite darkened by it, or the moral sentiments must sink to the low level of the ordinances of Nature: the worshipper must learn to think blind partiality, atrocious cruelty, and reckless injustice, not blemishes in an object of worship, since all these abound to excess in the commonest phenomenon of Nature.[38]

This difficulty is made more acute when trying to reconcile the God of nature with the God of revelation, for "the Author of the Sermon on the Mount is assuredly a far more benignant Being than the Author of Nature." Unfortunately for Christians, according to Mill, they are obliged to believe "the same being is the author of both." Mill advised them to

---

[33] Diary, 7 February [1854], *CW*, *27*, 652.
[34] "Utility of Religion," *CW*, *10*, 404.
[35] Early Draft, *CW*, *1*, 72.
[36] Nature, *CW*, *10*, 376.
[37] "Nature," *CW*, *10*, 384–88; see also 376, 382–83, and *passim* for other criticisms of deism.
[38] "Utility of Religion," *CW*, *10*, 423.

avoid trying to reconcile the two, which they usually did by resorting to the assumption that the purposes of Providence were mysterious.[39]

His critique of supernatural and Christian claims was presented most systematically and in greatest detail in his essay "Theism," written between 1868 and 1870, but, like the essays "Nature" and "Utility of Religion," not published until after his death. In his essay he still held—if anything, more emphatically than before—that physical science had "established, by conclusive evidence, matters of fact with which the religious traditions of mankind are not reconcilable." He also reaffirmed his conviction that "the creeds of the past are natural growths of the human mind, in particular stages of its career, destined to disappear and give place to other convictions in a more advanced stage."[40] He also held by his rejection of *a priori*, metaphysical arguments for the existence of a deity.[41] If anything, this view, following his *Examination of Sir William Hamilton's Philosophy* (1865), was even more confidently stated than in the 1850s. In addition, he repeated the argument that believers could not coherently affirm the omnipotence *and* the benevolence of the deity.[42] He also rejected any and all arguments for miracles.[43] Moreover, he rejected arguments for a first cause and appeals to the shared opinion of mankind.[44] And finally, Mill considered arguments that a design in nature supported a belief in a deity as the creator of that design, concluding that "though it has some force, its force is very generally overrated."[45]

Powerfully as these arguments were put forward, some of Mill's atheist friends, including Harriet Grote, were disappointed, for Mill, in assessing counter-arguments from believers, was anything but polemical or dogmatic. He did not rush to conclusions in the absence of conclusive proof,

[39] Ibid.
[40] "Theism," *CW*, *10*, 429–30.
[41] Ibid., 444–46.
[42] Ibid., 456; see also, 453, 457–59.
[43] Ibid., 471–81.
[44] Ibid., 435–43.
[45] Ibid., 446. In light of the arguments forcefully stated in "Theism" (and also considering Mill's personal rejection of Christianity and theistic belief: see above, text at notes 10–12), it is surprising that some scholars discern substantial residues of Christian belief or the adopting of Christian ideas in Mill's thought. Bernard Semmel, for example, writes that in the *Three Essays on Religion* Mill "sought to salvage as much as he could from traditional faith," but failed to note that what he salvaged did not amount to much. See *John Stuart Mill and the Pursuit of Virtue* (New Haven: Yale University Press, 1984), 173. Nicholas Capaldi argues that Mill's "vision is Christian. . . . His vision is Protestant. . . . Mill is close to Calvinism": "John Stuart Mill's Defence of Liberal Culture," *Political Science Reviewer* 24 (1995): 215. Eldon Eisenach claims that "Mill's ideas often became powerful tools to reform, transform and, therefore, potentially *extend* the reach of Christianity": "Mill's Reform Liberalism as Tradition and Culture," *Political Science Reviewer* 24 (1995): 99. If such claims are to be made, it would seem fitting to at least attempt to show how they can be reconciled with the arguments in "Theism," to say nothing about Mill's denials made to Comte and Carlyle and in the *Autobiography*.

and therefore he did not deny the possibility of immortality of the soul or the existence of God, nor did he disparage those who believed such things. On the other hand, neither did he profess belief in them himself; he only held there was no conclusive proof regarding them.[46] Yet for this he was accused of backsliding. His friend Bain thought such criticisms too harsh: "As is usual in such cases, the inch has been stretched to an ell." Taking into account all that was included in "Theism," Bain acknowledged that Mill remained "a thorough-going negationist. He admitted neither [Christianity's] truth nor its utility."[47]

Mill also attacked another defense of religion to which many in the nineteenth century retreated. This was the view that, even if untrue, religion should be supported because it was socially useful, it being an important source of morality and social stability. It was widely believed that without religious belief much of the motivation for moral conduct would disap-

[46] "Theism," CW, 10, 462; Morley, Recollections, 1, 99. Harriet Grote thought Mill supported the "vague poetic dreamy view of the Creator and of the immortality of the soul . . . the Christian religion is let off very easy by this archdestructive": Harriet Grote to Harriet Martineau, 14 December [1875], Martineau Papers, University of Birmingham. Regarding the prospect of life after death, Mill said that while "there is nothing to prove [it], there is as little in our knowledge and experience to contradict [it]." "Utility of Religion," CW, 10, 427. This did not mean, however, that he thought such hope was well-grounded, for he allowed that skeptics, as a matter of "imagination and feelings," could hope, but he also said "such vague possibility must ever stop far short of a conviction." Such hope, moreover, was at most a temporary need, for with human improvement, "When mankind cease to need a future existence as a consolation for the sufferings of the present, it will have lost its chief value to them." "Utility of Religion," CW, 10, 426.

[47] Bain, Mill, 136, 140. Although most of the arguments in "Theism" typically were used by atheists, Mill's qualifications, avoidance of dogmatism, and measure of uncertainty at the end of the essay perhaps makes it inappropriate to label him an atheist, especially as he did not call himself one. However, the aggressive, disdainful tone in "Nature" and "Utility of Religion," which he left unrevised, and the substantive arguments critical of theistic belief in "Theism" allow one to say he went far beyond a tepid agnosticism. If an atheist is defined as one who denies the existence of God, Mill cannot be called an atheist, for he made it clear that an atheist, by denying the existence of God, was dogmatic, as he could not provide proof for his claim. Yet Mill invites speculation about his belief by describing himself as a "refuser of Christianity"; and by his telling Comte that he had the "rare fate of never having believed in God." See above, text at note 11. His stopping short of the conclusion that theistic belief was utterly groundless was also a matter of tactics. See below, chapter 6, text at notes 133–39; and "Theism," CW, 10, 481–482. See also his statement that justice to Comte required "giving him praise on that point," i.e., his atheism: Mill to Harriet Taylor Mill, 9 January 1854, CW, 14, 126. Mill would have rejected the charge of backsliding, for in 1873, according to Helen Taylor, he contemplated publishing "Nature" without alterations, other than stylistic ones; and he regarded "Theism" as "fundamentally consistent" with the other two, earlier essays on religion. Helen Taylor, "Introductory Notice" (1874), CW, 10, 371–72. He also could have noted a similar formulation of his view about the evidence for the existence of God in an early letter to Carlyle. Mill to Thomas Carlyle, 12 January 1834. CW, 12, 206.

pear and irresponsibility, amorality, and perhaps worse would prevail. This was part of the received wisdom of the time. It was said that the clergy, including dissenting ministers, for generations had been teaching "that morality depended entirely on religion and religion on the Bible."[48] Carlyle claimed to know many who were shocked by the publication in England of David Friedrich Strauss' *Life of Jesus*, not on account of its views, which they shared, but because those views were made public.[49] Even so convinced an atheist as Harriet Grote thought religion was necessary for the many. "Two sorts of morals must be allowed in this world, one for the guidance of reflecting individuals *having a conscience*, the other for the vulgar, a religious morality in short."[50] Such an assumption about the uneducated populace underlay the attacks on Darwin for promoting Godlessness and therefore causing immorality and anarchy.[51]

The assumption that religion was necessary for morality was held by sophisticated persons, such as Henry Sidgwick.

> The reason why I keep strict silence now for many years with regard to theology is that while I cannot myself discover adequate rational basis for the Christian hope of happy immortality, it seems to me that the general loss of such a hope, from the minds of average human beings as now constituted, would be an evil of which I cannot pretend to measure the extent. I am not prepared to say that the dissolution of the existing social order would follow, but I think the danger of such dissolution would be seriously increased, and that the evil would certainly be very great.[52]

James Anthony Froude asked, "if the Christian sanction were lost, would the difference between right and wrong survive?"[53] This remained the conventional view, in spite of occasional dissent from it; for example, in

---

[48] Moncure Daniel Conway, *Autobiography, Memoirs and Experiences* (Boston, 1904), 2, 385.

[49] Ibid., 53.

[50] Harriet Grote to Richard Monckton Milnes, 25 March 1844, Trinity College Library.

[51] Adrian Desmond and James Moore, *Darwin* (London: Penguin, 1992), 577–83; Walter E. Houghton, *The Victorian Frame of Mind 1830–1870* (New Haven: Yale University Press, 1957), 59. Houghton offers additional evidence.

[52] Henry Sidgwick to J. R. Mozley, 30 July 1881, Arthur Sidgwick and Eleanor M. Sidgwick, *Henry Sidgwick: A Memoir* (London, 1906), 357. Sidgwick added that this consequence would not necessarily continue in the very distant future. On the development of Sidgwick's religious beliefs, see J. B. Schneewind, *Sidgwick's Ethics and Victorian Moral Philosophy* (Oxford: Clarendon, 1977), 21–40.

[53] Herbert Paul, *The Life of Froude* (New York, 1905), 45. The question was discussed in the Metaphysical Society in 1877. James Fitzjames Stephen, Lord Selbourne, James Martineau, and Dean Richard Church were among those upholding the view that a decline in religious belief would lead to a decline in morality. Frederick Harrison, W. K. Clifford, and Thomas Henry Huxley disagreed. However, all agreed that if religious belief could be shown to be false, it ought to be abandoned, regardless of the consequences for morality. "A Modern Symposium," *Nineteenth Century, 1* (April 1877): 331–58; (May 1877): 531–46.

about 1880, according to Professor Owen Chadwick, "some people said, discard religion and morality remains untouched. This was the view of a very small minority. To most people the old truth that unbelief causes immorality appeared as obvious as ever."[54]

Mill would have no part of such views, but the consensus on this issue indicates the extent of his departure from received opinion. The generally shared opinion, he argued, promoted religion only "as a supplement to human laws, a more cunning sort of police, an ancillary to the thief-catcher and the hangman."[55] Such an argument, moreover, reflected an effort to keep in line doubters whose convictions no longer sustained their religious beliefs.

> An argument for the utility of religion is an appeal to unbelievers, to induce them to practise a well meant hypocrisy, or to semi-believers to make them avert their eyes from what might possibly shake their unstable belief, or finally to persons in general to abstain from expressing any doubts they may feel, since a fabric of immense importance to mankind is so insecure at its foundations, that men must hold their breath in its neighborhood for fear of blowing it down.[56]

Since Mill regarded the morality which religion was supposed to support as pernicious, of course he asked, why support it? In any case, he argued that a wholesome morality could not be linked to a false religion: "If their [mankind's] religion is false it would be very extraordinary that their morality should be true."[57]

The argument about utility of religion, in Mill's view, was a way of shielding false religion from unanswerable criticism. Since he wished to deny Christianity this protection, he insisted that the question of usefulness of a doctrine be as open to free discussion as that of its truth. To counter the claim that religion was socially useful, he argued that morality in conduct only appeared to be produced by religion, whereas in fact it was the product of authority, early education, and, above all, public opinion. Authority was conferred by the general concurrence of mankind, which is "all powerful."[58] Early education, even without religion, was

---

[54] Owen Chadwick, *The Victorian Church* (London, 1966–1970), 2, 121.

[55] "Utility of Religion," *CW*, 10, 415. Of course there were a few who agreed with Mill in denying a causal connection between religious belief and moral conduct, for example, Frederic Harrison and W. K. Clifford (see above, note 54) and George Henry Lewes. All three were Comtists. On Lewes, see Rosemary Ashton, *G. H. Lewes: A Life* (Oxford: Clarendon, 1991), 232.

[56] "Utility of Religion," *CW*, 10, 403.

[57] "Enlightened Infidelity," unpublished letter to *The Reasoner*, after 2 June 1847, *CW*, 24, 1084.

[58] "Utility of Religion," *CW*, 10, 407.

also effective, as the example of Sparta suggested.[59] Most important, the "great effects on human conduct, which are commonly ascribed to motives derived directly from religion, have mostly for their proximate cause the influence of human opinion."[60] Consequently, belief in the supernatural "cannot be considered to be any longer required, either for enabling us to know what is right and wrong in social morality, or for supplying us with motives to do right and to abstain from wrong."[61]

When *On Liberty* was published in 1859, most of Mill's religious opinions were recorded in manuscripts, awaiting posthumous publication. These opinions were familiar to his closest friends, and some outside his immediate circle may have guessed what they were, but they were not known to the considerable number in the reading public that had read his *Political Economy* or his essays in the quarterly reviews. His critique of intuitionism, though it appeared in *Logic*, did not have an obvious bearing on religion, and, on the whole, *Logic* was not read as a statement of his religious opinions. His reticence about making his religious opinions public continued while he composed *On Liberty*, and thus, while those opinions were reflected in the thesis of *On Liberty*, their importance in that essay is obscured by Mill's deliberate camouflaging of their full import. Before turning to *On Liberty* to identify its religious themes and their connection with his plan for moral regeneration, it is necessary to look into the reasons for his lack of candor.

---

[59] Ibid., 409.

[60] Ibid., 411.

[61] Ibid., 417. Also, "History, so far as we know it, bears out the opinion, that mankind can perfectly well do without the belief in a heaven." Ibid., 427. Mill traced his opinions on this subject back to Bentham's and George Grote's *Analysis of the Influence of Natural Religion on the Temporal Happiness of Mankind* (1822): Early draft, *CW, 1,* 72.

Chapter Four

CANDOR OR CONCEALMENT

> You are doubtless aware that here an author who should
> openly admit to antireligious or even antichristian opinions,
> would compromise not only his social position, which I
> feel myself capable of sacrificing to a sufficiently high
> objective, but also, and this would be more serious,
> his chance of being read.
> (*John Stuart Mill*)

THAT MILL concealed his religious opinions in works published during his lifetime is evident. One need only compare such works with his other writing. In essays that were put aside for posthumous publication Mill did not conceal his atheism.[1] His most severe and systematic criticisms of Christian theology and of both natural and revealed religion appeared in two essays written during the mid-1850s—"Nature" and "Utility of Religion"—and in "Theism," composed in 1868–70. These three essays were not published until 1874, the year following his death. He also reminded his wife that in the draft of his autobiography (composed in 1853–54) there was "an unreserved proclamation of our opinions on religion."[2] In it he was forthright, and he called on others to be the same. "On religion in particular it appears to me to have now become a duty for all who . . . [are persuaded] that the current opinions are not only false but hurtful, to make their dissent known."[3] But this was not a call he would heed in 1854. It was for those reading his posthumously published *Autobiography*—as it turned out, in 1873.

In letters to trusted and like-minded friends, as in unpublished essays, he wrote as one with nothing to hide. He confessed his lack of faith and belief to Carlyle and Comte.[4] To his father's old friend Walter Coulson he put the question: "How can morality be anything but the chaos it now is, when the ideas of right and wrong, just and unjust, must be wrenched into accordance either with the notions of a tribe of barbarians in a corner of Syria three thousand years ago, or with what is called the order of

---

[1] On the suitability of the term 'atheist,' see above, chap. 3, n.47.
[2] Mill to Harriet Taylor Mill, 24 February [1854], *CW*, *14*, 168.
[3] Early Draft, *Autobiography*, *CW*, *1*, 46–47.
[4] See above, chapter 3, note 47 and text at notes 9–12.

Providence."[5] And writing to the radical journalist John Lalor, who until 1848 had been an editor of the *Morning Chronicle*, a paper to which he, like his father, had frequently contributed, he called Christianity "a child of the devil."[6] He also could be quite vehement on this subject. When his sister Mary expressed the hope that she might regard him as a Christian, Mill snapped: "There is . . . a total want of modesty in supposing that I am likely to receive instruction from you on the subject of my strongest convictions—which also were those of your father."[7]

Such forthrightness, however, entirely disappeared in what Mill wrote for immediate publication. What he had to say about Christianity or other religious matters on these occasions was written obliquely. Arguments which he thought important were not introduced and conclusions he had drawn were not stated. Some things were suppressed and others at most were only implied. For example, as already mentioned, his longstanding and relentless criticisms of intuitionism implicitly cast doubt on much of Christian theology. The reader of *Logic* could infer that Mill was deeply skeptical from his consideration of the grounds of belief and by applying his general conclusion to the particular example of religious belief.

Mill wanted it this way, for, as he said while writing *Logic*, "I try not to awaken any religious antipathy in the common reader"; but, he continued, "I have written in such a way that no reader, be he Christian or an unbeliever, can mistake the true nature of my opinions."[8] As he began working on his *Examination of Sir William Hamilton's Philosophy* (1865), he acknowledged that these had been his tactics. "The great recommendation of this project is, that it will enable me to supply what was prudently left deficient in the *Logic*, and to do the kind of service which I am capable of to rational psychology, namely, to its *Polemik*."[9] It should be said, however, that while in *Hamilton* he made up some of the deficiency, he by no means made up most of it.

A few discerning readers did recognize what Mill was doing. William George Ward, a Catholic scholar, for example, noted that if Mill's "principles be adopted as a full statement of the truth, the whole fabric of Christian Theology must totter and fall."[10] James Fitzjames Stephen recalled a conversation many years earlier with an Oxford student "who said that he had read every word of [the *Logic*] carefully, and that it contained not one word which was inconsistent with atheism. The remark was perfectly true." Stephen also said, "Probably hardly any work of our day has done

---

[5] Mill to Walter Coulson, 22 November 1850, *CW*, *14*, 53.
[6] Mill to John Lalor, 27 June [1852], *CW*, *14*, 92.
[7] Mill to Mary Mill Colman, 20 February 1858, *CW*, *15*, 547.
[8] Mill to Auguste Comte, 18 December 1841, *Correspondence of Mill and Comte*, 42.
[9] Mill to Alexander Bain [December 1861], *CW*, *15*, 752.
[10] Bain, *Mill*, 69.

so much to shake the foundations of theology as Mill's *Logic*, and if read in the light of its author's *Autobiography*, it is impossible not to believe that this result was intended."[11] Another reader, a stranger to Mill, wrote, "I do not know any passage either in the 'Logic,' or in your recent papers on 'Utilitarianism,' which would lead a person to suppose that the author considered the existence of God as established beyond a doubt."[12] And the evangelical colonial reformer, James Stephen, whose son James Fitzjames Stephen became Mill's notable critic, also recognized that "Mill is an opponent of Religion in the Abstract ... he evidently maintains that Super-human influences on the mind of man are but a dream; whence the inevitable conclusion, that all acts of devotion and Prayer are but a superstition. That such is his real meaning, however darkly conveyed, is indisputable."[13] Another reader of Mill's published work, Abraham Hayward, also understood that Mill was an atheist. He told Gladstone, "So far as I understand Mill's writings, he repudiates any religion founded on a God or a future state of rewards and punishments."[14] These judgments were based on analysis, insight, and inference; these discerning readers were able to recognize a position Mill held but did not make obvious. Mill's position might be evident now, in light of his opinions about religion revealed in his autobiography and other posthumously published writings. But during the years immediately following 1843, after the *Logic* was published, Ward's and Stephen's view was anything but typical, and to this day, Mill's *Logic* is mainly read as a treatise on scientific method and epistemology, and its implications for religion are regarded as having little importance.[15]

Mill's policy of concealment was contrary to the openness that he would have preferred. Uneasy about this policy, periodically he evaluated it. Bain reports, "He had long determined to throw off the mask entirely, when the time should be ripe for it. He . . . was prevented from an earlier avowal of these [unpopular religious opinions], solely by the circumstance that the silent course of opinion was serving the interests of progress better than any violent shock, on his part would have done."[16] The time,

---

[11] "The Laws of England as to the Expression of Religious Opinions," *Contemporary Review* 25 (February 1875): 473–74.

[12] Arthur Greene to Mill, 21 December 1861. Mill-Taylor Collection, British Library of Political and Economic Science, *1*, ff. 166–71. Greene made a similar observation in an earlier letter, to which Mill disingenuously replied, "neither in the Logic nor in any other of my publications had I any purpose of undermining Theism." Mill to Arthur Greene, 16 December 1861, *CW, 15*, 754.

[13] James Stephen to Macvey Napier, 14 May 1845, British Library, Add. 34625, ff. 210–12.

[14] Hayward to Gladstone, 20 May [1873], Add. 44207, f. 129.

[15] Bain said his religious opinions "could be inferred from his published writings," which does not mean that they were. Bain, *Mill*, 157.

[16] Ibid., 157–58.

however, seems never to have been ripe. As late as 1868 he was still being evasive, much to the annoyance of his stepdaughter, who upbraided him for his response to questions about his religious opinions when he was seeking reelection to Parliament in 1868. He did not deny being an atheist but pointed out that those calling him one probably were the persons calling Gladstone a Catholic; and he noted that dignitaries of the Church of England had found nothing contrary to Christianity in his writings. He suggested, "If any one again tells you that I am an atheist, I would advise you to ask him how he knows and in what page of my numerous writings he finds anything to bear out the assertion."[17] Helen Taylor was livid. "You actually invite the publication of this letter which makes me literally blush for you and must lower the opinion entertained of you by everyone who knows you and sees it. . . . Do not disgrace yourself as an open truthful man; do not shut the door to all future power of usefulness or religious liberty by such mean and wretched subterfuges." Recognizing that he was being anything but forthright, she also told him his responses were imprudent, as he adopted "a position which will be justly thrown in your teeth, if at a future time you should attempt to take up a nobler and bolder one."[18]

Conscientious, as he was, Mill felt morally vulnerable about his attempted deception, and his wish to find a defense for it was reflected in observations about concealment in other contexts. The question of secrecy or openness, for example, came up when considering the ballot. Earlier, following Bentham and his father and Grote, he had advocated the secret ballot. He reversed himself, however, in the 1850s and argued that votes should be open to public scrutiny. Although now opposing secret voting, and perhaps thinking he was inconsistent in avoiding public scrutiny of his religious opinions, he argued that secrecy sometimes was justified. Thus in *Representative Government* (1861), when discussing the ballot, he observed, "Secrecy [about one's opinions] is justifiable in many cases, imperative in some, and it is not cowardice to seek protection against evils which are honestly avoidable."[19]

On another occasion when arguing against secrecy for voters he insisted that in some circumstances it was quite alright to mislead others about one's opinions. He distinguished justifiable equivocation from the deceptions perpetrated by the "habitual equivocator."

[17] Mill to Frederick Bates, 9 November 1868, published in *The Times* and *Daily News*, 11 November. *CW, 16*, 1483.

[18] Helen Taylor to Mill, 12 November 1868, Mill-Taylor Collection, vol. 53, pp. 149–51, British Library of Political and Economic Science. Ann P. Robson, "Mill's Second Prize in the Lottery of Life," *A Cultivated Mind: Essays on J. S. Mill Presented to John M. Robson*, ed. Michael Laine (Toronto: University of Toronto Press, 1991), 231–32.

[19] *Representative Government, CW, 19*, 488.

We are often told, for example, that an equivocation is as bad as a lie. It is well for mankind that everybody is not of this opinion, and that not all who will equivocate will lie. For the temptation to equivocate is often almost irresistible; indeed, the proposition, that everything which can be termed an equivocation is necessarily condemnable, is only true in those cases and those relations in life in which it is a duty to be absolutely open and unreserved.[20]

By taking note of exceptions to the openness he was advocating, in these passages Mill seemed to be justifying his own lack of openness about his religious opinions.

Equivocation began much earlier, for his father had warned him about the dangers of being candid. "In giving me an opinion [about religion] contrary to that of the world," Mill explained, "my father thought it necessary to give it as one which could not prudently be avowed to the world." James Mill's own practice was in accord with his precept, for he wrote only "as much of his convictions as he thought the circumstances would in any way admit of." Thus at a very early age Mill learned the "lesson of keeping my thoughts to myself."[21] And this lesson continued to guide him, even though he knew that times had changed, making forthright speech less risky than it had been in his father's time. Measuring his own practice against his father's example, he speculated about how James Mill—a man with "intensity of moral conviction . . . [and] unpopular opinions on religion"—would conduct himself, had he been alive in the 1850s and 1860s. Mill was sure he would not engage in self-censorship or advocate it *unless* forthrightness led to loss of subsistence or to the "exclusion from some sphere of usefulness peculiarly suitable to the capacities of the individual."[22] Both exceptions, and especially the second one, could have been used by Mill to justify his self-imposed silence.

His sense of danger in connection with religion never left him. Throughout his life he was convinced that one could not safely cast doubt on Christianity. He told Carlyle that one could not write about the French Revolution for the English public "until the time comes when one can speak of Christianity as it may be spoken of in France." To describe it as having been valuable in the past but as "gone, never to return" was something "one could not *now* [1833] say . . . openly in England, and be read—at least by the many."[23] With the passage of time, his belief in the

[20] "Romilly's Public Responsibility and the Ballot" (29 April 1865), CW, 25, 1216.
[21] Early Draft, CW, 1, 6, 44.
[22] Early Draft, CW, 1, 46; *Autobiography*, CW, 1, 47. The second of the exceptions was not included in Early Draft but was added to *Autobiography*.
[23] Mill to Thomas Carlyle, 5 October 1833, CW, 12, 182.

necessity of concealing his opinions, if anything, hardened. "Here [he told Comte] an author who should openly admit to antireligious or even antichristian opinions, would compromise not only his social position, which I feel myself capable of sacrificing to a sufficiently high objective, but also, and this would be more serious, his chance of being read."[24] This was a recurring theme in his complaints to Comte about conditions in England. "The time has not yet come when we in England shall be able to direct open attacks on theology, including Christian theology, without compromising our cause. We can only evade the issue by simply eliminating it from all social and philosophical discussion."[25] And a year later his assessment was unchanged. "One ought to keep total silence on the question of religion when writing for an English audience, though indirectly one may strike any blow one wishes at religious beliefs."[26]

Mill's reticence continued into the 1850s when he was writing *On Liberty*. In 1854 he felt that the *Westminster Review*, edited by John Chapman, a freethinker, would not permit him to speak freely about Comte's atheism.[27] And in referring to the pseudonymously published *Analysis of the Influence of Natural Religion on the Temporal Happiness of Mankind* (1822) in the early draft of his autobiography (written 1853–54) and in "Utility of Religion" (written *c.* 1856), Mill mentioned Bentham's name in connection with it but not that of Grote, who, of course, was still living.[28] Even after Grote died, Mill in his *Autobiography* kept the secret of Grote's authorship.[29]

Mill again was reminded that atheism was a taboo subject after the death of Sir William Molesworth in October 1855. Molesworth, perhaps now most often remembered as the editor of *The Works of Thomas*

[24] Mill to Auguste Comte, 18 December 1841, *Correspondence Mill and Comte*, 42. Mill's judgment was shared by Richard Congreve, a tutor in Oxford and in orders. His religious faith had been shaken, and he was drawn to Comte's ideas. Responding to Comte's criticism of his lack of openness, he explained, "Had I unhesitatingly adopted Positivism, it was out of my power to make known my adoption, which would have exposed me to absolute ruin, as I had no independent means." Richard Congreve, "Personal Recollections of Auguste Comte," British Library, Add. 45259, f. 13.

[25] Mill to Auguste Comte, 3 April 1844, *Correspondence Mill and Comte*, 227.

[26] Mill to Auguste Comte, 8 July 1845, ibid., 317. See also letters of 28 January [1843], 27 January 1845, 13 August 1846: ibid., 130, 288, 377. Helen Talyor, in the Introductory Notice to Mill's posthumous *Three Essays on Religion*, claimed that shortly before he died he intended to publish "Nature" and the fifteen-year lapse since it was written reflected his usual slowness and deliberation but "was not withheld by him on account of reluctance to encounter whatever odium might result from the free expression of his opinion on religion": *CW, 10,* 371–72. Her explanation is not plausible, however, for in light of her having accused him of using "wretched subterfuges," she had to have been familiar with his practice of concealment. See above, text at notes 16–18.

[27] Mill to Harriet Taylor Mill, 9 January 1854, *CW, 14,* 126.

[28] Early Draft, *CW, 1,* 72; "Utility of Religion," *CW, 10,* 406.

[29] *Autobiography, CW, 1,* 73.

Hobbes (1839–1845), subscribed to Benthamite ideas and was one of the handful of philosophic radicals in Parliament during the 1830s. And most important for Mill, he had financed the *London and Westminster Review* from 1835 to 1840 when Mill was the actual though not the nominal editor. After his death Mill was approached about preparing an epitaph and an obituary, both for the *Westminster Review* and the *Edinburgh Review*, but he was also told that Molesworth's family wished to suppress any mention of his atheism.[30] Mill declined writing a biographical piece, asking,

> Is there not something monstrous in the fact, that in the case of a man universally applauded both for his public and his private life, yet his conscientious opinions on what all think the most important of all subjects, being diametrically opposite to the common ones, are not even permitted to be alluded to in any memoir or notice of him? Thus is buried with him his testimony to his most important convictions because they differ from those of the mob.[31]

Mill's response to censorship did not end here, for he composed an epitaph which illustrates how he dealt with the prohibition. He did not mention that Molesworth continued an atheist at the time of his death, but he made allusions to his having unorthodox opinions to which he was faithful to the end.

> A laborious & thoughtful student from an early age,
> both of speculative truth and of the practical questions of political life,
>   His opinions were his own.
> He lived to see some of them triumphant
>   partly through his efforts
> and died as he had lived, faithful to them all.

The statement that Molesworth's "opinions were his own," Mill explained, "is intended to imply, since it seems agreed not to express, that he held fast to other opinions than those mentioned."[32] Since Molesworth as a colonial reformer and member of the Aberdeen government was well known for his opinions on the practical questions of political life, the reference to Molesworth's interest in speculative truth was Mill's way of suggesting that Molesworth also had opinions about religion. The obscurity of these allusions indicates the extent of Mill's caution. They can hardly have conveyed any substantive information to anyone not already aware of Molesworth's atheism. By intimating, however weakly, what

---

[30] Mill to John Chapman, 27 October 1855, 1 November 1855; Mill to unidentified correspondents, 5 November 1855, 9 November 1855: *CW, 14,* 497–501.
[31] Mill to unidentified correspondent, 5 November 1855, ibid., 499.
[32] Ibid.

could not be made explicit, Mill perhaps was satisfying his conscience by proving to himself that he had not abjectly succumbed to social censorship.

Of course, Mill's friends understood his position—his atheism and his evasions, equivocation, and concealment. Alexander Bain explained, "He did not publicly avow his dissent from the orthodoxy of the country; but it was well enough known in a very wide private circle."[33]

<hr>

Mill was not alone among his contemporaries in concealing religious opinions. Jeremy Bentham, his father's patron and a source of intellectual guidance to John, was exceedingly cautious, as he wished to avoid offending those who might have implemented some of his legal and administrative reforms. Perhaps more relevant, he was fearful about the blasphemy laws, which in his time were still being enforced.[34] His most virulent critiques of Christianity were withheld from publication or published anonymously. One biographer reports, "he kept these revolutionary [religious] opinions to himself. He wrote page after page of denunciation, but as self-therapy, to purge himself of spleen." Such writings were put away, Bentham explaining they "are a little out of season."[35] When some of his extreme opinions were finally published (*Not Paul but Jesus* in 1823 and *Analysis of the Influence of Natural Religion on the Temporal Happiness of Mankind* in 1822), pseudonyms were used. And the editor of the collected works in 1843 excluded these titles from his edition.[36] Bentham, moreover, was careful about revealing his atheism in private conversation if a stranger was present.[37] When strangers were not

[33] Bain, *Mill*, 157–58. Although Mill revealed that he practiced prudent dissimulation and though his friends knew about it, modern scholarship is dubious. Collini, for example, says Mill did not hesitate to express his strong views. Introduction to *Essays on Equality, Law, and Education, CW, 21*, vii. Evidently it is assumed that because he advocated openness, he himself was open.

[34] Crimmins, *Secular Utilitarianism*, 11–13, 148–49; Bentham wished the word "blasphemy" were banished.

[35] Mary P. Mack, *Jeremy Bentham: An Odyssey of Ideas. 1748–1792* (London: Heinemann, 1962), 302–5.

[36] Ibid., 305. The *Analysis* made a powerful impression on Mill (see "Utility of Religion," *CW, 10*,406 *Autobiography, CW, 1*, 73); yet such was his caution that in "Bentham," in referring to its exclusion from the projected edition of Bentham's collected writings, Mill distanced himself from it by saying, "we think most of them [Bentham's religious writings] of exceedingly small value." He went on further to advocate an openness which he himself avoided: "the world has a right to whatever light they throw upon the constitution of his mind." "Bentham," *CW, 10*, 99; G. W. Smith, "Enlightenment Psychology and Individuality: The Roots of J. S. Mill's Conception of the Self," *Enlightenment and Dissent* 101 (1997).

[37] James E. Crimmins, "Bentham on Religion: Atheism and the Secular Society." *Journal of the History of Ideas* 47 (January–March 1986): 98.

in attendance, however, matters were different: Bain reports, "It is quite certain . . . that the whole tone of conversation in Bentham's more select circle, was atheistic."[38]

Within that circle no one was more firmly anti-Christian than Mill's confidante, George Grote, nor were there any who exceeded him in being careful not to reveal religious opinions to any but fellow-atheists or trusted friends. James Mill was said to have destroyed Grote's faith, and soon the newly emancipated Grote was proselytizing his atheism with his new wife, Harriet, who later said of her Christianity, she "was fairly argued out of it."[39] Grote also took on the mammoth task of composing the *Influence of Natural Religion on the Temporal Happiness of Mankind* from Bentham's vast accumulation of barely legible and disorganized notes, becoming, at the very least, sympathetic editor and, arguably, co-author. The book was published in 1822 under the pseudonym Philip Beauchamp but apparently not offered for sale. The radical printer Richard Carlile, himself an atheist, already in prison on convictions for blasphemous libel, was chosen as the publisher, on the ground that he was less vulnerable than others to a prosecution. Grote never wavered in his opposition to Christianity, and a year before he died his wife could say he "has a sort of *shiver* come over him, at the contact of a *parson*."[40]

Grote's secretiveness was quite extreme, but it cannot be attributed to the excessive timidity of a respectable banker with much to lose, for in Parliamentary elections and while in Parliament (1833–41) he did not hesitate to advocate radical measures, especially the secret ballot and an extended suffrage. With religion, however, he drew a line, and there is no evidence that he candidly expressed his religious opinions in public. As early as 1817 he complained about the "virulence and odium" that was directed against those who proclaimed their disbelief in the prevailing religion.[41] Although he proselytized atheism to his young sister-in-law, he also urged her not to deny holding unorthodox ideas, as religious people

---

[38] Bain, *James Mill*, 89; see also, Crimmins, *Secular Utilitarianism*, 148–49, 282. "My opinions on the subject of religion. . . . it is a fixt rule to me neither . . . to . . . declare them spontaneously in any address to the public, nor in private to comply [with] any call made upon me directly or indirectly for that purpose. . . . To avow them . . . in private would be . . . to give encouragement to a sort of prosecution which but too often, and never without indignation it has happened to me to see exercised. . . . this would, on every occasion be my reason and my sole reason for such silence. . . . Atheism is the crowning charge. As High treason is in the scale of the political atheism it the chosen imputation in the scale of religious tyranny." Jeremy Bentham to Richard Carlile, 10 April 1820, *The Correspondence of Jeremy Bentham*, ed. Stephen Conway (Oxford: Clarendon, 1989), 9, 418–20.

[39] *Amberley Papers. The Letters and Diaries of Lord and Lady Amberley*, eds. Bertrand and Patricia Russell (London, 1937), 2, 421.

[40] Harriet Grote to John Romilly, 1 February 1870, Romilly Papers, Public Record Office, 1/1192.

[41] George Grote, Notebook, 1817: University of London Library, MS 429/3, f. 294.

never believed such denials. "The only method is to maintain an obstinate silence and to say that as you interfere with no one else's opinions, you will tolerate no interference with your own."[42] His sister-in-law was uneasy about keeping her sentiments secret, but Grote assured her, "there are undoubtedly many occasions on which it is proper to keep them back."[43]

His judgment that it was dangerous to reveal religious disbelief continued to the time of his death in 1871. When in 1866 he reprinted the *Analysis* (1822), his name continued to be kept off the title page, and the privately printed book was distributed to friends but not sold. At the time it appeared, he told Lord Broughton (the former Monckton Milnes) that the use of pseudonyms was "a very unworthy strategem," which did not, however, prevent him from continuing his use of one.[44] His close friend Alexander Bain said that on the subject of utility as the basis of morals (which carried the implication that morality was not based on Christianity), Mill was one of the "few that [Grote] could declare his whole mind to."[45] Grote's reticence was carried on by his widow, who in 1874 still wished to keep Grote's name off the title page of the *Analysis*, at this time of a French translation of it.[46]

Grote's policy, on the whole, succeeded, for though he was defeated in 1867 as a candidate to be lord rector of the University of Aberdeen, apparently by a cry of infidelity being raised against him, his atheism was not sufficiently known to prevent his burial in Westminster Abbey in 1871. The greatest scandal was among his freethinking friends who assumed he would have wished to have had a non-religious burial.[47] Mill was among the pallbearers but, walking away from the Abbey, he told Bain, "It will not be long ere I am laid in the ground with a very different ceremonial than that."[48]

Toward the end of his life Grote had become ever more resigned to suppression. When the issue was, what God one will worship,

> [T]his is a point on which society is . . . resolved that no individual shall determine for himself, if they can help it. Each new-born child finds his religious creed ready prepared for him. . . . if the future man, in the exercise of his own

[42] George Grote to Frances Lewin, 20 December 1826, University College London, Add. 266, A2.20.

[43] George Grote to Frances Lewin, 8 April 1823 *Lewin Letters*, (London, 1909), 1, 102.

[44] George Grote to Broughton, 2 February 1866, British Library, Add. 47229, f. 286. Perhaps he thought the judgment not applicable to himself, as he said the use of pseudonyms was "unworthy for *any* person of rank and official station."

[45] Bain, *Mill*, 83.

[46] "Contemporary Literature," *Westminster Review* 101 (January 1874): 242. Alexander Bain to George Croom Robertson, 14 November [1874], University College London.

[47] Kate Amberley's Journal, 12 January 1867, *Amberley Papers*, 2, 10.

[48] Harriet Grote, *Life of George Grote*, 332. Alexander Bain to Helen Taylor, 12 May [1873], Mill-Taylor Collection, IV, f. 7, British Library of Political and Economic Science.

independent reason, acquires such convictions as compel him to renounce those Gods [established by his society], proclaiming openly that he does so—he must count upon such treatment as will go far to spoil the value of the present life to him.

Faced with this prospect, Grote said, "the man who dissents from his fellows upon fundamentals of religion, purchases an undisturbed life only by being content with that 'semi-liberty under silence and concealment,' for which Cicero was thankful under the dictatorship of Julius Caesar."[49] This was true for all societies, Grote said; some were more harsh than others, but "they all agree in antipathy to free, individual, dissenting reason." Consequently, "a writer has to consider . . . how much it will be safe for him to publish, having regard to the irritable sore places of the public judgment."[50] The restrictions led Grote to complain to Mill that "we are at present in a period where the philosopher is affectedly prostrate before the priest."[51] Grote also described his experience at the July 1864 meeting of the French Academy when the President bestowed the most remarkable encomiums on an essay by Taine, which was not, however, awarded the prize. The reason was "that the work of M. Taine *was deeply tainted with materialism.* 'Sans doute,' said the esteemed veteran of French literature in pronouncing his award, 'sans doute les opinions sont libres, *mais*'—It is precisely against this *mais*—ushering in the special anathematized or consecrated conclusion which it is intended to except from the general liberty of enforcing or impugning—in matters of philosophical discussion, that Mr. Mill, in the 'Essay on Liberty,' declares war as champion of Reasoned Truth."[52] Such were his fears that he concluded, "one who manifests active hostility against consecrated opinions ought to have a double share of prudence."[53]

---

[49] George Grote, *Review of the Work of Mr. John Stuart Mill, Entitled Examination of Sir William Hamilton's Philosophy* (1866; London, 1868), 46–48. Commenting on Protagoras' flight from Athens after revealing, in an unprovocative passage, his uncertainty about the existence of the gods, Grote observed, "Nor is it easy to see what a superior man was to do, who could not adjust his standard of belief to such fictions—or what he could say, if he said anything . . . in a treatise where the reader would expect to find much upon the subject." Grote, *History of Greece* (London, 1850), 8, 499–500.

[50] Grote, *Review of . . . Mill . . . [on] Hamilton's Philosophy*, 22, 47n. Grote presents a similar analysis in *Plato, and the Other Companions of Sokrates* (London, 1865), 2, 141–42. In the *History*, however, he claims that Periclean Athens was an exception, though only temporarily, as was revealed by the fate of Socrates. *History of Greece* (London, 1849), 6, 199–202.

[51] Mill to Auguste Comte, 27 January 1845, *Correspondance Mill and Comte*, 288.

[52] Grote, *Review of Mill*, 22–23. Grote also said, "The orthodox public do not recognize in any individual citizen a right to scrutinize their creed, and to reject it if not approved by his own rational judgment." Alexander Bain, "George Grote, Obituary," *Proceedings of the Royal Society of London* 130 (1871): vii.

[53] George Grote to Mill, 31 March 1856, Mill-Taylor Collection, *1*, 112, British Library of Political and Economic Science.

Grote's prudent concealment was practiced by others in Mill's circle of friends who generally shared opinions about politics and religion. They were, for the most part, disciples of Jeremy Bentham and James Mill. In the Utilitarian Society, a discussion group that included Mill and Grote, there were many skeptical discussions about the existence of God. At its second meeting, according to John Neal, "all [God's] attributes were seriously questioned by one or another of these fledglings, and subjected to what they called a 'searching analysis.' "[54] Such talk also entered into conversations in John Austin's drawingroom in 1831, with Mill present. Henry Reeve, the nephew of Austin's wife, recalled how "the conversation turned, as was not unusual among these philosophers, on the want of evidence of a superintending Deity and Providence in the affairs of the world."[55] Atheism was a bond among these young radicals. Much later Mill recalled how "mere negation of religion was a firm bond of union" among them.[56]

Within their circle there was a shared outlook, but looking outward, they perceived a hostile world. The fate of Richard Carlile, the publisher of Paine's *Age of Reason* and a variety of atheistic tracts, was much discussed.[57] While convinced about the soundness of their opinions, they recognized a clear though invisible barrier separating them from others in the public arena, where their opinions were forbidden. Within their circle they were candid with one another, while with those outside they were silent or evasive. Mill described this bifurcation in their dealings with the world: "nine tenths of society have a deportment and manner purely conventional, the other tenth have also the conventional for society and reserve the natural for their intimate friends."[58] It is not surprising, therefore, that Henry Reeve, who knew Mill and several of his friends quite well, was aware that the young Benthamites held "certain esoteric doctrines on the relation of man to God and to a future state, which they did not willingly make known." In this, Reeve believed, "they judged

[54] John Neal, *Wandering Recollections of a Somewhat Busy Life* (Boston, 1869), 56.
[55] Henry Reeve, "Autobiography of John Stuart Mill," *Edinburgh Review* 139 (January 1874): 115–16. Reeve implied that Mill was present during such conversations.
[56] Morley, *Recollections*, 61.
[57] Early Draft, *CW*, 1, 88.
[58] *Barclay Fox's Journal*, ed. R. L. Brett (Totowa, NJ: Rowman & Littlefield, 1979), 197 (entry 29 May 1840). An example of misleading discussion of religion by Mill's close friends is to be found in an essay by Charles Austin written while at Cambridge. The essay gives the appearance of belief and reverence but is entirely compatible with rejection of Christian claims. It inquires into the genuineness of the evidence on which the Bible is based and emphasizes that it is not considering "the authenticity of the history so conveyed." It concludes that the documents are authentic, but it adds that "the consequences that may be drawn from such a statement are foreign to our present purpose." Charles Austin, *The Argument for the Genuineness of the Sacred Volume, as Generally received by Christians, stated and explained* (Cambridge, 1823), 3, 147–48. The essay was awarded the Hulsean prize in 1822. Charles Austin enjoyed a reputation as a wit and prankster.

rightly—that if they disclosed to its full extent their absolute rejection of the principles of religious faith and of the accountability of man to God . . . they would stand but little chance of obtaining a hearing on any other subject."[59]

Mill must have been aware of a long tradition of concealment. He had read Gibbon's description of how philosophers in the age of the Antonines asserted, among themselves, the independent dignity of reason but also respected "both the interest of the priests and the credulity of the people"; and how philosophers of antiquity pitied the errors of the vulgar while practicing the ceremonies of their fathers and "concealed the sentiments of an Atheist under the sacerdotal robes."[60] He certainly was familiar with the ways some of the *philosophes* insinuated criticisms of Christianity while avoiding the risks of outright attacks.[61] And he may have alluded to this tradition in describing Guizot as possessing "the prudence of a wise man who lets some of his maxims go to sleep while the time is unpropitious for asserting them."[62]

The extent of his familiarity with the history of concealment of religious opinions is difficult to determine, but there is strong evidence that he assumed it was commonplace in his own time—that his contemporaries, in writing and conversation, concealed as a matter of prudence, and this confirmed his belief that it was still necessary. Already in 1834 he claimed that not less than one-fourth or one-third of the educated classes "are either actual unbelievers, or have only the faintest and most doubtful belief; though they do not chuse, by avowing their sentiments, to expose themselves to martyrdom."[63] And in the early draft of his autobiography, written when he was preparing to write *On Liberty*, he noted, "The world

---

[59] Henry Reeve, "Mill's Essays on Theism," *Edinburgh Review* 141 (January 1875): 4, 8.

[60] Edward Gibbon, *The History of the Decline and Fall of the Roman Empire* (London, 1828), *1*, 40–41 (chap. 2).

[61] *Examination of Sir William Hamilton's Philosophy*, CW, 9, 60; see below, chapter 5, text at note 61.

[62] Mill to Robert Barclay Fox, 23 December 1840, CW, *13*, 454–55. On the tradition of concealment, see, for example, Paul J. Bagley, "On the Practice of Esotericism," *Journal of the History of Ideas* 53 (April–June 1992): 231–47; Perez Zagorin, *Ways of Lying: Dissimulation, Persecution and Conformity in Early Modern Europe* (Cambridge, Mass.: Harvard University Press, 1990), *passim*.

[63] "Notes on the Newspapers" (4 June 1834), CW, *6*, 247. In 1819 Mill's friend W. J. Fox made a similar claim: "Deism has spread widely in our country; no inconsiderable proportion of the lower classes are honest and open unbelievers; and a larger proportion of the higher classes are, I fear, concealed unbelievers, who, while they discard Christianity themselves, think it an useful superstition to keep their inferiors in order." William Johnson Fox, *The Duties of Christians towards Deists: A Sermon Preached at the Unitarian Chapel . . . on occasion of the recent Prosecution of Mr. Carlile* (London, 1819), xii.

would be astonished if it knew how great a proportion of its brightest ornaments, of those most distinguished both for wisdom and virtue, are complete sceptics in religion."[64] This observation was repeated in *On Liberty*, where he claimed that many such persons are known only to their intimates to be unbelievers (239–40).

In observing this reticence about unbelief, Mill probably was correct. Other freethinkers, contemporaries of Mill's, at least acted as if they had something to hide, for they assumed that candid expressions of religious doubt would be penalized. Byron, not known for restraint or prudence, on this matter was cautious; in 1816 at a French inn he noticed that Shelley, during an earlier visit, had inscribed the word "atheist" in Greek after his own name in the guest book; Byron, assuming other English travelers would see it, defaced the word, believing he was doing Shelley a great service.[65] Hogg, in printing some of Shelley's letters in 1858, changed the word "atheist" to "philosopher."[66] Sarah Austin reported discussion of "how far one might dare be honest" in expressing opinions about religion and morals, in which an unnamed friend (Mill?) said these were matters about which one "must lie if he cannot stand martyrdom."[67] Thomas Moore agreed with Sarah Austin, who had told him that in Germany in spite of strong religious feelings, there was the fullest toleration for bold and infidel opinions. This provoked Moore to observe that it was "the very reverse of what existed in England, where a most worldly indifference prevailed as to real religion, while the slightest whisper of scepticism was sure to raise an outcry against him who dared to breathe it."[68] Carlyle recognized the truth of this, as he revealed in a conversation recalled by Alexander Bain: "Carlyle was denouncing our religion . . . Mill struck in with the remark—'Now, you are just the very man to tell the public your whole mind upon that subject.' This was not exactly what Carlyle fancied. He gave, with his peculiar grunt, the exclamatory—'Ho,' and added, 'it is someone like Frederick the Great that should do that.'"[69] Bain attributed Carlyle's "perplexing style of composition," including his "studied and

[64] Early Draft, *CW*, *1*, 46. Mill noted that Lord John Russell must know there are many disbelievers in public life, but they are not likely to avow unbelief; "if they did, they would emperil, among other things, all their chances of re-election." "Excluding Unbelievers from Parliament" (1849), *CW*, *25*, 1137.

[65] Leslie A. Marchand, *Bryon: A Portrait* (New York: Knopf, 1970), 250.

[66] David Berman, *A History of Atheism in Britain: From Hobbes to Russell* (London: Croom Helm, 1988), 186.

[67] Sarah Austin to Hermann Puckler-Muskau, 15 October 1832, Jagiellonian University Library, Cracow.

[68] *Memoirs, Journal and Correspondence of Thomas Moore*, ed. Lord John Russell (New York, 1857), *2*, 780. Brougham agreed with Sarah Austin about Germany: "Among the Germans at large all speculative opinions are freely ventilated, and all opposition to prevailing belief is fully tolerated." Henry Brougham, *Albert Lunel; or, the Chateau of Lanquedoc* (London, 1844), *2*, 71. This was a widely shared view of Germany, which Mill also held. See *CW*, *15*, 539, 550, 598; *32*, 108.

[69] Bain, *Mill*, 191.

ambiguous phraseology," to a determination to avoid being explicit about his religious convictions. This was an example of "compelled reticence on the part of the men best qualified to instruct mankind."[70]

Another contemporary, Harriet Martineau, also expected intolerance, though she refused to conceal her opinion; after she made public her rejection of Christianity she "anticipated excommunication from the world of literature, if not from society."[71] Macaulay also assumed intolerance when he noted that "in every age there are many concealed atheists who keep their opinions to themselves."[72] The belief that intolerance existed had the consequence, according to Buckle, that atheism was "skulking in hidden corners" and counting "its concealed proselytes to an extent of which only they who have studied this painful subject are aware."[73] An expectation of intolerance was widely shared among the literary and middle classes, and it led John M. Robertson, himself a proselytizing atheist, to conclude that up to mid-century it was "current doctrine that 'the wise man' conceals his opinions when they are unpopular."[74] Working-class radicals, in contrast, if they were atheists, were quite open about it.[75]

These varied observations support the suggestion made by a modern historian of British atheism, that during this period, and in the eighteenth century as well, avowed atheism was quite unusual and that most of the atheism that did exist was subterranean. Apart from Shelley's pamphlets, *The Necessity of Atheism* (1811) and *Refutation of Deism* (1814) and his political poem, *Queen Mab* (1813), there was little open confession of atheism from other than working-class advocates—Richard Carlile during the 1820s and, somewhat later, Charles Southwell, George Jacob Holyoake, Robert Cooper, and Charles Bradlaugh.[76]

Darwin was among those who feared being found out. His evolutionary ideas and even more unorthodox materialist philosophy took shape during the mid-1830s, and, according to Gruber, who studied the effect of the threat of persecution on the development of Darwin's scientific ideas,

---

[70] Bain, "Religious Tests and convictions," *Practical Essays* (New York, 1884), 274–75.

[71] Harriet Martineau, *Autobiography*, ed. Maria Weston Chapman (Boston, 1877), 2, 36–37; see also 1, 417, 548–49.

[72] Marginal comment in his copy of Francis Bacon, *Sylva Sylvarum*, in *Works*, 10 vols. (London, 1819), 2, 290: Copy of Notes, Trinity College Library, Cambridge. About Macaulay, Bain said, "His way of dealing with the subject [of religion] is so like the hedging of an unbeliever." *Practical Essays*, 274.

[73] Henry Thomas Buckle, "Mill on Liberty" in *Essays* (New York, 1863), 150.

[74] John M. Robertson, *A Short History of Freethought* (New York, 1906), 2, 402–3.

[75] Atheist missionaries, "unlike sceptics among the upper classes . . . never dissembled." F. B. Smith, "The Atheist Mission, 1840–1900," in *Ideas and Institutions of Victorian Britain*, ed. Robert Robson (London: Bell, 1967), 205. See Harriet Martineau, *A History of the Thirty Years Peace* (London, 1877), 2, 339; Holyoake: "In 1842, as I witnessed at the Gloucester Assizes, no barrister would defend any one accused of dissent from Christianity. . . . " *Bygones Worth Remembering* (London, 1905), 2, 210.

[76] Berman, *History of Athesim in Britain*, 105, 112–13, 120, 134–35, 169, 183, 203, 206, 220–21, 225–26.

"he was well aware of their explosive meaning for man's conception of his place in nature, and aware of the risk to himself if and when he presented these ideas in public." In his diary he wrote about the persecution of Galileo, and he experienced "some trepidation at the thought of exposing himself publicly as an atheist." Consequently he delayed publication of his ideas for twenty-three years—until 1859, the year *On Liberty* also appeared. Even then he pulled his punches and referred to the Creation, which led him to confess later that he "regretted that I truckled to public opinion."[77] Gruber notes that Lyell also was cautious, and he describes the extraordinary steps taken by Robert Chambers to conceal his authorship of his popularized account of the evolutionary outlook. Chambers had his manuscript transcribed in another person's handwriting and had it sent to the publisher from Manchester instead of Edinburgh, where he resided. Gruber concludes: "We are not wanting in evidence that an aura of fear and oppression surrounded scientific ideas challenging the literal interpretation of the Bible during the years when Charles Darwin was himself working out his ideas about evolution."[78]

Darwin's fears are described in even more extreme terms by his most recent biographers, who emphasize the oppressiveness of Victorian society. He was dealing with a "criminal subject" in an "hysterical climate." His worldly father advised concealing, and Darwin became guarded and "began devising ways of camouflaging his materialism." His dangerous speculations about the origin of species were recorded in a secret notebook and kept in a locked drawer. "Staring heresy in the face," he wore a "public mask" and was hesitant about sharing his ideas with colleagues and even close friends. "He was living a double life with double standards, unable to broach his species work with anyone except Eras [Erasmus, his brother], for fear he be branded irresponsible, irreligious, or worse." Thinking of his discovery as criminal and identifying with Galileo, he "saw himself in the torture chair" and had a nightmare of being executed. His many and dreadful physical symptoms may well have been generated by this state of mind. Understandably, he thought publication of his ideas suicidal.[79]

Such fears and the conditions that generated them were still in place at mid-century and beyond. They were in part the result of the legal author-

[77] Howard E. Gruber, *Darwin on Man: A Psychological Study of Scientific Creativity* (2nd ed. 1974; Chicago: University of Chicago Press, 1981), 29, 36–38, 40–41, 43–44.
[78] Ibid., 44, 45, 206, 209.
[79] Adrian Desmond and James Moore, *Darwin* (London: Penguin, 1992), xvi, 221, 233, 249, 259, 263, 294, 317, 320–23, 343, 348, 415, 670, 674–77; see also 250–53, 316. Like Grote, Darwin was buried in the Abbey.

ity to prosecute, for occasionally it was exercised. Prosecution for blasphemous libel was still possible throughout the nineteenth century. This was a matter of common law, in which blasphemous libel was defined, according to Blackstone, as an offense "against God and religion." It included denying the being or providence of the Almighty, contumelious reproaches of Christ, and all profane scoffing at the holy scripture or exposing it to contempt and ridicule. Its status was reinforced by the doctrine, traced back to Hale, that Christianity was part and parcel of the laws of England, and, therefore, "to reproach the Christian religion [was] to speak in subversion of the law." This was reaffirmed by Blackstone, and as late as 1883 James Fitzjames Stephen, who, as author of *The History of the Criminal Law*, spoke with authority, said, "The unexpressed assumption on which all legislation and government from the conversion of the English from heathenism to our own days has proceeded, has been the truth of Christianity."[80]

Blasphemous libel was a political offense, for it was assumed that public hostility to Christianity was damaging to the regime. Thus while blasphemous libel, as hostility to the Almighty, obviously had a religious dimension, it also had implications for the civil order, as it affected the peace and good order of society. Blackstone explained that, if the goal was "reforming the private sinner," ecclesiastical law could be brought to bear; but prosecution fell to the temporal courts in dealing with "the public affront to religion and morality, on which all government must depend for support."[81] This perspective was legally the most significant. This was confirmed by Starkie, a nineteenth-century commentator, who noted, "when it is considered that such impieties [of blasphemous libel] not only tend to weaken and undermine the very foundation on which all human laws must rest, and to dissolve those moral and religious obligations, without the aid of which more positive laws and penal restraints would be inefficacious, but also immediately tend to acts of outrage and violence . . . they necessarily become an important subject of municipal coercion and restraint."[82] Clearly it was the political consequences of public hostility to religion that justified making it a criminal offense, though only a misdemeanor. Parallel to this legacy of common law, there was

[80] William Blackstone, *Commentaries on the Laws of England*, ed. Thomas A. Green (Chicago: University of Chicago Press, 1979), 4, 59 (bk. IV, chap. 4); Thomas Starkie, *A Treatise on the Law of Slander and Libel* (2nd ed. [1830], Albany, 1843), 2, 127; John Macdonnell, "Blasphemy and the Common Law," *Fortnightly Review* 34 (June 1883): 780; James Fitzjames Stephen, *A History of the Criminal Law of England* (London, 1883), 2, 437, 473–74. Mill in 1823 criticized the doctrine that Christianity was part of English law. *CW*, 22, 6–8.

[81] Blackstone, *Commentaries*, 4, 58–59.

[82] Starkie, *Slander and Libel*, 2, 121–22; see also 125, 127, 130–31, 135; James Fitzjames Stephen, *Digest of the Criminal Law* (London, 1894), article 161.

among nonlawyers a general fear that atheism would undermine obligation and obedience and bring dissolution of social order.[83]

There was disagreement about the circumstances in which the law regarding blasphemous libel could be enforced, but such disagreement did
not justify an assumption that perhaps certain criticisms of Christianity
were immune from prosecution. It was held by some that if criticism was
not vituperative and not intended to injure or affront—for example, if it
had the character of philosophic inquiry into sacred subjects—it would
be exempt from prosecution. Others disagreed.[84] The very existence of
disagreement, however, left it uncertain whether denials of the truth of
Christianity, even if not cast in abusive or indecent language, would be
regarded as blasphemous libel in the eyes of the law. John Wade, compiler
of the radical *Black Book*, experienced this uncertainty. He noted that the
attorney general had stated in Parliament (in 1832) regarding libels, that,
if honestly and sincerely expressed, he would be "greatly disinclined to
prosecute." But Wade observed that "a public writer does not like to hold
his freedom by *courtesy*, he seeks the guarantee of a well-defined law."[85]
Such ambiguity made it somewhat risky for someone like Mill to be fully
candid in public discussions of religion.

In assessing this risk, a nonbeliever eager to speak out against Christianity might have considered how frequently the law concerning blasphemous libel was enforced. Enforcement varied over the course of the
century. Prosecutions, many leading to convictions, were quite frequent
up to the early 1830s, and they continued intermittently but infrequently
throughout the century and into the twentieth.[86] Richard Carlile was tried
and convicted several times during the 1820s.[87] The publisher of Shelley's
"Queen Mab" was prosecuted in 1841 and found guilty, but not called
up for judgment.[88] George Jacob Holyoake was convicted in 1842 and
sentenced to six months in prison.[89] Thomas Pooley, whose case was men-

[83] Walter Houghton, *Victorian Frame of Mind*, (New Haven 1957), 58–60.

[84] Starkie thought there were exceptions, Stephen not: Starkie, *Slander and Libel*, 121–
2, 125, 127, 130–1, 135; Stephen, *History*, 2, 274–5.

[85] John Wade, *History of the Middle and Working Classes* (3rd ed.; London, 1835), 465–
66. Dicey in 1868, noting that the law was unfavorable to liberty of religious discussion
and that public opinion was, on the whole, tolerant, argued that this left liberty on "a very
slender and insecure basis," for public opinion as it regarded liberty was "too uncertain,
indefinite, and capricious, to be called either systematically tolerant or systematically intolerant." A. V. Dicey, "The Legal Boundaries of Liberty." *Fortnightly Review* 9 (1 January
1868): 8–13.

[86] *Reports of State Trials*, new series, ed. John Macdonell (London, 1888), 1, 1387; William H. Wickwar, *The Struggle for the Freedom of the Press, 1819–1832* (London, 1928),
314–15.

[87] Joel Wiener, *Radicalism and Freethought in Nineteenth- Century Britain. The Life of
Richard Carlile* (Westport: Greenwood Press, 1983), 35, 44–48, 78, 253–54.

[88] *State Trials*, n.s., 4, 694.

[89] Ibid., 1381–82; George Jacob Holyoake, *The History of the Last Trial by Jury for
Atheism in England: A Fragment of Autobiography* (London, 1851), *passim*. In 1843 in

tioned in *On Liberty*, was convicted in 1857 and sentenced to three consecutive terms amounting to twenty-one months, but on judgment of insanity was released after five months.[90] These prosecutions, although not frequent, brought considerable penalties and/or costs and were sufficiently threatening that they could well have deterred many others.

The recognition that the government hesitated to prosecute did not eliminate the perception of risk, and prosecutions in 1882–83, 1908–9, 1911–17, and 1922 indicate that although the likelihood of prosecution was not great, the law was anything but a dead letter.[91] That Mill thought the law was to be taken seriously is indicated by his statement in *On Liberty* that there was little danger of its being put in force "against political discussion." By specifying political discussion he was making an exception of religious discussion. This implication is supported by his additional statement, "If the arguments of the present chapter [two] are of any validity, there ought to exist the fullest liberty of professing and discussing, as a matter of ethical conviction, any doctrine, however immoral it may be considered." By saying that such liberty ought to exist, he implied that it did not exist (228, 228n.).[92]

The risk of prosecution only drove some criticism of Christianity underground. This was Mill's view, and it was confirmed by Stephen in 1875 in arguing against the law as it was. Prosecutions for blasphemous libel, he said, did not check the growth of open skepticism among men such as Paine and Carlile who had nothing to lose in character or position, but

---

Scotland there were prosecutions for blasphemy. Matilda Roalfe was convicted for having published, i.e., sold, infidel books, and fined ten pounds as an alternative to imprisonment. Thomas Paterson was sentenced to fifteen months "for publications of Atheistical sentiments." At his trial, according to an admiring publication, he "had the moral hardihood to avow . . . his disbelief in God." *The Movement and Anti-Persecution Gazette*, ed. George Jacob Holyoake and M. Q. Ryall, no. 7 (27 January 1844): 56; no. 13 (16 March 1844): 105, 112; no. 16 (30 March 1844): 128; no. 28 (22 June 1844): 217. During the 1820s poor vendors of atheistic tracts were prosecuted and convcted in large numbers. Wickwar, *Struggle for the Freedom of the Press 1819–1832* (London, 1928), 96–114, 212–38.

[90] *State Trials*, n.s., 8, 1089; Timothy J. Toohey, "Blasphemy in Nineteenth Century England: The Pooley Case and Its Background," *Victorian Studies* 30 (spring 1987): 315–33. See also Gillian Hawtin, "The Case of Thomas Pooley, Cornish Well Sinker, 1857," *Notes and Queries* 219 (January 1874): 18–24.

[91] Most of these cases led to convictions with penalties ranging from fourteen days' to twenty-one months' imprisonment: Macdonell, "Blasphemy and the Common Law," 776; Paul O'Higgins, *Cases on Civil Liberties* (London: Woodfield, 1980), 65–95; Gerald Dacre Nokes, *A History of the Crime of Blasphemy* (London: Sweet & Maxwell, 1928), 159–60; Edward Royle, *Radicals, Secularists and Republicans: Popular Freethought in Britain, 1866–1915* (Manchester: University of Manchester Press, 1980), 33, 63, 224, 234, 272–75, 278, 280–83; John Edwin McGee, *A History of the British Secular Movement* (Girard, Kentucky, 1948), 71–72, 90. See also Hypatia Bradlaugh Bonner, *Penalties upon Opinion; or, Some Records of the Laws of Heresy and Blasphemy*, ed. F. W. Read (London: Watts & Co., 1934), 71–130.

[92] See also 240–41n, where he concludes from the statement by a member of the government that the government supported "the doctrine that all who do not believe in the divinity of Christ are beyond the pale of toleration."

"they forced serious and quiet unbelievers to take up a line of covert hostility to Christianity."[93] Mill was an example of what Stephen had in mind.

The legal armoury included more than the law of blasphemous libel. There were several statutes which served, as Starkie said, "to fortify the common law."[94] One such statute (9 & 10 William III, c. 35) made a person who had been educated as a Christian, or who had made at any time a profession of the Christian religion, ineligible to hold any ecclesiastical, military, or civil office (e.g., at India House?) if by writing, printing, teaching, or "advised speaking" he denied the Trinity, or denied the Christian religion to be true, or denied the Scriptures to be of divine authority. A first conviction led to forfeit of office; a second conviction disabled one to bring suit or to prosecute, to be a guardian of a child, to be an educator, to receive a legacy, or to hold office, and it called for three years in prison without bail. Stephen in 1875 asserted that the statute "is at this day in full force, and might at any moment be applied to any one who denies the Divine authority of the Bible, or the truth of the Christian religion, in private communication." Moreover, the court had no power, on a second conviction, to mitigate the penalties.[95]

Since the Act covered private conversation, Stephen ominously indicated that it could apply to conversation between a father and his son. Stephen acknowledged that the Act had not been put in force, but he took it seriously, especially as it imposed cumulative penalties on what was already an offense at common law. He speculated about how it might have applied to Mill and his father, in that the recently published *Autobiography* indicated that James Mill, who had been brought up as a Christian, had communicated his views on religion to his son. If James Mill had been prosecuted, he could have been saved from expulsion from India House only if employment by the East India Company had been regarded as private and not as civil employment. His son, however, since he had not been educated as a Christian and had not professed the Christian religion, could, if prosecuted under this Act, have mounted a valid defense. Stephen added, however, "Names of very distinguished living public servants, who might at any moment be utterly ruined (to the great injury of the public service) by the application of this Act, must occur to everyone." And he went on to say, "For obvious reasons I do not mention them here."[96]

---

[93] Stephen, "Laws of England as to the Expression of Religious Opinions," *Contemporary Review* 25 (Feb. 1875): 471.

[94] Starkie, *The Law of Slander and Libel*, 2, 135.

[95] Stephen, "Laws of England as to the Expression of Religious Opinions," 465–66. The law had been amended in 1813 to exempt Unitarians.

[96] Ibid., 467 See also Stephen, *Digest*, article 163.

Although Mill would have escaped the Act of 9 & 10 William III, Stephen noted that he had been vulnerable to other laws governing religious opinion, most importantly those that gave authority to the Ecclesiastical Courts. These courts "have to this day power to proceed criminally against any person whatever, clerical or lay, Protestant, Catholic, infidel, Jew, or anyone else—'in cases of atheism, blasphemy, heresy, or schism, and other damnable doctrines and opinions.' " The punishment was excommunication, which, Stephen explained, did not make Mill immune from penalty under this law. Stephen thought Mill could have been prosecuted for his *Three Essays on Religion*, had it been published while Mill still lived. Although excommunication hardly would have injured Mill, he could have been ordered to pay costs, enjoined to perform penance, or imprisoned up to six months until penance was performed. Thus the incidental effect of conviction would have been "that Mr. Mill might have been called upon to retract publicly the opinions contained in his book, under pain of six months' imprisonment."[97] Stephen's use of Mill as an example indicates that he believed Mill might well have experienced intimidation, fear, and censorship.

Stephen even went so far as to imagine a conversation in which Mill was asked, "Why don't you speak out like a man? Why don't you expose the superstitions and falsehoods, as you consider them, under which we are all groaning, boldly and decisively, and with all the powers of your mind? Why will you write about logic, and metaphysics, and liberty, when you really care about politics and religion?" Stephen, in this imaginary conversation, had Mill replying: "I will not do what you suggest for two reasons. First, I will not put it in the power of any bigot, who thinks he would do God service by so doing, to deprive me of my place at the India Office and to send me to gaol; and in the next place, you will find in the long run that the zig-zag mode of approach is good in controversy as well as in sieges. The sap and the mine must in time take us into the heart of the place. If we try to storm the town now, we shall simply be knocked on the head." Stephen was sure Mill would have written differently "if [he] had felt quite safe, legally and socially, in speaking his mind against Christianity, or the parts of it which he did not like."[98]

---

[97] Stephen, "Laws of England as to the Expression of Religious Opinions," 459–60, 465. Stephen added, "The living authors who might be proceeded against in the same way, are numerous and well-known, but it would be invidious to name them." If the conduct was a crime at common law, the Ecclesiastical Court did not have jurisdiction (465).

[98] Ibid., 475. Stephen made a similar analysis as early as 1859 in a review of *Dissertations and Discussions*. "It is characteristic both of the man and of the times in which he lives, that the subjects on which he has obviously thought and felt most deeply are not those on which he has written most largely. The subjects with which most . . . of his essays are concerned, are . . . morals, politics, and the social relations of mankind. There are various indications in different parts of the book that theology has also engaged his serious attention,

Penalties were not confined to prosecutions. Those few who proselytized freethinking opinions frequently faced hostile mobs, including stones being thrown through windows of lecture halls, the breakup of meetings, and harassment that sometimes made it necessary to flee. In addition, heretics faced a variety of economic and social penalties.[99] There was also the social stigma, which Mill thought even more effective than legal penalties. Buckle, among others, testified to the opprobrium that awaited those who investigated theological questions with skepticism.[100] One of the most notable of the penalized was James Anthony Froude. A copy of his *Nemesis of Faith* (1849), which portrayed but did not advocate skepticism, was thrown into a fire by the Senior Tutor of his college during a lecture, and Froude was cut by Fellows of his college and invited to resign his fellowship. Had he not resigned, he would have been expelled, as he put it, "in true heretic style. "[101] Although Harriet Martineau, in retrospect, thought she had been wrong, on the whole, to expect penalties for her views, she described hostile gossip and loss of friends that followed publication of her heresies.[102] The editor of the *Times*, asking Joseph Parkes to contribute a biographical sketch of Martineau, warned, "Remember that you are writing for the public and that you must speak of her religious opinions with all proper reprobation"; and, "Never forget how strong religion is in this country—or the affectation of it—much stronger than party or even interest."[103]

---

though none of the essays is especially devoted to it. It may seem at first sight strange that, this being the case, the most considerable of Mill's works should have been treatises on Logic and Political Economy. . . . It is difficult to avoid the conjecture that the choice of these subjects was determined, in a great measure, by the consideration that they were the only ones on which he would be sure of a full and fair hearing. . . . A discussion of them would give less offense to the feelings and less alarm to the prejudices of men than that of questions more nearly allied to the spiritual part of their nature." "Mr. Mill's Essays," *Saturday Review* 8 (9 July 1859): 47. For Stephen's authorship, see "Sir James Fitzjames Stephen's Publications and Selected Manuscripts," in Leon Radzinowicz, *Sir James Stephen 1829–1894 and his Contribution to the Development of Criminal Law*, Selden Society Lecture (London, 1957), 60.

[99] Edward Royle, *Radicals, Secularists, and Republicans*, 284 and *passim*. Edward Royle, ed., *The Infidel Tradition from Paine to Bradlaugh* (London: Macmillan, 1976), 214–15.

[100] Henry Thomas Buckle, "Mill on Liberty," *Essays* (New York, 1863), 149.

[101] Herbert Paul, *The Life of Froude* (New York, 1905), 47–52, 56; Alfred William Benn, *The History of English Rationalism in the Nineteenth Century* (London, 1906), 2, 42–5; F. Max Muller, *Auld Lang Syne* (New York, 1898), 88–91. Froude in 1858 rejoined the church, signed the 39 articles, and rejoined his old college: Rosemary Ashton, *G. H. Lewes: A Life* (Oxford: Claredon, 1991), 106.

[102] Martineau, *Autobiography*, 1, 471, 550; 2, 43, 46, 49. "The anticipation [of penalties] was very sincere at the time; and I took care that my comrade in the work [H. J. Atkinson] knew what my anticipation was" (36).

[103] John Delane to Joseph Parkes, 26 February [1855], 12 March 1855, University College London.

The belief that one might be penalized for extreme unorthodoxy was quite widespread among intellectuals at mid-century and beyond. George Henry Lewes did not hide his freethinking opinions within the Bohemian circle around Chapman, but outside he was cautious. The Chapman circle was like the coterie of Benthamites in that its members felt beleaguered— an enlightened enclave in a hostile world. Lewes's newspaper, *The Leader*, established in 1850, was devoted to free speech on all issues, especially religion, yet he kept Holyoake's name off the published list of sharehold- ers, because of his reputation for being an atheist.[104] Lewes complained about "the social persecution which embitters all departures from ac- cepted creeds."[105]

Such complaints were not isolated judgments, for there was much testi- mony about the threat of penalties from sophisticated men of letters. James Fitzjames Stephen, writing a year before *On Liberty* was published, testified to the "intellectual cowardice" of his countrymen: "most writers are so nervous about tendencies of their books, and the social penalties of unorthodox opinion are so severe, and are exacted in so unsparing a manner, that philosophy, criticism, and science itself too often speak amongst us in ambiguous whispers what ought to be proclaimed from the house tops."[106] A year later Stephen acknowledged that there was little social intolerance in the lay professions or among those with independent fortunes; however, "the least educated part of the clergy . . . and what is called the religious world, are very intolerant." Thus the injunction, "Thou shalt not say to stupid people things that would shock them" was one that "society at large either does or can enforce upon that thoughtful minority whose interests Mr. Mill has very properly so much at heart."[107] At about this time the American freethinker Moncure Conway was struck by the timid concealment of religious opinions among English rational- ists.[108] The way expectations of penalties produced acute anxiety is illus- trated by young Lord Amberley. As he was losing his belief in Christianity, he confessed in his diary: "I hope I may be able to make the avowal . . .

[104] Ashton, *Lewes*, 5, 84–87, 92, 109–111, 156, 235.

[105] Hock Guan Tjoa, *George Henry Lewes: A Victorian Mind* (Cambridge, Mass.: Har- vard University Press, 1977), 15; see also 35.

[106] James Fitzjames Stephen, "Buckle's History of Civilization in England," *Edinburgh Review* 107 (April 1858): 471.

[107] James Fitzjames Stephen, "Mr. Mill on Political Liberty (Second Notice)," *Saturday Review* 7 (19 February 1859): 213.

[108] Noel Annan, *Leslie Stephen: The Godless Victorian* (New York: Random House, 1984), 210; on the timidity of unbelievers, see 208–14. Henry Adams, in London during the 1860s, described those he called followers of Mill: "As a class, they were timid. . . . all tending to free-thinking, but never venturing much freedom of thought." *The Education of Henry Adams* (New York, 1931), 192.

but I dread the effect, as I should be thought dangerous, and I know not what else."[109]

One who was regarded as bold was Mill's publisher, William Parker. When publishing Buckle's short book of protest about a blasphemy trial which led to a conviction and severe sentence (*A Letter to a Gentleman Respecting Pooley's Case* [London 1859]), Parker "considered that he has crossed the Rubicon as a publisher, setting the clerical world at defiance, and espousing the promulgation of free-thought."[110] Apparently Parker's experience with Buckle's book decided him to send *On Liberty* to the printer without reading it, even though Mill warned Parker it would offend prejudices.[111] In contrast, John Murray refused to publish Harriet Martineau's *Eastern Life* (1848) because of its infidel tendencies.[112]

There were even ambiguous whispers during the 1860s in the writings of well-known agnostics, such as Herbert Spencer and T. H. Huxley, according to Robertson. These persons "felt cause to garble the extent of their unbelief" and spoke about true religion in a way that "implied that they were more anxious to be supposed essentially devout and God-fearing men than to be known as disbelieving the main points of the current faith."[113] In the case of Huxley, there certainly was harassment. When he became a candidate for a school board, he was assailed for his opinions about religion. He was variously called "atheist, infidel, and all the other usual hard names."[114] Huxley's experience was in keeping with the degree of tolerance others expected during the 1860s. G. H. Lewes and John Morley, successively editors of the new *Fortnightly Review*, were fearful about offending public opinion and therefore restrained themselves and their contributors on questions of theology.[115] Mill, seeking election to Parliament in 1865 and reelection in 1868, refused to answer questions about his religious opinions. And he thought it necessary to request Grote's permission to identify Grote as the author of the long anonymous review of *Examination of Sir William Hamilton's Philosophy*, in which Grote was critical of restrictions on philosophical atheists.[116]

While there was continued suspicion of atheism during the 1860s, other, less extreme unorthodoxy became increasingly acceptable. This be-

[109] *Amberley Papers*, 1, 278 (entry of 20 November 1863).

[110] Alexander Bain to Mill, 14 March [1859], National Library of Scotland. On Pooley, see above, text at note 89.

[111] Mill to John William Parker, 30 November 1858, CW, 15, 578–79.

[112] Desmond and Marsh, *Darwin*, 362.

[113] John M. Robertson [pseud. M. W. Wiseman], *The Dynamics of Religion: An Essay in English Culture History* (London, 1897), 295.

[114] T. H. Huxley to Charles Kingsley, 23 September 1860, Leonard Huxley, *Life and Letters of T. H. Huxley* (London, 1901) 1, 238.

[115] Alfred William Benn, *The History of English Rationalism in the Nineteenth Century* (London, 1906), 2, 354.

[116] Mill to George Grote, 25 December 1866, CW, 16, 1223.

came evident following the failure of the prosecution for heresy (initially in an ecclesiastical court and, on appeal, in the Privy Council) of two of the authors of *Essays and Reviews* (1860). These authors, of course, were churchmen, and the sense of freedom generated by their successful defense was not shared by atheists. Thus Sarah Austin in 1863 could say that "great progress has been made in England as to breadth and freedom of discussion. . . . Religions and political fanaticism are I think giving way before a general expansion of thought." Here, again, atheists were not beneficiaries, for she was referring to Acton and the recently founded Catholic journal, *Home and Foreign Review*.[117]

Liberalization occurred gradually, and the decade of the 1870s appears to have been transitional, for there is mixed testimony from contemporary observers who saw signs of both new openness and the old intolerance. Walter Bagehot in 1874 sensed the presence of a new liberty to say things which ten years earlier would have led to obloquy and being "turned out of society." Yet he also discerned a strong wish in many believers to persecute skeptics, and because of this he recognized that on some occasions it would be best to speak in terms of a parable.[118] Leslie Stephen in 1880 testified to the continuation of restraints, for while he acknowledged that a radically skeptical frame of mind was quite widespread, he also admitted that "open atheism is not common in decent English society," and among Members of Parliament, where atheism existed, it was concealed.[119] Professor Owen Chadwick suggests there was some openness at that time, at least for men of letters, but he also notes that the easy, candid, and private discussions in the Metaphysical Society caused surprise and that the society was a rare example of tolerance. He also acknowledges that in late Victorian times "a man's influence might still be a little diminished in some circles if he were known to be agnostic."[120] The historian of the Metaphysical Society was aware "how high religious feelings could run in the seventies and how still unresolved were the problems of free expression of religious opinion." Indeed, claims for "freedom of religious thought and the discussion of religious questions . . . were still suspect in England."[121] The perception of restrictions was shared by Trollope—or, at least, by one of the characters he created, Elias Gotobed, who, while preparing a lecture in the 1870s, said, "I am told that as long as I do

---

[117] Sarah Austin to Count Leo Thun, 1 April 1863. Status Oblastni Archiv Litomerice. Referring to *Essays & Reviews*, Brown asserts "that religious and doctrinal liberty would be as secure as the right to vote." Brown, *Metaphysical Society*, 286. On *Essays and Reviews*, see Owen Chadwick, *Victorian Church*, 2, 133 and 135.

[118] "The Metaphysical Basis of Toleration" (1874), *The Works and Life of Walter Bagehot*, ed. Mrs. Russell Barrington (London, 1915), 6, 219–20, 232–34, 237.

[119] "Mr. Bradlaugh and His Opponents," *Fortnightly Review* 34 (August 1880): 177–78.

[120] *Victorian Church*, 2, 6, 125–26.

[121] Brown, *Metaphysical Society*, 171, 180.

not touch Her Majesty's family, or the Christian religion . . . I may say anything."[122]

Mixed testimony came from Mill's young friend John Morley, who during the 1870s edited the *Fortnightly Review*. He referred to "the singular tolerance of free discussion which now prevails in England—[but] I do not mean that it is at all perfect."[123] It was so imperfect that a year later he acknowledged knowing many who rejected Christianity but felt constrained to assent to it publicly.[124] Such pressures led him in 1872 to describe contemporary religious discussion as a "pantomime stage-play, in which muffled phantoms of debate are made to gesticulate inexpressible things in portentously significant silence." This debate was "demoralized by cowardice of heart and understanding, when each controversial man-at-arms is eager to have it thought that he wears the colours of the other side."[125] Morley was not immune from this harsh judgment, for he himself counseled lack of candor when Huxley asked him whether he should publish his views on Christian miracles.

> Though I am strong for liberty of prophesying in all its forms and degrees, I think it would be wiser for your own peace and freedom from vexatious interruption, to let it alone. . . . I am quite sure it will land you in a row, compared with which any previous row of my time will seem peace and quietness. People don't much object to denial of "miracles" in a vague general way, but they will be very differently affected by a denial, a reasoned and provocative denial, by a man in the very front rank of modern reasoners, of the arch-miracle which is the base of their whole system of belief.[126]

The dangers Mill described seem to have been still in place.

The survival of this sense of danger was also evident in Mill's like-minded friend Alexander Bain. How like-minded is not evident in Bain's *Autobiography*, but privately he boasted to Mill of "the five or six infidels that I have had some hand in maturing."[127] And Mill was able to tell Comte that Bain was "a conquest of the first order for our common philosophy."[128] In recognition of their affinities, Mill felt, "Were I to die tomorrow, I could feel certain of leaving a successor."[129]

---

[122] *The American Senator* (New York: Oxford University Press, 1986), 357 (chap. 51).

[123] John Morley, "The Death of Mr. Mill," *Fortnightly Review*, n.s. 13 (1 June 1873): 673.

[124] John Morley, *On Compromise* (London, 1874,) 132.

[125] Morley, *Voltaire*, quoted by John M. Robertson [pseud. M. W. Wiseman], *Dynamics of Religion* (London, 1897), 301.

[126] John Morley to Thomas Huxley, 9 January 1876, Huxley Collection, Imperial College, London, vol. 23, pp. 24–25.

[127] Alexander Bain to Mill, 14 March [1859], National Library of Scotland.

[128] Mill to August Comte, 30 August 1843, *Correspondence Mill and Comte*, 185.

[129] Mill to Auguste Comte, 5 October 1844, ibid., 258. Bain said about James Martineau, "the virulence of his language towards Auguste Comte, on Comte's best points—his Athe-

Sharing Mill's outlook, Bain also shared Mill's anxieties, and they were revealed when, soon after Mill's death, Helen Taylor, Mill's stepdaughter, indicated she might publish translations of Mill's correspondence with Comte or allow Comte's disciples to publish the correspondence in France. Bain was alarmed and insisted that all references to himself be omitted. Such omissions would also be a service to others, including Grote.

> I do not think that it is yet time to speak out Grote's strong opinions, seeing that he never gave utterance to them in his own person. In such a matter as religion, whoever happens to be on the unpopular side, should be allowed to bring out his views, or not, as he pleases, and in the way he thinks best.[130]

This plea carries conviction, and it allows us to discount Bain's assertion, made to Harriet Martineau, that Mill "might have come out much sooner, without any harm to himself, or to any interest that he cared for."[131]

Bain's fears were also evident in his planning of the biographies of Mill and his father which ultimately were published in 1882. He considered publishing chapters in *Mind*, the journal which he founded in 1876, and which George Croom Robertson edited. "I begin to fear," he told Robertson, "that my plan of overhauling the two Mills should not begin with the first number [of *Mind*]. The Atheistic stamp upon both would need to be worn out a little before we make too much of them. The branding of outspoken irreligion is still in full exercise."[132] Bain's uneasiness continued throughout the writing of his book on Mill. As he completed the fourth chapter, he felt as if he had negotiated a mine field.

> I have a very touchy close upon the 'Religion' [i.e., *Three Essays on Religion*]. I have finished his wife, for the present; and felt I must risk something, not to show the white feather. Very guarded of course; but some may read between the lines.[133]

---

ism, makes him to me quite odious." Alexander Bain to George Grote, 2 August 1866, University College London, Add. 88/2.

[130] Alexander Bain to Helen Taylor, 6 November 1874, Mill-Taylor Collection, 4, ff. 65–68, British Library of Political and Economic Science.

[131] The account of Mill's religious views in the recently published *Autobiography* was the occasion for this comment. Alexander Bain to Harriet Martineau, 4 November 1873, University of Birmingham Library. Bain's worries were made worse by Helen Taylor's menacing tone. She was furious with Bain for having shown sheets of *Three Essays on Religion* to a friend, who then allowed them to be seen by a journalist, who published extracts before the book appeared. Bain to Helen Taylor, 21 March 1875. Mill-Taylor Collection, 4. f. 27. British Library of Political and Economic Science.

[132] Bain to G. C. Robertson, 25 October [1874], University College London, Add. 88/4.

[133] Bain to G. C. Robertson, 27 October [1881], University College London, Add. 88/6, ff. 33—34. Bain refers to *Mill*, 134–39. Bain asked the biographer of David Hume, John Hill Burton, "Why was Hume never dragged before the Civil Courts, under the statutes that make it penal to utter heretical opinions? seeing that, in our time, it has been possible to get

The fate of the atheist Charles Bradlaugh serves as a reminder that the transitional 1870s did not quickly lead to a new era of complete openness. He was not allowed to take his seat in the House of Commons in 1880, even though successful in the election, as he refused to comply with the formal requirement that he swear an oath on the Bible. This, however, was not the sole explanation of his exclusion from Parliament, for, as a prominent, fearless proselytizing atheist, he was the object of widespread public revulsion.[134] Bradlaugh was harassed and members of his family were subjected to vindictiveness.[135] Bradlaugh's unpopularity had already affected Mill adversely, for Mill's subscription to Bradlaugh's election expenses in 1868, which was known to the electorate, significantly contributed to his defeat in 1868.[136]

The Metaphysical Society provided evidence that the religious censorship which Mill and Bain feared was weakening. In a paper read to the Society in 1878, there was clear acknowledgment that few would defend penalties for religious opinion—and this came from William Connor Magee, Bishop of Peterborough, who was anything but pleased with this development. The question was asked, are such penalties immoral? and he acknowledged, "Most persons now-a-days would unhesitatingly answer this question in the affirmative."[137] The Bishop in his assessment agreed with James Fitzjames Stephen's statement in 1875 that the existing laws authorizing punishments for blasphemy and heresy were "in hopeless and direct opposition to the general current of principle and opinion in the present day."[138]

---

convictions against Atheists and profaners." Bain to John Hill Burton, 4 December 1875, National Library of Scotland, MS 9400, ff. 187–88.

[134] Walter L. Arnstein, *The Bradlaugh Case: A Study in Late Victorian Opinion and Politics* (Oxford: Clarendon, 1965), 54, 58–9; Hypatia Bradlaugh Bonner,: *Charles Bradlaugh: A Record of His Life and Work* (London, 1898), *1*, 137; *2*, 20–7, 316, 324.

[135] David Tribe, *President Charles Bradlaugh, M.P.* (London: Elek, 1971), 72, 226–7. On hostility to atheists, see Owen Chadwick, *Victorian Church*, *1*, 527. Stephen opposed penalties for unbelievers but said he understood that sincere Christians would try to deter criticism "by denouncing such opinions as dangerous and immoral, and by imposing social penalties on their advocates." "Laws of England as to the Expression of Religious Opinions," 447.

[136] Mill denied that it contributed. *CW*, *16*, 1459, 1487, 1502; *17*, 1541; on its negative effect, see Bruce Kinzer, Ann P. Robson, and John M. Robson, *A Moralist In and Out of Parliament, John Stuart Mill at Westminster, 1865–1868* (Toronto: University of Toronto Press, 1992), 229–49, 278, 280, 289.

[137] "The Ethics of Persecution," 11 June 1878, *Papers read before the Metaphysical Society* (privately printed, n.d.). This essay was a response to and acknowledgment of victory to Mill in chapter two of *On Liberty* .

[138] James Fitzjames Stephen, "Laws of England as to the Expression of Religious Opinions," *Contemporary Review*, 25 (February 1875), 467.

When the Bishop acknowledged that most persons regarded penalties for opinions as immoral, of course he had in mind those whose education gave them advanced, sophisticated views. Among such persons scientific advances reenforced the assumption that there could be a naturalistic explanation for any event,[139] and with the growth in size and confidence of this class of person, religion was put on the defensive. The aggressiveness and conviction of the rationalists within the Metaphysical Society, Brown tells us, "did much to persuade the theists that the day of theological and ecclesiastical influence over the minds of 'free spirits' had already drawn to a close."[140] The change, however, took place in slow motion. The claim to free inquiry was made by the small number of intellectually adventurous men of letters—such as George Jacob Holyoake, T. H. Huxley, Leslie Stephen, George Henry Lewes, and James Fitzjames Stephen. For most, including most of the educated classes, the idea of extending freedom to inquiry about religion caused considerable uneasiness. The state of the public mind in 1878 was described by A. J. Balfour, who acknowledged that the spirit of the age included criticism and scrutiny of inherited faith by men of letters. However,

> Of people who pass for educated probably the largest number regard [this] with . . . passive dislike. In their secret hearts they object to any change of opinion because it must be inconvenient and may be dangerous. . . . Next to them came a set of people, intellectually somewhat more restless who regard the spirit of the age with mixed feelings of fear and admiration. It seems to them a fine thing to be above prejudice. . . . But though agreeable . . . they cannot help thinking these new ways a little alarming. Who can tell where it will all end?[141]

Thus all but the boldest inquirers were likely to feel uneasy when faced with searching inquiry into the foundations of religious belief.

The state of mind described by Balfour, of course, followed Mill's death. The small changes in the direction of greater tolerance were noticed by Mill, though they did not keep him from engaging in self-censorship. He was aware of some acceptance of fully free inquiry in the old English universities. "Whereas they formerly seemed to exist mainly for the repression of independent thought, and the chaining up of the individual intellect and conscience, they are now [1867] the great foci of free and manly enquiry, to the higher and professional classes."[142] He took note of

---

[139] See below, text at note 146.

[140] Brown, *Metaphysical Society*, 136.

[141] A. J. Balfour, unpublished introduction to *Defense of Philosophic Doubt*, Balfour Papers, British Library, Add. 49892, ff. 1–10 (13–21 October 1878).

[142] "Inaugural Address Delivered to the University of St. Andrews," *CW*, 21, 250. The old universities "are now very much changed, and free enquiry and speculation on the deepest and highest questions, instead of being crushed or deadened, are now more rife there

this change in an addition to the early draft of his autobiography. "More recently a spirit of free speculation has sprung up, giving a more encouraging prospect of the gradual mental emancipation of England."[143] Morley also reported that shortly before his death Mill was astonished by the recently developed "liberty of expressing unpopular opinions in this country without social persecution."[144] This change may have encouraged him to include the notorious "to Hell I will go" passage in the *Examination of Sir William Hamilton's Philosophy* (1865). Apart from this, however, the small increase in public tolerance did not affect Mill's practice of concealment. The *Examination*, after all, was a long, abstruse, technical, philosophical discourse, written for those who were philosophically sophisticated. When he faced the populace, as he did during the elections of 1865 and 1868, he was evasive about religion, and throughout the sixties he continued to withhold from publication his essays "Utility of Religion" and "Nature."[145]

The restrictive atmosphere changed substantially only late in the century—well after Mill's death. The gradual erosion of belief among the educated classes came with the expectation that religion had to be compatible with naturalistic explanations.[146] A loss of political power by the religious party (as Noel Annan has argued) also contributed. Whatever the causes, those looking back from this century recognized the change. Annan located it during Leslie Stephen's generation; before that time, he said, there was pusillanimity.[147]

The historian Lecky also placed the transformation late in the century: "No change in English life during the latter half of the nineteenth century is more conspicuous than the great enlargment of the range of permissible opinions on religious subjects. Opinions and arguments which not many years ago were confined to small circles and would have drawn down grave social penalties, have become the commonplaces of the draw-

---

than almost anywhere else in England." Mill to Mrs. Henry Huth, 7 January 1863, *CW*, 15, 819.

[143] *Autobiography*, CW, 1, 247.

[144] Morley, "The Death of Mr. Mill," *Fortnightly Review*, n.s. 13 (1 June 1873): 673.

[145] It has been held, however, that for including the "to Hell I will go" passage Mill was courageous and heroic, and that it opened up a new irreligious era. Berman, *History of Atheism in Britain*, 235, 237, 242, 244, 246.

[146] The state of religious belief among the working classes may have been quite different. There was much fear that it had eroded, but it has been argued that as late as 1900, although there was either indifference or hostility to the churches, rejection of their message was quite rare. K. S. Inglis, *Churches and the Working Classes in Victorian England* (Toronto: University of Toronto Press, 1963), 329. Pelling also concludes that claims about extensive antireligious views among the working classes are exaggerated. It is difficult, he says, to find evidence of a strong atheist or anti-Christian feeling in London: Henry Pelling, *Popular Politics and Society in Late Victorian Britain* (London: Macmillan, 1968), 27.

[147] Noel Annan, *Leslie Stephen: His Thought and Character in Relation to his Time* (London: MacGibbon & Kee, 1951), 157.

ingroom and of the boudoir."[148] The consensus about the timing of the change indicates that Mill's factual assumptions underlying his policy of prudent concealment were well founded.

Whatever the precise date that divided a period of openness and candor from an earlier time when nonbelievers felt threatened by legal or social penalties, the change occurred well after publication of *On Liberty*. Stephen again provides useful testimony: "The present generation," he wrote in 1883, "is the first in which an avowed open denial of the fundamental doctrines of the Christian religion has been made by any considerable number of serious and respectable people." Before this time a denial of the truth of religion was akin to high treason. "A man who did not believe in Christ or God put himself out of the pale of human society."[149] Mill when he wrote *On Liberty* could well have believed that the public avowal of atheistic views was risky. He might have assumed he was personally at risk, and he certainly would have been justified in believing that freethinkers, agnostics, and atheists did not enjoy freedom of religious opinion. These assumptions affected what he wrote in *On Liberty* and how it was written.

[148] William Edward Hartpole Lecky, *Democracy and Liberty* (1896: reprint Indianapolis: Liberty Classics, 1981), 431.
[149] Stephen, *History of Criminal Law*, 2, 438. In another, more ambiguous statement Stephen located the change during the previous twenty or so years.

Chapter Five

ARGUMENTS ABOUT CHRISTIANITY IN *ON LIBERTY*

> Let anyone read the autobiography of Mr. John Mill,
> compare it with his works, and ask himself whether
> every one of them does not show the clearest traces of a
> deep-seated hostility to religion . . . and of a settled
> determination . . . to sap the very foundations of religion,
> by means of a mode of attack which no law short of the
> Spanish Inquisition could possibly reach.
> (*James Fitzjames Stephen*)

THE REALITY of penalties and the practice of dissimulation provided the immediate context of Mill's writing about religion in *On Liberty* and elsewhere. These things influenced what he wrote and determined the way he wrote. He made it clear that about religion he would not publish all his thoughts, and he implied that in what he wrote he would practice the kind of equivocation which he regarded as justifiable. Yet the need to conceal affected more; it also shaped the substance and the rationale for the book. His purpose was to establish liberty for those who would implement his plan for moral reformation. There were, in general, two functions that had to be performed, one destructive, the other constructive. The first involved eliminating old moral, religious, and social beliefs that were objectionable as well as being obstacles to the emergence of better alternatives; the second involved visualizing and encouraging the growth of a new moral and social order. Mill wished to promote both these activities, and in *On Liberty* he criticized the social and legal constraints that made it difficult for these functions to be performed.

The time was ripe for such changes, he believed. Vast, long-term subterranean changes were underway. One of the strongest tendencies was toward "a general demolition of old institutions and opinions." It had begun in France, and the process was underway in England, indeed, the English were "in the middle of *their* Revolution."[1] Mill, of course, welcomed these changes: "I confidently hope for . . . complete subversions

---

[1] "Duveyrier's Political Views of French Affairs" (1846), *CW, 20,* 297–98.

of the foundations of 'society' [such] as were made by Christianity, the Reformation, and the enfranchisement of the slave."[2]

In *On Liberty* he also mentioned the Reformation as an example of the undermining of authority and greatly increased political consciousness that would be one of the fruits of full liberty (243). This process of breaking down the old order had priority, for, as he explained, "there is still too much to be undone, for the question, 'what is to be done,' to assume its due importance."[3] Therefore, while thinkers in advance of their time prepared for ultimate reconstruction, the immediate need was for criticism, undermining, and destruction. *On Liberty*, which justified the freedom that would make it possible to engage in these activities, was supposed to hasten the process of history.[4]

Custom and established beliefs were among the things that were to be destroyed, and since Christianity, Mill was convinced, was closely tied to much that had to go, it became one of his prime targets. Its theology, on the whole, was not considered in *On Liberty*. Nor were church institutions. There was, however, an analysis of Christian morality (which will be examined in chapter seven, below).[5] There was also an analysis of the effect of open discussion on Christian belief, which is a major theme of Mill's chapter two.

Christian belief survived, Mill thought, only because it was protected from radical criticism by atheists and freethinkers. Such persons, Mill knew from personal experience, were, at the very least, inhibited. In fact, the rejectors of Christianity were the only persons excluded from the general toleration that was in place. They were the only ones threatened by penalties, familiar with fear, and needing to equivocate and conceal. This was repression, and it prevented the free and open discussion (and, by extension, publication) that was the subject of chapter two—"Liberty of Thought and Discussion."[6]

The repression of atheism, he acknowledged, was not as great as in the past, yet it was sufficient to silence and intimidate. "It is true we no longer put heretics to death," and modern feeling would not allow punishments that led to extirpation, but there were prosecutions, at least occasionally, and legal requirements for the swearing of religious oaths (239). The latter were absurd, for while they assumed "atheists must be liars," testimony from atheists who were willing to lie was admitted; but "those

---

[2] "Stability of Society" (1850) *CW*, *25*, 1181.

[3] "Duveyrier's Political Views," *CW*, *20*, 299.

[4] Already in 1831 he observed, "destruction must precede renovation." Mill to John Sterling, 20–22 October 1831, *CW*, *12*, 77.

[5] See chapter 7, text between notes 39 and 41, below.

[6] "The liberty of expressing and publishing opinions may seem to fall under a different principle . . . but, being almost of as much importance as the liberty of thought itself . . . is practically inseparable from it." *On Liberty, CW, 18*, 225–26.

who brave the obloquy of publicly confessing a detested creed rather than affirm a falsehood" were not allowed to testify (240). Such things were "but rags and remnants of persecution" (240), a legacy from the past which, however, could be reinvigorated by the religious revival that was taking place.

Worse than legal punishments and restrictions, however, there was "the social stigma . . . which is really effective, and so effective is it, that the profession of opinions which are under the ban of society is much less common in England, than is, in many other countries, the avowal of those which incur the risk of judicial punishment" (241). For most, "opinion, on this subject, is as efficacious as law; men might as well be imprisoned, as excluded from the means of earning their bread." And Mill concluded, "Our merely social intolerance kills no one, roots out no opinions, but induces men to disguise them, or to abstain from any active effort for their diffusion" (241).

Because atheists and freethinkers were to be the main beneficiaries of the enlarged liberty of thought and discussion that he proposed, his second chapter contains many allusions to such persons. They were infidels and heretics and the one-sided asserters who compelled attention to their arguments (253). He urged that they be protected from abuse by Christians: there was "much more need to discourage offensive attacks on infidelity, than on religion" (259). Christians, he said, "should themselves be just to infidelity" (257). Early in the chapter he announced that if his arguments were valid, they would show "there ought to exist the fullest liberty of proposing and discussing . . . any doctrine, however immoral it may be considered" (228n.)—a statement to be understood in light of the fact that the only doctrine widely regarded as immoral that he continuously alluded to in this chapter was atheism. He again defended the rejectors of Christianity when criticizing a member of the government for defining toleration in a way that excluded them. Toleration, the official had said, "meant the complete liberty to all, freedom of worship, *among Christians, who worshipped upon the same foundation.*" Mill noted that, according to this argument, "all who do not believe in the divinity of Christ are beyond the pale of toleration" (241n.).[7] Mill confirmed that his second chapter was written to enlarge freedom for atheists and freethinkers by telling a correspondent that in reading *On Liberty* she would discover "why I think such men as Mr. B[radlaugh] ought to be allowed to say what they have got to say, and not be abused for their opinions so long as they do nothing wrong."[8]

---

[7] The official distinguished Hindoos and Mahomedans from Christians, but Mill applied his observation to rejectors of Christianity.

[8] Mill to Mrs. Elizabeth Lambert, 28 November 1868, *CW*, *16*, 1492. Such were "the principles I have openly proclaimed especially in my book on Liberty, viz that atheists . . .

He maintained his conviction that atheism was suppressed in spite of the widespread belief that freedom of conscience was well established. "Yet so natural to mankind is intolerance in whatever they really care about, that religious freedom has hardly anywhere been practically realized, except where religious indifference . . . has added its weight to the scale." Even in tolerant countries, "in the minds of almost all religious persons . . . the duty of toleration is admitted with tacit reserves." Thus even open-minded but religious persons will exclude those who do not believe in a God and in a future state. "Wherever the sentiment of the majority is still genuine and intense," Mill concluded, "it is found to have abated little of its claim to be obeyed" (222).

In focusing his argument on liberty for atheists and other critics of Christianity, he acknowledged that liberty in most other areas was fairly well-established. Thus there was no need to plead for liberty in general or for political liberty. "The time, it is to be hoped, is gone by, when any defense would be necessary of the 'liberty of the press' as one of the securities against corrupt or tyrannical government" (228). There would be moments of panic when freedom of political discussion might be interfered with, but Mill was confident that "the era of pains and penalties for political discussion has, in our own country, passed away" (228n.). Thus to Villari he explained that his book was not about political so much as "social, moral, and religious liberty."[9] If Mill had had an opportunity to respond to Macaulay's observation about *On Liberty*—that Mill "is

---

may be & often are, good men, . . . & are entitled like all other persons to be judged by their actions . . . and not by their speculative opinions." Mill to Richard Marshall, 5 November 1868, *CW*, *16*, 1479. Mill's advocacy of liberty of expression for heretics was not confined to *On Liberty*. He criticized Lord John Russell for not allowing "sceptics and infidels" to be admitted into Parliament. And in making way for Jews, Russell "opens the door of parliament just wide enough to allow one particular class of dissenters from Christianity to slip in, and closes it, as far as depends upon him, against all others." "The Attempt to Exclude Unbelievers from Parliament" (1849), *CW*, *25*, 1135. Also: "[A] great difference in the conscientious convictions of human beings ought to make a visible difference of some kind or other in their conduct, but in point of fact it seldom does. Certain it is that neither Lord John Russell, nor any other man of the world, would trust the unbelievers less in any relation of life, or would consider them less eligible for the great majority of public functions, than the average of Christians." "Excluding Unbelievers from Parliament" (1849), *CW*, *25*, 1137. When the Evidence Amendment Act passed in 1869, allowing the substitution of an affirmation for an oath in the swearing of witnesses in courts of law, Mill called it "a great triumph of freedom of opinion," Mill to G. J. Holyoake, 8 August 1869, *CW*, *17*, 1630. Earlier, he wrote: "But if you exclude discussion on any one doctrine of religion, you must, by parity of reason, exclude it on all. It is in vain to say that Atheistical opinions shall alone be excluded. What reason is there why this more than any other subject should be prevented from undergoing a thorough examination?" "Free Discussion [I]" (1823), *CW*, *22*, 11. "The equal administration of law is due to the Infidel as well as to the Christian." "Debate on the Petition of Mary Ann Carlile" (1823), *CW*, *22*, 24. And: "[T]he same reasons which make him a friend to toleration in other cases, bind him also to tolerate Infidelity." "Law of Libel and Liberty of the Press" (1825), *CW*, *21*, 14.

[9] Mill to Pasquale Villari, 30 June, 1857, *CW*, *15*, 534; see also 539, 550.

really crying 'Fire!' in Noah's flood"—he would have insisted that Macaulay's assumption of abundant liberty, while generally correct, did not extend to atheists and freethinkers.[10] Mill's perception of restriction in England allowed him, rather curiously, to look enviously at France: with bold leadership in England "we could hope to conquer soon that freedom which France happily enjoys: the freedom of saying everything. This above all is what we lack at present."[11] Even for discussion of religious matters, there was ample liberty—provided those engaging in the discussion were Christians. Mill was aware of intense disagreement among Christians about theology—indeed he thought there was too much of it and regarded it as an utter waste of time and talent.[12]

Mill's close friends understood that he wished to extend liberty to atheists. Alexander Bain said the book "is everything that I expected or wished, and more. The chapter on Freedom of Opinion would have deserved the highest encomiums even without the analysis of the Christian morality; while, with that, it gives one already the sense of breathing a freer atmosphere," and he reported that Grote "thinks that you have decidedly extended the standing ground for *irreligious* opinions."[13]

Mill's focus on liberty of expression for atheists shows that he went far beyond the traditional doctrine of liberty of the press, which justified ample liberty but not for those who undermined religion. Milton and Blackstone were among the most prominent spokesmen for the traditional theory, and with regard to toleration generally, Locke was also part of this tradition. But Mill, like his father and Bentham, held Blackstone, as the most notable theorist of the common law, in contempt. Blackstone had argued that Christianity was part and parcel of the law of England and in his *Commentaries* had offered a rationale for the offense of blasphemous libel and, following Locke, he withheld toleration from atheists.[14] Mill's distance from traditional doctrine is revealed even more clearly in his judgment of Milton, who in *Areopagitica* argued against censorship prior to publication but also defended severe punishment for those who published atheistical opinions, arguing that they would unlaw law itself. Mill must have recalled this when an admirer coupled his name

---

[10] George Otto Trevelyan, *The Life and Letters of Lord Macaulay* (Oxford: Oxford University Press, 1932), 2, 380.

[11] Mill to Auguste Comte, 13 August 1846, *Correspondence Mill and Comte*, 377. Also, "This freedom of speech you enjoy in France is compensation for many woes. We are still very far from such a state, but who knows? In a period of moral transition, things may move faster than they seem." Mill to Comte, 28 January [1843], ibid., 131.

[12] Diary, 7 February [1854], *CW*, 27, 652.

[13] Alexander Bain to Mill, 14 March [1859], National Library of Scotland.

[14] Helen Taylor, adopting Mill's position, criticized Huxley for endorsing Locke on the withholding of toleration from atheists. Helen Taylor, "The New Attack on Toleration," *Fortnightly Review* 16 (1871): 718.

with Milton's. "It is not agreeable to me to be praised in the words of a man whom I so wholly disrespect as Milton, who with all his republican-ism had the soul of a fanatic and despot and tyrant."[15] Many, however, have insisted on regarding Mill as comfortably fitting into the same tradi-tion as Milton and Blackstone. James Fitzjames Stephen, for example, initially thought Mill was reminding Englishmen "of truths which for the most part they look upon as established"; and, "we know of nothing in English literature since the Areopagitica more stirring, more noble . . . than these two chapters [2 and 3] of Mr. Mill's Essay."[16] This view still prevails; one modern commentator refers to "the classical argument for tolerance formulated by John Milton and John Locke and restated by John Stuart Mill."[17]

Among those who were to benefit from the enlarged liberty, Mill seems to have had himself in mind. In fact, his arguments, while cast in general terms, often sounded like a *cri de coeur* from one who felt personally oppressed and desperate for the opportunity to speak his mind freely.[18]

When Mill was composing *On Liberty*, he had more than thirty years' experience of feeling constrained as the result of acting on his father's advice to conceal his religious opinions. It was an experience of holding back and self-censorship that made him feel uneasy and, by the 1850s, somewhat ashamed. He described the policy of concealment as "morally prejudicial" because in any discussion of religion one had to choose "avowal or hypocrisy."[19] He came to disapprove of concealment, saying, in the past, "I was much more inclined, than I can now [1853–54] ap-prove, to put in abeyance the most decidedly heretical part of my opin-ions, which I now look upon as almost the only ones the assertion of

[15] Mill to John Lalor, 27 June [1852], *CW, 14*, 91.

[16] "Mr. Mill On Political Liberty," *Saturday Review* 7 (12 February 1859): 186, 187.

[17] F. A. Hayek, *The Constitution of Liberty* (Chicago: University of Chicago Press, 1960), 30. Himmelfarb recognizes the important ways Mill differed from Milton and Locke. Edi-tor's Introduction, Mill, *On Liberty* (Harmondsworth: Penguin, 1974), 9. Stewart Justman, on the other hand, arguing that Mill was part of the tradition of civic republicanism, claims he had close affinities with Milton: *The Hidden Text of Mill's* Liberty (Savage, Md.: Row-man and Littlefield, 1991), 6, 75–105.

[18] In *On Liberty*, "for once he becomes passionate . . . In . . . stepping forward as the champion of individual liberty, a new spirit seems to have taken possession of him. He speaks like a martyr, or the defender of martyrs." Max Muller, "On Freedom," *Contempo-rary Review* 36 (1879): 369.

[19] Early Draft, *CW, 1*, 44. Leslie Stephen in 1877, perhaps reacting to what he read about this in Mill's *Autobiography*, called the practice "a system of pious frauds" and urged that it be ended as being "neither creditable nor safe." Leslie Stephen, "An Apology for Plain-speaking," *Essays on Freethinking and Plainspeaking* (New York, 1877), 328.

which tends in any way to regenerate society."[20] This is not to say that he stopped practicing concealment. As J. M. Robertson said, "Privately they [Mill and Carlyle] would speak of the need for speaking out, without speaking out."[21] During the mid-1850s when he was condemning his own self-censorship, he also wrote the essays "Nature" and "Utility of Religion," intending to withhold them from the public; and the statement suggesting disapproval of concealment is from his autobiography, which he had no intention of publishing during his lifetime.

Despite his condemnation of concealing, he found excuses to continue practicing it,[22] which, however, did not remove Mill's feeling that he was in a false position. Henry Reeve, who as Sarah Austin's nephew had known him since boyhood, made a discerning observation: "This species of dissimulation was painful to the sincere and courageous nature of John Mill."[23]

Courage was the problem. Mill admired it and he possessed it. This he demonstrated in the London Debating Society, where he put forth advanced views on a wide range of subjects; in his position as intellectual leader of the Philosophic Radicals during the 1830s when he made bold assertions of radical political principles; in his published critique of Bentham and defense of Coleridgean ideas, which outraged many of his associates; and in his conduct relating to Mrs. Taylor, whom he met when he was twenty-four. Only with regard to religious opinions could he find himself wanting. He implicitly condemned himself in *On Liberty* where, after describing how social intolerance induces men to disguise their religious opinions, he noted that "the price paid for this sort of intellectual pacification, is the sacrifice of the entire moral courage of the human mind" (242).[24] The principle by which he judged himself was put forth in a work contemporary to *On Liberty* in which he advocated open, nonsecret voting: enlightened morality condemns concealment, and "if it be one of the paramount objects of national education to foster courage and public spirit, it is high time now that people should be taught the duty of asserting and acting openly on their opinions. Disguise in all its forms is a badge of slavery."[25]

[20] Autobiography, *CW*, *1*, 237, 239. Early Draft, *CW*, *1*, 236, 238.

[21] John M. Robertson, *A Short History of Freethought Ancient and Modern* (2d. ed.; New York, 1906), *2*, 401.

[22] See chapter 4, text at note 16.

[23] Henry Reeve, "Autobiography of John Stuart Mill," *Edinburgh Review* 139 (January 1874): 94.

[24] Earlier he linked submission to social pressure and cowardice: The gentleman class suffers from "a moral effeminacy, an inaptitude for every kind of struggle. They . . . cannot brook ridicule, they cannot brave evil tongues. . . . This torpidity and cowardice . . . is new in the world." "Civilization" (1836), *CW*, *18*, 131–32.

[25] *Thoughts on Parliamentary Reform* (1859), *CW*, *19*, 337.

Mill's discomfort with his own failure to live up to his standard was reflected in his comment about an impoverished man who had been denied poor relief because he would not affirm having religious belief. This person, Mill said, "has the manliness to speak out, with simplicity and without ostentation, the fact of his unbelief."[26] Aware of the discrepancy between his standards and his conduct, Mill must have been stung by Comte's reaction to his insistence that in England one could not safely declare one's atheism. In France, Comte declared, philosophers who complained about restraint would "have to recognize that they are involuntarily guilty of a lack of inner courage or of firm convictions." Not letting up, he added, "true freedom is not granted; it is seized!"[27] These considerations also affected his judgment of Charles Bradlaugh, who, in spite of faults, had qualities Mill admired but felt he did not possess—"a courageous willingness to face opprobrium, an urgent need to speak the truth, [and] a kind of necessity to fight against all falsehood & hypocrisy."[28] As late as 1870 he still pondered this deficiency. A visitor reported that "many times . . . he returned with regret to the lack of courage that everywhere withholds writers from supporting new ideas."[29]

Mill felt intimidated and victimized. Here he was, with so much to say, yet he was silenced. It is not difficult to recognize a description of his own situation in *On Liberty*: "With us, heretical opinions do not perceptibly gain, or even lose, ground in each decade or generation; they never blaze out far and wide, but continue to smoulder in the narrow circles of thinking and studious persons among whom they originate, without ever lighting up the general affairs of mankind" (241). He was distressed by being prevented from playing the intellectual role as architect of moral

[26] "Notes on the Newspapers" (4 June 1834), *CW*, 6, 247. He also described "the famous atheist, [Richard] Carlile, who really had no other notable merit than his courage." Mill to Auguste Comte, 15 December 1842, *Correspondence Mill and Comte*, 120. John Neal harshly described Mill's position: "He learned to question the attributes, and being of God, though never willing to be called an atheist, but only, at the worst, a free-thinker and philosopher. But his want of moral courage I foresaw." John Neal, *Wandering Recollections of a Somewhat Busy Life* (Boston, 1869), 292.

[27] Auguste Comte to Mill, 6 May 1846, 3 September 1846, *Correspondence Mill and Comte*, 372, 381.

[28] Mill to Thomas Dyke Acland, 1 December 1868, *CW*, 16, 1500.

[29] Georg Brandes, *Eminent Authors of the Nineteenth Century: Literary Portraits*, trans. Rasmus B. Anderson (New York, 1886), 130. John Morley, in a posthumous estimate, proclaimed Mill's forthrightness while also acknowledging its absence: "Probably no English writer that ever lived has done so much as Mr. Mill to cut at the very root of the theological spirit, yet there is only one passage in the whole of his writings . . . which could possibly give any offence to the most devout person. His conformity . . . never went beyond the negative degree, nor even passed beyond the conformity of silence. That guilty and grievously common pusillanimity which leads men to make or act hypocritical professions, always moved his deepest abhorrence. And he did not fear publicly to testify his interest in the return of an atheist to parliament." "The Death of Mr. Mill," *Fortnightly Review*, n.s. 13 (1 June 1873): 672.

reform that he laid out in Book VI of the *Logic* and which he speculated about in his diary and in letters to his wife. Existing constraints, he complained—again, this was in *On Liberty*—were an obstacle to anyone playing that role.

> A state of things in which a large portion of the most active and inquiring intellects find it advisable to keep the general principles and grounds of their convictions within their own breasts, and attempt, in what they address to the public, to fit as much as they can of their own conclusions to premises which they have internally renounced, cannot send forth the open, fearless characters, and logical, consistent intellects who once adorned the thinking world. (242)[30]

The consequences were clear: public discussion was constricted and distorted. "The ban placed on all inquiry which does not end in the orthodox conclusions" had a narrowing effect—"mental development is cramped, and . . . reason cowed, by the fear of heresy" (242). Among the best of those intimidated were some with "promising intellects combined with timid characters, who dare not follow out any bold, vigorous, independent train of thought, lest it should land them in something which would admit of being considered irreligious or immoral" (242).[31] The speculative thinker was victimized, and since so much depended on those few persons, humanity itself suffered.

Apart from the loss to society, Mill took note of the corrupting effects on the thinking person. "Now if those men who . . . find themselves unable to accept any dogmatic religion whatever, not even the dogmas of natural religion, are to continue to wrap up their doubts in mystery, to be afraid to speak out, and to be the object of abuse whenever they do, a strong premium is put upon dishonesty on their part."[32] Once again, it seems likely that he was thinking of his own circumstances when this was written.

If these statements were self-descriptions it is necessary to recognize that *On Liberty*, in addition to its general argument, also is autobiographically revealing. It was a passionate plea for a freedom he had been denied, and this would explain his statements, which appear to be generalizations from his own experience, that social intolerance induced men to disguise their heretical opinions. In this light, his surprising assertions that his country was "not a place of mental freedom" (241) and that "every one

---

[30] "This is not a place for speculative men, except (at most) within the limits of ancient and traditional Christianity." Mill to Gustave d'Eichthal, 12 November 1839, *CW*, *13*, 413.

[31] Grote seems to have had the same phenomenon in mind when he referred to "that fear of offending the current religiosity which enfeebles the style of so many." George Grote to Mill, 12 January 1867, Pierpont Morgan Library

[32] Mill to Thomas Dyke Acland, 1 December 1868, *CW*, *16*, 1499–1500.

lives as under the eye of a hostile and dreaded censorship" (264) express a perspective that was highly personal, and if not uniquely his own, it was one that arose from the situation of opponents of Christianity who were eager to break their shackles and make religion a political issue.[33]

———————

Mill had high expectations from the liberation of atheists and freethinkers. There would be unrestrained, bold criticism of claims made on behalf of Christianity—claims about the divinity of Jesus, miracles, the ethical value of Christian morality, and the benevolence and omnipotence of the deity judged in light of the misery that could be witnessed everywhere. As a result of candid discussion, Mill expected there would be erosion of Christian belief, which was one of the things required by his plan for moral reform. Thus religious notions would be "put on the logical rack" and subjected to "the discipline which purges the intellect itself."[34] This would follow from the Socratic *elenchus* which, through full freedom of thought and discussion, would be applied to religious belief in his own time.

The rationale for liberty of thought and discussion was cast in general terms, especially at the beginning of chapter two, and this has masked the extent of his specific concern with the credibility of Christian belief. The issue was defined as one of establishing the truth of an opinion. There were those with "received opinions" and those whose opinions have been suppressed. The opinions might be about politics or science or religion. Whatever the subject, it was a matter of truth versus error. Although Mill's second chapter was an account of discussion as a way of sifting truth from error, his intense interest in the truth and error of religion, and especially of Christianity, was indicated by the frequency with which he referred to Christianity (Jesus, Catholicism, Protestants, Savonarola, persecution of Christians, the Reformation, Christian morality, the early Christians, the Apostles, Saint Paul, Calvin, Knox, Christian ethics) in this chapter. It consists of forty-three paragraphs, and such references are to be found in twenty-seven of them, and in some, Mill's discussion is detailed and elaborate.

Having stated his argument in general terms, Mill quickly made it clear that he would focus on his favorite example—that of Christianity.

———

[33] Once again Henry Reeve wrote discerningly that the acrimony with which Mill spoke of English society could be traced to the fact that "this entire liberty was denied him, or at least was only accorded under social penalties, which even he was not prepared to pay." "Autobiography of John Stuart Mill," *Edinburgh Review* 139 (January 1874): 94.

[34] "Grote's Plato" (1866), CW, *11*, 411–12.

> In order more fully to illustrate the mischief of denying a hearing to opinions
> because we, in our own judgment, have condemned them, it will be desirable
> to fix down the discussion to a concrete case; and I choose, by preference, the
> cases which are least favourable to me—in which the argument against freedom
> of opinion, both on the score of truth and on that of utility, is considered the
> strongest. Let the opinions impugned be the belief in a God and in a future
> state, or any of the commonly received doctrines of morality. (234)

Of course the commonly received doctrine he chose to consider was that
of Christian morality. "As this is of all cases the most important in practice, none can be fitter to test the general maxim" (254).[35] That religion
was at the forefront of his thinking was also evident in other places. He
considered whether a doctrine could be useful even though not true, without mentioning the specific religious context (233–34), which would have
been obvious to his contemporaries, for at the time the argument that
Christianity ought not be questioned even if its claims could not be sub-
stantiated was widely discussed.

All this was in keeping with Mill's acknowledgment of the way he analyzed problems: "My practice being to study abstract principles in the
best concrete instances I could find."[36] In chapter two of On Liberty, he
apparently was focusing as much on the best concrete instance, Christianity, as on the abstract principle of discovering truth through discussion.

Mill's expectations that Christianity would crumble if subjected to criticism by atheists and freethinkers was revealed in his account of the way
free discussion would affect belief in Christianity in each of three conceivable circumstances. First, the suppressed opinion, that is, the opinion held
by rejectors of Christianity, might be true (229–43). Second, the received
opinion, that is, belief in Christianity, might be true (243–52). And third,
those holding the suppressed opinion and those believing in Christianity
might share the truth (252–57). With each of these alternatives (even

---

[35] Ryan recognizes that "Mill's chief target is the Victorian intolerance of criticisms of
Christianity." Alan Ryan, J. S. Mill (London: Routledge, 1974), 140. James Fitzjames Stephen also saw that this was a matter of great concern for Mill: "Mr. Mill on Political Liberty," Saturday Review, 12 February 1859, p. 186. Some commentators have suggested that
Mill's work breathed the spirit of Protestantism, as both emphasized appeals to individual
conscience. In his discussions of Christianity and Christian morality, however, Mill does not
exempt Protestantism, nor does he specify variants of Christianity other than Protestantism.
Thus he says, "By Christianity I here mean what is accounted such by all churches and
sects—the maxims and precepts contained in the New Testament." On Liberty, CW, 18,
248. His most favorable assessment of Protestantism appears in his polemic against Comte:
Auguste Comte and Positivism, CW, 10, 321. However, in his critique of Christian morality
in On Liberty, he makes clear that Protestantism shares responsibility for it. CW, 18, 255.

[36] Early Draft, CW, 1, 166. In the Autobiography he amended this passage, inserting after
"practice": "(learnt from Hobbes and my father)." Autobiography, CW, 1, 167. See also,
"Nature," CW, 10, 373.

the second and third), as Mill analyzed them, Christianity would be undermined.

In considering the first of these circumstances—in which it was assumed that the received opinion (Christianity) was untrue, Mill argued as if the falsity of the opinion in itself might not lead to disbelief. For he recognized that its defenders would try to forestall this outcome by adopting the view that, even if untrue, religious belief was useful. As already intimated, Mill was familiar with this widely shared argument. He had been exposed to discussion of it in Bentham's and Grote's *Analysis of the Influence of Natural Religion on the Temporal Happiness of Mankind* (1822), which he had carefully studied.[37] He also had read Tocqueville's defense of religious belief as politically useful, especially in a democracy. Tocqueville held that in a democracy there were no legal obstacles to the people authorizing any action, no matter how evil; and therefore religion, as a source of moral restraint, made it less likely that the sovereign populace would even contemplate immoral actions. At the time he was planning *On Liberty* Mill said of the notion that even untrue religions were useful: it was the most important issue "in this age, in which real belief in any religious doctrine is feeble, but the opinion of its necessity for moral and social purposes almost universal."[38]

Mill regarded appeals to the utility of religion as the last-ditch defense of Christianity, and in *On Liberty* he sought to undermine it.

> In the present age—which has been described as "destitute of faith, but terrified at scepticism"—in which people feel sure, not so much that their opinions are true, as that they should not know what to do without them—the claims of an opinion to be protected from public attack are rested not so much on its truth, as on its importance to society. There are, it is alleged, certain beliefs, so useful, not to say indispensable to well-being, that it is as much the duty of governments to uphold those beliefs, as to protect any other of the interests of society. (233)

Such an assumption, he insisted, should be challenged. "The usefulness of an opinion is itself matter of opinion: as disputable, as open to discussion, and requiring discussion as much as the opinion itself" (233). Mill went further to imply how he would judge the usefulness of Christianity, for he asserted, "The truth of an opinion is part of its utility" (233) and that "no belief which is contrary to truth can be really useful" (234). Since these observations were part of his consideration of the possibility that Christianity was untrue, the reader was invited to draw the conclusion

[37] Early Draft, *CW*, *1*, 72.
[38] ibid.

that Christianity, if untrue, could not be useful—a conclusion he made explicit in the unpublished "Utility of Religion."

Mill made the same point with a rhetorical flourish by describing the rationale for the persecution of Christianity by Marcus Aurelius. Roman society, though in a deplorable condition,

> was held together, and prevented from being worse, by belief and reverence of the received divinities. As a ruler of mankind, [Marcus Aurelius] deemed it his duty not to suffer society to fall in pieces; and saw not how, if its existing ties were removed, any others could be formed which could again knit it together. The new religion [i.e., Christianity] openly aimed at dissolving these ties: unless, therefore, it was his duty to adopt that religion, it seemed to be his duty to put it down. (236)

Thus it was an argument for the usefulness of religion—a religion to which Christianity was a rival and a threat—that justified persecution of Christianity. Mill was suggesting that Christians in his time were as blind and unjust as Marcus Aurelius had been. "No Christian more firmly believes that Atheism is false, and tends to the dissolution of society, than Marcus Aurelius believed the same things of Christianity" (237).

Mill included the same arguments in "Utility of Religion," but there they had a sharper edge. He made it clear that if the claim for the usefulness of religion were not challenged, discussion and criticism of Christianity would be stifled, and this would prevent Christianity's demise. Unbelievers—those "who, having consciously ceased to find the evidences of religion convincing"—were withheld from saying so, "lest they should aid in doing an irreparable injury to mankind."[39]

There was another path to the erosion of Christian belief, and this was laid out in his consideration of the second possibility as to how Christianity would fare in the face of fully free discussion. In this second set of possible circumstances it was assumed that Christianity was true.

Even if true, the arguments for Christian belief in Mill's time were not fully comprehended by most persons, and this made Christianity vulnerable. If received opinion, though true, "is not fully, frequently, and fearlessly discussed, it will be held as a dead dogma, not a living truth" (243). Such opinion "is but one superstition the more" (244). The grounds of belief are lost and the meaning, as well. "Instead of a vivid conception and a living belief, there remain only a few phrases retained by rote; or, if any part, the shell and husk only of the meaning is retained, the finer essence being lost" (247). In these circumstances, the doctrine is "received pas-

---

[39] "Utility of Religion," *CW*, *10*, 404.

sively, not actively," and those who accept it "give it a dull and torpid assent" (248). This erosion was experienced with most ethical and religious creeds, especially Christianity: "To what an extent doctrines intrinsically fitted to make the deepest impression upon the mind may remain in it as dead beliefs, without being ever realized in the imagination, the feelings, or the understanding, is exemplified by the manner in which the majority of believers hold the doctrines of Christianity" (248). This was shown by the failure of most Christians to conduct themselves in accordance with the precepts and teachings of their religion. "The doctrines have no hold on ordinary believers—are not a power in their minds" (249).[40]

This was the condition of Christianity in the absence of full discussion, and in spite of its weakness, Mill still found Christian belief objectionable, as it was an obstacle to the emergence of a new and better alternative. "The creed remains as it were outside the mind, incrusting and petrifying it against all other influences addressed to the higher parts of our nature" (248). As he put it in his diary, such creeds "live on with a sort of life in death until they are replaced. So the religions of the world will continue standing, if even as mere shells and husks."[41]

This very condition, however, made Christianity vulnerable, for as a dead belief, even if true, it could not survive free discussion. Since the grounds for believing it to be true were not understood, the criticisms that would be introduced with free and candid discussion from which atheists and freethinkers were not excluded would lead to the erosion of belief. Mill expected that "real freedom of speculation" would have the effect of "making [all persons] unbelievers."[42] Once discussion takes place, he explained in On Liberty, "beliefs not grounded on conviction are apt to give way before the slightest semblance of an argument" (244). Or, as he said in Utilitarianism, moral belief will, "when intellectual culture goes on, yield by degrees to the force of analysis."[43]

After considering two contrasting assumptions—that the received opin-

---

[40] The early Christians were an exception (249). He lived "in this age, in which real belief in any religious doctrine is feeble." Early Draft, CW, 1, 72. "We are in an age of weak beliefs, and in which such belief as men have is much more determined by their wish to believe than by any mental appreciation of evidence." "Utility of Religion," CW, 10, 403.

[41] Diary, February 15, [1854], CW, 27, 654.

[42] "Utility of Religion" (1874), 72.

[43] Utilitarianism, CW, 10, 230. Or, as he had put it earlier, "To discuss, and to question established opinion, are merely two phrases for the same thing." "Spirit of the Age" (1831), CW, 22, 233. He added, "When all opinions are questioned, it is in time found out what are those which will not bear a close examination. Ancient doctrines are then put upon their proofs; and those which were originally errors, or have become so by change of circumstances, are thrown aside. Discussion does this." In "Utility of Religion," he wrote: "exactly in proportion as the received systems of belief have been contested, and it has become

ion was false, and that it was true—Mill turned to a third possibility in which the two opposing opinions shared the truth, each possessing a portion of it. Discovering new truths, in his view, involved reconciling and combining opposite opinions, and he now searched for a way to do just this with Christianity and the rejection of Christianity.[44] Since, as Mill formulated this part of his argument, each were partly true and partly false, the way they would combine would have a decisive impact on Christianity and on his conception of how to implement his plan for moral reform.

As Mill foresaw the clash of opinions, a very considerable portion of Christianity would be shown to be untrue, and therefore was destined to disappear. This part consisted, first, of Christian theology, which he had criticized in writings composed but not published during the period when *On Liberty* was planned; and consisted second, of Christian morality, which he described very critically in *On Liberty*. There it was portrayed as promoting passivity, acceptance, failure to actively pursue virtue, and above all, selfishness.[45] Mill alluded to the results of this clash of opinions in telling Bain that "undoubtedly both good [i.e., utilitarian] ethics and good [i.e., anti-intuitionist] metaphysics will sap Xtianity if it persists in allying itself with bad. The best thing to do in the present state of the human mind is to go on establishing positive truths (principles and rules of evidence of course included) and leave Xtianity to reconcile itself with them the best way it can."[46]

The only part of Christianity that was immune to Mill's criticisms, and therefore the only part that would survive, was the character and teaching of Jesus. For the historical Jesus, Mill had great admiration, but this did not affect his condemnation of Christianity as it existed in his time, which, as Mill described it, seems to have had little to do with Christ himself. The aspects of Christianity that were condemned were traced to developments from which Jesus was distanced or to features of the religion that emerged after the religion was founded. The separation of Jesus from much of what is conventionally associated with Christianity is especially evident in the contrast drawn between Jesus and Paul. In *On Liberty* Paul was portrayed as a persecutor of Christians (236) and his teaching was condemned as incomplete and as being too accommodating to Greek and

---

known that they have many dissentients, their hold on the general belief has been loosened." "Utility of Religion" (1874), 79.

[44] He also said in 1865, "The great thing was to consider one's opponents as one's allies; as people climbing the hill on the other side." (1865): *Amberley Papers*, ed. Bertrand and Patricia Russell, *1*, 373.

[45] See chapter 7, text between notes 39 and 41, for an account of Mill's critique of Christian morality.

[46] Mill to Alexander Bain, 14 November 1859, *CW*, *15*, 646.

Roman law, including the laws that sanctioned slavery (255). He also called St. Paul "The first great corrupter of Xtianity."[47]

Later developments of Christianity made it even more objectionable. The recorded precepts of the founder of Christianity, Mill said, "have been entirely thrown aside in the system of ethics erected on the basis of those deliverances by the Christian Church" (256). Moreover, "What is called Christian, but should rather be termed theological, morality, was not the work of Christ or the Apostles, but is of much later origin" (255). It originated, Mill tells us, in the Catholic Church during the first five centuries of its existence and in Protestantism, as well. Catholic church morality, he claimed, "though not implicitly adopted by moderns and Protestants, has been much less modified by them than might have been expected" (255). Thus the target of Mill's criticisms was a Christian morality that was a product of the entirety of Christianity since the period of its founding.[48]

In contrast to all this, there was the moral character and teaching of Jesus, and memory of it was the portion of Christianity which, Mill expected, would survive fully free discussion. What was admirable in that character, however, had nothing to do with claims of divinity or with miraculous powers. Jesus was a "man who left on the memory of those who witnessed his life and conversation . . . an impression of his moral grandeur" (235). This judgment appeared in *On Liberty* and was repeated elsewhere. The author of the Sermon on the Mount was a "benignant Being" whose "precepts . . . as exhibited in the Gospels—rising far above the Paulism which is the foundation of ordinary Christianity—carry some kinds of moral goodness to a greater height than had ever been attained before."[49] Thus Mill attributed to Jesus alone the Christian virtues of charity, humility, and compassion, and he denied that Christianity generally encouraged them. To the Catholic philosopher William George Ward, Mill wrote reassuringly: "You need not have supposed any inclination in me to speak with irreverence of J[esus] C[hrist]. He is one of the very few historical characters for whom I have a real and high

---

[47] Mill to William George Ward, [spring 1849], CW, *14*, 27. "I grant that some of the precepts of Christ as exhibited in the Gospels—rising far above the Paulism which is the foundation of ordinary Christianity—carry some kinds of moral goodness to a greater height than had ever been attained before." "Utility of Religion," CW, *10*, 416. Bentham had been a severe critic of Paul in *Not Paul, but Jesus*. Crimmins, *Secular Utilitarianism*, 234–38.

[48] Mill's view has affinities with a Unitarian perspective in which Christ is regarded as a morally noble person and organized Christianity as a perversion of Christ's teaching; see Brown, *Metaphysical Society*, 130; and "Coleridge," CW, *10*, 159 for Mill's characterization of Unitarianism.

[49] "Utility of Religion," CW, *10*, 416, 423.

respect."[50] The moral example provided by Jesus, which to be compelling did not require acceptance of Christian theology or belief in the supernatural, was the part of Christianity that would endure free discussion.

Mill's admiration for Jesus did not mean that he regarded moral regeneration as an extension of what was best in Christianity or as an application of Christ's teachings. He was clear that the "doctrines and precepts of Christ . . . contain, and were meant to contain, only a part of the truth."

> Many essential elements of the highest morality are among the things which are not provided for, nor intended to be provided for, in the recorded deliverances of the Founder of Christianity, and which have been entirely thrown aside in the system of ethics erected on the basis of those deliverances by the Christian Church. (256)

Therefore, he continued, "other ethics than any which can be evolved from exclusively Christian sources, must exist side by side with Christian ethics [i.e., those of Jesus] to produce the moral regeneration of mankind" (256–57).[51] Such a combination of Christian and secular sources could be accomplished; "the sayings of Christ . . . are irreconcilable with nothing which a comprehensive morality requires" (256).

This suggestion that something in Christianity might exist side by side with a radically different ethical principle was not a retraction from his condemnation of Christian morality; rather, it referred only to the teachings of Jesus, which, according to Mill, were not incorporated into Christian morality. His opposition to Christian morality was not modified by acknowledging the moral stature of Jesus. As he said, the valuable effect of holding up the character of Jesus as a model "is available even to the absolute unbeliever."[52] His praise for Jesus, however, did not diminish his argument that a non-Christian ethics was essential for moral regeneration.

Mill's argument that the teachings of Jesus could be separated from Christianity as a religion resting on assumptions of divine origins and authority, and his claim that those teachings could be combined with a secular ethics, was in keeping with one of the themes developed in "Utility of Religion," that morality could exist without the support of supernatural religion. There he argued that morality in conduct only appeared to

---

[50] Mill to William George Ward, [spring 1849], CW, 14, 27. Mill also spoke of the "reverence for Christ, in which I myself participate." Mill to Arthur W. Greene, 16 December 1861, CW, 15, 754.

[51] "I think it a great error to persist in attempting to find in the Christian doctrine that complete rule for our guidance, which its author intended it . . . only partially to provide" (256).

[52] "Theism," CW, 10, 487.

be produced by religion whereas in fact it was the product of authority, early education, and, above all, public opinion. Authority is conferred by the general concurrence of mankind, which is "all powerful."[53] Early education even without religion, was also effective, as the example of Sparta suggested.[54] Most important, the "great effects on human conduct, which are commonly ascribed to motives derived directly from religion, have mostly for their proximate cause the influence of human opinion."[55] Consequently, belief in the supernatural "cannot be considered to be any longer required, either for enabling us to know what is right and wrong in social morality, or for supplying us with motives to do right and to abstain from wrong."[56] Thus even if Christianity disappeared, morality would survive. Apart from depreciating claims made for religion, these arguments also allowed Mill to assert his own: "A large portion of the noblest and most valuable moral teaching has been the work, not only of men who did not know, but of men who knew and rejected, the Christian faith" (257).

While he made it clear that the teachings of Jesus would have to be supplemented with a secular ethics, in *On Liberty* he only hinted at what the principles of these secular ethics would be. He did say in chapter one of *On Liberty*, "I regard utility as the ultimate appeal on all ethical questions; but it must be utility in the largest sense, grounded on the permanent interests of man as a progressive being" (224). Of course, in this extraordinarily ambiguous statement he did not have in mind the utilitarianism of Bentham or his father, for he had distanced himself from it in his 1838 essay on Bentham; and in his contemporary essay *Utilitarianism* he re-defined happiness to make it incompatible with the happiness which was the end of individual action in Benthamite utilitarianism.[57]

If he had been less ambiguous about the secular ethics which were necessary for regeneration, he would have had to say more about his revised utilitarianism, and this would have involved an explanation of his ideal of altruism, which was his alternative to the selfishness that contaminated Christian morality and so much else in the established culture. There are allusions to his ideal of altruism in *On Liberty*—for example, he upheld

[53] "Utility of Religion," *CW*, *10*, 407.

[54] Ibid., 409.

[55] Ibid., 411.

[56] Ibid., 417. Also, "History, so far as we know it, bears out the opinion, that mankind can perfectly well do without the belief in a heaven." Ibid., 427.

[57] *Utilitarianism* was published in *Fraser's Magazine* in 1861 and as a book in 1863, but it was written in 1854 and revised in 1860, according to Bain, who notes that it is "closely connected [with *On Liberty*], both in date of composition and in subject matter." Bain, *Mill*, 112. For additional discussion of the allusion to utility in *On Liberty*, see below, chapter 6, text between notes 97 and 98.

obligation to the public as an ideal and contrasted it with modern selfishness (256); and he asserted the "need of a great increase of disinterested exertion to promote the good of others" and ranked self-regarding virtues as being "only second in importance, if even second, to the social [virtues]" (277). But he more clearly reveals his wish to have the principle of altruism established in *Utilitarianism*;[58] and he conveys his full sense of its importance only in observations about the religion of humanity, which he laid out in several of the other essays written during these same years. The allusions to this theme in *On Liberty* and elaboration of it in other contemporary works in ways entirely compatible with the argument of *On Liberty* reminds us that *On Liberty* should not be read in isolation but as one part of a coherent program which is fully revealed only by examining all the essays he planned with Harriet Taylor Mill during the mid 1850s.

Mill intended to stimulate doubts that would slowly erode Christian belief, but he had no wish to confront Christians with arguments that proved their religion to be without evidence or foundation. Such arguments were reserved for posthumous publication. It cannot be said that he refrained from criticizing Christianity, but neither did he make his criticisms obvious. His harsh observations about Christian morality, for example, were combined with admiring, reverential comments about Jesus, and this device must have disguised from many readers the full import of his argument.

While there was little in the book—and especially in chapter two—that was confrontational, he laid out a program of fully free discussion that would have eroded Christian belief.[59] This was the predictable outcome of each of the three scenarios he outlined. Whichever one was adopted, discussion would undermine. Mill did not draw the conclusions, but he defended the free discussion that would lead to the conclusion he eagerly awaited. Therefore he could *not* have said about *On Liberty* what he claimed with respect to *Utilitarianism*, "I have not written it in any hostile spirit towards Xtianity."[60] The hostile spirit combined with indirection and the pulling of punches that is evident in *On Liberty* is analogous to some eighteenth-century writing against Christianity which, as he described it, consisted of a declaration that Christian doctrine was contrary to reason but that this was without consequence, as religion was a matter

[58] *Utilitarianism, CW, 10,* 218–19, 232.
[59] Bentham, it has been claimed, adopted the same strategy. Crimmins, *Secular Utilitarianism,* 157–58.
[60] Mill to Alexander Bain, 14 November 1859, *CW, 15,* 645–46.

of faith, not reason. This was a mode of argument by which "assailants of received opinions . . . might have an opportunity of ruining the rational foundation of a doctrine without exposing themselves to odium by its direct denial." Mill called this "a mere fetch," that is, a contrivance or trick, and much of chapter two of *On Liberty* was his fetch and his way of avoiding the odium that would have been the consequence of candor.[61]

Initially Mill was concerned about public reaction to *On Liberty*. In sending a copy to the pamphleteer and editor George Jacob Holyoake, who was an atheist, he asked him to delay publishing a review, explaining, "It is likely enough to be called an infidel book in any case; but I would rather that people were not *prompted* to call it so."[62] He need not have worried, for while reviewers disagreed about his religious opinions, some being more discerning than others, there were notable examples of blindness. The *Times* even concluded a long review by saying the book "deserves to be studied attentively by every statesman . . . and by every English gentleman who desires to hand down to his children the liberty of thought and action in which he has himself been brought up."[63] In light of reactions such as this, Bain could hardly believe the obtuseness of the public. "It amazed me not a little to see the continued reluctance of people to write you down an infidel. . . . Think of the 'Times' calling the book 'The English gentlemen's gift to his son.' "[64] A reaction similar to that in the *Times* came from Thomas Hare, Mill's correspondent and originator of the idea of proportional representation. He assumed congeniality between Mill's position and Christianity: "The fundamental teachings of Christianity, apart from dogma, few would appreciate better than Mr. Mill."[65]

The failure to recognize the importance—or even the presence—of Mill's anti-Christian theme may reflect the effectiveness of Mill's deliberate blurring of it, but not all readers were undiscerning. James Martineau, the Unitarian clergyman, recognized that Mill had opinions which were

[61] *An Examination of Sir William Hamilton's Philosophy*, CW, 9, 60. He used the term "fetch" in the same sense but in the context of political controversy in a letter to Thomas Hare, 4 February 1860, CW, 15, 668. And about Baden Powell he said, "What can he mean by holding that miracles are *impossible*, and yet that those of the new testament may be received as matters of faith, though not of science. Is this last a mere saving clause, as when Voltaire said nearly the same thing? If so, he must intend it to be seen through, as Voltaire did." Mill to Alexander Bain, 11 April 1860, CW, 15, 696.
[62] Mill to George Jacob Holyoake, [February 1859], CW, 15, 593.
[63] *Times*, 4 March 1859, 11.
[64] Bain to Mill, 14 March [1859], National Library of Scotland.
[65] Thomas Hare, "John Stuart Mill," *Westminster Review* 101 (January 1874): 137. An extreme example of uncritical reading came from Lady Stanley, whose late husband had been Bishop of Norwich. She was delighted to discover many parallels between arguments of *On Liberty* and the Bishop's *Canterbury Sermons*. Catherine Stanley to George Grote, 15 March 1859, bound in Grote's copy of *On Liberty*, Goldsmith's Library, University of London.

held back. "No writer, it is probable, was ever more read between the lines," and he noted "a certain air of suppression occasionally assumed by Mr. Mill himself."

> It seems hardly becoming [Martineau continued] in an author who has attained the highest rank of influence in the intellectual councils of his time, to write as if there were something behind which, as a veracious thinker on human life and morals, he would like to say, but which, under the pitiable bigotry of society, must be reserved for an age that does not persecute its benefactors.[66]

Mill appreciated Martineau's understanding of his situation and told Bain the review was worth reading.[67]

A few other clerical writers also recognized the incompatibility of Mill's arguments with Christianity, but they voiced isolated protests that had little impact on most contemporary discussion of *On Liberty*. In one of these, published in *The English Churchman*, the author expressed "regret and indignation, that so many professing Christians of our day have spoken of this book with an approbation unaccompanied with one single word of rebuke or reclamation; without a suspicion that the independence from control which Mr. Mill seeks to assert may be rebellion against the highest Power that exists." The reviewer went on to note that "the animus which runs through the whole of his discussion is essentially destructive. . . . The individual, then, has no moral superior. The idea of God, the only intellectual sovereign that the subjects of revelation can know, is excluded."[68] Those who recognized that Mill had targeted Christianity and all theism were, however, few in number and quite obscure; most reviewers, even when addressing one aspect or another of Mill's views on Christianity (but not his atheism), displayed neither alarm nor panic.[69]

---

[66] James Martineau, "John Stuart Mill" (1859), *Essays, Reviews and Addresses* (London, 1891), *3*, 534–35.

[67] Mill to Alexander Bain, 15 October 1859, *CW, 15*, 640.

[68] "R.P.," "Mr. John Stuart Mill's Work on Liberty—No. 3," *The English Churchman*, 29 September 1859, 934. This is one of eighteen articles on Mill's book, published from 15 September 1859 to 5 April 1860. Mill said of this article and one other (in *Dublin University Magazine* 54 [October 1859]: 387–410), "People are beginning to find out that the doctrines of the book are more opposed to their old opinions and feelings than they at first saw, and are taking the alarm accordingly." Mill to Bain, 15 October 1859, *CW, 15*, 640. Another who discerned Mill's ultimate purpose was his old friend Caroline Fox, who recorded her reaction in her diary: "I am reading that terrible book of John Mill's . . . he lays it on one as a tremendous duty to get oneself contradicted, and admit always a devil's advocate into the presence of your dearest, most sacred Truths, as they are apt to grow windy and worthless without such tests, if indeed they can stand the shock of argument at all. . . . Mill makes me shiver." *Memories of Old Friends*, *2*, 269–70.

[69] Rees, in his survey of early reactions to *On Liberty*, reports "a chorus of indignant protest," but he failed to distinguish between criticisms of Mill's opinions about various aspects of Christian belief, such as its being a merely formal profession of faith, or its having fallen into decay, or that Calvinism fostered a narrow type of character, and criticisms of

For Mill, it mattered little that most of his contemporaries were not affronted by his religious skepticism, for he regarded *On Liberty* as a pemican that in the future would nourish those who would go on chipping away at Christian belief. By having this effect it would accentuate the intellectual anarchy of the transitional era and set the stage for the emergence of a better faith, that is, the religion of humanity.

Mill's atheism. The former are easily found, the latter appeared infrequently. Whichever the type, however, Rees thought they had little importance: "If vehemence and volume were to be accepted as the criteria of importance we should have to devote more space to this topic than to any other single question. But it can be dealt with quite briefly." Rees, *Mill and His Early Critics*, 33–34. The brevity with which he dealt with it indicates his estimate of its significance for understanding *On Liberty*.

Chapter Six

THE RELIGION OF HUMANITY

> Having had the rather rare fate in my country of never
> having believed in God, even as a child, I always saw in the
> creation of a true social philosophy the only possible base for
> the general regeneration of human morality, and in the idea
> of Humanity the only one capable of replacing that of God.
> (*John Stuart Mill*)

THERE WAS widespread interest in the religion of humanity during the middle decades of the nineteenth century. This "religion," which was supposed to promote a widely shared, communal, anti-individualistic morality without the aid of conventional religious belief, attracted Mill's interest, and his growing belief in its utility from the 1840s onward had far- reaching implications for his evaluation of Bentham and James Mill and their version of utilitarianism; for his political agenda, including his plan for moral regeneration; and for his views about the value of liberty and for the argument of *On Liberty*.

Mill discovered the religion of humanity in the writings of Auguste Comte, where it was presented as a novel conception of ethics and social life. It held up duty as an ideal and sought to fundamentally change motives and habits to generate widespread altruism—a word invented by Comte. The goal was to discourage selfishness by making private motives coincide with the public good. This was to be achieved by teaching an authoritative morality and deterring violations of it through moral education and the application of social pressures. Mill found this secular religion appealing, not only because morality was divorced from supernatural religion, but for its being a radical alternative to the pervasive selfishness he discerned in commercial society and mass culture.

Although Mill found the conception of a religion of humanity in Comte's writings beginning in 1848, there were affinities between it and his political thought as it evolved from the late 1820s when he became deeply dissatisfied with Benthamism and adopted fundamentally different ideas. (This does not mean that he did not continue to speak the language of Benthanism and seek to combine the old ideas with the new.) The new opinions appeared most clearly in a series of newspaper articles in 1831 called "Spirit of the Age." In them he endorsed the St. Simonian distinction between transitional and natural states of society, labels for which, later on, he sometimes substituted Comte's categories, critical and organic.[1] His conception of the natural or organic state is significant as it anticipated his later conception of a religion of humanity. Of course, the linkage between the St. Simonian conception of a natural or organic state of society and the idea of a religion of humanity is not accidental, for Comte in the 1820s had already shared ideas with St. Simon and contributed to the development of St. Simonian thought.

In "Spirit of the Age" Mill presented the historical generalization that societies alternated between natural and transitional states. In natural states of society there is unity, harmony, stability, and, he implies, contentedness, whereas in transitional states there is disagreement, conflict, discontent, and a restless desire for change. The shift to a transitional state occurs when there is disintegration of the institutions at the end of a natural period and arises from doubts about its legitimizing beliefs. Thus a transitional era occurs when mankind "have outgrown old institutions and old doctrines, and have not yet acquired new ones."[2] While the generalization about alternation between these two states of society was supported with historical examples, the assumption that it would prove valid in the future and that a new organic era would emerge was a manifestation of something like utopian desire.

While the superiority of the natural or organic state of society arose from its harmony and stability, it was also appealing for the role it gave to intellectuals—those responsible for originating and disseminating opinions and beliefs. There would be "a body of moral authority" which would rest with those possessing the greatest knowledge and competence. The opinions originating with such persons would be widely accepted. "The opinions and feelings of the people are, with their voluntary acquiescence, formed for them, by the most cultivated minds which the intelligence and morality of the times calls into existence."[3] Mill was aware of the implication of a prospective organic state of society for the role he might play. He confessed having "the unshakable confidence of playing a role not only in the initial diffusion, but even in the establishment of the final philosophy."[4]

Such deference to the authority of superior persons was made necessary by the practical obstacles faced by most persons seeking knowledge required for sound judgment. At best such persons were "half-instructed—and we cannot expect the majority of every class to be any thing more." Mill offered the example of physical science: in such a field, would a layman challenge a consensus of experts? During a transitional period when

---

[1] Early Draft, CW, 1, 170.
[2] "Spirit of the Age" (1831), CW, 22, 230.
[3] Ibid., 304.
[4] Mill to Auguste Comte, 15 June 1843, Correspondence Mill and Comte, 164.

there was disagreement among those claiming authoritative knowledge, it was understandable that an individual would rely upon private judgment. But it was preferable, if the best educated and most competent were in agreement, for most persons to defer to authority, even in moral and political matters. Therefore the majority "must place the degree of reliance warranted by reason, in the authority of those who have made moral and social philosophy their peculiar study. . . . [R]eason itself will teach most men that they must, in the last resort, fall back upon the authority of still more cultivated minds."[5]

In keeping with this view of authority, Mill evaluated "received opinion" quite differently than in *On Liberty*, where it was depreciated as the opinion adopted by the many unthinking persons guided by the customs of existing society. From the perspective, however, in which it was assumed that natural or organic states of society were preferable to transitional states, received opinion was not necessarily a bad thing. To believe received opinion (or, as he also called it, received doctrine) during a transitional era, when it might have originated in an earlier but now discredited natural era and when those claiming moral authority were in sharp disagreement, was, of course, unwarranted. But when the authorities were competent and united, as they were (Mill believed) in physical science, and as the Catholic clergy were in the middle ages, and as they would be in a future organic state of society, it was reasonable to be guided by it.[6] Mill indicated that in a natural state, even with respect to moral and political philosophy, received opinion should command our obedience.

The authority and unity of the natural state would also be reflected in political life. Those enjoying political authority would not face challenges from within the political class or from those with moral authority. "Worldly power [would be] . . . habitually and undisputedly exercised by the fittest persons." Because they were the fittest, they would have the allegiance of the populace, which "habitually acquiesce[s] in the laws and institutions which they live under."[7] Thus in politics as well as in the realm of morality, it was expected that in the natural state there would be stability, authority, and loyalty.

Transitional states, in contrast, would be anything but stable. Institutions and doctrines that were supported during the natural state would become obsolete, as the people ceased to have faith in them. This erosion of legitimacy would be increased by the inaccessibility to positions of authority for those fittest to hold them and by sharp conflict with those

---

[5] "Spirit of the Age," *CW*, 22, 244.

[6] Ibid., 240, 244, 290. "The Catholic clergy, at the time when they possessed this undisputed authority in matters of conscience and belief, were, in point of fact, the fittest persons who *could* have possessed it." Ibid., 305.

[7] Ibid., 252.

holdovers from the earlier natural era who still held on to positions of authority. "Mankind will not be led by their old maxims, nor by their old guides." Since the old authorities would be discredited and new ones would have not been established, there would be reliance on private judgment. This, however, made agreement elusive, and the result would be diversity carried so far as to bring "intellectual anarchy."[8]

Mill easily recognized his own age as being transitional, making "the times . . . pregnant with change." A revolution was taking place "in the human mind, and in the whole constitution of human society."[9] The "Spirit of the Age" appeared in 1831, the year of the Reform Bill agitation, when there was a great deal of unrest, including street disturbances and occasional riots, and fear of revolution. Intellectual diversity, political conflict, and distrust of authority—the hallmarks of transitional periods—were abundantly evident. This transitional era had, of course, begun very much earlier with the Reformation, which signaled the breakdown of medieval, Catholic unity over which the clergy had presided. All the features of a transition were accentuated with the French Revolution,[10] and Mill regarded his own country in 1831 as dealing with the same historical forces that produced the events of 1789. England lagged by a generation, and he and the other radicals—bold, freethinking opponents of church, crown, and aristocracy—were (as he explained in his autobiography) playing the role of the *philosophes*, not eager for violence but dreaming of a transformation.[11] It was a time of danger, but the young Mill increasingly would regard a transitional period also as a time of opportunity for great change.

By introducing the concepts of natural and transitional states of society into his thinking, Mill established a dichotomy which remained a permanent feature of his thought and facilitated his developing the belief, a decade or so later, that a religion of humanity could be established. The natural-transitional distinction was a particular example of a dichotomy between social and moral conditions as they existed in an unsatisfactory present and those conditions as they might, perhaps would, exist in the future. Of course at an earlier time Mill, like his father and Bentham, distinguished between present unsatisfactory circumstances and a future when greatly improved conditions might come into existence. But after having adopted St. Simonianism, Mill thought about social and moral change quite differently. The future to which he looked forward was regarded, not as an extension of the present, arrived at incrementally, but as fundamentally different, the result of a transformation. It was as if he

---

[8] Ibid., 231, 233, 238–39, 252.
[9] Ibid., 228–29.
[10] Ibid., 292, 305–6.
[11] Early Draft, CW, 1, 110.

had an eschatology—of course, secular—which allowed him to visualize an end to history when values, motivations, and institutions would be fundamentally different. The natural or organic state represented such an end, and later he visualized the religion of humanity in the same way.

Contemplating such a transformation made it necessary to assume that the transitional era in which he lived would not continue forever. The label 'transitional' implies impermanence, and St. Simonian doctrine encouraged Mill to expect that the working out of sociological and intellectual forces would bring such a state of society to an end. Men will "be held together by new ties, and separated by new barriers; for the ancient bonds will now no longer unite, nor the ancient boundaries confine."[12] His assumption of impermanence was clearly revealed in his statement that from St. Simon and Comte "I obtained a much clearer conception than before of the peculiarities of an age of transition in opinion, and ceased to mistake the moral and intellectual characteristics of such an age, for the normal attributes of humanity."[13]

This expectation that the transitional state was bound to come to an end was also revealed in his belief that contemporary institutions were provisional—a word which, as W. J. Ashley pointed out, was "constantly in Mill's mouth [with regard to economic and industrial matters]."[14] He "regarded all existing institutions and social arrangements as being . . . 'merely provisional.' "[15] Mill explained to Comte that, if he wrote about political economy, "it will be in the way of never losing sight of the purely provisional character of all concrete conclusions. I would make a special effort to distinguish the general laws . . . necessarily common to all industrial societies, from the principles of distribution and of the exchange of wealth, principles which by necessity assume a particular state of society without prejudicing whether this state must or even can last indefinitely."[16] Comte was being assured that private property would be regarded as not necessarily having either permanent existence or enduring value. With this perspective Mill was uneasy in using the language of class, for it referred to "an existing, but by no means a necessary or permanent, state of social relations."[17]

---

[12] "Spirit of the Age," CW, 22, 229.

[13] Early Draft, CW, 1, 172.

[14] W. J. Ashley, "Introduction," xxii, Principles of Political Economy by John Stuart Mill (London, 1909).

[15] Autobiography, CW, 1, 241.

[16] Mill to Auguste Comte, 3 April 1844, Correspondence Mill and Comte, 228; see also 237, 247; Ashley, "Introduction," xvii, xviii, xx, xxiii; Iris Wessel Mueller, John Stuart Mill and French Thought (Urbana: University of Illinois Press, 1956), 105, 116–20.

[17] Principles of Political Economy with Some of Their Applications to Social Philosophy, CW, 3, 758. Comte was not satisfied with Mill's concession, saying "he regretted Mill's work on Political Economy, as not conceived in a philosophic spirit, as in fact diverting him

Because existing opinions and institutions were provisional, Mill could visualize vast, transformational change as being within the realm of possibility, and thus he held that "one must never suppose what is good in itself to be visionary because it may be far off."[18] And with the same hopeful perspective he affirmed "the practicability of Utopianism."[19] Large-scale change, moreover, was more than a hope; in keeping with his assumption that foundations were crumbling, he even discerned signs of deep-seated change. "There is a spontaneous education going on in the minds of the multitude." The poor were out of their leading-strings, he explained, and he confidently forecast they will not be led and governed by their superiors (unless, of course, the superiority was deserved by virtue of intellect and knowledge). And with a new secular religion in mind, he added, "The poor will not much longer accept morals and religion of other people's prescribing."[20]

Such broad changes were not only observed and accepted—they were welcomed. The present transitional age, like all such periods, was characterized by "anomalies and evils,"[21] and its termination would "conduct us to a healthier state," which would be stable, unchanging, and tranquil, such as he described in the chapter on the stationary state in the *Political Economy*. Thus he looked forward to the time when England would "emerge from this crisis of transition, and enter once again into a natural state of society."[22]

Mill continued to provide a place in his thinking for a vision of a greatly transformed, morally superior society. This was especially evident in his essays "Bentham" (1838) and "Coleridge" (1840) where one again finds the dichotomy between imperfect society as it existed and a vision of how it might be. He continued to make the assumptions and use the categories that originated in St. Simonism and later were to provide the foundation on which he constructed his version of the religion of humanity. Bentham was severely criticized in both essays, though Mill also made it clear that he was eager to find redeeming features in Bentham's theories, partly from loyalty he felt for his father's old patron and his own former mentor. Bentham in spite of his contributions, however, on balance, was judged

---

from the true direction of social inquiries." Richard Congreve, "Personal Recollection of Auguste Comte," British Library, Add. 45259, f.6.

[18] Mill to Alexander Bain, 17 March 1859, CW, *15*, 606.

[19] "Rationale of Representation," CW, *18*, 42.

[20] *Principles of Political Economy*, CW, *3*, 762–64.

[21] Early Draft, CW, *1*, 180.

[22] "Spirit of the Age," CW, *22*, 316.

inadequate—for he assumed the permanence of a transitional era and did not address issues relevant to a natural or organic state of society.

This gap in Bentham's political theorizing was made evident by considering how he addressed the three great questions of government. Bentham provided the answer to only one of them, namely, by what means are abuses of authority to be checked? Bentham's well-known remedy was to make office holders responsible, and this was to be achieved with democratic institutions, particularly universal suffrage, secret ballot, and frequent elections. By these and other devices, "he exhausted all the resources of ingenuity in devising means for riveting the yoke of public opinion closer and closer round the necks of all public functionaries." While Mill thought Bentham carried this too far, he acknowledged that Bentham's democratic checks on political authority were useful and necessary, at least in some circumstances.[23] Their value was greatest when those in positions of authority were irresponsible and corrupt and perhaps despotic. This was likely during transitional periods when those holding such positions, holdovers from the previous era, no longer possessed the moral and intellectual qualifications for office.

Bentham's deficiencies were made obvious by considering his political philosophy in relation to the other two great questions. They were, first, to what authority is it for the good of the people that they should be subject? and second, how are they to be induced to obey that authority? Whereas Coleridge did provide answers to these two questions, Bentham did not even recognize their importance. Bentham, as was suitable in an age of transition, was "the great questioner of things established" and "the great *subversive*, or . . . the great *critical*, thinker of his age and country."[24] He, and the eighteenth-century philosophers on whom he drew, could "tear away"; that was all they aimed at, but

> They had no conception that anything else was needful. At their millennium, superstition, priestcraft, error and prejudice of every kind, were to be annihilated; some of them gradually added that despotism and hereditary privileges must share the same fate; and, this accomplished, they never for a moment suspected that all the virtues and graces of humanity could fail to flourish, or that when the noxious weeds were once rooted out, the soil would stand in any need of tillage.[25]

They did not understand, in other words, that "society requires to be rebuilt," nor that "the very first element of the social union, obedience to a government of some sort, has not been found so easy a thing to establish

---

[23] "Bentham" (1838), *CW*, *10*, 106–9.
[24] Ibid., 79.
[25] "Coleridge" (1840), *CW*, *10*, 132.

in the world."[26] Establishing authority, Mill held, was one of the ways to rebuild society. By "attempting to new-model society without the binding forces which hold society together," Bentham's theories were of no use to those seeking to introduce a new natural state of society.[27]

The problem with Bentham, then, was his failure to visualize anything beyond the transitional state of society. His thought (and by implication James Mill's and that of the eighteenth century, which James Mill and Bentham represented) expressed the destructive impulses of the transitional condition. It continued the struggle against the previous organic era, in Bentham's case, the old regime of church and aristocracy derived from medieval feudalism. Thus Bentham was skeptical, critical, negative, and subversive; at demolition he was very effective.[28] "The assault on ancient institutions has been, and is, carried on for the most part with his weapons." Through his influence, "the yoke of authority has been broken."[29] This was useful, but Bentham was unable to see beyond a transitional era. His narrow conception of human nature prevented him from recognizing the capacity for those feelings that made obligation and authority possible. The cultivation of affections was "a blank in Bentham's system." He did "nothing . . . for the spiritual interests of society." He also had nothing to say about national character, which was essential for success and greatness, nor did he understand that it "alone enables any body of human beings to exist as a society." "A philosophy of laws and institutions [which Bentham did create], not founded on a philosophy of national character, is an absurdity. But what could Bentham's opinion be worth on national character?"[30]

Mill revealed his quest for the theoretical basis of a natural state in his essay on Bentham. But in the companion essay on Coleridge he went beyond criticism of Bentham's inadequacies and showed how Coleridge filled the gap left by Bentham and the eighteenth-century philosophers. Coleridge, Mill argued, provided principles that explained how a natural state of society would function. This kind of society, to have stability, authority, and obedience, had to meet certain conditions.

First: There has existed, for all who were accounted citizens,—for all who were not slaves, kept down by brute force,—a system of education, beginning with infancy and continued through life, of which, whatever else it might include, one main and incessant ingredient was *restraining discipline*. To train the human being in the habit, and thence the power, of subordinating his personal

---

[26] Ibid., 132, 137.
[27] Ibid., 138.
[28] Ibid., 131–32.
[29] "Bentham," *CW, 10*. 78–79.
[30] Ibid., 98–99.

impulses and aims, to what were considered the ends of society; . . . this was the purpose, to which every outward motive that the authority directing the system could command, and every inward power or principle which its knowledge of human nature enabled it to evoke, were endeavored to be rendered instrumental.[31]

In the absence of such a restraining discipline, there would be serious consequences. Mill did not use the phrase 'transitional state' in the essay on Coleridge, but his description was similar to the account of a period of transition given in "Spirit of the Age." When this happened, "the natural tendency of mankind to anarchy reasserted itself; the State became disorganized from within; mutual conflict for selfish ends, neutralized the energies which were required to keep up the contest against natural causes of evil." Ultimately this led to progressive decline, with the nation becoming "either the slave of a despotism, or the prey of a foreign invader."[32] To avoid such a condition, Mill made clear, a socialization process instilling shared values was necessary.

Mill continued his sociological analysis of the conditions that would provide the stability and consensus for a natural state of society.

> The second condition of permanent political society has been found to be, the existence, in some form or other, of the feeling of allegiance, or loyalty. This feeling may vary in its objects, and is not confined to any particular form of government; but whether in a democracy or in a monarchy, its essence is always the same; viz. that there be in the constitution of the State *something* which is settled, something permanent, and not to be called in question; something which, by general agreement, has a right to be where it is, and to be secure against disturbance, whatever else may change. This feeling may attach itself . . . to a common God or gods. . . . Or it may attach itself to certain persons. . . . Or finally (and this is the only shape in which the feeling is likely to exist hereafter) it may attach itself to the principles of individual freedom and political and social equality, as realized in institutions which as yet exist nowhere or exist only in a rudimentary state. But in all political societies which have had a durable existence, there has been some fixed point; something which men agreed in holding sacred; which, wherever freedom of discussion was a recognised principle, it was of course lawful to contest in theory, but which no one could either fear or hope to see shaken in practice; which, in short (except perhaps during some temporary crisis), was in the common estimation placed beyond discussion.[33]

Here again, as he observes that in the absence of this second condition there will be excessive conflict and social disintegration, Mill alludes to

[31] "Coleridge," *CW, 10*, 133.
[32] Ibid.
[33] Ibid., 133–34.

the transitional state. Without shared allegiance to the fundamental principles of the regime, there will be "internal dissension." When the questioning of these fundamental principles becomes "the habitual condition of the body politic, and when all the violent animosities are called forth, which spring naturally from such a situation, the State is virtually in a position of civil war."[34] Here Mill again implicitly condemns the transitional state for allowing, even encouraging, selfishness and conflict.

Mill completes his analysis by identifying another feature of a society in a natural or organic state.

> The third essential condition of stability in political society, is a strong and active principle of cohesion among the members of the same community or state. We need scarcely say that we do not mean nationality in the vulgar sense of the term. . . . We mean a principle of sympathy, not of hostility; of union, not of separation. We mean a feeling of common interest among those who live under the same government, and are contained within the same natural or historical boundaries. We mean, that one part of the community do not consider themselves as foreigners with regard to another part; that they set a value on their connexion; feel that they are one people, that their lot is cast together, that evil to any of their fellow-countrymen is evil to themselves; and do not desire selfishly to free themselves from their share of any common inconvenience by severing the connexion.[35]

Although Mill did not use the words 'transitional' and 'natural' in the essays on Bentham and Coleridge, the conceptual understanding of the two kinds of society represented by these terms had a central place in his thinking when he assessed the importance of these figures. His preoccupation with these types of society persisted and his wish to put an end to one of them and to promote the other ultimately led to his adopting the Comtean idea of a religion of humanity.

In the *Logic* (1843), Mill continued to structure his thought to allow for the recognition of a natural or organic kind of society as a real alternative to the continuation of a transitional state of society. Drawing on Comte, he identified two sociological sciences, one, social statics, which explained how to maintain a natural state of society, once it was achieved; and the other, social dynamics, which explained the path of change that would show how the transitional state might be brought to an end and the natural state might be reached.

Social dynamics was closely tied to his theory of history, as it provided "a true explanation of the social past and the prophesy of an indefinite future."[36] Social statics, on the other hand, "ascertains the conditions of

---

[34] Ibid., 134.
[35] Ibid., 134–35.
[36] Mill to Auguste Comte, 8 December 1843, *Correspondence Mill and Comte*, 213.

stability" and seeks to establish a theory of consensus. The account of the three conditions of political society laid out in the essay on Coleridge was incorporated into the *Logic* where those conditions were presented as illustrations "of the kind of theorems of which sociological statics would consist."[37] The importance of this subject to him is indicated by his ambition to produce a work on general sociology; and the magnitude of this ambition is indicated by his definition of sociology: "I understand by Sociology not a particular *class* of subjects included *within* Politics, but a vast field *including* it—the whole field of enquiry and speculation respecting human society and its arrangements, of which the forms of government, and the principles of the conduct of governments are but a part."[38]

He also had a related ambition—to write a book on the science of ethology—and this also would have served his goal of improving society and bringing a natural state of society into being. Ethology was the science of character, collective as well as individual, and its purpose was to illuminate the practical activity of educating character and the conduct that issued from it. In the formal and stilted language of the *Logic*, ethology was to discover "the origin and sources of all those qualities in human beings which are interesting to us, either as facts to be produced, or to be avoided, or merely to be understood: and the object is, to determine . . . what actual or possible combinations of circumstances are capable of promoting or of preventing the production of those qualities."[39] Bain said he cherished this subject "with parental fondness," and late in 1843, with the *Logic* published, he expected it to be the subject of his next book.[40] In *On Liberty* and other writings of the 1850s Mill provided more detailed and concrete accounts of how to promote wholesome and how to prevent depraved qualities of character, and though he never produced the book on ethology, in these later works he revealed some of the conclusions of his ethological speculations.

Mill's thought was characterized by the use of paired antinomies that referred to two types of society—the disordered, non-cohesive, transi-

---

[37] *Logic, CW, 8,* 918, 921.

[38] Mill to John Chapman, 9 June 1851, *CW, 14,* 68. Bain located Mill's wish to produce a treatise on sociology in 1842–43 but reported that he despaired: Bain, *Mill,* 79. Harriet Martineau reported hearing that Mill "will by and by publish a book on Sociology, according much with Comte's views." Martineau to George Jacob Holyoake, 6 October [1851], British Library, Add. 42 726, f.2.

[39] *Logic, CW, 8,* 869, 873–74, 904–5.

[40] Bain, *Mill,* 78; Mill to Auguste Comte, 8 December 1843, *Correspondence Mill and Comte,* 213. On his failure to write a book on ethology, see Bain, *Mill,* 79. In 1844 he noted, "my meditations on ethology will not be ripe for some time." Mill to Auguste Comte, 3 April 1844, *Correspondence Mill and Comte,* 228. In 1859 it continued to be on his writing agenda: Mill to Bain, 14 November 1859, *CW, 15,* 645. He still thought such a work necessary in 1869: "Of all difficulties which impede the progress of thought, and the formation of well-grounded opinions on life and social arrangements, the greatest is now

tional state, and the harmonious natural state. His initial distinction between transitional and natural later became a contrast between critical
and organic.[41] He had several other ways of describing these two social
states, and they closely paralleled one another. He also called them, respectively, negative and positive; destructive and constructive; the kind of
society in which Bentham's philosophy was most useful and the kind calling for Coleridge's; and the kind studied by social dynamics and the kind
examined by social statics. One served the interests of Progression, the
other the interests of Permanence;[42] and one was promoted by Progressive
writers, the other by Conservatives.[43]

By arguing that an organic state of society with authority, order, and
cohesion was desirable, Mill forged a link with conservative thought, not
in place of, but in combination with the intellectual tradition he labeled
"progressive." In doing this he acknowledged that the kind of liberal or
radical reform which aimed only to remove the institutions and practices
of the old regime was not sufficient. Thus he criticized those who advocated this kind of reform, saying, "the *philosophes* saw, as usual, what
was not true, not what was." The "essential requisites of civil society
[they] unfortunately overlooked." They did not understand that all re-
gimes needed foundations. In seeking to weaken bad government, they
weakened the foundations of all government. They devoted themselves to
"discrediting all that still remained of restraining discipline, because it
rested on the ancient and decayed creeds against which they made war
. . . [and to] unsettling everything which was still considered settled . . .
and in uprooting what little remained in the people's minds of reverence
for anything above them." They were mistaken in not recognizing the
value, in past times, of the old creeds and institutions and that those old
forms "still filled a place in the human mind, and in the arrangements of
society, which could not without great peril, be left vacant." Put differently, "they threw away the shell without preserving the kernel; and attempt[ed] to new-model society without the binding forces which hold
society together."[44] Consequently the reforms proposed by the *philosophes* were not so much defective as insufficient. Other institutions and
practices had to be established as substitutes for those which were disap-
pearing, just as Christianity had to be replaced by a secular religion.

---

the unspeakable ignorance and inattention of mankind in respect to the influences which
form human character." *Subjection of Women* (1869), CW, *21*, 277.

[41] Early Draft, CW, *1*, 170.

[42] "Coleridge," CW, *10*, 152

[43] "Bentham," CW, *10*, 77.

[44] "Coleridge," CW, *10*, 136–39. This part of Mill's perspective was anticipated in his
early approval for "speculative Tories" who "are duly sensible that it is good for man to be
ruled: to submit both his body and mind to the guidance of a higher intelligence and virtue."
Mill to John Sterling, 20–22 October 1831, CW, *12*, 84.

With this perspective, Mill drew from the *philosophes* (and from their English spokesman, Bentham) and also from the counter-revolutionary side (represented by Coleridge). Thus he concluded in 1865, "we hold the amount of truth in the two [sides] to be about the same. M. Comte has got hold of half the truth, and the so-called liberal or revolutionary school possesses the other half."[45] St. Simon and Comte, from whom Mill derived his appreciation for an organic state of society, were explicit about their strategy of bringing the revolutionary era to a close and substituting a new regime that would have structural similarities with, while being sub-stantively different from, the pre-revolutionary, Christian regime of the past. In St. Simon's case, this perspective was derived from Bonald, and Comte shared it with de Maistre, and since Mill took so much of it from both St. Simon and Comte, he also had links, though in his case they were indirect, with these conservative theocratic writers.[46] This connection makes it difficult to classify Mill unambiguously as a spokesman for lib-eral and Enlightenment ideals. It should be noted that this affinity with some who put forth anti-Enlightenment views is also reflected in parallels between Mill's thought and Rousseau's. These similarities included their views on equality, the mutability of human nature, commercial civiliza-tion and its effects on self-definition and motivation, selfishness, and, above all, on religion, both Christianity and its replacement, for Mill thought about the religion of humanity much as Rousseau did about civil religion.

The paired antinomies of variously described transitional and natural states of society remained a pervasive presence in Mill's thought.[47] Given the connection between the several ways he invoked the distinction be-tween transitional and natural states, there were analogies between the natural state, the organic state, the ideal condition represented by Cole-

[45] *Auguste Comte and Positivism* (1865), CW, 10, 313.

[46] See Keith Baker, "Closing the French Revolution: Saint Simon and Comte," in *The French Revolution and the Creation of Modern Culture, 3, The Transformation of Political Culture 1789–1848*, ed. Francois Furet and Mona Ozouf (Oxford: Pergamon, 1987), 326–30; Frank Manuel, *The Prophets of Paris* (Cambridge, Mass.: Harvard University Press, 1962), 257, 285–86. Introduction, *The Doctrine of Saint-Simon: An Exposition, First Year, 1828–1829*, ed. Georg G. Iggers (Boston: Beacon Press, 1958), xlii–iii. Comte: "History has too much ignored the immortal school which arose at the commencement of the nineteenth century under the noble presidency of De Maistre, and was worthily completed by Bonald with the assistance of Chateaubriand's poetry. These teachers succeeded in systematically discrediting negativism by proving that its vices . . . were the necessary result of the doc-trine. . . . The demonstration . . . brought about a vague reaction against the preceding cen-tury. . . . Thenceforward there was a general recognition of the constant need of a religion of some sort." Comte, *System of Positive Policy* (1853; New York: Burt Franklin, 1966), 3, 518–19. On de Maistre's influence on Comte, see Mary Pickering, *Auguste Comte: An Intellectual Biography, Volume 1* (Cambridge: Cambridge University Press, 1993), 261–65, 305, 313.

[47] Reference to transitional periods can be found at CW, 1, 172, 246, 259; 13, 564; 24, 815; *Correspondence Mill and Comte*, 109, 131, 173; Diary, 22 January [1854], CW, 27, 645.

ridge, and permanent political society as described in *Logic*, and this understanding of natural states included Mill's conception of a religion of humanity, as it too would provide a widely shared, authoritative morality that shaped character in accordance with its moral ideals.

The idea of a religion of humanity was latently present in Mill's thinking long before he encountered Comte's full account of it in 1848. It was present by virtue of Comtean ideas about a natural, organic state of society, and it was strongly suggested by what Mill adopted from Comte's writings about historical development, scientific method, and sociology in the latter's *Cours de philosophie positive* (1830–1842). Mill's enthusiastic response to this book is recorded in his letters to Comte, beginning in 1841, a time when Mill was completing his *Logic* (1843). Having found Comte's first five volumes so helpful and so promising, he delayed composition of book VI of *Logic*, the most politically substantial part of his treatise, until he had an opportunity to study Comte's sixth and last volume of the *Cours*. "I still hunger for your book," he wrote in 1842, and when it arrived, he gave it "successive rereadings" and confessed, "I share your conviction very deeply and fully support the conclusions of your work." The impact of Comte's book was so great that Mill acknowledged that he "felt the kind of jolt that your works have often given me, the result of sudden insight into a great and luminous new idea."[48] His sense of shared ideas and beliefs was such that he referred to "our philosophic sympathy," "our feeling of solidarity," and "our enterprise."[49]

Mill as he read the *Cours* was quick to discern the connection between what Comte wrote there and the possibility of what only later would be called a religion of humanity. After reading Comte's final volume but before Comte published his account of the religion of humanity Mill reported:

> What is now taking shape in my mind is a first specific formulation of the grand
> general conclusion to your treatise: my realization that positive philosophy,
> once it is conceived as a whole, is capable of fully assuming the high social
> function that so far only religions have fulfilled, and [at that], quite imperfectly
> so.

[48] Mill to Auguste Comte, 10 September, 23 October, 15 December 1842, *Correspondence Mill and Comte*, 100, 109, 118–19. On Mill's conversion to Comtean ideas, see Pickering, *Comte*, 535–36. On Mill's postponing composition of book VI of *Logic*, see Mill to Comte, 9 June, 11 July, 23 October 1842; 28 January, 13 March 1843, *Correspondence Mill and Comte*, 75, 82–83, 108, 130, 138.

[49] Mill to Auguste Comte, 22 March, 9 June 1842; 17 January 1844, ibid., 59, 74, 221. Comte referred to "our philosophical revolution" and to the "convergence" and "concordance" of their ideas. Auguste Comte to Mill, 30 September, 30 December 1842; 16 May 1843, ibid., 107, 127, 155.

Elaborating on this, he went on to say,

> I always saw in the creation of a true social philosophy the only possible base for the general regeneration of human morality, and in the idea of Humanity the only one capable of replacing that of God.[50]

This testimony was supplemented by evidence in book VI of *Logic*, which itself was the immediate intellectual context to Mill's quest for a new secular religion that could lead to moral and social regeneration. There he adopted Comtean ideas and acknowledged Comte as the source of them, though most of these footnote acknowledgments to the *Cours* were removed from the second and subsequent editions. He borrowed Comte's theories about the three successive stages through which all fields of inquiry developed (the theological, metaphysical, and positive) and about social dynamics and social statics, both of which pointed to an end of history with the transformation of existing society.[51] Comte's implicit historical generalization had "that high degree of scientific evidence, which is derived from the concurrence of the indications of history with the probabilities derived from the constitution of the human mind." This delighted Mill and satisfied his eschatological needs, leading him to observe, "what a flood of light it lets in upon the whole course of history." It allowed one to foresee not only a positive, scientific future for social science but also "the correlative condition of other social phenomena," that is, the natural, organic state of society, shaped and defined by a new secular religion, which would be made possible by the development of social science.[52]

---

[50] Mill to Auguste Comte, 15 December 1842, ibid., 118.

[51] *Logic*, CW, *8*, 917–8. About the *Cours*, Mill said, "He makes some mistakes, but on the whole, I think it very nearly the grandest work of this age." Mill to Alexander Bain, 15 October 1841, CW, *13*, 487 (for date of letter, see Bain, *Mill*, 63). Comte thanked Mill for acknowledgments in the *Logic*: "Every time the occasion presented itself, I received the full philosophic appreciation which you considered my due." Comte to Mill, 16 May 1843, *Correspondence Mill and Comte*, 153–54. See also CW, *1*, 216, 255n. Frederic Harrison, who became a positivist, looked back on his reading of *Logic* and realized how much it exposed him to Comte's teaching. Recalling his experience as a student at Wadham College, Oxford (*c.* 1857), he said, "I was practically a Comtist, under the teaching of Mill, Lewes, and Littré; . . . Congreve had never mentioned to us the name of Comte, nor did we know anything more of Positivism than what we read in Mill's Logic, and Littre's sketch." Frederic Harrison, "Early Reminiscences of John Henry Bridges," in *Recollections of John Henry Bridges M.B.*, with an introduction by M.A.B. [Mary A. Bridges] (London: Privately printed, 1908), 74. Another positivist, Richard Congreve, recognized the Comtean themes in *Logic*. Referring to 1849, he noted, Comte's "name had become more and more familiar to English readers. By the publication of Mill's Logic attention had been called to his high importance as a thinker." "Personal Recollections of Auguste Comte," British Library, Add. 45 259, f.1. That Mill's name was linked to Comte's is evident in the rumor that he was translating Comte's *Cours*. Harriet Martineau to George Jacob Holyoake, 6 October [1851], British Library, Add. 42 726, f.2.

[52] *Logic*, CW, *8*, 928

Comte's teaching did more than inform Mill's strategic goals, for it also was a source of tactical guidance for one eager to hasten the pace of historic development and direct it to its proper ends.

> By its aid we may hereafter succeed not only in looking far forward into the future of history of the human race, but in determining what artificial means may be used, and to what extent, to accelerate the natural progress in so far as it is beneficial; to compensate for whatever may be its inherent inconveniences or disadvantages; and to guard against the dangers or accidents to which our species is exposed from the necessary incidents of its progression. Such practical instructions, founded on the highest branch of speculative sociology, will form the noblest and most beneficial portion of the Political Art.[53]

By recognizing that the religion of humanity was implied by what Comte had written about science, history, and sociology, Mill anticipated a development that in fact occurred six years later.[54]

When Mill encountered Comte's proposal for a religion of humanity in 1848 he experienced a sense of illumination, as if he had been shown the way to clarity about ideas that previously had been somewhat inchoate. A new work of Comte's, *Discours sur l'ensemble du positivisme* (Paris, July, 1848), he said, "is well calculated to stir the mind and create a ferment of thought, chiefly, I think, because it is the first book which has given a coherent picture of a supposed future of humanity with a look of possibility about it" and for "making much clearer, than to me they ever were before, the grounds for believing that the *culte de l'humanité* is capable of fully supplying the place of a religion, or rather (to say the truth) of *being* a religion."[55] It was not exactly a conversion experience, like the one in 1822 when he discovered in Bentham's *Treatise of Legislation* the principle of utility, which "fell exactly into its place as the keystone which held together the detached fragmentary portions of my knowledge and beliefs." At that time the new idea "gave unity to my conceptions of things" and provided "a creed, a doctrine, a philosophy;

---

[53] Ibid., 929–30.

[54] The phrase 'religion of humanity' was not used in the *Cours* but the idea it represented was implied there: Pickering, *Comte*, 691; see also 535–37. See also T. R. Wright, *The Religion of Humanity: The Impact of Comtean Positivism on Victorian Britain* (Cambridge: Cambridge University Press, 1986), 41, 43.

[55] Mill to John Pringle Nichol, 30 September 1848, *CW*, *13*, 738–39. According to Moncure Daniel Conway, Paine was the inventor of the phrase, which appeared in *The Crisis* and in *Age of Reason*. *The Writings of Thomas Paine*, ed. Moncure Daniel Conway (1894–96; New York: AMS Press, 1967), 4, 6. Mill quoted from *The Crisis* and may well have been familiar with *Age of Reason*: *CW*, *20*, 163. Mill may also have been familiar with W. J. Fox's essay "The Religion of Humanity" (1849), which probably had been a lecture; however, it shows no Comtean influence; see William Johnson Fox, *The Religious Ideas* (London: British & Foreign Unitarian Association, 1907), 140–50.

in one (and the best) sense of the word, a religion."[56] These words, written after his discovery of Comte's religion of humanity, seem an even better description of Comte's impact on him than of Bentham's, but, as on the earlier occasion, in 1848 Mill found that the goal toward which his thoughts were moving had been given sharp definition.

Mill's eagerness to see the religion of humanity become reality was masked by his severe criticisms of Comte's version of it. Mill's posterity especially found it easy to conclude that the Mill of *On Liberty* could not approve of a religion of humanity, for in *On Liberty* he identified Comte as a religious thinker who asserted the right of spiritual domination and accused him of aiming to establish "a despotism of society over the individual, surpassing anything contemplated in the political ideal of the most rigid disciplinarian among the ancient philosophers" (227). This judgment was reenforced in the widely read *Autobiography*, where he created the impression that Comte's perspective and *On Liberty* were polar opposites. There he accused Comte of carrying his doctrines to the "extremest consequences" by planning "the completest system of spiritual and temporal despotism, which ever yet emanated from a human brain, unless possibly that of Ignatius Loyola." The contrast with themes in *On Liberty* were highlighted:

> a system by which the yoke of general opinion, wielded by an organized body of spiritual teachers and rulers, would be made supreme over every action, and as far as is in human possibility, every thought, of every member of the community, as well in the things which regard only himself, as in those which concern the interests of others. . . . Yet it [Comte's *Système de politique positive*] leaves an irresistable conviction that any moral beliefs, concurred in by the community generally, may be brought to bear upon the whole conduct and lives of its individual members with an energy and potency truly alarming to think of. The book stands a monumental warning to thinkers on society and politics, of what happens when once men lose sight, in their speculations, of the value of Liberty and of Individuality.[57]

Mill clearly rejected Comte's religion of humanity, which does not mean, however, that he did not have one of his own.

While Mill still lived, his contemporaries had even less reason than those who survived him to recognize that he favored a religion of human-

---

[56] Early Draft, *CW*, *1*, 68. Pickering calls Comte's impact as "Mill's second spiritual conversion." *Comte*, 536.

[57] *Autobiography*, *CW*, 1, 221.

ity. Although he used the phrase 'religion of humanity' in correspondence and in writings that were not to be published before he died, in work published while he was still alive he did not use the phrase, except in *Auguste Comte and Positivism* (1865), where he could hardly avoid using it, and here, while he made a few favorable observations about it, his criticisms of Comte's proposal for a religion of humanity were so severe that the impression is easily gained that Mill rejected it out of hand.

Comte's version of the religion of humanity, Mill explained, led to an overly authoritarian, oppressive regime. It would establish a corporation of philosophers which would be denied riches and excluded from political authority but would enjoy reverence and "have the entire direction of education: together with, not only the right and duty of advising and reproving all persons respecting both their public and their private life, but also a control . . . over the speculative class itself." This arrangement would coexist with a temporal government made up of "an aristocracy of capitalists" which, while it would be unchecked by a representative system or by popular bodies, would be subject to counsel from the spiritual power of the philosophers—an arrangement which, Mill noted, even Comte called 'dictatorship.'[58] There would be little regulation by law but a great deal of "pressure of opinion, directed by the Spiritual Power." Consequently, "liberty and spontaneity on the part of individuals form no part of the scheme." Also, there would be uniformity, "a state of things which instead of becoming more acceptable, will assuredly be more repugnant to mankind, with every step of their progress in the unfettered exercises of their highest faculties." The result would "involve nothing less than a spiritual despotism"—as Mill said elsewhere, Comte's proposal was liberticide.[59] Although Comte would have allowed free discussion for all those denied moral authority, freedom of inquiry by those in the speculative class would be denied, as they would be subject to direction by the corporation of philosophers. Comte was accused of not allowing free play of intellect. "Of all the ingredients of human nature, he continually says, the intellect most needs to be disciplined and reined-in." Thus he would have the Spiritual Power "stigmatize as immoral, and effectually supress, . . . useless employments of the speculative faculties," i.e., those that did not benefit mankind.[60] For Mill, this was unacceptable. The vast scope Comte would give to the Spiritual Power granted "absolute and undivided control of a single Pontiff for the whole human race." Mill was "appalled at the picture of entire subjugation and slavery, which

---

[58] *Auguste Comte and Positivism*, CW, *10*, 326, 351.
[59] Ibid., 314–15, 327. Mill to Harriet Taylor Mill, 15 January 1855, CW, *14*, 294.
[60] *Auguste Comte and Positivism*, CW, *10*, 326–27, 352–53.

is recommended to us as the last and highest result of the evolution of Humanity."[61]

Mill also took Comte to task for his opinions about women and the family, especially for subordinating wives to husbands and women generally to men.[62] He also challenged Comte's belief that biological science proved a natural hierarchy of the sexes in which women had the subordinate place.[63] This question repeatedly arose during their six-year correspondence, and though Mill, eager to collaborate with Comte and appreciative of his general theories, appeared diffident and at first played down their disagreement, in the end, under pressure from Harriet Taylor, he made it clear his opinion was not to be altered.[64] They also disagreed about divorce, for Comte wished to uphold the family as the prime source of social feelings and unselfishness. Therefore he regarded marriages as "rigidly indissoluble," while Mill believed "these two institutions [property and marriage] may be destined to undergo more serious modifications than you [Comte] seem to think." Although he could not foresee how the institution of marriage would change, he did indicate in *On Liberty* that he regarded divorce, in certain circumstances, as justifiable.[65]

This was not all. Comte naively expected his utopia would be easily reached. Also, he wished to make altruism the source of all motivations: he was "a morality-intoxicated man." Moreover, his understanding of psychology was flawed; on the subject of political economy he was superficial; he did not understand English Protestantism; and he expected that a scientific basis would be found for phrenology.[66]

---

[61] Ibid., 351. *Auguste Comte and Positivism* reflected Mill's longstanding wish to distance himself from Comte. Although his appraisal was published in 1865, he had been looking for an opportunity to write about Comte since 1854, because of "the great desire I feel to atone for the overpraise I have given Comte [in the first edition of *Logic*] and to let it be generally known to those who know me what I think on the unfavourable side about him." Mill to Harriet Taylor Mill, 17 January 1854, *CW*, *14*, 134.

[62] *Auguste Comte and Positivism*, *CW*, *10*, 311.

[63] Comte to Mill, 16 July 1843, *Correspondence Mill and Comte*, 179–80.

[64] Mill to Comte, 30 August, 30 October 1843, ibid., 183–85, 199, 205. On seeing some of the correspondence, Harriet wrote: "Comte's [part of the correspondence] is what I expected—the usual partial and prejudiced view of a subject which he has little considered. . . . I am surprised to find in your letters to find [sic] your opinion undetermined where I had thought it made up. I am disappointed at a tone more than half apologetic with which you state your opinions. . . . I only wish that what was said was in the tone of conviction, not of suggestion. This dry root of a man is not a worthy coadjutor scarcely a worthy opponent." Harriet Taylor to Mill, n.d., Mill-Taylor Mill Collection, 2, ff. 723–24, British Library of Political and Economic Science.

[65] *Auguste Comte and Positivism*, *CW*, *10*, 345; Mill to Comte, 15 June 1843, *Correspondence Mill and Comte*, 165. On divorce, see above, chapter 1, text at notes 27 and 28. Comte used the phrase "the subjection of women." Comte to Mill, 5 October 1843, ibid., 191.

[66] *Auguste Comte and Positivism*, *CW*, *10*, 296–97, 305, 321, 325–26, 335–36. Mueller, *Mill and French Thought*, 116–17. Wright, *Religion of Humanity*, 42, 48.

Their disagreements were reenforced by deterioration of what had been a cordial and mutually flattering relationship during the initial period of their six-year correspondence. Mill had reason to be annoyed, for Comte was difficult and irritating, nor did Comte conceal his extraordinary conceit, carrying this so far that he avoided reading newspapers and periodicals and even most books, calling this cerebral hygiene. He even proposed setting aside one hundred worthy works of science, philosophy, poetry, and history and then committing "a systematic holocaust of books in general."[67] Mill was familiar with other manifestations of Comte's eccentricity, as he was exposed to it during their correspondence—his paranoia, his accusations against Grote and Molesworth when they refused to continue their financial support, and his recriminations against Mill because he was reluctant to contribute to a new positivist journal Comte had proposed.[68] After eagerly agreeing to meet Comte in Paris, Mill, irritated by Comte, outraged by some of his proposals, especially regarding women and the family, and reflecting Harriet Taylor's anger, never called on him.

Yet, in spite of all this, Mill retained considerable respect for Comte. No doubt recalling his intellectual debt to him, Mill paused to observe, "Others may laugh, but we could far rather weep at this melancholy decadence of a great intellect." In the end, he classed Comte with thinkers responsible for "grand thoughts, with most important discoveries, and also with some of the most extravagantly wild and ludicrously absurd conceptions and theories which ever were solemnly propounded by thoughtful men." He contemplated the "frightful aberrations a powerful and comprehensive mind may be led [into] by the exclusive following out of a single idea."[69] Mill told Herbert Spencer how much he owed Comte and that "in speculative matters (not in practical) I often agree with him," which was Mill's way of indicating that he accepted the main features of Comte's theoretical perspective while disagreeing about particular proposals for policies or institutional arrangements.[70] Thus he acknowledged that Comte was "one of the most fertile thinkers of modern times."[71] And when Comte died (in 1857) he wrote Harriet, "It seems as if there would be no thinkers left in the world."[72]

Notwithstanding his criticism of Comte's conception of the religion of humanity, Mill had good things to say about it. He endorsed Comte's

[67] *Auguste Comte and Positivism*, CW, 10, 330–31, 357. Comte spoke about "my philosophic mission" and "my basic contribution to the great human regeneration." Ibid., 347, 369.

[68] Mill promised to help financially, but Comte refused. He arranged for contributions from Grote and Molesworth.

[69] Ibid., 351, 367–68.

[70] Mill to Herbert Spencer, 3 April 1864, CW, 15, 934–35.

[71] *Hamilton*, CW, 9, 314.

[72] Mill to Harriet Taylor Mill, [16 September 1857], CW, 15, 537.

suggestion that a religion might exist without belief in a God and that it would be instructive to consider adopting such a religion. He went further to assert that Comte "was justified in the attempt to develope [sic] his philosophy into a religion" and that "all other religions are made better in proportion as, in their practical result, they are brought to coincide with that which he aimed at constructing." He also approved of Comte's wish to have altruism replace egoism, but he criticized him for making heroic levels of altruism obligatory.[73] He also acknowledged, "There are many remarks and precepts in M. Comte's volumes, which, as no less pertinent to our conception of morality than to his, we fully accept."[74] His praise in *Auguste Comte and Positivism* was hardly excessive and it constitutes but a few of the total of 106 pages, many of them studded with criticisms. It is understandable that Mill's contemporaries did not find in his book on Comte strong evidence of his belief in a religion of humanity.

An exception to this can be found in a pamphlet by one of Comte's leading English disciples, John Henry Bridges, who wrote in response to the critical tone of Mill's *Auguste Comte and Positivism*. Eager to gain Mill's support for positivism and to nullify his criticisms, Bridges assessed the extent of Mill's disagreements. He acknowledged some differences, which he regarded as minor, and he argued that Comte was less hostile to liberty than Mill claimed. On the other hand, the common ground was emphasized, especially regarding a theory of history and the religion of humanity. Mill did, after all, "accept, or at least admiringly appreciate, the Religion of Humanity."[75]

Mill's acceptance of the idea of a religion of humanity, though not Comte's particular conception of it, is evident in another work published during his lifetime. In *Utilitarianism* he endorsed the idea of a religion of humanity without, however, mentioning it by name. Identifying it with "the ideal perfection of utilitarian morality," he said it would require,

first, that laws and social arrangements should place the happiness, or (as speaking practically it may be called) the interest, of every individual, as nearly as possible in harmony with the interest of the whole; and secondly, that education and opinion, which have so vast a power over human character, should so use that power as to establish in the mind of every individual an indissoluble association between his own happiness and the good of the whole; . . . so that not only he may be unable to conceive the possibility of happiness to himself, consis-

[73] *Auguste Comte and Positivism*, CW, *10*, 332–35.
[74] Ibid., 339–40.
[75] J. H. Bridges, *The Unity of Comte's Life and Doctrine: A Reply to Strictures on Comte's Later Writings, addressed to J. S. Mill, M.P.* (London, 1866), 31. On other points of agreement, 4–8, 10; on liberty, 42, 47; on disagreement, 8, 20, 22, 42–43, 47, 49. There is no indication that Mill read the pamphlet, though later they did correspond about Ireland. Mill to J. H. Bridges, 16 November 1867, CW, *16*, 1328–30.

tently with conduct opposed to the general good, but also that a direct impulse to promote the general good may be in every individual one of the habitual motives of action, and the sentiments connected therewith may fill a large and prominent place in every human being's sentient existence.[76]

This feeling of unity, he also said, could be "taught as a religion," and he recommended Comte's *Système de politique positive* as a work that has "abundantly shown the possibility of giving to the service of humanity, even without the aid of belief in a Providence, both the psychical power and the social efficacy of a religion; making it take hold of human life, and colour all thought, feeling, and action." In this passage Mill went further than in anything else published while he continued to live to endorse the idea of a religion of humanity, but even here distanced himself from Comte's version of it by announcing in the same sentence that he had "the strongest objections to the system of politics and morals set forth in [Comte's Système]." And (still in the same sentence) he warned that such a religion might be so powerful "as to interfere unduly with human freedom and individuality."[77]

The full extent of Mill's belief in the desirability of a religion of humanity is fully revealed only in private communications and in essays he was unwilling to have published until after his death. The most forthright of these occurs in "Utility of Religion" which was composed in 1855 but held back for posthumous publication. Here he made explicit reference to the religion of humanity four times, describing its main features and comparing it with supernatural religion.[78] Acknowledging that religion might be valuable for an individual, he asked

whether in order to obtain this good, it is necessary to travel beyond the boundaries of the world which we inhabit; or whether the idealization of our earthly life, the cultivation of a high conception of what *it* may be made, is not capable of supplying a poetry, and, in the best sense of the word, a religion, equally fitted

[76] *Utilitarianism*, CW, *10*, 218; see also 231–32. The essay was written 1854, revised 1860: Bain, *Mill*, 112.

[77] *Utiliarianism*, CW, *10*, 232. See also 215, 218–19, 227, 231–32, 248 for other allusions to the religion of humanity. Wright claims that in *Utilitarianism* Mill made his faith in the religion of humanity public; this may be questioned, however, for while he made allusions to the religion of humanity, in this essay he continued to avoid naming it. Wright, *Religion of Humanity*, 45. There are allusions to it also in *Inaugural Address, Delivered to the University of St. Andrews* (1867) and in *Subjection of Women*. CW, *21*, 254, 294–95.

[78] "Utility of Religion," CW, *10*, 422, 425, and twice on 426. As Pickering has noted, Mill scholarship has underestimated Mill's debt to Comte: *Life of Comte*, 538. While Mill's interest in a religion of humanity has been noted in the literature, the difficulty of reconciling it with individual liberty has been generally ignored. Exceptions to this include Cowling, *Mill and Liberalism*; and Richard Vernon, "J. S. Mill and the Religion of Humanity," in *Religion, Secularization and Political Thought*, ed. James E. Crimmins (London: Routledge, 1989), 169.

to exalt the feelings, and (with the same aid from education) still better calculated to ennoble the conduct, than any belief respecting the unseen powers.[79]

Of course, society also would benefit, for the ennobling of conduct consisted of promoting disinterestedness and acting in accord with the highest feelings and convictions.

> To call these sentiments by the name morality, exclusively of any other title, is claiming too little for them. They are a real religion; of which, as of other religions, outward good works (the utmost meaning usually suggested by the word morality) are only a part, and are indeed rather the fruits of the religion than the religion itself. The essence of religion is the strong and earnest direction of the emotions and desires towards an ideal object, recognized as of the highest excellence, and as rightfully paramount over all selfish objects of desire. This condition is fulfilled by the Religion of Humanity in as eminent a degree.[80]

Such a secular religion would not only fulfill its functions, it "would fulfill them better than any form whatever of supernaturalism. It is not only entitled to be called a religion: it is a better religion than any of those which are ordinarily called by that title." So central was it to his thinking that in 1854 when, facing the prospect of rapidly deteriorating health, he planned how to use his time in writing essays which he regarded as most valuable for posterity, one was to be about the religion of the future.[81]

In "Theism," another of his posthumous essays on religion, he also made it clear that he subscribed to "that real, though purely human religion, which sometimes calls itself the Religion of Humanity and sometimes that of Duty." And he added, "that it is destined . . . to be the religion of the Future, I cannot entertain a doubt."[82]

Mill's enthusiasm for a religion of humanity was also revealed in a diary in which he recorded what he regarded as his most valuable thoughts.

> The best, indeed the only good thing (details excepted) in Comte's second treatise [*Système de politique positive, ou traité du sociologie instituant la religion de l'humanité*], is the thoroughness with which he has enforced and illustrated the possibility of making *le culte l'humanité* perform the functions and supply the place of a religion. If we suppose cultivated to the highest point the sentiments of fraternity with all our fellow beings, past present, and to come, of veneration for those past and present who have deserved it, and devotion to the good of those to come; universal moral education making the happiness

---

[79] "Utility of Religion," *CW, 10,* 420.
[80] Ibid., 422.
[81] Ibid.; Mill to Harriet Taylor Mill, 7 February [1854], *CW, 14,* 152.
[82] "Theism," *CW, 10,* 488–89. Frederic Harrison notes that the three posthumous essays on religion revealed a definite acceptance of the religion of humanity. *Tennyson, Ruskin, Mill; and other Literary Estimates* (London: Macmillan & Co., 1900), 300–301.

and dignity of this collective body the central point to which all things are to trend and by which all are to be estimated, instead of the pleasure of an unseen and merely imaginary Power; the imagination at the same time being fed from youth with representations of all noble things felt and acted greater to come: there is no worthy office of a religion which this system of cultivation does not seem adequate to fulfill. It would suffice both to alleviate and to guide human life. Now this is merely supposing that the religion of humanity obtained as firm a hold on mankind, and as great a power of shaping their usages, their institutions, and their education, as other religions have in many cases possessed.[83]

These themes were also candidly stated in a letter to one of Comte's disciples. While proclaiming his disagreements with Comte about morals and politics, Mill added: "as for religion . . . it is there without doubt that my opinions are most similar to those of M. Comte. I entirely agree with him on the negative part of the question, and in the affirmative part, like him, I hold that the idea of the whole of humanity, represented above all by the minds and the characters of the elite, past, present, and future, not only for exceptional people but for all persons, can become the object of a sentiment capable of replacing with advantage all actual religions."[84]

Mill approved of Comte's general idea of a religion of humanity, not the particular way Comte chose to have it put in place. Rejection of Comte's "details"—the practical application of his theory—did not mean that Mill rejected the general idea. Masked behind the public facade of severe criticism, Mill cultivated a strong belief in the importance of Comte's religion for the future of mankind. In fact, Mill tied all his hopes for moral regeneration to a futurity in which the religion of humanity would be the most important feature. Since Comte's proposal was tarnished by its details, Mill developed his own more acceptable version. As Bain noted, he was led to the religion of humanity in the first instance by Comte, but "the filling-up is his own."[85]

At the core of Mill's conception of a religion of humanity, as in Comte's, was a belief that altruism ought to inform social relationships, and this judgment followed from a prior belief that selfishness was destructive and

[83] Diary, 24 January [1854], CW, 27, 646.
[84] Mill to Barbot de Chement, 7 August 1854, CW, 14, 237.
[85] Bain, Mill, 134, and also see 71. "Mill realized that he would have to develop Positivism independently, without the aid of its founder." Wright, Religion of Humanity, 43. Since Mill's affinities with Comte cast doubt on the interpretation of Mill as a defender of expansive liberty, there is a tendency in recent scholarship to emphasize Mill's criticisms of Comte and to ignore the opinions they shared. See, for example, John C. Rees, John Stuart Mill's On Liberty, 133–34.

unworthy. Disapproving comments about selfishness appear ubiquitously in Mill's writing. There was a "deeprooted selfishness which the whole course of existing institutions tends to generate."[86] Amongst them was commerce, which promoted an "engrossing selfishness."[87] A commercial people tended to be mean and slavish (169). Such self-seeking appeared in many guises—in the quest for "worldly or selfish success"; in "supposed favours of the supernal powers"; in the indulgence of self-will; and in self-conceit.[88] Of course, the reference to supernal powers was explained elsewhere as the Christian appeal to a selfish wish for immortality. It was also condemned when observed in the conventional exchanges of social life; as Harriet Mill put it, "The spirit of Emulation in childhood and of competition in manhood are the fruitful sources of selfishness and misery."[89] Mill also discerned its presence in the numbers of children one had, for it was selfish to ignore Malthus's prudent warnings and have so many children that the labor market became swamped, driving down the rate of wages for everyone, including those unselfish who practiced restraint.

The problem of selfishness initially arises in our unfortunate nature. "The truth is that there is hardly a single point of excellence belonging to human character, which is not decidedly repugnant to the untutored feelings of human nature."[90] The distinctive and most problematic of those untutored feelings is selfishness. "The strongest propensities of un-cultivated or half-cultivated human nature . . . [are] the purely selfish ones." If not restrained, they tend "to disunite mankind, not to unite them,—to make them rivals, not confederates." The remedy is civilization: "Social existence is only possible by a disciplining of those more powerful propensities, which consists in subordinating them to a common system of opinions."[91]

Existing civilization, however, only reenforced the selfish tendencies in human nature, for it encouraged and justified selfishness. This had not been the case always, for in earlier times there had been natural or organic

[86] Early Draft, CW, 1, 240.

[87] Mill to Gustave d'Eichthal, 15 May 1829, CW, 12, 31.

[88] Diary, 9 April [1854], CW, 27, 667. Mill's critique of selfishness, in combination with his call for civic and social virtue, his use of models drawn from antiquity, his alleged invocation of virtu, and his presumed affinity with Milton, have been interpreted by some as evidence that he drew on civic republican thought. The most strained example of this interpretation is to be found in Stewart Justman, The Hidden Text of Mill's Liberty, 2–6, 22, 26, 35, 49, 51–61, 103, 111, 116, 118, 139, 151–56, 165 and passim.

[89] "An Early Essay by Harriet Taylor" (1832), Hayek, Mill and Harriet Taylor, 279. That his wife shared his estimate of selfishness and may even have felt more strongly about it is implied in his telling her, "I cannot persuade myself that you do not greatly overrate the ease of making people unselfish." Mill to Harriet Taylor, 21 March [1849], CW, 14, 19.

[90] "Nature," CW, 10, 393; see also 396.

[91] Logic, CW, 8, 926.

eras. Ancient Greece for example, approximated such a condition, as did the middle ages.[92] But with the decay of medieval unity, a transitional era emerged, and Europe's institutions and beliefs, if anything, fostered selfishness. Civilization, as it developed in modern Europe, distorted individual character, leading to "the concentration of it within the narrow sphere of the individual's money-getting pursuits."[93] Only a few persons, by virtue of self-cultivation, overcame selfishness; most however, were mired in it.

The contrast between altruism and selfishness as polar opposites and defining types of morality and social relationships was closely tied to Mill's modifications of the utilitarianism to which he had been introduced by Bentham and his father. Earlier he had believed that reform could be accomplished by educating people as to their real interest, which, once they understood it, they would promote.[94] This assumption changed, however, with the distinction between kinds of pleasure, a lower kind that was sensual, animallike, suitable for pigs, and a higher kind that was elevated, and gratifying to the intellect, feelings, imagination, and moral sentiments. Mill had no doubts about which of the two kinds of experience was the higher and which the lower, for those who had experienced both invariably chose the life that provided the higher pleasures.[95] Whereas the person who sought the higher pleasures was capable of subordinating selfish desires and cultivating "a fellow-feeling with the collective interests of mankind," his opposite was characterized by selfishness, which was the principal cause of an unsatisfactory life.[96] Such a person was "a selfish egotist, devoid of every feeling or care but those which centre in his own miserable individuality."[97]

Mill's revision of utilitarian doctrine may help explain the cryptic statement about utility near the beginning of *On Liberty*. Following his claim that his arguments about liberty were not based on the idea of abstract right, as something independent from utility, he wrote: "I regard utility as the ultimate appeal on all ethical questions; but it must be utility in the largest sense, grounded on the permanent interests of man as a progressive being" (224). Utility consisted of maximizing happiness, but in Mill's revised utilitarianism the definition of happiness was fundamentally altered

[92] Early Draft, *CW, 1*, 240.

[93] "Civilization," *CW, 18*, 129.

[94] *Logic, CW, 8*, 890–91, on "the interest philosophy of the Bentham school." Cf. the puzzling denial that there is selfishness in Bentham's doctrines in a letter to the editor of the *Westminster Review*. Mill to William E. Hickson, 15 October 1851, *CW, 14*, 78.

[95] *Utilitarianism, CW, 10*, 210–14. Cf. Diary, 23 March [1854], *CW, 27*, 663. Also cf. Plato, *Republic*, 582a, b.

[96] *Utilitarianism, CW, 10*, 215.

[97] Ibid., 216.

to consist of higher pleasures. Such happiness would be generally available only in the distant future when cultural regeneration would have occurred and "the permanent interests of man as a progressive being" would be provided for. Since only then would such happiness be available to all, promotion of it was "the ultimate principle of Teleology."[98] These observations suggest that by rejecting low, selfish pleasures and approving higher pleasures, which included concern for others, Mill's revised utilitarianism, encouraged the altruism that was at the core of his religion of humanity.

Meanwhile, most persons were mired in the selfish search for low pleasures which were readily available during the present transitional era. Only a few advanced thinkers resisted such influences and managed to achieve nobleness of character and to foresee the organic state of society that ultimately would emerge. One must suspect that he regarded his wife and himself to be among those few, that is, to be authentic, not narrow, Bentham-like, utilitarians, and this linkage between his revised utilitarianism ("utility in the largest sense") and an understanding of "the permanent interests of man as a progressive being" allowed him to regard Socrates, Plato, Aristotle, and Jesus as utilitarians.[99] About Jesus, Mill said, "In the golden rule of Jesus of Nazareth, we read the complete spirit of the ethics of utility. To do as one would be done by, and to love one's neighbor as oneself, constitute the ideal perfection of utilitarian morality."[100]

Selfishness was not a necessary condition for Mill. "The deep rooted selfishness which forms the general character of the existing state of society, is *so* deeply rooted, only because the whole course of existing institutions tends to foster it.[101] But existing institutions could be altered. Human nature, he insisted, was pliable, and the institutions that shaped it were historically determined and therefore, in theory, subject to change, even to fundamental change.[102] "Mankind are capable of a far greater amount of public spirit," he explained, "than the present age is accustomed to suppose possible."[103] Any kind of regime, even communism, might be established.[104] In theory, therefore, what appeared to be natural, including selfishness, could be altered, even eliminated, by altering institutions and

[98] *Logic*, CW, *8*, 951. In the 1865 edition he added a footnote referring to *Utilitarianism* for vindication of this principle. Ibid., 951n.

[99] On Socrates, *Utilitarianism*, CW, *10*, 205; Mill to George Grote, 10 January 1862, CW, *15*, 764. On Plato, "Bentham," CW, *10*, 88, 90. On Aristotle, *On Liberty*, CW, *18*, 235.

[100] *Utilitarianism*, CW, *10*, 218.

[101] *Autobiography*, CW, *1*, 241.

[102] Early Draft, CW, *1*, 186. Mill recommended that a student take up history, as "nowhere else will he behold so strongly exemplified the astonishing pliability of our nature." "Civilization," CW, *18*, 145.

[103] *Political Economy*, CW, *2*, 205.

[104] *Representative Government*, CW, *19*, 405.

culture. Selfishness, therefore, was less an individual's responsibility than a matter of cultural influence. Unusual persons could overcome such influence, but for most persons to elevate themselves above the pursuit of low, selfish pleasures, a "social transformation" was required, and this would be accompanied by "an equivalent change of character."[105] To accomplish this was the goal of Mill's cultural politics.

The change in character Mill looked for would make happiness less a matter of individuals searching for it, each on his or her own behalf, and more a matter of "social instincts," that is, the shaping of wishes and expectations in ways that reduced selfishness and promoted altruism.[106] This was to be accomplished by a new ethos which valued altruism and made selfishness shameful. Such would be the creed of the new religion of humanity, which "carries the thoughts and feelings out of self, and fixes them on an unselfish object, loved and pursued as an end for its own sake."[107] Education and opinion would habituate each person to associate his own happiness with the good of others. The strengthening of social ties will "give to each individual a stronger personal interest in practically consulting the welfare of others; it also leads him to identify his *feelings* more and more with their good."[108] When this occurred the best system of morals would be in place, as everyone would have a "just regard for the good of all."[109] The result would be an end to the conflicts and selfishness of an age of transition: there would be a "sense of unity with mankind, and a deep feeling for the general good."[110]

––––––––––

Mill claimed the religion of humanity was capable of providing motivations that would make compliance with its ethical principles not a matter of heroic virtue but rather one of routine—a matter of "habitual exercise."[111] To achieve this, education was necessary, that is, moral education that shaped character and instilled the ethos of the new religion of humanity. Pointing to the example of Sparta, he held that "the power of education is almost boundless."[112]

[105] Early Draft, *CW*, *1*, 238.

[106] *Auguste Comte and Positivism*, *CW*, *10*, 310.

[107] "Utility of Religion," *CW*, *10*, 422. "Nearly every respectable attribute of humanity is the result not of instinct, but of a victory over instinct. . . . All worth of character was [at an earlier stage of existence] deemed the result of a sort of taming; a phrase often applied by the ancient philosophers to the appropriate discipline of human beings." "Nature," *CW*, *10*, 393.

[108] *Utilitarianism*, *CW*, *10*, 231.

[109] Diary, 9 April [1854], *CW*, *27*, 667.

[110] "Utility of Religion,", *CW 10*, 422. On the introduction of the term 'altruism' into England, see Brown, *Metaphysical Society*, 124; Collini, *Public Moralists*, 60–65, 69–71.

[111] "Utility of Religion," *CW*, *10*, 423.

[112] Ibid., 409.

Education of this type aimed to shape not the cognitive faculties but the feelings. The intellectual component in moral conduct was not eliminated, but the feelings and involuntary desires were given prominence. It was not enough to understand virtue; it was necessary to desire it. In addition to possessing "a clear intellectual standard of right and wrong," it was also necessary for moral education to "educate the will . . . [by] exalting to the highest pitch the desire of right conduct and the aversion to wrong."[113] The religion of humanity was designed to serve both of these functions: it will have "the twofold character of a religion, viz., as the ultimate basis of thought and the animating and controlling power over action."[114] And he had no doubt it would be effective. "If the Religion of Humanity were as sedulously cultivated as the supernatural religions are (and there is no difficulty in conceiving that it might be much more so), all who have received the customary amount of moral cultivation would up to the hour of death live ideally in the life of those who are to follow them."[115]

The science of Ethology which Mill hoped to develop also had as its goal the shaping of character, both individual and collective, and he assumed it would allow for the deliberate formation of the kind of character suitable for the religion of humanity. "When the circumstances of an individual or of a nation are in any considerable degree under our control, we may, by our knowledge of tendencies, be enabled to shape those circumstances in a manner much more favourable to the ends we desire, than the shape which they would of themselves assume."[116] According to Bain, "He was all his life possessed of the idea that differences of character, individual and national, were due to accidents and circumstances that might possibly be, in part, controlled; on this doctrine rested his chief hope in the future."[117]

Although Mill did not produce the work on ethology he had planned when completing his *System of Logic* (1843), he set out its goals in greater detail during the years that followed. Ethology, as he thought of it, was to produce the kind of character required by the religion of humanity, that is, it would form the desires so that those which were selfish would be diminished and those which were altruistic would become predominant. Since education was omnipotent: its "very pivot and turning point . . . [is] a moral sense—a feeling of duty, or conscience, or principle, or

---

[113] *Hamilton, CW,* 9, 453.
[114] Diary, 15 February [1854], *CW,* 27, 654; see also 11 March [1854], 27, 660.
[115] "Utility of Religion," *CW,* 10, 426.
[116] *Logic, CW,* 8, 869–71; see also 905.
[117] Bain, *Mill,* 79.

whatever name one gives it—a feeling that one ought to do, and to wish for, what is for the greatest good of all concerned."[118]

In all this Mill shared Comte's view about the character and function of education, though, of course, there were some differences.[119] Comte, Mill pointed out, required that motivations should be shaped so that one desired only the good of others. Moreover, he proposed that it be obligatory to seek the good of others. To these Comtean notions Mill objected. As to motivations, Mill accepted as legitimate that there would be desires for the gratification of egoistic propensities. Rather than obliterate them, Mill aimed to direct them and to provide that they not predominate. "The moralization of the personal enjoyments we deem to consist, not in reducing them to the smallest possible amount, but in cultivating the habitual wish to share them with others, and with all others, and scorning to desire anything for oneself which is incapable of being so shared."[120]

Mill also differed with Comte about it being obligatory that one seek the good of others. He accused Comte of being like Calvin, making whatever is not a duty into a sin. Mill insisted that "between the region of duty and that of sin there is an intermediate space, the region of positive worthiness. . . . There is a standard of altruism to which all should be required to come up, and a degree beyond it which is not obligatory, but meritorious."[121] Within this region, Mill would encourage altruism and hoped that it would emerge spontaneously. Meeting the minimum level of altruism and encouraging a higher amount was his conception of "the moral rule prescribed by the religion of Humanity. But above this standard there is an unlimited range of moral worth, up to the most exalted heroism, which should be fostered by every positive encouragement, though not converted into an obligation." Having distinguished his position from Comte's, however, Mill went on to endorse Comte's goal. "It is as much a part of our scheme as of M. Comte's, that the direct cultivation of altruism, and the subordination of egoism to it, far beyond the point of absolute moral duty, should be one of the chief aims of education, both individual and collective."[122]

Believing that education could inculcate morality and form character, Mill had no difficulty in dismissing supernatural religion, which commonly was assumed to have a large role in promoting these results. In

[118] Mill to Harriet Taylor, [c. 31 March 1849], CW, 14, 22.

[119] For Comte, education was to "restore . . . the sense of duty"; he provided for "a rational system of education, throughout which, even in its intellectual department, moral considerations will predominate." System of Positive Polity, 1, 260.

[120] Auguste Comte and Positivism, CW, 10, 339; see also 335–39.

[121] Ibid., 337.

[122] Ibid., 339.

"Utility of Religion" (1855) Mill cast doubt on the necessity of supernatural religion for this purpose, arguing that whereas religion received credit for generating and gaining adherence to morality, in fact, moral conduct depended upon education and public opinion. "It is usual to credit religion as such with the whole of the power inherent in any system of moral rules inculcated by education and enforced by opinion."[123] Mill concluded that the system of moral rules incorporated in a religion of humanity would be obeyed without the sanction of supernatural religion. "The sense of unity with mankind, and a deep feeling for the public good, may be cultivated into a sentiment and a principle capable of fulfilling every important function of religion . . . it [the religion of humanity] is not only capable of fulfilling these functions, but would fulfill them better than any form whatever of supernaturalism."[124]

He tried to make this argument plausible by comparing altruistic morality and patriotism. Both called for putting aside selfish concerns and acting for the good of society. Since many persons act to confer benefits on their country that will come into existence long after they are dead, "we cannot doubt that if this and similar feelings were cultivated in the same manner and degree as religion they would become a religion."[125] Mill assumed that patriotic feelings might be extended to include all of humanity. Just as patriotic emotions overcame selfishness, "the love of that larger country, the world, may be nursed into similar strength." Nor would such feelings be found only among the most eminent of the species. With cultivation, all would be capable of being moved by them.[126]

An important part of Mill's educational scheme was to cultivate reverence for secular heroes who were, in a sense, substitutes for a deity. Such persons were to be models for imitation and sources of inspiration. Moral conduct would not depend on "a problematical future existence" but on "the approbation . . . of those whom we respect, and ideally of all those, dead or living, whom we admire or venerate." These might include dead parents or friends, and "the idea that Socrates, or Howard or Washington, or Antoninus, or Christ, would have sympathized with us, or that we are attempting to do our part in the spirit in which they did theirs, has operated on the very best minds, as a strong incentive to act up to their highest feelings and convictions."[127] Other candidates for heroic status included Pericles, Marcus Aurelius, and Turgot; and among those he knew person-

---

[123] "Utility of Religion," *CW*, *10*, 407; see also 407–10.

[124] Ibid., 422.

[125] Diary, 17 March [1854], *CW*, *27*, 661.

[126] "Utility of Religion," *CW*, *10*, 420–21.

[127] Ibid., 421–22. See also Mill's comment on Gorgias where he traces love of virtue and noble feeling to admiration rather than argument. "We acquire it from those whom we love and reverence . . . from our ideal of those, whether in past or in present times, whose lives

ally, John Sterling, Armand Carrel, and, of course, Harriet Taylor Mill.[128] This theme he also shared with Comte, for whom such heroes were servants of humanity during their lifetimes and, after they died, became symbols of the pursuit of the Comtean ideal of order combined with progress. Like Comte, he also extended the object of reverence to the future; we might "sustain ourselves by the ideal sympathy of the great characters of history, or even in fiction, and by the contemplation of an idealized posterity."[129]

Jesus was especially important to Mill as a moral guide and exemplar. He was "a standard of excellence—a model for imitation." Moreover, admiration for Jesus did not require that one accept claims of his divinity. "Whatever else may be taken away from us by rational criticism, Christ is still left." He is "the ideal representative and guide of humanity; nor . . . would it be easy, even for an unbeliever, to find a better translation of the rule of virtue from the abstract into the concrete, than to endeavour so to live that Christ would approve our life." He "is available even to the absolute unbeliever and can never more be lost to humanity." Stripped of his connection with Christianity, the historical Jesus survives in Mill's thought as a hero of the religion of humanity.[130]

How would the great change take place? He knew what the ideal was, "but to discern the road to it—the series of transitions by which it must be reached . . . —is a problem."[131] He understood that while a transformation was required, it would have to be accomplished gradually. "It must be a development from the state at which we are now arrived, worked

---

and characters have been the mirror of all noble qualities." *CW, 11,* 150. On Socrates, see also Early Draft, *CW, 1,* 48, 114; "Grote's *History of Greece* [5]"(1850), *CW, 25,* 1163–64; *On Liberty, CW, 18,* 235.

[128] On Pericles, see ibid., 266. "Pericles . . . was his greatest hero of autiquity": Bain, *Mill,* 154. On Marcus Aurelius, see *On Liberty, CW, 18,* 236–37. On Sterling, see the eulogy in a letter to Comte, 5 October 1844, *Correspondence of Mill and Comte,* 257–58; in 1848 Mill intended to write a biography of Sterling. Caroline Fox, *Memories of Old Friends,* 2, 97. On Turgot, see John Morley, "The Death of Mr. Mill," *Fortnightly Review,* n.s. 13 (1 June 1873): 671. Although Mill wrote about Carrel (1800–1836) in 1837, long before his conception of a religion of humanity was fully formed, he described him in heroic terms. Although only the editor of a republican newspaper, "he was the greatest political leader of his time," and, "ripened by years and favoured by opportunity, he might have been the Mirabeau or the Washington of his age, or both in one." He "left us his memory, and his example," and his life proved that "a hero of Plutarch may exist amidst all the pettinesses of modern civilization." "Armand Carrel" (1837), *CW, 20,* 169–70, 215.

[129] *Inaugural Address, CW, 21,* 254.

[130] "Theism," *CW, 10,* 487–88. Of course Mill was familiar with Carlyle's *On Heroes, Hero-Worship, and the Heroic in History* (1841), though he did not agree with all Carlyle said. Diary, 12 February, 7 April [1854], *27,* 653, 666.

[131] Diary, 22 January [1854], *CW, 27,* 645.

out by many minds, for . . . it is a task far beyond the powers of any one." Thus it would be the effect of "the silent workings in men's minds" over a long period.[132]

During this slow development, Mill expected Christianity to have a role to play; this was unavoidable, for, weak as it was, it would not quickly disappear. "[T]here is little prospect at present [1840] that philosophy will take the place of religion." From philosophy, of course, he had learned that a secular religion promoting altruism was superior to Christianity. Yet while one could not expect philosophy to replace religion in the immediate future, or even "that any philosophy will be generally received in this country," it might make headway, if it were "supposed not only to be consistent with, but even to yield collateral support to, Christianity." This prospect increasingly dictated Mill's tactics in discussing Christianity; thus he asked, "What is the use, then, of treating with contempt the idea of a religious philosophy?"[133] This consideration led him to look for ways in which some aspects of Christianity might be combined with philosophy, that is, with his religion of humanity, which is just what he held out as a possible outcome of free discussion in chapter two of *On Liberty*. Rationally based ethics, it will be recalled, would, in this scenario, combine with admiration for Jesus as a moral exemplar though without divine status. Thus while asserting that the evidence for Christianity is "too shadowy and unsubstantial, and the promises it holds out too distant and uncertain, to admit of its being a permanent substitute for the religion of humanity," he acknowledged that "the two may be held in conjunction."[134]

In visualizing a combination of his religion of humanity with Christianity Mill clearly was not retreating from his critique of Christianity. This is evident in his looking forward to a new system of morals that "will be a development of Xtianity, *properly understood*" (emphasis added).[135] And he revealed his expectations in conversation with John Morley not long before he died: "Thinks we cannot with any sort of precision define the coming modification of religion, but anticipates that it will undoubtedly rest upon the solidarity of mankind, as Comte said, and you [Morley]

---

[132] Mill to Auberon Herbert, [29 January 1872], *CW, 32*, 235–36.

[133] "Coleridge," *CW, 10*, 160. In 1831 he writes to avoid destroying Christian belief, not because it is true, but because it gives sense of duty. *CW, 12*, 76. Cf. argument about utility of religion in chapter 3.

[134] "Utility of Religion," *CW, 10*, 425.

[135] Mill to Auberon Herbert, [29 January 1872], *CW, 32*, 235–36. In conversation in May 1840 Mill foresaw "finally a reduction of the creed of the universal Christian church to a few general articles in which all can unite and nominal distinctions be thenceforth abolished, tho' each individual be still allowed full freedom of opinion. This is the great consummation to be desired." *Barclay Fox's Journal*, ed. R. L. Brett (Totowa, N.J.: Rowman & Littlefield, 1979), 194.

and I believe."[136] This is compelling evidence that he regarded the combination as one in which Christianity would be subordinated to his religion of humanity. Meanwhile he could deny without disingenuousness that he would "willingly weaken in any person the reverence for Christ, in which I myself very strongly participate." And he could assert, "I am an enemy to no religions but those which appear to me to be injurious either to the reasoning powers or the moral sentiments."[137] Of course, he believed Christian religion had these consequences.

Given his expectations for the future development of Christianity, and ever one to trim the formulation of his arguments to serve his rhetorical and political purposes, Mill wrote "Theism," in which he offered a few small concessions to Christian believers, avoided dogmatism, did not disparage Christian belief, and sought to reduce enmity between skeptics and Christians. Unlike in eighteenth- and early nineteenth-century controversy, one could now (1868–70) observe "the more softened temper in which the debate is conducted on the part of unbelievers. . . . [T]he position assigned to Christianity or Theism by the more instructed of those who reject the supernatural, is that of things once of great value but which can now be done without; rather than, as formerly, of things misleading and noxious *ab initio* [from the beginning]."[138]

Having begun "Theism" by declaring an armistice in what had been his war against Christianity, Mill closed the essay by holding up Jesus as a hero for the religion of humanity. He was "in the very first rank of the men of sublime genius of whom our species can boast." He was, moreover, "the greatest moral reformer." Even after rational criticism has undermined theological claims, the influences of Jesus on moral character "are well worth preserving," for they are "excellently fitted to aid and fortify that real, though purely human religion, which sometimes calls itself the Religion of Humanity."[139]

It is evident that Mill anticipated dilution of Christian belief and sought to disguise his attempts to promote this outcome with praise for Jesus in terms entirely compatible with the secular religion he expected ultimately to emerge. Far from backsliding in "Theism," as dogmatic atheists charged, he was being conciliatory as a matter of tactics. This practitioner of the inherently extreme politics of cultural revolution was adopting a posture of moderation.

[136] John Morley, "The Death of Mr. Mill," *Fortnightly Review*, n.s. 13 (1 June 1873): 676.
[137] Mill to Arthur W. Greene, 16 December 1861, CW, *15*, 754; see above, 102.
[138] " Theism," *CW*, *10*, 429.
[139] Ibid., 487–88.

Mill's quest for a religion of humanity in which altruism prevailed led to his sympathizing with socialism. Socialism he defined as a system of cooperative production which involved "the association of the labourers themselves on terms of equality, collectively owning the capital with which they carry on their operations, and working under managers elected and removable by themselves."[140] Such a system would "cut up by the root the present partial distribution of social advantages, and would enable the produce of industry to be shared." There would be less inequality, though not necessarily complete equality. He was puzzled as to why the prospect of socialism provoked so much "frantic terror."[141] But Mill was not frightened, and his sympathy for it developed in spite of his having been taught the doctrines of political economy which emphasized the value of private property, markets, and competition.

Since Mill believed equality to be ethically compelling, he was impatient with all indications of its absence—with what he called the "unjust distribution of social advantages."[142] The poor as well as women were victims of this injustice, and moral regeneration required the elimination of inequities. Bain, after many conversations on this matter, reported that Mill believed in "the natural equality of human beings in regard of capacity," and Bain thought him dogmatic on this issue and blind to empirical evidence that might suggest the need to qualify his opinion. "This region of observation must have been to him an utter blank."[143] This opinion long preceded publication of *Subjection of Women*, and it shows up in his disapproval of society being divided into the idle and the industrious, his objection to the inheritance of great wealth (286), and his agreement with Comte that the idle rich ought to be eliminated—this was "destined to be one of the constitutive principles of regenerated society."[144]

> As I look upon inequality as *in itself* always an evil [he wrote], I do not agree with any one who would use the machinery of society for the purpose of promoting it. As much inequality as necessarily arises from protecting all persons in the free use of their faculties of body & mind & in the enjoyment of what these can obtain for them, must be submitted to for the sake of a greater good: but I certainly see no necessity for artificially adding to it, while I see much for

[140] *Political Economy*, CW, 3, 775. See also *Subjection of Women*, CW, 21, 294: "The true virtue of human beings is fitness to live together as equals."
[141] "Vindication of the French Revolution of February 1848," CW, 20, 352.
[142] Ibid., 351.
[143] Bain, *Mill*, 84, and also 131, 146.
[144] Early Draft, CW, 1, 238; *Auguste Comte and Positivism*, CW, 10, 347. He looked forward to "putting an end to the division of society into the industrious and the idle." *Political Economy*, CW, 3, 793.

tempering it, impressing both on the laws & on the usages of mankind as far as possible the contrary tendency.[145]

Thus it is no surprise that for Mill "the art of living with others consists first and chiefly in treating and being treated by them as equals."[146]

With this belief about equality, Mill naturally was critical of private property as a major source of inequality and was sympathetic with the idea of workers' cooperatives, as they aimed to overcome it.[147] "It appears to us," Mill concluded, "that nothing valid can be said against socialism in principle; and that the attempts to assail it, or to defend private property, on the ground of justice, must inevitably fail."[148]

Mill's critique of inequality extended to competition, which was responsible for "arming one human being against another, making the good of each depend upon evil to others, making all who have anything to gain or lose, live as in the midst of enemies."[149] This opinion was shared with Harriet Mill, who, as already noted, believed that competition was one of the "fruitful sources of selfishness and misery."[150] And it was introduced into the well-known chapter on the stationary state in the *Political Economy*:

> I confess I am not charmed with the ideal of life held out by those who think that the normal state of human beings is that of struggling to get on; that the trampling, crushing, elbowing, and treading on each other's heels, which form the existing type of social life, are the most desirable lot of human kind, or anything but the disagreeable symptoms of one of the phases of industrial progress.[151]

Mill concluded that "the best for human nature is that in which, while no one is poor, no one desires to be richer, nor has any reason to fear being thrust back by the efforts of others to push themselves forward."[152]

Mill's strong sympathies for socialism had affinities with his religion of humanity: both regarded selfish individualism as a major source of society's ills, and both sought to establish an ethos that countered such selfishness. He shared with many socialists their critique of established

---

[145] Mill to Arthur Helps, [1847?], *CW*, *17*, 2002.

[146] Ibid., 2001. Cf. Comte: *Auguste Comte and Positivism*, *CW*, *10*, 304. For "the English, of all ranks and classes, . . . the very idea of equality is strange and offensive to them." Mill to Giuseppe Mazzini, 15 April 1858, *CW*, *15*, 553.

[147] Early Draft, *CW*, *1*, 238; Mill to Frederick J. Furnivall, 19 November 1850, *CW*, *14*, 50; Mill to Peter Deml, 22 April 1868, *CW*, *16*, 1389; *Political Economy*, *CW*, *2*, 201–14.

[148] "Newman's Politcal Economy," *CW*, *5*, 444.

[149] Ibid.

[150] Harriet Taylor, "An Early Essay," Hayek, *Mill and Harriet Taylor*, 279.

[151] *Political Economy*, *CW*, *3*, 754.

[152] Ibid.

institutions and values, but here his approval stopped. French socialists, he explained, "have generally very wide and silly notions and little that one can sympathize with except the spirit and feelings which actuate them."[153] Consequently he accepted much of their critique of existing society but not their remedy. "Socialism, as long as it attacks the existing individualism, is easily triumphant; its weakness hitherto is in what it proposes to substitute. The reasonable objections to socialism are altogether practical, consisting in difficulties to be surmounted, and in the insufficiency of any scheme yet promulgated to provide against them."[154]

When he specified his objections in a work on socialism which he was working on during his last years, he criticized socialists for being ignorant of economic facts and for not understanding political economy.[155] Mill recognized the many varieties of socialism—British and French, revolutionary and moderate, Proudon's and Fourier's, small, communitarian and large, centrally organized—and he regarded the remedies proposed by all of them as problematic. Among other things, he thought they could not provide adequate incentives—what he called "motives to exertion."[156] Also, and even more objectionable, socialist schemes were too managing and paternalistic and incompatible with liberty and individuality.

> In Communist associations private life would be brought in a most unexampled degree within the dominion of public authority, and there would be less scope for the development of individual character and individual preferences than has hitherto existed among the full citizens of any state belonging to the progressive branches of the human family.[157]

Related arguments were included in *On Liberty*, where he offered objections to government interference even in cases not involving infringements of liberty. Individuals will perform most activities better than government, as they are more interested in the outcome; moreover, mental education will be improved if citizens rely on themselves rather than on government; and finally, the power of government ought not be expanded unnecessarily (305–6).[158]

Mill's combination of approval for socialist goals and skepticism about its practical means was abundantly evident in his *Principles of Political Economy*, even as, with revisions, he tilted the balance more favorably to socialism. His criticisms of inequalities and poverty were very evident; yet

[153] Mill to Henry Samuel Chapman, 28 May 1849, CW, *14*, 33.
[154] "Newman's Political Economy," CW, *5*, 444.
[155] "Chapters on Socialism," CW, *5*, 727.
[156] Ibid., 739–43.
[157] Ibid., 746.
[158] These arguments were presented more elaborately in *Political Economy*, book V, chap. 11. CW, 3, 936–71.

he also valiantly defended what he called the competitive principle for being an obstacle to monopoly and an engine of increased productivity. However, in the third edition, many criticisms of contemporary socialist proposals were deleted and "replaced by arguments and reflexions of a decidedly socialistic tendency."[159]

Attracted to socialism, yet aware of its limitations, Mill reconciled these views by invoking his theory of history. Criticisms of socialism were valid, not as statements of ethical theory, but as judgments based on acceptance of present realities which were historically contingent and, in the large scheme of things, transitory. Intense competitiveness was ethically objectionable but perhaps one of the unavoidable "disagreeable symptoms of one of the phases of industrial progress." One endures such symptoms but does "not accept the present very early stage of human improvement as its ultimate type."[160] Thus political economy had limited value, for it was based on assumptions about institutions and motivations that were not necessarily permanent features of human life. This, however, "does not take away the value of the propositions, considered with reference to the state of Society from which they were drawn."[161]

Mill had two different judgments on these matters, depending on whether he looked at them in the context of existing conditions or from a perspective located in a distant future when transformation of such conditions will have taken place. Thus, "the competition of the market may represent a practical necessity, but certainly not a moral ideal."[162] And "the *laissez faire* doctrine, stated without large qualifications, is both unpractical and unscientific; but it does not follow that those who assert it are not, nineteen times out of twenty, practically nearer the truth than those who deny it."[163]

Such statements show Mill thoroughly grounded, even if not comfortable or satisfied, in the present realities. But they coexisted in his outlook with others that arose from his utopian wish to visualize the transformation of the present into a radically different historical stage of society that would be organic rather than transitional. Thus he was open to socialist experiments that might discover new directions for social and economic

---

[159] Early Draft, *CW, 1*, 240.

[160] *Political Economy, CW, 3*, 754.

[161] *Logic, CW, 8*, 904. For a comprehensive discussion of Mill on socialism, see Samuel Hollander, *The Economics of John Stuart Mill* (Toronto: University of Toronto Press, 1985), 2, 770–824. While Hollander recognizes Mill's openness to alternative institutional arrangements, he emphasizes Mill's caution and therefore attributes much less significance to his socialism than to his acceptance of existing arrangements which required private property and competition (774–76).

[162] *Auguste Comte and Positivism, CW, 10*, 341.

[163] Ibid., 303. These statements make it untenable to assert that "Mill is an unequivocal defender of a market economy." see Nicholas Capaldi, "John Stuart Mill's Defence of Liberal Culture," *Political Science Reviewer* 24 (1995): 239.

development, and he made statements favorable to socialism as it might be in the distant future when selfishness, which under present circumstances made socialist proposals impractical, will have disappeared, to be replaced by a regenerated moral character.[164] Thus he said Comte's political views were mischievous, "except *qua* socialist, that is, calling for an entire renovation of social institutions and doctrines, in which respect I am entirely at one with him."[165]

Having both criticized and expressed sympathy for socialism, he was bound to believe that he was misunderstood when interpreters seized on one side of the argument about the merits of socialism. When a translator of the *Political Economy* into German introduced his work as a refutation of socialism, Mill protested. "I certainly was far from intending that the statement it contained of the objections to the best known Socialist schemes should be understood as a condemnation of Socialism regarded as an ultimate result of human improvement."[166] In saying this, he showed himself to be, in his own mind, as much a visionary as a realist, that is, one who assumed that changes sufficient to allow socialism to become practical might well occur. Thus he said, "I look forward to alterations extending to many more, and more important points than the relation between masters and workmen: I should not expect much practical benefit from a modification of that single relation, without changes fully as great in existing opinions and institutions on religious moral and domestic subjects."[167] He also looked forward "to changes in the present opinions on the limits of the right of property and which contemplate possibilities, as to the springs of human action in economical matters."[168] Thus Mill was justified in saying that he had moved, "so far as regards the ultimate prospects of humanity, to a qualified Socialism"; and, in a stronger statement, in which he spoke for his wife as well as himself, "our ideal of future improvement was such as would class us decidedly under the general designation of Socialists."[169]

Mill in much of what he wrote as philosopher, political theorist, and even as economist, was involved in a religious project. He claimed that his plan for moral reform would create a religion, though one that was secular, and that it was superior to supernatural religions, including Christianity.

---

[164] "Chapters on Socialism," *CW*, *5*, 749–50.

[165] Mill to John Pringle Nichol, 30 September 1848, *CW*, *13*, 739.

[166] Mill to Dr. Adolf Soetheer, 18 March 1852, *CW*, *14*, 85. The same argument appears in Mill to John Jay, [November 1848], *CW*, *13*, 740–41.

[167] Mill to unidentified correspondent, 9 June 1851, *CW*, *14*, 70.

[168] Yale Fragment of autobiography, *CW*, *1*, 256.

[169] *Autobiography*, *CW*, *1*, 199; Early Draft, *CW*, *1*, 238.

In keeping with these claims, he insisted that he—and other nonbeliev-ers—had religious feelings.

> If a person has an ideal object, his attachment and sense of duty towards which are able to control and discipline all his other sentiments and propensities, and prescribe to him a rule of life, that person has a religion: and though every one naturally prefers his own religion to any other, all must admit that if the object of this attachment, and of this feeling of duty, is the aggregate of our fellow-creatures, this Religion of the Infidel cannot, in honesty and conscience, be called an intrinsically bad one.[170]

Consequently, Mill was indignant against the *Weekly Dispatch* for as-serting that skeptics believed nothing. "I affirm that nearly all the persons I have known who were, and are, eminently distinguished by a passion for the good of mankind, hold the opinions respecting religion which your article stigmatizes, that is, that nothing can be known on the subject."[171] He explained that Christians were not the only ones to uphold charity and good actions, for "this is also the fundamental doctrine of those who are called Atheists. . . . Honesty, self sacrifice, love of our fellow-crea-tures, and the desire to be of use in the world, constitute the true point of resemblance between those whose religion however overlaid with dogma is genuine, and those who are genuinely religious without any dogmas at all."[172] Confident and self-justifying, he went even further in saying that the best of the unbelievers "are more genuinely religious, in the best sense of the word religion, than those who exclusively arrogate to themselves the title."[173]

Mill seems to have had a religious temperament that came into conflict with the conclusions of his reasoning. To Carlyle he wrote that he had "the strongest wish to believe" but acknowledged he was without faith.[174] Bain recognized that he was "at bottom a religious man."[175] In these cir-cumstances, the religious dimension of his thought was temperamentally congenial, for he tended to define his own role in religious terms. Once again one recalls his claim that by subscribing to Bentham's doctrines he

---

[170] *Auguste Comte and Positivism*, CW, *10*, 333.

[171] "Religious Sceptics," unpublished letter to *Weekly Dispatch*, [1 February 1851], CW, *25*, 1182–83.

[172] Mill to Thornes Dyke Acland, 1 December 1868, CW, *16*, 1499.

[173] Early Draft, CW, *1*, 46; see also "Utility of Religion," CW, *10*, 422.

[174] Mill to Thornes Carlyle, 12 January 1834, CW, *12*, 206.

[175] Bain, *Mill*, 139–40. Crimmins has noted that Bentham, as well as Comte and Mill, thought of his intellectual project in religious terms. *Secular Utilitarianism*, 286–88. Cowl-ing has also emphasized Mill's bent for proselytizing, his theological interest, and the reli-gious dimension of his thought. *Mill and Liberalism*, 77, 81, 87, 93. According to Élie Halévy, Mill was religious by nature; referred to by Karl W. Britton, "John Stuart Mill on Christianity," in James and John Stuart Mill. Papers of the Centenary Conference, ed. J. M. Robson, Michael Laine (Toronto: University of Toronto Press, 1976), 33.

had acquired a creed and a religion, and on that and other occasions, as after more than one encounter with Comtean ideas, he experienced what appeared to be conversions. Bain noted that his religion of humanity had features that made it "a real analogue of religion."[176] He also possessed, according to Morley, the "ingenuous moral ardour" that is associated with some religious temperaments.[177] And Connop Thirlwall noted, "People who only knew him by his literary character supposed him to be a man of cool temperament. He is evidently . . . a man of vehemently passionate susceptibility. The snow covers a volcano."[178]

The specific role Mill sought for himself in his religious project was limited by the need to face the fact that the religion of humanity would be in place only in the distant, even remote, future. He experienced "the misfortune of having been born and being doomed to live in almost the infancy of human improvement." In these circumstances, at most he could only do something "towards helping on the slow but quickening progress towards that ultimate consummation."[179] Thus he worked to hasten the demise of the existing obsolete, transitional society (and this was how *On Liberty* was to serve his plan of moral reform), but beyond this, he described his vision of the new religion and the kind of society it would sponsor. "To see the futurity of the species" was his (and Harriet Taylor Mill's) task.[180] "My own work lies rather among anticipations of the future," he explained.[181] It may seem farfetched to those who think of him as the exemplar of cold, detached rationality, but in visualizing a utopian future, Mill cast himself in the role of prophet, and in 1854, when he was expecting to die from lung disease, he wondered whether in future ages he would be remembered as a benefactor to humanity.[182]

---

[176] Bain, *Mill*, 139–40.

[177] "The Death of Mr. Mill," *Fortnightly Review*, n.s. 13 (1 June 1873): 671.

[178] Letter of 19 November 1868, *Letters to a Friend by Connop Thirlwall, late lord bishop of St. David's*, ed. Arthur Penryn Stanley (London, 1881), 171. Fredrick Harrison used the same metaphor in describing Mill: *Tennyson, Ruskin, Mill*, 298. Caroline Fox in 1840 noted it "a new thing for John Mill to sympathize with religious characters; some years since, he had so imbibed the errors which his father instilled into him, as to be quite a bigot against religion." *Memories of Old Friends*, 1, 213.

[179] Diary, 14 April [1854], *CW*, 27, 668.

[180] *Subjection of Women*, *CW*, 21, 294.

[181] Mill to Pasquale Villari, 28 February 1872, *CW* 17, 1873.

[182] Diary, 15 April [1854], *CW*, 27, 668.

Chapter Seven

INDIVIDUALITY AND MORAL REFORM

> . . . individuality should assert itself. Where, not the person's own character, but the traditions or customs of other people are the rule of conduct, there is wanting one of the principal ingredients of human happiness, and quite the chief ingredient of individual and social progress.
>
> *(John Stuart Mill [261])*

MILL'S CELEBRATION of individuality in chapter three of *On Liberty* is passionate and compelling. He presents a picture of a free-spirited, independent person with a distinctive personality who lives in accordance with original and worthy ideas and values. The person with individuality is spontaneous, original, and makes choices in accordance with strong desires that reflect individual character rather than with what is fashionable or customary. Such a person, moreover, is courageous and thus not afraid to defy society. Of course Mill believed that these qualities of individuality were inherently valuable. He indicates that individual spontaneity had "intrinsic worth" and deserved "regard on its own account" (261). And he argued that individuality allowed for the greatest development of human qualities—"it brings human beings themselves nearer to the best thing they can be" (267). Human nature, after all, was more like a tree than a machine, and thus it ought "to grow and develope [sic] itself on all sides, according to the tendency of the inward forces which make it a living thing." (263)

Mill celebrated individuality, however, less for its intrinsic value than for its usefulness in helping bring about distant and (in the largest sense of the word) political ends. The few statements upholding it for its inherent value are greatly outnumbered by the many passages emphasizing its instrumental value. Those with individuality were to contribute to society and this they were to do by criticizing and undermining existing society which was still in the transitional state and also by promoting the emergence of a new organic society. Thus, while for Mill individuality as he described it was his ideal of character, his portrayal of it in chapter three of *On Liberty* included attributes that would allow those with this kind of character to contribute to the implementation of his plan for moral reform. Some of the features of individuality would be useful during the first, destructive phase of his plan, and others would be valuable during the reconstruction that was supposed to follow. Like Mill himself, those with individuality were engaged on two fronts, simultaneously tearing down and building up, acting progressively and conservatively, serving the goals of Bentham and of Coleridge, of progress and of permanence.

That Mill thought of those with individuality as doing the things required to bring about moral and cultural transformation is indicated in an obscurely placed but clear passage in chapter three in which he identifies the functions they were to perform.

> There is always need of persons not only to discover new truths, and point out when what were once truths are true no longer, but also to commence new practices, and set the example of more enlightened conduct, and better taste and sense in human life. (267)

Here Mill specifies three things that must be done to implement his plan for moral transformation. To identify beliefs that were once true but which were no longer true was the task of freethinkers and atheists who were to be liberated to take part in the free discussion of Christianity as outlined in chapter two of *On Liberty*. They were also to cast doubt on beliefs that validated customs and traditions which might have been suitable in an earlier age but which no longer were useful. Having undermined the old and established but no longer serviceable beliefs, the possessors of individuality were also to discover new ethical beliefs to replace the old ones. Mill's defense of altruism and his speculations that led to his radically revised conception of utilitarianism were part of this project. And, finally, by having those with individuality develop new practices, Mill provided for the incorporation of the new ethical beliefs into a cultural and institutional setting. Or, as he put it elsewhere, there was one thing "all good customs presuppose—that there must have been individuals better than the rest, who set the customs going."[1] His new religion of humanity was intended to achieve this goal. By specifying these three tasks for those with individuality, Mill made it clear that individuality, attractive as it was as a type of character, gained its greatest significance by performing these functions which were necessary to move history forward.

This account of Mill's conception of individuality—emphasizing that it was much more than an ideal of character and that it called upon those who possessed it to lead the way toward a transformation of moral values and social institutions—should be consistent with the understanding of

[1] "Nature," *CW, 10,* 394.

individuality put forth by William Maccall, whom Mill identified as one who anticipated what he had to say in *On Liberty.* "The doctrine of Individuality had been enthusiastically asserted, in a stile of vigorous declamation sometimes reminding one of Fichte, by Mr. William Maccall, in a series of writings of which the most elaborate is entitled *Elements of Individualism* [1847]."[2]

Maccall (1812–1888) lived on the margins of intellectual life as a lecturer, pamphleteer, and contributor to newspapers. Earlier he had been a Unitarian minister, having embraced Unitarianism following a period of youthful religious skepticism. He was acquainted with Carlyle and Mill, both of whom, holding him in some respect, tried to encourage and help him, in Mill's case by introducing him to London editors. At the end of the century when the *Dictionary of National Biography* was being prepared, he was regarded as worthy of inclusion.[3]

Maccall's ideas do not coincide with Mill's, but there are striking affinities between them. In using the term "individuality," rather than individualism, Maccall already set himself apart, for while the word had long been in use, it was anything but commonplace. He spoke of the "Individuality of the Individual" and thought of it as invigorating the will, and as self-development, which is achieved "when the Individual is faithfullest to his Individual Nature."[4] Maccall's individuality, like Mill's, was at war with Conventionalism and also with selfishness, cowardice, prejudice, and habit. Opposition to convention led to spontaneity and diversity (called multiformity) which, however, would be compatible with unity in the future.[5] Maccall's conception of individuality, moreover, was anything but individualistic, for, like Mill's, it emphasized responsibility to others and it rejected isolation and selfishness. He regarded humans as sympathetic beings, that is, as capable of altruism. His was "the most social of all Systems," and he held that "the more faithful an Individual is to his Individual Nature, the more he develops his social nature." The individual and humanity, he also said, "should be one, not torn asunder and mutilated for the sake of each other as they have usually been."[6]

[2] *Autobiography, CW, 1,* 260.

[3] *Dictionary of National Biography,* 12, 434. Biographical details can also be found in William Maccall, *Elements of Individualism: A Series of Lectures* (London, 1847), 14–16; David Alec Wilson, *Carlyle to Threescore-and-Ten* (London: K. Paul, Trench, Trubner & Co., 1929), 10–11, 342; *Carlyle at His Zenith* (London: K. Paul, Trench, Trubner & Co., 1927), 65–67.

[4] William Maccall, *The Outlines of Individualism: A Lecture delivered at the John Street Institution, London, On the 16th of October, 1853* (London, 1853), 3, 7; *Elements,* 103, Mill very likely saw *Outlines,* for, though he mentioned *Elements,* he also referred to "a series of writings" by Maccall.

[5] Ibid., 4–7, 9, 214, and see also 318.

[6] Ibid., 8, 96–97, 110, 113. Cf. Burke on the danger that "the commonwealth itself would . . . crumble away, be disconnected into the dust and powder of individuality, and at length

Maccall also shared Mill's estimate of Christianity. He rejected supernaturalism and condemned Christianity, as "it changes Society into an arid and joyless thing." It was also "eminently hostile to the best interests of mankind," and therefore, "To Christianity . . . Individualism proclaims eternal war."[7] He even called himself "the leader of the Heretics."[8] In any case, Christianity "is drawing to a close. We are now entering on the Moral Phase of Humanity's Growth," and thus the Doctrine of Individuality was his "substitute for a dying or dead Christianity."[9]

These ideas provided the context for Maccall's ambition to usher in a "moral and spiritual reformation of Society."[10] He looked forward to millions of persons being "so transformed morally, so transformed religiously, [that they] are the materials for a future Community in which should prevail what I call Pantheistic Harmony."[11] Thus he called himself a "Prophet of Individuality," seeking, like Socrates and Jesus, "a grand spiritual revolution."[12]

Indications that Mill thought of those with individuality as being responsible for the undermining of existing beliefs and institutions and promoting the emergence of a new, harmonious, organic society can be found in his specific descriptions of this type of character. On the negative side, they would be critical and skeptical in the struggle against established, obsolete beliefs and institutions. Thus those with individuality were to be nonconformists, ignoring customs and social pressures that arose from mass opinion. By their "example of nonconformity, the mere refusal to

----

dispersed to all the winds of heaven." *Reflections on the Revolution in France* (1790), ed. Thomas H. D. Mahoney (Indianapolis: Bobbs-Merrill, 1955) 109.

[7] *Outlines*, 4, 10, 12, 25.

[8] William Maccall, *The Song of Songs* (London, 1862), 16–17.

[9] *Outlines* 3, 12–13.

[10] *Elements*, iv.

[11] *Outlines*, 9. It is noteworthy that the other person to whom Mill acknowledged indebtedness for ideas used in *On Liberty*, Josiah Warren, also combined a belief in individualism with a search for social cohesion and unity that would be compatible with individualism. From Warren Mill took the phrase "the sovereignty of the individual." *Autobiography*, *CW*, 1, 261; and Warren also assumed his anarchism would issue in cooperation and harmony. Josiah Warren, *Equitable Commerce* (1852), 22, 26, 99, 100, 103, 106.

[12] *Elements*, 346, 348. There were other similarities; like Mill, Maccall contrasted established Christianity with the teachings of Jesus; and he contrasted Voltaire and Rousseau much as Mill did Bentham and Coleridge. In spite of their affinities, Maccall gave *On Liberty* a critical review, dated October 1859 and reprinted in *New Materialism* (London, 1873), 10–18, in which he suggested plagiarism: "Mr. Mill is never directly or consciously a plagiary; but he is only a higher kind of compiler, and his brain has prodigious facility and rapidity of appropriation and assimilation. This is not exactly theft, as the article which came to him with much warmth and colour, contrives in his hands completely to lose both. It is of course not known to Mr. Mill that any one in England every zealously promulgated the doctrine of Individuality before." Ibid., 17.

bend the knee to custom, is itself a service," for it helps break through "the tyranny of opinion" (269). Such persons represent the progressive principle and therefore will resist "the sway of Custom" (272).

On the positive side, such persons were to be bold, inventive, exploratory in seeking new ideas and new practices. Thus in the quest for new truths, those with individuality would display originality (262, 267, 268), even genius (268, 269), and they would employ all their faculties (262) while open-mindedly exploring new possibilities. When they turned to the parallel task—to "commence new practices, and set the example of more enlightened conduct" (267)—those with individuality engaged in experiments in living (261). In searching for new modes of conduct, they made reasoned and discriminating choices instead of following custom or imitating others (262–63). In this search they were animated by strong desires and impulses (263–64), great mental vigor (269), and much energy (262, 263). In setting an example and innovating, far from being unobtrusive, to have an impact, they had to be assertive (266), even eccentric (269), and this required that they also be unafraid, bold, and morally courageous (269). They were, moreover, to be determined and purposeful. Once a course of action is chosen, the person with individuality will display "firmness and self-control to hold to his deliberate decision" (263). With these qualities, such persons will be the opposite of inert (262), imitative (262), indolent (263), passive (263), narrow (265), weak in feelings or energy (272); and especially they will not be "starved specimens of what nature can and will produce" (263). On the contrary, they would stand out as having distinctive characters (264).

The attributes of individuality—both those serving the undermining task and that of reconstruction—were necessary for the leaders of the moral and social transformation Mill sought. This does not mean that all those with individuality would be engaged in cultural politics. Some had the necessary qualities but only to a moderate degree, and others might choose other ways of life or have other goals (John Sterling, for example).[13] But among those with individuality—in any case, "a small minority" (267)—a few would serve as a vanguard seeking social transformation. Those who did this in past ages—Socrates, Plato, Jesus, for example—were heroic figures in Mill's religion of humanity.

Clearly there was a moral qualification for those who played this role. Their goal was to discourage, suppress, eliminate selfishness, and therefore they spurned this attribute in their own conduct and promoted its opposite in others. This creates a direct link between them and Mill's revised utilitarianism, which included the claim that helping others pro-

---

[13] Without naming him, John Sterling was eulogized in these terms in Mill to Comte, 5 October 1844, *Correspondence Mill and Comte*, 257–58.

vided a greater quality of happiness than merely helping oneself. Therefore there is a close affinity between those with individuality, who form the vanguard leading the way to the moral transformation of society, and those who lived in accordance with Mill's revised utilitarianism, namely, those who recognized the superiority of the higher pleasures over those that were low, self-indulgent, and piglike.[14] Among the higher pleasures in Mill's revised utilitarianism he included the quest for the greatest happiness: "the happiness which forms the utilitarian standard of what is right in conduct, is not the agent's own happiness, but that of all concerned."[15] Thus the person who experienced the highest pleasure—who came closest to meeting Mill's revised utilitarian standard—conducted himself with sensitiveness and thoughtfulness, displayed sympathy with others and "social feeling," and such a person would wish for "harmony between his feelings and aims and those of his fellow creatures."[16] He also "cultivated a fellow-feeling with the collective interests of mankind."[17] This theme in *Utilitarianism* makes it altogether suitable that Mill included clear allusions to the religion of humanity in that work.[18] And the linkage between the persons seeking higher pleasures (in *Utilitarianism*) and those with individuality of character (in *On Liberty*) is confirmed by noting that in *On Liberty*, as in *Utilitarianism*, this person promoted "strengthening the tie which binds every individual to the race" (266), that is, such a person promoted altruism and the religion of humanity. *Utilitarianism* thus provided an account of the morality that drives those with individuality of character and which was promoted by them, and it also elaborated on Mill's account of the qualities of character that made those with individuality eligible to lead the struggle for moral and social transformation.

In addition to their moral qualities, such leaders of cultural transformation also needed to have intellectual distinction: those with "more pronounced individuality . . . stand on the higher eminences of thought" (269). Elsewhere he alluded to their being in the "speculative class."[19] While such distinction was necessary, clearly not all intellectuals qualified, as Mill made clear by his disdain for most contemporary writers. He heaped derision on "that very feeble and poor minded set of people, taken generally, the writers of this country." Instead of rejecting existing society and paving the way to future transformation, they pretended to be "an aristocracy of scribblers, dividing social importance with the other aris-

---

[14] On the similarities between the person with individuality and the person appreciating higher pleasures in *Utilitarianism*, see G. W. Smith, "The Logic of J. S. Mill on Freedom," *Political Studies* 28 (1980): 250.

[15] *Utilitarianism*, CW, 10, 218; see also 213.

[16] Ibid., 233.

[17] Ibid., 215.

[18] Ibid., 218.

[19] *Auguste Comte and Positivism*, 314.

tocracies, or rather receiving it from them and basking in their beams."[20] On another occasion he explained, "I set no value whatever on writing for its own sake and have much less respect for the literary craftsman than for the manual labourer except so far as he uses his powers in promoting what I consider true and just. . . . there is already an abundance, not to say superabundance, of writers who are able to express in an effective manner the mischievous commonplaces which they have got to say."[21] This depreciatory judgment of most intellectuals was introduced into *On Liberty*, where he noted that for the mass of the people, "Their thinking is done for them by men much like themselves, addressing them or speaking in their name, on the spur of the moment, through the newspapers" (269).

In contrast to the common run of intellectuals, those in the vanguard were to have advanced opinions and to be in advance of their age. This allowed them to anticipate a future transformation and prepare for it. In *On Liberty* he identified such persons as those on behalf of whom he was pleading—"those who have been in advance of society in thought and feeling" (222). Mill, it will be recalled, thought his special contribution as a member of the speculative class was to anticipate the future. In making this claim he identified with the small group whose political role he laid out in chapter three of *On Liberty*, and it is difficult to avoid noticing that several of the attributes of those with individuality of character describe Mill himself, notably "the most passionate love of virtue, and the sternest self-control" (264). His claim for such persons was made even more explicitly in *Subjection of Women*, where he seems to have alluded to Harriet Taylor Mill. Anticipation of the future "has always been the privilege of the intellectual elite . . . to have the feelings of that futurity has been the distinction, and usually the martyrdom, of a still rarer elite."[22]

The achievements of such persons could be spectacular, for they were the prophets of a new, radically different ethos. Those with exceptional character could have a determining, formative influence, either as practical organizers or as speculative thinkers, especially the latter. "Those who introduce new speculative thoughts or great practical conceptions into the world, cannot have their epoch fixed beforehand," that is, they will be recognized and appreciated only in the distant future, since the detailed features of the future society cannot be known ahead of time. Such persons determine "whether there shall be any progress." He offered the

---

[20] Diary, 12 February [1854], *CW*, 27, 653.

[21] Mill to the Secretary of the Neophyte Writers' Society, 23 April 1854, *CW*, 14, 205. He also said, "I have on most of the subjects interesting to mankind, opinions to which I attach importance and which I earnestly desire to diffuse; but I am not desirous of aiding the diffusion of opinions contrary to my own."

[22] *Subjection of Women*, *CW*, 21, 294.

examples of Confucius, Lycurgus, Socrates, Plato, Christ, and St. Paul.[23] Such persons were among "the more intelligent and active minded few," and without such persons, he explained, there would have been no Reformation, no Commonwealth, and no Revolution of 1688, and, he must have thought, no religion of humanity.[24]

Although Mill was defining a role for such intellectuals in the grand politics of cultural transformation and was not drawing on an established tradition of writing about the intelligentsia, there are similarities between his design and some late twentieth-century accounts of the way intellectuals visualize their own character. In the modern self-image they are often portrayed as being outsiders, rebellious, oppressed by society, antibourgeois, agnostic, heretical, original, opposed to custom and tradition, and believing themselves the bearers of superior moral values. Given this affinity, Mill's speculative thinker can be regarded as a prototype of what emerged as a distinguishable social type in the twentieth century.

Among Mill's contemporaries, Harriet Taylor Mill was one whom he regarded as having the qualities of individuality. The similarity between Mill's language while eulogizing his wife and while praising individuality as the highest type of human character suggests that he may have modeled his account of individuality on her. She had great originality, even genius. Harriet also was independent-minded—in her there was "complete emancipation from every kind of superstition," including that of religion.[25] She herself boasted about living among people who were "like myself absolute unbelievers." Freedom from religious belief, which she had achieved, was necessary for individuality of character. As she explained, "I do not believe that lofty character is in these times consistent with the utter prostration or indolence of intellect requisite for belief in the low puerilities which now usurp the name of religion."[26] She also had "strength of noble and elevated feeling," which made her unselfish—as Mill put it, she "thoroughly identified . . . with the feelings of others." In addition, Mill attributed "deep and strong feeling" to her, employing language similar to that used for the person with individuality—strong "desires and impulses" (263).[27] (Carlyle described her as "veevid.")[28] And she possessed the dis-

---

[23] *Logic, CW, 8,* 938–39.

[24] Mill to John Chapman, 6 June 1851, *CW, 14,* 68.

[25] Early Draft, *CW, 1,* 192, 194. "Who can tell how many of the most original thoughts put forth by male writers, belong to a woman by suggestion, to themselves only by verifying and working out? If I may judge by my own case, a very large proportion indeed." *Subjection of Women, CW, 21,* 316.

[26] Draft, Harriet Taylor to Arthur Helps, [1847?], *CW, 17,* 2001 n.

[27] Early Draft, *CW, 1,* 192, 194.

[28] Bain, *Mill,* 169 n.

tinctive character of the person with individuality: she had "an air of natural distinction, felt by all who approached her."[29]

Mill attributed to her attitudes and ambitions similar to those which made persons possessing individuality useful as instruments for the implementation of his plan for moral transformation. Like them, she complained about "the monstrous evils and immoralities of our social system."[30] He also noted that her thought "was high and bold in its anticipation for a remote futurity," that is, in thought and feeling she was in advance of her age. Alluding even more clearly to the attributes of individuality, he said she was "like all the wisest and best of mankind," that is, she was among those who were "dissatisfied with human life as it is and whose feelings are wholly identified with its radical amendment."[31] Thus she possessed the features of mind and character that allowed her to visualize the future, for she had "entire faith in the ultimate possibilities of human nature [which] was drawn from her own glorious character," and this was reflected in her quest for "perfect distributive justice as the final aim, implying therefore a state of society entirely communist in practice and spirit, whether also in institutions or not."[32] This aspect of her outlook led Mill to speak vehemently when describing her as an "apostle of progress," a role he also ascribed to those with individuality.[33] Thus she was the "source of a great part of all that I have attempted to do, or hope to effect hereafter for human improvement."[34]

———

The liberation of those with individuality—those similar in character to Harriet Taylor Mill—was powerfully advocated in chapter three of *On Liberty*. Already in chapter two of *On Liberty* Mill argued that such persons should be free to point out that certain widely held beliefs were untrue. Now in chapter three he tried to undermine the obstacles to the discovery of new beliefs and the development of new practices. Neither in chapter two nor in chapter three did Mill connect the liberation of atheists and those with individuality with the implementation of the plan

---

[29] Early Draft, *CW*, *1*, 192. Mill's reverence is comparable to Comte's for Clotilde, and his analysis of Comte's appreciation of Clotilde seems applicable to his own feelings about Harriet Taylor. Comte "formed a passionate attachment to a lady whom he describes as uniting everything which is morally with much that is intellectually admirable, and his relation to whom, besides the direct influence of her character upon his own, gave him an insight into the true sources of human happiness, which changed his whole conception of life. . . . the adoration of her memory survived, and became . . . the type of his conception of the sympathetic culture proper for all human beings. "*Auguste Comte and Positivism, CW*, *10*, 331.

[30] Draft, Harriet Taylor to Arthur Helps, [1847?], *CW*, *17*, 2001 n.

[31] *Autobiography*, *CW*, *1*, 199; Early Draft, *CW*, *1*, 196.

[32] Mill to Louis Blanc, 4 March 1859, *CW*, *15*, 601.

[33] Bain, *Mill*, 166. Bain recalled this from conversation in which Mill spoke vehemently.

[34] Early Draft, *CW*, *1*, 192.

for moral and social transformation which he set forth in other writings of this period. However, since the consequences he anticipated from their liberation—the replacement of established customs and beliefs, including Christianity, with a new ethos and new institutions—would have gone far toward the implementation of his plan, we should assume that Mill regarded *On Liberty* as one of the instruments for achieving his overarching purpose.[35]

To liberate those with individuality Mill had to undermine the customs and attitudes that prevented exploration and experimentation, and he had to discredit the penalties for deviations from established modes of conduct. Thus he criticized the existence of general expectations as to how one ought to conduct one's life and the pressures to conform to them. "In our times, from the highest class of society down to the lowest, every one lives as under the eye of a hostile and dreaded censorship" (264).[36] Consequently people ask, what is suitable to someone in their position, rather than giving free play to what is distinctive in their character. "Thus the mind itself is bowed to the yoke . . . conformity is the first thing thought of . . . they exercise choice only among things commonly done" (265). What is peculiar to themselves—what might grow into individuality of character—is stifled. As for those already aware of their individuality, including persons of genius, they are "*more* individual than any other people—less capable, consequently, of fitting themselves, without hurtful compression, into any of the small number of moulds which society provides" (267).

Social expectations were enforced in more or less subtle ways. There was an intolerance of being different that was revealed in depreciatory remarks, as if one "had committed some grave moral delinquency" (270). Mere eccentricity was a matter for reproach, and this Mill called "the tyranny of opinion" (269). And most important, there was custom—he spoke of the "despotism of custom" (273)—which denied choice. The truly human faculties involving feeling, mental activity, and moral judg-

[35] This is just how the prominent positivist Richard Congreve regarded *On Liberty*, without, however, discerning Mill's intention, for he recognized that its recommendations would contribute to the social transformation he and other Comtists would have welcomed. Surveying the scientific and literary world, assuming it was hostile to positivism, he said, "If I were to say what I think the most favorable event for the cause we advocate of the last year, in reference to this branch of our opponents, I should select the work of their most eminent name, Mr. J. S. Mill, [and his book] on Liberty." Richard Congreve, *The Propagation of the Religion of Humanity: A Sermon Preached at South Fields, Wandsworth, Wednesday, 19th Moses, 72 [19th January 1860], on the anniversary of the birth of Auguste Comte, 19th January, 1798* (London: John Chapman, 1860), 17.

[36] Cf. an observation by Harriet Taylor in 1832. "The opinion of Society . . . is a combination of the many weak, against the few strong; an association of the mentally listless to punish any manifestation of mental independence." "An Early Essay by Harriet Taylor," in F. A. Hayek, *Mill and Harriet Taylor*, 275–76.

ment were "exercised only in making a choice. He who does anything because it is the custom, makes no choice." A person with individuality was constrained: "Customs are made for customary circumstances, and customary characters; and his circumstances or his character may be uncustomary" (262).[37]

There is another theme in chapter three. Assuming that those with individuality would be the leaders of the movement for moral and cultural transformation, and having identified the obstacles to the development and expression of individuality, Mill also presented a contrast between two types of character—those with individuality and those responsible for creating the obstacles. The two types of character had an adversarial relationship. It was a contest between the few and the many, the agents of progress and those who prevented it, the advanced thinkers and the "stupid classes."[38] On the outcome of the struggle between them hinged the fate of Mill's plan for moral reformation.

While those with individuality had a character that was clearly identified, their adversaries, with the opposite type of character, although not given an identifying label, are also clearly described in chapter three of *On Liberty*. In addition to being conformist and shaped by custom, these persons are described as being "inert and torpid, instead of active and energetic" (262) and also "indolent and impassive" (263). Their predominance brought about the consequence Mill most deplored—complacency, acceptance of society as it existed, the absence of independent judgment that might lead to dissatisfaction with, or moral outrage against, the existing order. As a consequence of being adversaries to those with individuality, they were also obstacles to the achievement of moral transformation.

Mill's overarching concern with the achievement of moral transformation thus significantly influenced his argument in chapter three of *On Liberty*. The two types of character are described in ways that defined their roles in the historical drama that, according to Mill's theory of history, was unfolding just beneath the surface of the more visible events of public life. In a work contemporary to *On Liberty* he labeled these two types as active and passive. Those with individuality would be *active* in promoting moral and cultural transformation, while those who were

---

[37] "The great majority of mankind are, as a general rule, tenacious of things existing: habit and custom predominate with them . . . a people are as tenacious of old customs and ways of thinking in the crisis of a revolution as at any other time." "Vindication of the French Revolution of February 1848," *CW*, *20*, 359–60; see also 345.

[38] *Early Draft*, *CW*, *1*, 28.

customary, inert, and complacent would be *passive*, thus preventing the desired outcome. In *Representative Government* (1861) he addressed a fundamental question—which of these two types contributes more to "the general good of humanity." The active type, which had all the features of individuality as described in *On Liberty*, of course contributed more, for it "struggles against evils" and, rather than bending to circumstances, "endeavours to make circumstances bend to itself."[39]

The difference between these two types of character was reinforced by Christianity, which contributed to making the passive type hostile to individuality and to moral reform. The contrast was especially clear in his criticism of Calvinism, as it attempted to crush willfulness in human nature so that "human capabilities are withered and starved." And this was not confined to a narrow sect, for the Calvinist theory "is held, in a mitigated form, by many who do not consider themselves Calvinists." All around him Mill saw that "there is at present a strong tendency to this narrow theory of life, and to the pinched and hidebound type of human character which it patronizes" (265). These features of Calvinism, which were widely disseminated in the dominant culture, made enemies of those with the active type of character, but, more than this, Calvinism also reinforced and provided justification for passivity. In the Calvinist theory, Mill went on to explain, "all the good of which humanity is capable, is comprised in obedience," and this he linked to Christian morality generally.

> Its ideal is negative rather than positive; passive rather than active; Innocence rather than Nobleness; Abstinence from Evil, rather than energetic Pursuit of Good: in its precepts (as has been well said) "thou shalt not" predominates unduly over "thou shalt." . . . It is essentially a doctrine of passive obedience; it inculcates submission to all authorities found established; who indeed are not to be actively obeyed when they command what religion forbids, but who are not to be resisted, far less rebelled against, for any amount of wrong to ourselves. (255)

Thus the passive character, as a consequence of Christian influences, was also made self-denying, obedient, abject, and servile (256, 266, 271). The antithesis between it and his own ideal was evident in his comparison of "Pagan self-assertion," which promoted the Greek ideal of self-development exemplified by Pericles, with "Christian self-denial," which fostered abnegation (265–66). Simple Christian faith, he explained, could only "co-exist with a torpid and inactive state of the speculative faculties."[40] The Christian ideal would have to be overcome before those with individ-

---

[39] *Considerations on Representative Government*, CW, 19, 406–7.
[40] "Utility of Religion," CW, 10, 425.

uality could perform their function as a vanguard leading the way to cultural transformation. This consideration reinforced the opposition to Christianity which underlay chapter two of *On Liberty.*

Far from being an abstraction, for Mill the passive type of character was embodied in his own countrymen. The English were the "most wedded to their own customs, of all civilized people."[41] He went further to observe "how invariably the instinct of the English people is on the side of the *status quo.* . . . English opinion is sure to be against the side . . . that seems to be attempting to alter an existing order of things."[42] Because they were so unadventurous when it came to ideas, the English, he said, "are certainly a remarkably stupid people."[43]

The most typically English, he believed, were the middle classes, and they were objectionable for being complacent and passive and, even as reformers, unambitious. Tied to the culture of commerce, they were selfish, and this was evident in tawdry ambitions and status pretensions. Their energies "are almost confined to money-getting." In identifying the "hostile and dreaded censorship" that leads to suppression of the unique impulse of individual character and therefore to conformity, he described the thinking of such persons: "They ask themselves, what is suitable to my position? what is usually done by persons of my station and pecuniary circumstances? or (worse still) what is usually done by persons of a station and circumstance superior to mine?" (264). Here in *On Liberty* he did not make explicit the linkage of this behavior to the middle classes, but in letters he left no doubt about it. For example, "the degraded moral state of the middle classes in this country" he traced to "their absorption in the effort to make the greatest possible shew at needless and useless expense."[44] And again, "Our middle class moreover have but one object in life, to ape their superiors."[45] He alluded to the middle classes in referring to those who have "given hostages to Mrs. Grundy" and to those "kept down in that mediocrity of respectability which is becoming a marked characteristic of modern times."[46]

[41] Diary, 26 January [1854], *CW*, *27*, 647.

[42] Diary, 17 January [1854], *CW*, *27*, 644.

[43] Diary, 10 January [1854], *CW*, *27*, 641. This meaning of the word 'stupid' is similar to what Mill meant when, in a famous passage, he referred to the Tories as the stupidest, i.e., unchanging, party. *Representative Government, CW*, *19*, 452n; *Autobiography, CW*, *1*, 277. Cf. Bagehot's appreciation of what he called stupidity, i.e., sane common sense and distrust of extreme, theoretical conclusions. He regarded it essential for perpetuating liberty. Norman St. John-Stevas, "Walter Bagehot 1826–1877," in *Walter Bagehot*, ed. N. St. John-Stevas (London: N.p., 1959), 49; "Letters on the French Coup d'Etat of 1851," *The Collected Works of Walter Bagehot*, ed. N. St. John-Stevas (London: The Economist, 1968), *4*, 51.

[44] Mill to John Lalor, 3 July 1852, *CW*, *14*, 93.

[45] Mill to Gustave d'Eichthal, 15 May 1829, *CW*, *12*, 32.

[46] *Subjection of Women, CW*, *21*, 332–33.

The middle classes were linked not only to conformity but also to another of the targets in *On Liberty*—intolerance and persecution. "Where there is the strong permanent leaven of intolerance in the feelings of a people, which at all times abides in the middle classes of this country, it needs but little to provoke them into actively persecuting those whom they have never ceased to think proper objects of persecution." This was a residue from the religious persecutions in past times, and much of what in Mill's time passed for a revival of religion was in reality "the revival of bigotry" (240).

The middle classes were also closely tied to public opinion, which was the source of the tyrannical tendencies in democracies and the means by which individuality was stifled.

> In politics it is almost a triviality to say that public opinion now rules the world. The only power deserving the name is that of masses, and of governments while they make themselves the organ of the tendencies and instincts of masses. This is as true in the moral and social relations of private life as in public transactions. Those whose opinions go by the name of public opinion, are not always the same sort of public: in America they are the whole white population; in England, chiefly *the middle class*. But they are always a mass, that is to say, collective mediocrity. (268; emphasis added)

He also interpreted this in light of Tocqueville's argument about the despotic tendencies of democratic majorities. He not only used Tocqueville's phrase, "tyranny of the majority," in *On Liberty* (219), but in reviewing the second part of Tocqueville's treatise, he anticipated the argument of *On Liberty* in noting the expanding "yoke of bourgeois opinion," and observing, "Hardly anything now depends upon individuals, but all upon classes, and among classes mainly upon the middle class." All the flaws and dangers ascribed to democracy by Tocqueville were explained by Mill, insofar as they were found in England, as a consequence of "the democracy of the middle class."[47] Mill, having begun as an enthusiastic advocate of democracy, early developed a concern that intellectual leadership would not thrive in a democracy; this concern was intensified by his distaste and contempt for the middle class.

Given the inclinations and values of the middle class, his conclusion that it was "the ascendant power" (286) meant the prospects for individuality were poor. Since middle class hegemony meant that those with individuality would be denied power and influence, Mill ended his chapter three with an analysis of the circumstances that allowed the passive, weak,

---

[47] "De Tocqueville on Democracy in America [II]" (1840), *CW*, *18*, 194–95. There is a remarkable contrast between Mill's vituperation against the middle class and James Mill's famous eulogy of the middle classes in his essay "Government."

conformist, and intolerant to predominate. "The circumstances which surround different classes and individuals, and shape their characters, are daily becoming more assimilated" (274). This result was brought about by political changes, educational developments, the increase of commerce, and above all, by "the ascendancy of public opinion" (275). These changes combined "to raise the low and to lower the high" (274), bringing a general leveling somewhere in the middling range where the features of character Mill condemned were to be found. Consequently there was "so great a mass of influences hostile to Individuality" (275).

This was among the considerations that led Mill to his well-known contempt for much in English life and culture. Dominated by the middle class, England fostered the kind of character faced by those with individuality in the struggle for the cultural ethos, and it embodied values and aspirations that were in polar opposition to what persons with individuality wished to establish. It was insipid, trivial, and vulgar.[48] The English preferred hierarchy to equality.[49] They derived no happiness from the exercise of the sympathies, that is, they were incapable of altruism.[50] English character, he told Harriet, "is starved in its social part."[51] There was a "low moral tone [in] English society."[52] Human nature among the English was stunted: "by dint of not following their own nature, they have no nature to follow" (265). Clearly he did not exaggerate in telling Comte, "I have stood for quite some time in a kind of open opposition to the English character, which arouses my animosity in several respects."[53] His opinions led the usually sympathetic Bain to complain that "his habitual way of speaking of England, the English people, English society, as compared with other nations, was positively unjust."[54]

His depreciation of the English contrasted with admiration for Continental ways, especially those of the French, and this reflected his belief that in France, in contrast to England, severe critics of things established and visionaries of better worlds were not persecuted. In conversation Mill observed of the French, "Their first opinions—those which they have simply imbibed from tradition and prejudice—they have forsaken, and their

---

[48] Early Draft, *CW, 1*, 234; Mill to Harriet Taylor Mill, [5 January 1854], *CW, 14*, 121.

[49] Mill to Guiseppe Mazzini, 15 April 1858, *CW, 15*, 553.

[50] Early Draft, *CW, 1*, 156.

[51] Mill to Harriet Taylor, 19 February [1849], *CW, 14*, 9.

[52] Early Draft, *CW, 1*, 60.

[53] Mill to Auguste Comte, 26 March 1846, *Correspondence Mill to Comte*, 365. Also, "the nuisance of England is the English": Mill to Harriet Taylor Mill, 2 January [1855], *CW, 14*, 277.

[54] Bain, *Mill*, 161. Also, "I *do* think . . . that an average Athenian was a far finer specimen of humanity on the whole than an average Englishman—but then unless one says how low one estimates the latter, one gives a false notion of one's estimate of the former." Mill to Harriet Taylor, 17 March 1849, *CW, 14*, 18.

minds are anxiously open to truth."[55] At Paris "it needs little or no courage . . . to make the openest profession of any kind of opinions or feelings whatever. It is the very place which a speculative man should desire for promulgating his opinions, for you startle nobody, you are sure of an audience." And he lamented, "How different here."[56] Thus in France (and also in Germany), having a systematic point of view derived from general theories about philosophy or history was not an obstacle to being heard, and this made intellect relevant to politics, allowing Mill to say, "the whole problem of modern society . . . will be worked out . . . in France and nowhere else."[57] In contrast, in England, intellect was depreciated, those with ambitious ideas had to conceal them to gain a hearing, and politics did not benefit from new ideas.[58] He complained about "the characteristic distrust of our countrymen for all ambitious efforts of intellect. . . . we have no faith in, and no curiosity about the kind of speculations to which the most philosophic minds of those nations [France and Germany] have lately devoted themselves."[59] Macaulay, whose writings were immensely popular in England, was the object of Mill's contempt, for he had not a single thought of German or French origin, and therefore was "an intellectual dwarf." This Mill said in 1855, the year of publication of the third and fourth volumes of Macaulay's immensely popular *History of England.*[60] Mill concluded that, because of the dearth of ideas, England "is dead, vapid, left quite behind by all the questions now arising."[61] And most significant, England was not "as ripe as most of the Continental countries for . . . great improvement."[62]

It was against all this that the few with individuality carried on their struggle. It was a moral class struggle in which the intellectually and morally superior few opposed all the others, most notably in the middle class but in the classes above and below, as well. In this struggle mental superi-

---

[55] Caroline Fox's journal, 10 April 1840, *Memories of Old Friends, 1,* 164. Mill had "sympathy with everything French. . . . He always dealt gently with her faults, and liberally with her virtues." Bain, *Mill,* 78.

[56] Mill to Thomas Carlyle, 25 Nov. 1833, *CW, 12,* 192.

[57] Mill to Henry Samuel Chapman, 28 May 1849, *CW, 14,* 32.

[58] "Comparison of the Tendencies of French and English Intellect" (1833), *CW, 23,* 445; see also "Smart's Outline of Sematology" (1832), *CW, 23,* 425.

[59] "Guizot," *CW, 20,* 260. He noted in his diary: "The characteristic of Germany is knowledge without thought; of France, thought without knowledge; of England, neither knowledge nor thought" 9 March [1854], *CW, 27,* 660.

[60] Mill to Harriet Taylor Mill, 16 February [1855], *CW, 14,* 332. "It would certainly be unfair to measure the worth of any age by that of its popular objects of literary or artistic admiration. Otherwise one might say the present age will be known and estimated by posterity as the age which thought Macaulay a great writer." Diary, 11 February [1854], *CW, 27,* 653.

[61] Mill to Henry Samuel Chapman, 28 May 1849, *CW, 14,* 34.

[62] Mill to Karl D. Heinrich Rau, 7 July 1852, *CW, 14,* 95. He was referring to the formation of cooperative associations.

ority faced mediocrity; the self-disciplined opposed the self-indulgent; and the vanguard seeking a new ethos carried on against old, entrenched, customary values and religion. In all transformations there was such a struggle between "the stupidity and habitual indifference of the mass of mankind [who] would bear down by its dead weight all the efforts of the more intelligent and active minded few."[63] Mill visualized the forthcoming cultural transformation he was promoting as pitting the same adversaries against each other. It was a struggle between two types of character. On one side was his ideal character, which was active, self-assertive, high-minded, experimental, unafraid, original. On the other was the character produced by custom and Christian morality, which was passive, self-denying, obedient, low, vulgar, unadventurous, abject, servile, and conformist. The "progressive principle" supported by the first sort of character was antagonistic to "the sway of Custom," which produced the second sort of character and led to stationariness. Indeed, "the contest between the two constitutes the chief interest of the history of mankind" (272). And where tradition and custom prevailed at the expense of individuality, "there is wanting one of the principal ingredients of human happiness, and quite the chief ingredient of individual and social progress" (261).

[63] Mill to John Chapman, 9 June 1851, CW, *14*, 68.

Chapter Eight

HOW MUCH LIBERTY?

> The spirit of improvement is not always a spirit of liberty, for
> it may aim at forcing improvements on an unwilling people.
> *(John Stuart Mill [272])*

WHILE MILL enjoys a reputation as an unequivocal defender
of liberty and as one who asserted its claims against the restrictions imposed by society, including its customs, "received
opinions," and expectations, his reputation is not fully deserved, for his
plan for moral reform would have led to many restrictions on individual
liberty, and this was a consequence he foresaw and accepted. So great was
his wish to stamp out selfishness that the achievement of moral reform
coexisted with and sometimes superseded individual liberty.

Liberty would be diminished in two ways. First, as shown in chapter
one, the harm principle would be applied broadly and enforced extensively, and liberty in all social relations, especially in the family, would be
adversely affected. Not only conduct but also inclinations, or, as Mill
called them, dispositions, would be subject to punishment. And punishments, were not merely to be legally defined and enforced, but moreover
were also to include the unregulated, spontaneous, and therefore arbitrary reactions of opinion, what Mill called moral reprobation, moral
retribution, and social stigma.

It was not only the harm done to others that would lead to a diminution
of liberty, however, for Mill provided that self-regarding conduct, which
was defined as not causing harm to others, also would "suffer very severe
penalties" (278). The threat to liberty following from this kind of conduct, only briefly mentioned in chapter one above, is the subject of this
chapter, which will also focus on the responsibility of those with individuality of character for penalizing those engaging in objectionable self-
regarding conduct.

By introducing penalties for self-regarding conduct, which he did in
chapter four of *On Liberty*, Mill expanded the contest between the adversaries struggling against each other in chapter three of *On Liberty*—
between those with individuality and those who were complacent, passive, customary, intolerant, and resistant to challenge and change.
Whereas in chapter three these adversaries were characterized as either
resisting or advancing the movement of history, in chapter four Mill was

even more judgmental as he emphasized the aesthetic and moral dimensions of the two types of character. One side was "deprav[ed]" and "inferior" (278–79), and their adversaries, those with individuality, while not so clearly labeled, were by implication, wholesome and superior. One side represented the higher pleasures, the other the lower; one side, Socrates, the other, the fool or the pig, as he described them in *Utilitarianism*. He and Harriet had complained about "a morbid feebleness of conscience" among their contemporaries,[1] but those battling their moral inferiors were to be confident and assertive. In their struggle against depravity—it was really a moral crusade—those with individuality took on a new function. Previously Mill had them criticizing old beliefs and institutions, inventing new ones, and commencing new practices (267). Now, in addition, they were to take an active part in discrediting and discouraging the depraved and inferior in the move toward a morally regenerated, reconstructed society. Whereas in chapter three those with individuality were victims of intolerance and were threatened with being submerged by the collective mediocrity of the emerging mass society, in chapter four they take the initiative against those with characters inferior to their own.

When Mill turned to self-regarding conduct he displayed a readiness to pass judgment and have those of whose conduct he disapproved suffer penalties just as he did when considering conduct that injured others. Once again there was a discrepancy between his general principle and its application. According to the principle, power over an individual was not justified for that person's own good, either physical or moral. "He cannot rightfully be compelled to do or forbear because it will be better for him to do so, because it will make him happier, because, in the opinion of others, to do so would be wise, or even right" (223–24). The choice of pleasures should be left to the individual, as they are his concern (198). Elaborating, no one "is warranted in saying to another human creature of ripe years, that he shall not do with his life for his own benefit what he chooses to do with it. He is the person most interested in his own well-being. . . . Individuality has its proper field of action. . . . [I]n each person's own concerns, his individual spontaneity is entitled to free exercise" (277).

Yet, in spite of these statements, Mill identified conduct that caused no direct harm to others that would be penalized. If a person's conduct reflects "qualities which conduce to his own good," he is admired, but "if he is grossly deficient in those qualities, a sentiment the opposite of admiration will follow."

There is a degree of folly, and a degree of what may be called (though the phrase

---

[1] Harriet Taylor and Mill, "The Acquittal of Captain Johnston" (1846), CW, 24, 866.

is not unobjectionable) lowness or depravation of taste, which, though it cannot justify doing harm to the person who manifests it, renders him necessarily and properly a subject of *distaste*, or, in extreme cases, even of *contempt*: a person could not have the opposite qualities in due strength without entertaining these feelings. Though doing no wrong to any one, a person may so act as to compel us to judge him, and feel to him, as a fool, or as a being of an inferior order. (278; emphasis added)[2]

Becoming more concrete, Mill described depravity in a person "who shows rashness, obstinacy, self-conceit—who cannot live within moderate means—who cannot restrain himself from hurtful indulgences—who pursues animal pleasures at the expense of those of feeling and intellect" (278). Persons displaying such conduct were to become the objects of distaste and perhaps contempt. And such conduct made one "a selfish egotist, devoid of every feeling or care but those which centre in his own miserable individuality." This label—*miserable* individuality—appeared in the contemporary work *Utilitarianism* (1861). In contrast, the characteristics without the label were discussed in chapter four of *On Liberty*, where they offer a little-noticed juxtaposition to Mill's eulogy to individuality in chapter three.[3]

An indication that for Mill depravity was not uncommon comes from realizing that sexual indulgence, in some circumstances, was regarded as depraved. When he referred to the "lowness or depravation of taste" of the persons who pursue "animal pleasures at the expense of those of feeling and intellect" (278), he alluded, among other things, to sex. He regularly associated it with what was low and animallike, and he was convinced that "great improvement in human life is not to be looked for so long as the animal instinct of sex occupies the absurdly disproportionate place it does therein."[4] This judgment was extended to marriage, in which there was degradation and slavery of women who, as wives, were "victim of man's animal instinct."[5] These views were reflected in *Subjection of Women*, where he claimed that in marriage a woman is made

---

[2] James Mill also recommended that certain "bad actions" be "restrained by the common disapprobation of society"—"by the common hatred and contempt of mankind; such as ingratitude, common lying, disobligingness, and others." "Toleration," *The Philanthropist* 2, no. 6 (1812): 119.

[3] *Utilitarianism* (1863), *CW*, *10*, 216. Cf. "miserable self-seeking" in "Remarks on Bentham's Philosophy" (1833), *CW*, *10*, 16. Such conduct is alluded to at the end of "Nature," where it is traced to the spontaneous course of nature. *CW*, *10*, 402.

[4] Diary, 26 March [1854], *CW*, *27*, 664. Robson points out that for Mill man's animality was distinguished and markedly separate from his humanity. John M. Robson, "Rational Animals and Others," *James and John Stuart Mill: Papers of the Centenary Conference*, ed. John M. Robson and Michael Laine (Toronto: University of Toronto Press, 1976), 148–49.

[5] Mill to Professor [Henry?] Green, 8 April 1852, *CW*, *14*, 88–89. He approved the separation of men and women in workhouses, saying, "I consider it an essential part of the moral training." Mill to Edward Herford, 22 January 1850, *CW*, *14*, 45.

the instrument of an animal function contrary to her inclinations; the institution of marriage reminded him of "how many are the forms and gradations of animalism and selfishness, often under an outward varnish of civilization and even cultivation."[6] If this were not sufficient condemnation, Mill added to his charge by linking sex and sensuality with despotism. And his belief that sexual indulgence was often depraved was supplemented by his Malthusianism, which, as became evident in his definition of harm, still had a prominent place in his social and economic thought. His Malthusianism thus made sexual indulgence a source of harm to others—to children that might not be properly cared for and who later would suffer and cause others to suffer in an overcrowded labor market. The strength of these convictions about sexual indulgence was matched by the fullness of his expectation that the desire for such indulgence can be obliterated. He confidently asserted, "These [animal] instincts may be modified to any extent, or entirely conquered, in human beings . . . by other mental influences, and by education."[7] And elsewhere he claimed that "there is not one natural inclination which [education] is not strong enough to coerce, and, if needful, to destroy by disuse."[8] He told Lord Amberley that "this particular passion will become with men, as it is already with a large number of women, completely under the control of reason."[9]

The description of depraved conduct that would call forth distaste or contempt was not in an isolated passage, nor was it carelessly introduced, nor was it confined to sexual conduct. In other places he identified self-regarding but objectionable conduct. For example, he referred to "vices

[6] *Subjection of Women*, CW, 21, 285, 288. These views were shared by Harriet Taylor; in an early essay on marriage she stated that marriage arrangements gave women "reason to barter person for bread." "On Marriage (1832–33?)," CW, 21, 377. See also Packe, *Life of Mill*, 125.

[7] *Logic*, CW, 8, 859.

[8] "Utility of Religion," CW, 10, 409, Also see "Nature," CW, 10, 398: "[I]t must be allowed that we have also bad instincts which it should be the aim of ed[u]cation not simply to regulate but to extirpate, or rather (what can be done even to an instinct) to starve them by disuse."

[9] Mill to Lord Amberley, 2 February 1870, CW, 17, 1693. Of course, Mill could not have known that Lady Amberley would soon be having sexual relations with her eldest son's tutor, who, since he suffered with consumption, was discouraged from marrying; but apparently she felt it unfair that he remain celibate. Alan Ryan, *Bertrand Russell: A Political Life* (New York: Oxford University Press, 1988), 7. On this subject, Harriet Taylor Mill agreed with her husband: although she regarded sensuality as not in itself unworthy, she thought it incorrect to believe "that the exercise of the sexual function is in any degree a necessity" or that "the non exercise of [it] is necessarily a deprivation." "Popular Fallacies," Mill-Taylor Collection, Box III, no. 107. Mill's views on these matters may have reflected his own inclinations. Bain observes, "in the so-called sexual feelings, he was below average . . . he made light of the difficulty of controlling the sexual appetite"; and that "while his estimate of pure sentimental affections were more than enough, his estimate of the sexual passion was too low." Bain, *Mill*, 90, 149. See also. Early Draft, CW, 1, 236.

or follies" which might injure one's property or deteriorate one's bodily or mental faculties. In this connection he mentioned gambling, drunkenness, incontinence, idleness, and uncleanliness—all indications that one was "incapable of self-government" (280).[10] And he referred to the "defect of prudence or of personal dignity," which leads to "loss of consideration," that is, to distaste or contempt (279); and to "the vicious or the self-indulgent" persons whose conduct provokes "painful or degrading consequences," namely, harsh judgments by others, including distaste or contempt (283). In each of these examples, Mill's disapproval is evident in his judgmental language—low, inferior, vicious, self-indulgent, folly. This disapproval is in keeping with his characterization of "miserable individuality" and his distinction between low and high pleasures. Clearly he believed that it was wiser, more right, and better to choose the higher rather than the lower and to be self-disciplined rather than self-indulgent; and that (as explained in *Utilitarianism*) the lower pleasures could not provide genuine happiness. Since he welcomed penalties—distaste and contempt—for the lower, inferior, depraved persons, he evidently was not giving a complete statement of his position regarding liberty when (as already quoted) he wrote that a person "cannot rightfully be compelled to do or forbear because it will be better for him to do so, because it will make him happier, because in the opinion of others, to do so would be wise, or even right" (223–24). Nor was his approach to penalties consistent with the statement that "liberty consists in doing what one desires" (294).

There is no question that Mill regarded pressure on those with miserable individuality as a penalty, even though their conduct was self-regarding: "a person may suffer very severe penalties at the hands of others, for faults which directly concern only himself" (278).[11] Recognizing that this was a challenge to his distinction between self-regarding conduct and conduct that harmed others, Mill claimed that the depraved, inferior person "suffers these penalties only in so far as they are the natural, and, as it were, the spontaneous consequences of the faults themselves, not because they are purposely inflicted on him for the sake of punishment" (278). This defense of his distinction is undermined, however, by his advocacy of such harsh judgments. The condemned conduct is "justly censured,"

---

[10] He especially condemned the idleness of the rich; he approved Comte's proposal that the life of the idle rich be "deemed so disgraceful, that nobody with the smallest sense of shame would choose to be guilty of it." *Auguste Comte and Positivism*, CW, 10, 347. See also Early Draft, CW, 1, 238.

[11] Such penalties were different from legal penalties for self-regarding conduct justified by society's right to prevent crime: "The right inherent in society to ward off crimes against itself by antecedent precautions, suggests limitations to the maxim, that purely self-regarding misconduct cannot properly be meddled with in the way of prevention or punishment" (295).

he said (283), and thus "There is need of a great increase of disinterested exertion to promote the good of others" (277). "I . . . mean that the feelings with which a person is regarded by others, *ought* . . . to be . . . affected by his self-regarding qualities or deficiencies" (277–78; emphasis added). This passage was embedded in a sentence with a double negative. The full statement was, "I do not mean that the feelings with which a person is regarded by others, ought not to be in any way affected by his self-regarding qualities or deficiencies. This is neither possible nor desirable."

This statement about penalties for self-regarding conduct was foreshadowed already in his first chapter, where he qualified the promise of liberty for self-regarding conduct by mentioning *consequences* that might accompany such conduct. The region of human liberty, he explained, included the liberty of tastes and pursuits and of framing a plan of life to suit one's own character, and, in addition, the liberty "of doing as we like, subject to such *consequences* as may follow" (226; emphasis added). This warning was repeated in another discussion of "a person's conduct [that] affects the interests of no person besides himself" (276), i.e., self-regarding conduct. "In all such cases there should be perfect freedom, legal and social, to do the action and *stand the consequences*" (276; emphasis added). And again, with regard to "the personal concerns of individuals . . . the decision ought to rest with those who are to *abide the consequences*" (282; emphasis added). These repeated references to consequences that might attend self-regarding conduct seem to point to the penalties referred to in Mill's statement that a person might "suffer very severe penalties" for self-regarding conduct.[12]

The penalties for self-regarding conduct were akin to social pressure. To be the object of distaste and contempt and to have it revealed that others regard one as depraved and inferior is to be pressured, and, as Mill well understood, such pressure was an encroachment on individuality and it would diminish liberty to engage in the activities that were being condemned. In *On Liberty* he was reticent about indicating the character of this pressure but he did say the target should be warned beforehand, "as of any other disagreeable consequences to which he exposes himself" (278). Beyond this, those passing judgment may avoid the society of the condemned person (though they should not parade the avoidance) and going further, others are to be cautioned against him. While "we shall not treat him like an enemy of society," we are justified in "leaving him to

---

[12] See also 260, 296.

himself" (280). Although Mill does not use the word, this is ostracism, which he associated with ancient Greece, a place that, on account of many of its practices, he held up as exemplary. For example, he praised Athenian government for being, in common with democracies, "a government of unlimited publicity, and *freedom of censure* and discussion" (emphasis added).[13]

Mill was proposing the use of shame to pressure the depraved and inferior—those with miserable individuality. He was less reticent about describing this kind of pressure in an essay contemporary to *On Liberty* but which was not to be published until after his death. In "Utility of Religion" he described the great potential influence of the wish to avoid shame. The "regard for the sentiments of our fellow-creatures is in one shape or other, in nearly all characters, the pervading motive."[14] This was a matter of self-interest, as most persons are "spurred from behind by the love of distinction and the fear of shame."[15] Apart from animal passions, the strongest drives in human nature were derived from public opinion, and he classified them into those with attractive power, including love of glory, praise, admiration, and respect, and their opposites: "the fear of shame, the dread of ill repute, or of being disliked or hated, are the direct and simple forms of its deterring power." The deterrents acted in two ways: There was "the painfulness of knowing oneself to be the object of those sentiments"; and, in addition,

> it includes all the penalties which they can inflict: exclusion from social intercourse and from the innumerable good offices which human beings require from one another; the forfeiture of all that is called success in life; often the great diminution or total loss of means of subsistence; positive ill offices of various kinds, sufficient to render life miserable, and reaching in some states of society as far as actual persecution to death.[16]

Here Mill was describing the range of penalties that could flow from the kind of pressure he was prepared to use. Obviously he was not endorsing all of them, though in *On Liberty* he mentioned some of them, notably "the moral coercion of public opinion" (223) for conduct that harmed others and, for self-regarding conduct, exclusion from social intercourse and ill offices which would render life miserable.

In the same essay he mentioned shaming as one of the ways morality could be enforced if a religion of humanity were established. Then moral-

---

[13] "Grote's History of Greece [5]" (1850), *CW*, 25, 1161. Bain called Mill "a Greece-intoxicated man." Bain, *Mill*, 94. Social excommunication was also advocated by Comte. *System*, 1, 300; 2, 339–40.

[14] "Utility of Religion," *CW*, 10, 411.

[15] Early Draft, *CW*, 1, 240.

[16] "Utility of Religion," *CW*, 10, 410–11.

ity would be complied with by both "superior natures" and inferiors, though with different motivations. The superior natures would act morally from sympathy, benevolence, and the passion for excellence, and "in the inferior, from the same feelings cultivated up to the measure of their capacity, with the superadded force of shame."[17] This was consistent with *Utilitarianism*, where he identified external sanctions for morality as including "the fear of displeasure from our fellow creatures";[18] and the foundation for utilitarian morality, he claimed, would be the social feelings of mankind—"the desire to be in unity with our fellow creatures."[19] This was a powerful principle of human nature, one that would become even stronger as civilization advanced, that is, as the religion of humanity became reality.

Mill's wish to use shaming to improve the character of selfish and miserably individualistic persons is evident in his views on the ballot. Whereas earlier, in keeping with his acceptance of orthodox Benthamism, he had been a strong advocate of the secret ballot, by the time *On Liberty* was written his opinion changed radically. Now Mill wanted voters to cast their ballots openly, in full view of their fellow citizens. The purpose, he claimed, was not to influence how votes were cast but to force voters to be prepared to explain and defend the ways they voted. Since voting for representatives was a public act which concerned others, electors and non-electors, "all such acts should be done in the face and subject to the comments and criticisms of the entire public. I wish that the elector should feel an honourable shame in voting contrary to his known opinions, and in not being able to give for his vote a reason which he can avow."[20] He acknowledged that noxious influences might be the result—voters dependent on landlords, employers, or customers might vote to satisfy such persons—but he felt the salutary consequences outweighed such considerations. On the other hand, with a secret ballot, the voter could give full effect to his selfish preferences. But if open, "the feeling of responsibility to others may keep him right."[21] Thus "the only restraint on a majority of knaves, consists in their involuntary respect for the opinion of an honest

---

[17] Ibid., 421. Also, "Mankind would be in a deplorable state if no principles or precepts of justice, veracity, beneficence, were taught publicly or privately, and if these virtues were not encouraged, and *the opposite vices repressed*, by the praise and blame, the favourable and unfavourable sentiments of mankind." Ibid., 407 (emphasis added).

[18] *Utilitarianism*, CW, 10, 228.

[19] Ibid., 231. Also, "how large a portion of the motives which induce the generality of men to take care even of their own interest, is derived from regard for opinion—from the expectation of being disliked or despised for not doing it. . . . Men are seldom found to brave the general opinion of their class, unless supported by some principle higher than regard for opinion, or by some strong body of opinion elsewhere." *Political Economy*, CW, 2, 371–2.

[20] Mill to James Beal, 17 April 1865, CW, 16, 1033.

[21] *Representative Government*, CW, 19, 331.

minority."[22] He had no illusions about what he was recommending: "We are for leaving the voter open to the *penalties of opinion*" (emphasis added).[23] This was an application of "a principle so important in forming the moral character either of an individual or of a people."[24]

In advocating the application of pressure of opinion to discourage objectionable conduct, Mill carefully treated the opinion of the superior natures—those with individuality—quite differently than *public* opinion, which reflected values and beliefs prevailing in existing society. It was a distinction he made carefully, even if not explicitly. While he accepted that public opinion could be directed against those who harmed others—this was the "moral reprobation" (279) and the expression of "the moral coercion of public opinion" (223), which he defended—he emphasized that *public* opinion, as it was in existing society, could not be legitimately used against self-regarding conduct. "Society has no business, *as* society, to decide anything to be wrong which concerns only the individual" (296). Thus a Muslim majority ought not forbid pork eating; a Spanish majority ought not forbid Protestant worship; a Catholic majority ought not forbid marriage by non-Catholic clergymen; and Puritan majorities, whether in seventeenth-century England or nineteenth-century America, ought not forbid amusements (285–86). Interference by public opinion with self-regarding conduct was especially objectionable in nineteenth-century England, where it was prejudiced and more than usually intrusive.

To control the self-regarding conduct of the depraved and inferior and of those with miserable individuality, in contrast to conduct that harmed others, Mill thus insisted that public opinion could not be used; but opinion of certain individuals whose views were formed independently of public opinion could be directed against such self-regarding conduct. Such opinion included expressions of distaste and contempt and other acts of shaming by those with wholesome individuality. Whereas public opinion reflected the beliefs and norms of existing society, the depraved and inferior were to be censured by individuals acting in support of principles

---

[22] Ibid., 336.

[23] "Romilly's Public Responsibility and the Ballot" (1865), *CW*, 25, 1215.

[24] Mill to Henry Samual Chapman, 8 July 1858, *CW*, 15, 558. Grote, the most prominent advocate of a secret ballot, was dismayed by Mill's position. The ballot, he said, "connects itself with the full liberty of *private judgment*. . . . The importance of guarding the full liberty of individual judgment and the expression thereof, against the tyranny and persecution of bystanders, (often themselves conscientious), appears to me even greater in my old age, than it did when *I* was younger. No man has gone further in upholding this right than John Mill, and that by excellent arguments in his Essay on Liberty. But when I read his arguments against the Ballot they really disallow and even condemn, all right of private judgment, on the part of the voter. I know no two things more contradictory, than the Essay on Liberty and the reasonings against the Ballot." George Grote to John Romilly, 19 April 1865, Romilly Papers, Public Record Office, PRO 1/119/1.

which, though superior to what existed, were not yet widely accepted, and therefore could not be represented as society's norms. Since the censuring was to be directed against those he labeled depraved and inferior, their adversaries, by implication, were elevated and superior, in other words, those with individuality of character. While he made it clear in *On Liberty* that censuring would take place, in this work he did not identify those who were to pass judgment on the inferiors as the persons with individuality, though he came close in saying, "We have a right . . . to act upon our unfavourable opinion of any one, not to the oppression of his individuality, but in the exercise of ours" (278).

He was more explicit in other writings. In "Utility of Religion," where he described how those with inferior natures would be shamed into compliance with a higher morality, he labeled those who were not inferior, that is, those who did the shaming, as "superior natures."[25] He also described them as assertive, confident, bold initiators, and therefore even in a democracy—especially in a democracy—they had this role. "The sovereignty of the whole people does not mean the passiveness of individuals—the rejection of all impulse, of all guidance, of all initiative, on the part of the better and wiser few."[26] He also referred to this function as performed by the superior natures in *Political Economy*, where he said that "it is allowable in all, and in the more thoughtful and cultivated [i.e., those with individuality] often a duty, to assert and promulgate, with all the force they are capable of, their opinion of what is good or bad, admirable or contemptible, but [since compulsion was the prerogative of society and/or government] not to compel others to conform to that opinion."[27] He also said these persons would be members of "the speculative class" but without the public authority Comte would have conferred on such a class. The promulgation and diffusion of principles of conduct is desirable, Mill acknowledged; and it also was useful to inculcate duties, even to specific individuals. "A function of this sort, no doubt, may often be very usefully discharged by individual members of the speculative class; but if entrusted to any organized body [as Comte proposed], would involve nothing less than a spiritual despotism."[28]

By exempting those with individuality from the charge of being spiritual despots, in spite of their being censorious and their heaping contempt upon those with miserable individuality, Mill allowed them considerable power. He complained about the "moral police" who presumed to act on behalf of the public, but the label seems applicable to those he called

---

[25] "Utility of Religion," *CW*, *10*, 421.
[26] "Vindication of the French Revolution of February 1848," *CW*, *20*, 335.
[27] *Political Economy*, *CW*, *3*, 938.
[28] *Auguste Comte and Positivism*, *CW*, *10*, 314.

superior natures who expressed distaste and contempt as they sought to morally reform their inferiors. He eloquently pleaded for toleration of such persons in chapter three of *On Liberty*, yet it was only his confidence that their adversaries were morally loathsome that saved him from having to recognize that he had granted them the privilege of being themselves intolerant.[29]

Mill's analysis of certain self-regarding vices in chapter five of *On Liberty* illustrates how individual opinion of the superior natures rather than public opinion would operate to penalize selfish, self-indulgent conduct of those with miserable individuality. He considers fornication, drunkenness, gambling, and idleness in chapter five. Drunkenness, he emphasized, "is not a fit subject for legislative interference" (295), except, of course, for cases where it causes harm to others. And he said the same about idleness: except for cases involving persons receiving public support or where it constitutes breach of contract, it "cannot without tyranny be made a subject of legal punishment" (295). These statements, with their emphasis on *legal* punishment, imply that drunkenness and idleness were kinds of conduct that were not punishable and therefore were to be tolerated. This is how Henry Fawcett interpreted *On Liberty*—as justifying "everybody to get drunk just as much as he pleases."[30] But recalling the passages in chapter four in which Mill described how individuals, acting not on behalf of society but on their own, would and should censure those whose conduct was self-regardingly selfish, indulgent, and animalistic, it should be clear that those who indulged in drunkenness and idleness would still suffer penalties, though not punishments enforced by law. This is confirmed by his observation that "a man who is intemperate in drink, is discountenanced and despised by all who profess to be moral people."[31]

Similar arguments were made about fornication and gambling. They "must be tolerated" (296), which in the context of his discussion clearly meant they must be permitted under the law. As with drunkenness and idleness, however, both activities perfectly illustrate the low, pig-like pleasures that were selfish and animalistic and which were justly censured.

---

[29] Mill refers to moral police at 281, 283–84, 287. In the *Autobiography* he asserted, "The forbearance, which flows from a conscientious sense of the importance to mankind of the equal freedom of all opinions, is the only tolerance which is commendable, or, to the highest moral order of minds, possible." *CW*, *1*, 53. See also G. W. Smith, "The Logic of J. S. Mill on Freedom," *Political Studies* 28 (1980): 250.

[30] Frederic William Maitland, *The Life and Letters of Leslie Stephen* (London: Duckworth & Co., 1906), 246. A Temperance reformer understood Mill's position the same way. George Vasey, *Individual Liberty, Legal, Moral, and Licentious, in which the Political Fallacies of J. S. Mill's essay "On Liberty" are pointed out* (London, 1877).

[31] *Political Economy*, *CW*, *2*, 368. For additional discussion of drunkenness, see 282, 287–88, 293, 298.

That fornication should be judged in this way is evident if one recalls his characterization of sexual indulgence as a manifestation of animalism and as a lower type of pleasure.[32] Presumably Bain had these examples in mind when he told Mill, "the applications, though brief, suggest much."[33]

Since in each of these examples—and they were not the only ones that could have been used—the censuring would have involved "the distaste or the contempt" (282) of those who did the censuring, as well as ostracism and shaming, it is difficult not to regard such social pressure as encroachments on individuality and threats to liberty. Mill clearly acknowledged that such persons were to be coerced when he said that "the spirit of improvement is not always a spirit of liberty, for it may aim at *forcing* improvement on an unwilling people" (272; emphasis added).[34]

It might be objected that Mill's approval for the use of opinion to exert pressure on the depraved and inferior appears inconsistent with the well-known passage in which he asserts "one very simple principle, as entitled to govern absolutely the dealings of society with the individual in the way of compulsion and control." This principle was self-protection, which meant that "the only purpose for which power can be rightfully exercised over any member of a civilized community, against his will, is to prevent harm to others" (223). It should be noted, however, that Mill restricts the application of this principle to "the dealings of *society* with the individual" (emphasis added), and in another passage within the same paragraph, to the actions of "mankind." Therefore his simple principle is not

[32] Mill used other examples, though less prominently. Along with gambling, drunkenness, and idleness, he mentions uncleanliness and incontinence (280). These, too, he made immune from legal punishment, unless these faults caused injury to others, but, even though not legally punished, they were subject to censure. (By incontinence Mill probably meant, as the OED explains, want of self-restraint, especially with reference to sexual appetite, though in his translation of *Phaedrus* he defined it more generally as a desire that "drags us irrationally to pleasure." Introduction to Plato, *The Phaedrus*, *CW*, 11, 68–69.)

[33] Bain to Mill, 14 March [1859], National Library of Scotland. Yet in the literature there is a widely shared belief that Mill would have (or should have) approved fornication and sexual freedom. According to Ryan, "What Mill was concerned to argue was that fornication was a matter for the persons concerned and no one else, and thus not a matter for moral condemnation." Ryan, *J. S. Mill*, 152. Also, according to Sidgwick, Mill's doctrine "would exclude from censure almost all forms of sexual immorality committed by unmarried and independent adults," a view that Sidgwick thought "Certainly opposed to common sense." Henry Sidgwick, *The Methods of Ethics* (7th ed.; Indianapolis: Hackett, 1981), 478, n.2. And Jeremy Waldron, who considers the example of public copulation, seems disappointed to discover that Mill would prohibit it, and he finds "this passage the most difficult to reconcile with the overall tendency of Mill's argument." "Mill and Moral Distress." *Liberal Rights*, 130.

[34] Mill had written about Bentham, "To say either that man should, or that he should not, take pleasure in one thing, displeasure in another, appeared to him as much an act of despotism in the moralist as in the political ruler." "Bentham" (1838), *CW*, *10*, 96. Therefore Mill must have understood that Bentham would have regarded him as endorsing moral despotism.

inconsistent with his approval of penalties for some self-regarding conduct, as long as such penalties are not imposed on behalf of existing society.

Mill's advocacy of penalties for self-regarding faults may also appear inconsistent with his strong statement in *Political Economy* that "there is a part of the life of every person who has come to years of discretion, within which the individuality of that person ought to reign uncontrolled either by any other *individual* or by the public collectively" (emphasis added). By protecting individuality from other individuals, however, he was not contradicting his assertion of the right of the superior natures to express distaste and contempt or to shame those with self-regarding vices, for the context of this statement makes it clear that he was defending individuality from "authoritative intrusion by agents of government or society." And in the same paragraph he proclaimed that it was the duty of those who were superior to forcefully assert their opinions about what was bad and contemptible, in other words, to express distaste and contempt.[35]

By acting censoriously, the superior natures—those with individuality—were acting as the vanguard in a move toward the cultural transformation that would be achieved when the religion of humanity was established. Since selfishness had to be eliminated before altruism could prevail, the moral vanguard directed its harsh judgments against it—both the kind that caused harm to others and the self-regarding but depraved kind, which also led to conduct that had a "pernicious effect" (278). There was an affinity between the two. Both emanated from selfishness. The former, which caused harm to others, involved encroachment on the rights of others, "selfish abstinence" from defending others, the love of domineering, engrossing more than one's share of advantages, pride, "egotism which thinks self and its concerns more important than everything else" (279). The latter—self-regarding but depraved conduct—also involved gratification of selfish desires: self-conceit, self-indulgence, and sensuality (278).

The campaign against selfishness that Mill tried to organize was directed not merely against a small minority of offenders but against the entire culture. He believed there was a "deeprooted selfishness which the whole course of existing institutions tends to generate."[36] These institu-

---

[35] *Principles of Political Economy*, CW, 3, 938.
[36] Early Draft, CW, 1, 240. Mill was not alone in this view, for, according to Collini, many Victorian moralists had an "obsessive antipathy to selfishness." *Public Moralists*, 65. Later Mill became more specific: "All the selfish propensities, the self-worship, the unjust self-preference, which exist among mankind, have their source and root in, and derive their principal nourishment from, the present constitution of the relation between men and women." *Subjection of Women*, CW, 21, 324.

tions were intertwined with Christianity, which he regarded as inherently selfish. All existing morality was implicated. "What is called morality in these times is a regulated sensuality; in the same manner exactly as the love of gain is regulated by the establishment of a law of property."[37] It is not surprising, therefore, that almost no one escaped the contamination. He noted the "low moral and intellectual condition of the masses";[38] and "the present low state of the human mind" (269). To bring about a social transformation, he explained, "an equivalent change of character must take place both in the uncultivated herd who now compose the labouring masses, and in the immense majority of their employers."[39] The poor as well as the rich were involved, making it necessary to "unbrutalise them."[40] Focusing on the large middle ground between the few fiends and the few angels, Mill remarked on "how many are the forms and gradations of animalism and selfishness."[41]

When Mill visualized the success of the moral vanguard, he expected a diminution of individual liberty. Before this success occurred, that is, during a period of transition, there would be comparatively few kinds of conduct that were a matter of duty and obligation. However, with moral and social improvement, the realm of obligatory conduct enlarged, as more and more kinds of conduct were included within it. Thus "the domain of moral duty, in an improving society, is always widening. When what once was uncommon virtue becomes common virtue, it comes to be numbered among obligations."[42] Clearly, the greater the obligations, the more frequent the occasions to punish those failing to do their moral duty or the more frequent the restraint in anticipation of such a consequence. In either case, the realm of choice was made smaller.

Chapter four of On Liberty—with its expansion of Mill's definition of harm to include disposition to do harm, its provision of penalties even for self-regarding conduct, its advocacy of using social pressure to restrain selfishness, its indictment of what in a contemporary work he called

---

[37] Diary, 4 March [1854], CW, 27, 659. See also Diary, 25 January [1854], ibid., 646, where vanity is described as a "moral defect; a form of selfishness; a dwelling on, and caring about, self and what belongs to it, beyond the just measure; especially what flatters its self-importance."

[38] Mill to John Holmes, 19 January 1858, CW, 15, 546.

[39] Early Draft, CW, 1, 238. Shirley Letwin discerned Mill's wish to improve the tastes of the uncultivated. "On Liberty was not a defence of the common man's right to live as he liked; it was more nearly an attack on him": Shirley Robin Letwin, The Pursuit of Certainty (Cambridge: Cambridge University Press, 1965), 301. She regarded On Liberty as congenial to those who wish to impose their own views on "the less fortunate mass of people in want of uplifting" (308).

[40] Mill to Rev. Henry William Carr, 7 January 1852, CW, 14, 80.

[41] Subjection of Women, CW, 21, 288.

[42] Auguste Comte and Positivism, CW, 10, 338. This passage is discussed, and its context provided, in the text at notes 74ff. below.

"miserable individuality"—complements but also modifies the picture in chapter three of ample liberty in an environment with few penalties and few justifications for them. Chapter four with its harsh realities conveys an impression quite different from chapter three, and in interpreting *On Liberty*, reliance on chapter three combined with neglect of chapter four is misleading. Perhaps Bain had this in mind when he said chapter four "helps us better to his real meaning."[43]

Many scholars have not appreciated the full import of the passages in which Mill provided penalties for self-regarding conduct and called for expressions of distaste and contempt.[44] In fact, these crucial passages are not often noticed in commentaries, perhaps because they make it difficult to uphold any of the conventional interpretations, all of which take the position that Mill did not approve of interference with self-regarding conduct. These crucial passages also raise questions about the distinction, widely attributed to Mill, between self-regarding conduct, which was not to be interfered with, and conduct that concerns others, which, if it harmed them, could be punished.

Among the commentators who avoid discussion of these crucial passages is the editor of the most recently published reprint of *On Liberty*. Explaining that for Mill interference is justified only if the interests of other persons are harmed, this editor goes on to argue that this makes it difficult to justify intervention where the conduct is "regarded as merely offensive or disagreeable." And he adds, "the onus of producing evidence of 'harm' [is] on the proposers of interference, and, even more important, it rules out intervention on any other basis."[45] These assertions could not have been made, if it had been noticed that Mill said an individual "may suffer very severe penalties . . . for faults which directly concern only himself." And as for justification being needed for interference with conduct that is "offensive or disagreeable," this observation could not have been made if Mill's argument about distaste or contempt for depraved conduct had been considered.

Another critic who neglects Mill's approval of distaste or contempt as penalties for certain kinds of self-regarding conduct is C. L. Ten. For Mill

[43] Bain, *Mill*, 107.

[44] One might have expected Cowling to draw support from Mill's advocacy of distaste, contempt, and shaming; yet in arguing that Mill allowed coercive pressures, he ignores what Mill said about these things and refers only to education as the source of coercive pressures. Surprisingly, he quotes *On Liberty* only seventeen times. *Mill and Liberalism*, 102–4.

[45] Stefan Collini, Introduction, xvi–xvii, to Mill, *On Liberty with the Subjection of Women and Chapters in Socialism* (Cambridge: Cambridge University Press, 1989). These assertions are surprising in light of Collini's recognition elsewhere that Mill might have adopted "coercive premises" and that his was "hardly the voice of the textbook stereotype of liberal individualism." *Public Moralists*, 71.

to allow intervention, he tells us, the case "must rest on reasons other than, for example, the mere dislike or disapproval of the conduct." Also, "certain reasons for intervention—paternalistic, moralistic, and gut reactions—are irrelevant, whereas the prevention of harm to others is always relevant."[46] But what else are expressions of distaste and contempt if not gut reactions, and moralistic ones, at that? Ten's insistence that Mill does not allow disapproval on the basis of mere dislike does not occur in an isolated passage. He also asserts that for Mill, "The distress suffered by people when others act in ways which they strongly dislike or find repugnant should be discounted. . . . conduct must be harmful to others before it can be the subject of legal penalties or *coercive social pressures*" (emphasis added). Mill in fact does argue that there is no justification for the *majority* to act in this way, but Ten fails to notice that Mill does allow the minority of those with individuality of character to interfere with the self-regarding conduct of those whose behavior they (in Ten's words) "strongly dislike or find repugnant."[47] Ten also claims that the heart of Mill's liberalism is the "rejection of paternalism and of moralism, or the view that we may impose on all persons our opinion of right conduct even when by so doing we do not prevent harm to others." But it is difficult to know what is being done by those displaying distaste and contempt if they are not imposing their opinions of right conduct.[48]

In yet another example, it is asserted that Mill's liberty principle "affirms that individuals are rightfully granted absolute liberty in a distinct 'private' or 'self-regarding' sphere of actions"; and that "the liberty principle assigns *absolute* libertarian rights to any individual with respect to this private sphere of self-regarding actions."[49] Once again, Mill's statement about the severe penalties that may be suffered for self-regarding conduct has been ignored.

In still another example, Jeremy Waldron argues that Mill advocated "open struggle between competing conceptions of the good life" even if it meant accepting "the dangers of peoples practicing life-styles that are actually depraved." It is difficult to reconcile this with Mill's proposal that those he labeled depraved be subjected to penalties, including shaming and expressions of distaste and contempt.[50]

[46] Ten, *Mill on Liberty*, 41, and also 109, 113; see also above, chapter 1, text at notes 18–20. Ten alludes to Mill's account of distaste and contempt without quoting the passages where the words are used.

[47] C. L. Ten, "Mill's Place in Liberalism," *Political Science Reviewer* 24 (1995): 193; see also 181, 194, 199.

[48] Ibid., 181.

[49] Jonathan Riley, *Liberal Utilitarianism: Social Choice Theory and J. S. Mill's Philosophy* (Cambridge: Cambridge University Press, 1988), 208–9.

[50] Jeremy Waldron, "Mill and Moral Distress," in *Liberal Rights* (Cambridge: Cambridge University Press, 1993), 133; see also 118–26. Waldron suggests that a liberal ought to reject Bentham's panopticism, which allowed everyone to cast sidelong glances at others, as it

Judge Devlin made the same error, for he too assumed that in setting up a barrier to society's control of conduct in the private sphere, i.e., self-regarding conduct, Mill permitted complete freedom from interference. Mill's conception of a free society, he tells us, was one that "sought to control vice simply by passive resistance and good works."[51] But this statement fails to take account of all that Mill wrote about expressions of distaste and contempt and shaming and penalties for self-regarding vices.

To take another example, Richard Friedman attributes to Mill "an urgent concern to protect liberty against interceders from *all* areas of human affairs; and this is reflected in Mill's principle of liberty, which is intended to fix a limit on coercion *whatever its source* in the community" (emphasis added).[52] Once again, in making this assertion Friedman neglects the interceders identified by Mill in his provision for and justification of all the devices for shaming briefly mentioned in *On Liberty* and elaborately described in "Utility of Religion."

Unlike many recent commentators, some of Mill's contemporaries did notice the crucial passages that are difficult to reconcile with the conventional interpretation. Most notably, Harriet Martineau was not misled: "I think you will find, on a second reading [of *On Liberty*] . . . that Mill does not reject the penalty of *opinion* on self-regarding vices."[53]

Not all who have recently offered interpretations of *On Liberty* have ignored the crucial passages regarding penalties for self-regarding con-

---

denied "freedom from the public gaze . . . [which] is an indispensable condition for the nurture of moral agency." "Theoretical Foundations," ibid., 58–59. But this criterion would not allow Mill to be called a liberal.

[51] Patrick Devlin, "Mill on Liberty in Morals," in *The Enforcement of Morality* (London: Oxford University Press, 1965), 106.

[52] Richard Friedman, "A New Exploration of Mill's Essay *On Liberty*," *Political Studies* 14 (October 1966): 286. For other examples, see Berger, *Justice, Happiness, and Freedom*, 259, 274; John Gray, *Mill on Liberty: A Defence* (London: Routledge, 1983), 77–78, 103, 119; F. A. Hayek, *Constitution of Liberty* (Chicago: University of Chicago Press, 1960), 146; Bernard Semmel, *John Stuart Mill and the Pursuit of Virtue* (New Haven: Yale University Press, 1983), 167, 196, *passim*. While these and many other commentators have largely ignored Mill's proposals that shaming and the pressures of opinion be used to shape and direct conduct and character, Gertrude Himmelfarb, upholding the "two Mills" thesis, recognizes this side of Mill's perspective but locates it only in the "other Mill," i.e., in most of his writings other than *On Liberty*, and neglects the presence of this theme in *On Liberty*. The argument that *On Liberty* authorizes license is not compatible with the passages on distaste, contempt, and shaming. See her *On Liberty and Liberalism*, 139, where she sharply distinguishes the other works which emphasize "the development of the social character of man" from *On Liberty* in which "Mill looked . . . in precisely the opposite direction, the development of man's individuality."

[53] Harriet Martineau to Rev. R. P. Graves, 20 May 1859, *Selected Letters*, ed. Valerie Sanders (Oxford: Clarendon, 1990), 180. James Fitzjames Stephen also noticed Mill's argument about distaste and contempt, and he recognized its implications: "Mr. Mill on Political Liberty," *Saturday Review*, 12 February 1859, 187; also in *Liberty Equality Fraternity* (2d ed., 1874), ed. R. J. White (Cambridge: Cambridge University Press, 1967), 58–59. See also, Bernard Bosanquet, *Philosophical Theory of the State* (London, 1899), 63; and Frederic Harrison, *Tennyson, Ruskin, Mill*, 283.

duct. For example, John C. Rees, one of the more prominent commentators on *On Liberty*, takes note of their presence but does not seem to take them at all seriously. Rather than recognize that they are not compatible either with the longstanding interpretation of *On Liberty* or with his revision of it, he suggests that the distasteful and contemptible conduct to which Mill referred was "perhaps misleadingly [called] 'self- regarding conduct.' " He also assumes that Mill's words resulted from "unintentional, loose use of language." Thus by denying the significance of this part of Mill's argument, Rees seeks to uphold his claim that the only conduct subject to penalty is that which harms the interests of others. "According to the doctrine of *On Liberty* encroachments [on individuality] constitute an improper interference with 'self-regarding' conduct: the individual is being held accountable for actions that cause no harm to others."[54] But this invites the obvious objection: expressions of distaste and contempt are very likely to be regarded as encroachments on individuality. Rees, moreover, claims that "Mill does not say that men will be coerced or pressed into a life of higher cultivation of the mind. . . . if a man should choose what Mill would consider a depraved form of life he is to suffer no more than 'the loss of consideration' and 'the inconveniences strictly inseparable from the unfavorable judgment of others.' "[55] But it is difficult to know what Mill intended in the passages on distaste and contempt if he did not expect that men would be "pressed" into a less depraved way of living. Rees refuses to acknowledge that distaste and contempt constitute coercive pressure, and he makes light of what would be involved in becoming the target of distaste and contempt; and while it is correct that Mill avoided saying depraved persons would be coerced, he certainly allowed and even advocated that they be "pressed," and such pressures would be applied in a way that would make the person feeling such pressure also feel coerced.[56]

H.L.A. Hart also notes Mill's references to distaste and contempt, but, like Rees, he does not draw the implication for liberty from what Mill said. For one thing, Hart misrepresents what Mill said, indicating that Mill provided only that the target of harsh judgments be warned about possible feelings of distaste and contempt, whereas Mill justified and advocated the expression of such feelings. Hart senses that Mill was on dan-

[54] John C. Rees, *John Stuart Mill's* On Liberty, ed. G. L. Williams (Oxford: Clarendon, 1985), 40, 46, 146, 173. For another example of unwillingness to accept Mill's words and arguments, see Waldron's discussion of Mill's consideration of violations of good manners being "Offences against others." Waldron acknowledges this to be "a difficult passage to accommodate," and he concludes it should be "charitably overlooked." "Mill and Moral Distress," *Liberal Rights*, 131.

[55] Rees, *Mill's* On Liberty, 134–35.

[56] For another example of one who, though aware of the passages on distaste and contempt, insists that they do not reduce liberty or autonomy, see Richard J. Arneson, "Mill versus Paternalism," *Ethics* 90 (July 1980): 476, 478, 485.

gerous ground, for he acknowledges that "Mill here comes perilously near to sanctioning coercion." Yet surprisingly he concludes that although Mill "erred in that direction [of coercion]," his references to distaste and contempt did not involve punishment or loss of liberty.[57]

In another example of a Mill scholar acknowledging the presence of the crucial passages about distaste and contempt, Alan Ryan takes note of Mill's argument that there should be penalties for objectionable self-regarding conduct, but, like Rees and Hart, he denies that these passages undermine Mill's defense of liberty. He points to Mill's observation that the penalties are a natural ill-consequence of the objectionable self-regarding conduct and claims that distaste and contempt "are not a case of coercion" and do not constitute punishment. "Punishment involves the intention to inflict harm; in this case the harm is a side effect of each person exercising his freedom." But this does not explain why Mill called such consequences "penalties"—a word, if not synonymous with, at least akin to, the word "punishment," which Mill used for the consequence he recommended for conduct that harmed others. Nor does it explain why, if the consequences were merely side effects, Mill advocated that disapproving judgments of such self-regarding conduct be made more often. Such advocacy indicates that Mill recognized such judgments were to be deliberate and intended and were not natural side effects, and this allows us to conclude that he meant what he said when he stated that there could be penalties for self-regarding conduct.[58]

—————

Mill's provision for penalties on self-regarding conduct and his calls for expressions of distaste and contempt have been explained as mere persuasion with respect to matters beyond the realm of morality.

[57] H.L.A. Hart, *Law, Liberty, and Morality* (Stanford: Stanford University Press, 1963), 77. In contrast to Hart and many others, Schoeman recognizes the full import of the crucial passages in chapter four of *On Liberty*: "The problem is that only a fine line prevents these tactics [of expressing distaste or contempt] from evolving into intimidation and harassment, particularly when one's own critical assessment is widely shared. Oddly, . . . Mill unleashes an activism that has no limitation in scope. Anything about another's life becomes open game for our probing challenges. . . . Mill exposed [others] to social confrontation in a way that may intensify the social control that concerned Mill so profoundly. . . . Mill has . . . exposed people to social pressures to account for themselves and to conform to others' expectations." Ferdinand David Schoeman, *Privacy and Social Freedom* (Cambridge: Cambridge University Press, 1992), 31–32, 34. See also the observation by G. W. Smith, that Mill's "attempt to mark out a sphere of privacy, is misleadingly interpreted if it is read simply as a 'hands off' command to society and the state. . . . The private sphere is not a social vacuum; neither does the individualist who enjoys its protection escape the moralizing influences of the economic and political institutions and practices of his society." "Freedom and Virtue in Politics: Some Aspects of Character, Circumstances and Utility from Helvetius to J. S. Mill," *Utilitas* 1 (May 1989): 132.

[58] Alan Ryan, *The Philosophy of John Stuart Mill* (2d ed.; Atlantic Highlands, N.J.: Humanities Press International, 1990), 235, 237–39, 243. See also Ryan, *J. S. Mill*, 145–46.

The scholars who recognize that Mill was eager to discourage objectionable self-regarding conduct usually try to defend Mill's position as a strong advocate of individual liberty by arguing that Mill allowed only attempts to persuade persons displaying the objectionable conduct, and that such persuasion did not constitute punishment and was not coercive. There is some evidence for this interpretation in Mill's text, even though it is not all the evidence he provided. He did say one should remonstrate, advise, reason with, entreat; and that the distinction between "loss of consideration" and punishment for harm to others was "not a merely nominal distinction" (279). The withholding of consideration, he said, might only involve showing the person with self-regarding defects "how he may avoid or cure the evils his conduct tends to bring upon him." Thus he will be "an object of pity, perhaps dislike, but not of anger or resentment" (280). By focusing on these statements, it is concluded that to try to influence and improve the self-regarding conduct of others is not to interfere with their liberty: to advise, remonstrate, and persuade, after all, is not to punish. Thus Ryan argues that, according to Mill, self-regarding faults do not harm others and do not constitute violations of morality, and therefore only entreaties, warnings, exhortations, and persuasion are appropriate. And such activities, he insists, should not be construed as being coercive.[59]

This position—that those with self-regarding faults may be subjected to persuasion but not coercion—has been reinforced by linking Mill's principle of liberty to his arguments about morality and justice in *Utilitarianism* and *Logic*. This interpretation has been developed by spokesmen for the so-called "revisionist" position, and notably by Alan Ryan, though others have contributed to it.[60] In *Utilitarianism*, Ryan points out, Mill explains that if a wrong is done, it is justifiably punished; it might be punished through legal punishment or through moral condemnation of public opinion or by conscience, which reflects society's moral rules. One such wrong is doing harm to an identifiable person, and thus *Utilitarian-*

R. J. Halliday makes a similar argument. *John Stuart Mill* (New York: Barnes & Noble, 1976), 118.

[59] Ryan, *The Philosophy of John Stuart Mill*, 236, 254; see also Ryan, "John Stuart Mill and the Open Society," *Listener* 89, no. 2303 (17 May 1973): 635; "Mr. McCloskey on Mill's Liberalism," *Philosophical Quarterly* 14 (July 1964): 257. For other examples, see G. L. Williams, "Mill's Principle of Liberty," *Political Studies*, 24 June 1976), 131–35; Rees, *John Stuart Mill's* On Liberty, 131–32, 139–54; Ten, "Mill's Place in Liberalism," *Political Science Reviewer* 24 (1995): 200; Hart, *Law, Liberty, Morality*, 75–77.

[60] See above, chapter 1, text at note 7. Other revisionists include John C. Rees, John Gray, Fred Berger, Richard Wollheim, Geraint Williams, among others. All argue that Mill's defense of liberty is consistent with his utilitarianism, but they do not always interpret his utilitarianism in the same way. For comment on variants of the revisionist position see John Gray and G. W. Smith, Introduction, 1–21, in *J. S. Mill's On Liberty in Focus* (London: Routledge, 1991); and John Gray, *Mill on Liberty: A Defence* (London: Routledge, 1983), 1–14, 131 n.17.

ism is linked to *On Liberty*, for the harm principle in the latter work is interpreted as an application of the more comprehensive doctrine presented in *Utilitarianism*. Through this linkage Ryan shows that the punishments justified in *On Liberty* are used to enforce morality, but, Ryan emphasizes, the morality that is enforced is not the privately held "moral" opinions of most citizens, but rather morality in a very specific sense.[61]

To explain the specific meaning of enforceable morality, Ryan turns to *Logic*, where he finds a distinction between acts that really are wrong and therefore punishable and those that are foolish or unaesthetic and therefore subject to disapproval but not punishment. This distinction, which is also made in *On Liberty*, especially in chapter four, appeared in the part of *Logic* where Mill analyzed the Art of Life. He divided it into three parts—Morality, Prudence, and Aesthetics. Morality is concerned with right and wrong; Prudence with what is wise or foolish; Aesthetics with what is noble or base. Morality, on one side, makes categorical commands and defines obligations—it is concerned with conduct that might harm the interests of others. Prudence and Aesthetics, however, are concerned with self-regarding conduct. To behave well with regard to them is not a matter of duty or obligation. The parallel with the argument of *On Liberty* is evident: Morality, which defines obligations (such as the obligation not to harm others) is enforceable, and therefore violations of it can subject one to coercion; but deviations from what is recommended by the rules of Prudence or Aesthetics are self-regarding and not subject to coercion.[62]

The distinction between Morality, on the one side, and Prudence and Aesthetics, on the other, is assimilated to the argument of *On Liberty* in yet another way by Ryan, for it allows him to distinguish legitimate from illegitimate enforcements of morality. In Ryan's interpretation, Mill does allow the enforcement of morality, but only the morality that is deliberately formed with the purpose of defining the moral rules that make social existence possible, including provision for preventing harm to assignable persons. Quite different from this kind of morality are the "moral" judgments emanating from uninformed and prejudiced persons who wish to impose their feelings and opinions on others. Such feelings and opinions are often regarded as having a moral character; they constitute what is

---

[61] Ryan, *Philosophy of John Stuart Mill*, 213–46. See also Mill, *Utilitarianism*, CW, 10, 246–47; J. O. Urmson, "The Interpretation of the Moral Philosophy of J. S. Mill," *Philosophical Quarterly* 3 (1953): 36–39; D. G. Brown, "Mill on Liberty and Morality," *Philosophical Review*, 81 (April 1972), 146–58; John Gray, Introduction, *On Liberty and Other Essays*, ed. John Gray (Oxford, Oxford University Press, 1991), xii, xv.
[62] Ryan, *Philosophy of John Stuart Mill*, 215, 219, 233, 237–38, 240, 245; Ryan, "Mr. McCloskey on Mill's Liberalism," *Philosophical Quarterly*, 14 (July 1964), 255, 258–59.

called private morality, and this was what Devlin had in mind when he called for the enforcement of morality. But according to Ryan, such feelings and opinions only reflect what Mill called the "likings and dislikings of society" (222), and they arise from "constructing bogus moral rules out of mere likings."[63] Such judgments, possibly praiseworthy but often prejudiced and misguided, are really prudential or aesthetic in character, for they concern the wisdom or foolishness and the nobility or baseness of self-regarding conduct. This argument has the effect of narrowly circumscribing the province of morality and harm, and therefore it allows for an expansive realm in which liberty will thrive.[64]

This entire argument, which justifies coercion for violations of a narrowly defined harm and, at the same time, classifies all other conduct as being subject *only* to the standards of Prudence and Aesthetics, implies that it is inconceivable that Mill would approve of applying coercive pressures to persons whose conduct caused no harm to others. Thus Ryan and others are dismissive of suggestions that Mill's advocacy of distaste and contempt constitute such coercive pressures. He and others place exaggerated emphasis on Mill's references to persuasion, and they neglect his more severe ways of dealing with self-regarding faults.

There are several difficulties with this position. One arises from Mill's use of much stronger language than that of mere persuasion, advice, and warning. Expressions of distaste and contempt comprise more than persuasion by means of rational discussion. Also, Mill called these things penalties, a word he could have easily circumvented to avoid the implication of coerciveness. Adding to the difficulty, in "Utility of Religion" he described the deterring power of shame, which caused "*fear* of shame," "*dread* . . . of being disliked or hated," and "*painfulness*" of knowing that one is regarded in this way (emphasis added). He also described a range of penalties, including ostracism, denial of various good offices, and

---

[63] Alan Ryan, "Mr. McCloskey on Mill's Liberalism," *Philosophical Quarterly*, 14 (July 1964), 256; see also 259; *Philosophy of John Stuart Mill*, 244–45. The distinction between enforceable morality and non-enforceable private morality underlies the argument that morality-dependent harms are self-regarding. See Richard Wollheim, "John Stuart Mill and the Limits of State Action," *Social Research*, 40 (1973), 9, 15–17; Jeremy Waldron, "Mill and the Value of Moral Distress,"*Liberal Rights*, 117–20. In the literature, homosexuality is a favorite example of conduct disapproved by misguided, non-enforceable private morality which, it is assumed, Mill would have tolerated. But there is nothing that he said about "animal pleasures" (see text at note 4) that might not apply to homosexuality as much as it did to heterosexuality. He would not have legally prohibited it, nor would he have disapproved because it was a target of those reflecting the "dislikings of [contemporary] society." But to the extent that it involved the pursuit of "animal pleasures at the expense of those of feeling and intellect," it would be an example of self- regarding vices that would be subject to expressions of distaste or contempt by those promoting higher pleasures.

[64] There are striking parallels between the part of Mill's position that Ryan highlights and passages in Locke's *A Letter Concerning Toleration*, ed. James H. Tully (1689; Indianapolis, Hackett, 1983), 27, 35, 47.

loss of means of subsistence.[65] These things are almost never mentioned by the commentators who argue that Mill allowed only noncoercive persuasion when trying to improve the conduct or quality of life for those with self-regarding faults. The passages in "Utility of Religion" (an essay composed as *On Liberty* was being planned and written) are not even used by those who are prepared to support their interpretations by drawing on works other than *On Liberty*. Even Mill's references in *On Liberty* to distaste and contempt are not often mentioned or they are treated as insignificant.[66]

While it can be reasonably argued that Mill's references to persuasion did not imply coercion, the coercive dimension of shaming and expressions of distaste and contempt cannot be so easily discounted. Persuasion can be an appeal to reason but, obviously, causing fear, dread, and pain are appeals of a different kind; and many of the other penalties mentioned by Mill—all for self-regarding faults—can be as coercive as the punishments for harm done, which, of course, he sanctioned. Where along the scale, beginning with persuasion and becoming increasingly severe, Mill's penalties became coercive and punishing is a question for which there is no clear answer, but it is clear that there is a threshold beyond which his penalties are experienced as if they were akin to punishments and where they become coercive. Bain took this view, for, though initially he held that disesteem is not the same as punishment, he quickly abandoned this position. He pointed out that there are many degrees of demerit, and "the point where punishment in any proper sense could be said to begin would be about the middle of the scale." In other words, mildly stated disapproval is disesteem but not punishment, but more intensely expressed disapproval becomes punishment.[67]

From the perspective of the person exposed to distaste, contempt, or shaming, it would be difficult to distinguish between these manifestations of disapprobation coming from the superior natures and the "moral coercion of public opinion" (223), which Mill provided as a punishment for harm done to others. Ryan emphasizes that the latter would be organized

---

[65] "Utility of Religion," *CW, 10,* 410–11; see also Early Draft, *CW, 1,* 240. See above, text between notes 12 and 17.

[66] See above, text at notes 44ff.

[67] Bain, *Mill,* 108–9. R. J. Halliday recognizes that one must ask, "which kinds of persuasion were compatible with liberty; could persuasion, in fact, be distinguished from compulsion?" And he observes, "If persuasion cannot be distinguished from compulsion there is little point in the categorisation of human behaviour into self-and other-regarding conduct." "Some Recent Interpretations of John Stuart Mill," *Philosophy, 43* (January 1968), 12. Frederic Harrison recognized the difficulty. "Mill has left it exceedingly vague what is the line that he draws between the 'persuasion,' exhortation, instruction, and apparently even the boycotting, which he admits, and the 'moral coercion of public opinion,' which he regards as iniquitous." *Tennyson, Ruskin, Mill,* 283. See also McCloskey, *John Stuart Mill: a Critical Study,* 117–118.

whereas the former would be individual and diverse.[68] But this is a distinction clearer to him than it would be to the person against whom distaste, contempt, shaming, and the other penalties would be directed. That person, at the very least, would experience humiliation, and very probably he would be intimidated. The distaste, contempt, and shaming, moreover, would not be expressed unemotionally, as if in the spirit of reasoned persuasion, for Mill made it clear that the inferior, depraved person would experience fear, dread, and pain, emotions not likely to be caused by calmly expressed, reasoned argument.[69]

Another difficulty with the argument that interprets Mill's principle of liberty in light of his narrow definition of the province of morality in *Logic*—and this is a difficulty with most commentary on *On Liberty*—is that it fails to recognize what for Mill is an important source of moral authority located in those with individuality of character. In most of the existing interpretations, it is assumed that Mill classified attempts to coerce into those initiated by society, through its legal institutions and through "the moral coercion of public opinion" (223), and those that are initiated by misguided persons who seek to impose their views which are not genuinely moral but merely reflect the "likings and dislikings of society." The first of these are legitimate claims to moral authority and the second are, of course, illegitimate. This assumption ignores Mill's account of the function of those with individuality. In advance of society, and in anticipation of the future when a religion of humanity would be in place, these superior natures with elevated character make judgments reflecting the morality, not of existing society, but of the society of the future. They also are enforcers of morality—the future morality that they help to create. Their enforcing involves penalties rather than punishments, but the pain suffered by the penalized is not less severe than what is experienced by those who are punished by the agents of existing society.[70]

---

[68] *The Philosophy of John Stuart Mill*, 237, 240, 244. By distinguishing [socially] organized actions from those that are individual, Ryan does not avoid the social dimension of the attempts by individuals to influence self-regarding conduct of others, for Mill acknowledged that "to give advice . . . to any one, is a social act" (296). Since disapproval by individuals would be perceived as social, doubt may be cast on Ryan's statement that Mill was concerned "with [i.e., disapproving of] *all* forms of social pressure." *Philosophy of John Stuart Mill*, 235.

[69] "Utility of Religion," CW, *10*, 410–11. Bain, in a work commended by Mill (*Utilitarianism*, CW, *10*, 246n.), described how distaste, contempt, and shaming would be experienced: "Censure, Disapprobation, Dispraise, Abuse, Libel, Scorn, Infamy increase the feeling of self-humiliation, or at least increase the pain of it. . . . they themselves affect the mind with misery and terror, and the sense of outer darkness. . . . when a man has strongly roused our disfavour we are not content with slighting his personal qualities, but are ready to damage his happiness in many other ways. . . . The feeling of Shame is . . . the dread of being condemned, or ill-thought of, by others." *The Emotions and the Will* (London, 1859), 141–42.

[70] Mill's providing this role for the "superior natures" in relation to the inferior and depraved calls for qualification of the argument that Mill was anti-paternalist, such as that

When describing the exercise of moral authority by the superior natures on behalf of future society, Mill rather consistently refers to their attempts to enforce the superior future morality as the imposition of *penalties*, whereas the legitimate enforcements of existing morality he calls *punishments*. Although, obviously, there are affinities between these two things, there are also differences; and an examination of the similarities and differences between punishments and penalties will confirm that Mill regarded the superior natures—those with individuality—as having the responsibility to promote and enforce a new morality that anticipates the coming ethos of altruism. There are many similarities. Penalties, like punishments, are imposed deliberately. Those who impose them are the self-controlled superior natures. Penalizing, Mill says, is a matter of "right, and it may be our duty" (278); therefore it is not the result of thoughtless impulse. This is confirmed by Mill's recommendation that such penalizing take place.[71] Moreover, penalties—distaste, contempt, ostracism, shaming, humiliation—would be experienced no differently than one of Mill's two types of punishment. While obviously they are different from a legally imposed fine or a prison sentence, the "fear . . . dread . . . painfulness" they produce is indistinguishable from the experience of being exposed to the "moral coercion of public opinion" (223), which for Mill was one of the punishments for harm done to others. In addition, penalties, like punishments, were intended to deter, or, as Mill put it, they were to improve, which, of course, included abandonment of undesirable conduct. And finally, liberty is limited by both penalties and punishments, for both establish disincentives for repeating the conduct that calls for one or the other. Penalties and punishments are different, however, with regard to the morality that justifies the suffering caused by each. Punishments are used to enforce the moral rules established by the law or opinion of existing society, such as the society's rules intended to prevent harm; penalties, on the other hand, are imposed on behalf of future morality that condemns selfishness and promotes altruism. And the instruments for enforcement are also different: for punishments they are the legal establishment and public opinion; for penalties they are those bold, courageous, strong-minded, creative initiators, that is, those with individuality, who take it upon themselves to promote moral regeneration.

---

made by Nicholas Capaldi ("John Stuart Mill's Defence of Liberal Culture," *Political Science Reviewer* 24 (1995), 225, 240) or Gerald Dworkin, that for Mill, choosing is a good independent of what is chosen. "Paternalism," in *Philosophy of Law*, eds. Joel Feinberg and Hyman Gross (Encino, 1975), 179.

[71] This includes the so-called natural penalties (278, 282); see above, 366. Whereas Mill's recommendation that penalties be imposed implies that the imposition be deliberate, one of his types of punishment, by contrast, would be quite spontaneous. It is difficult to visualize deliberation preceding the punishment which consisted of the expression of "the moral coercion of public opinion." (223)

The affinities between penalties and punishments reflect the difficulty of distinguishing too sharply a province of morality, in which there are enforceable obligations, from a province concerned with aesthetics and prudential matters, in which noncoercive judgments are made. Although Mill described these differing jurisdictions in *Logic*, when, in *On Liberty* and elsewhere, he recommended how judgments should be made, he allowed that moral considerations affected the judgments which, according to the definitions in *Logic*, were supposed to be concerned with matters of taste and prudence. In other words, the distinctions set out in *Logic* became quite blurred in practice. This was most evident in his use of the language of morality to describe the self-regarding conduct he wished to have stamped out. Thus in the campaign carried on by those with individuality of character against those he called depraved, the goal was to make them less selfish and more considerate of others, that is, to change their morality. This struggle of superiors against inferiors was a moral struggle. It was undertaken by those whose conduct was approved by Mill's revised utilitarian standard, and it was directed against those with miserable individuality whose conduct, as he characterized it in *Utilitarianism*, was low and piglike. This was part of his argument about what was preferable and what came closest to meeting the utilitarian (that is, an ethical) standard. The penalties were imposed for self-regarding conduct that was not only contrary to good taste or maxims about what is prudent; it also violated a moral standard.

The mixing of moral with aesthetic and prudential judgments was made evident in Mill's criticism of Bentham, who, he explained, did not believe it justified to pass judgment about another person's good or bad taste. Such judgments Bentham regarded as unjust and prejudiced. But Mill rejected this, arguing that matters of taste—"men's likings and dislikings, on things in themselves indifferent [i.e., self-regarding]"—were "pregnant with the most important inferences as to every point of their characters." A person's tastes, Mill explained, "show him to be wise or a fool, cultivated or ignorant, gentle or rough, polished or coarse, sensitive or callous, generous or sordid, benevolent or selfish, conscientious or depraved."[72] Thus taste, a matter for aesthetic judgment, has implications for character, including selfishness, which clearly are matters of moral judgment.

The failure to recognize the claim to moral authority by those with superior natures is a consequence of not taking into account the importance of the historical dimension of Mill's thinking. The theory of history that assumed alternating transitional and organic eras underlay Mill's reflections and speculations about liberty, morality, authority, and the reli-

[72] "Bentham," *CW, 10,* 113.

gion of humanity, and consequently he believed that what was suitable in one state of society would be inappropriate in another. The things that would change included morality, the scope of moral authority, the identity of the persons exercising moral authority, and the balance between moral demands and individual liberty.

Notwithstanding the context provided by Mill's theory of history, *On Liberty* and related writings on ethics are often regarded as settling Mill's principle of liberty once and for all, and thus there is a failure to recognize that for Mill there was a movable boundary between the realm of morality (and therefore obligation and the subjection to coercion for violations of moral rules) and the realm of prudence (and therefore immunity from the coercion applied by agents of existing society). During the present transitional era there were limitations on the claims of morality which Mill recognized as valid. "There is a standard of altruism to which all should be required to come up, and a degree beyond it which is not obligatory, but meritorious." If one acts in praiseworthy ways without having been obligated to do so, one deserves "gratitude and honour, and . . . moral praise." But if one fails to do so, one ought not be coerced (at least, not by those enforcing the morality of existing society). This distinction, while usable during the existing transitional era, becomes outmoded, however, as circumstances change, for, after explaining this distinction, Mill, in the same paragraph, describes how moral obligations and therefore vulnerability to coercion can greatly increase. Everyone, Mill explains, is expected to perform certain good offices and disinterested services; this is customary, and these offices and services are required of those who avail themselves of the advantages of society. And a person "deserves moral blame if, without just cause, he disappoints that expectation." What is expected of one will vary, however, depending on what customs are in place—it will depend on what it is that "the moral improvement attained by mankind has rendered customary."[73] Thus the boundary between morality and prudence (and therefore between obligation and liberty) can change. "Through this principle *the domain of moral duty, in an improving society, is always widening. When what once was uncommon virtue becomes common virtue, it comes to be numbered among obligations*, while a degree exceeding what has grown common, remains simply meritorious" (emphasis added).[74] Thus the scope of enforceable

[73] Mill alludes to substantive changes in custom in *On Liberty* where he notes that "it is important to give the freest scope possible to uncustomary things, in order that it may in time appear which of these are fit to be converted into customs" (269).

[74] *Auguste Comte and Positivism*, CW, *10*, 337–38. This passage was not quoted by Rees, who, however, quoted earlier parts of the paragraph in which this passage appeared; the earlier part of the paragraph suggests that there are fixed limits to the scope of obligation.

morality and obligation increases and the extent of liberty diminishes. Mill could not have more clearly revealed his expectation that the realm of self-regarding conduct, where liberty was supposed to be protected, would be reduced. This is what he alluded to in *On Liberty* where he referred to "the adjustment of the boundaries between it [liberty] and social control" (261).

Mill was concerned with beliefs as well as conduct, and his proposals for altering beliefs about individual goals and obligations, which were incorporated into his views about the need for a religion of humanity, also had far-reaching implications for individual liberty.

There is a prima facie difficulty in reconciling individual liberty with such a future organic state of society, and it arises with regard to both a liberty of conduct and a liberty of thought and discussion. The difficulty has its origin in the extent of cohesiveness required by a society with a religion of humanity. Such a society is an extension of the type of regime which Mill, following the St. Simonians, first called natural and later organic. Whatever label he used, he thought of it in contrast to the transitional state, which was characterized by disagreement, conflict, the absence of established authority, and intellectual anarchy—a state in which individual liberty flourished. The organic era, which was expected to follow a transitional period, ushered in agreement, authority, cohesion, and stability. There would be "a large body of received doctrine, covering nearly the whole field of the moral relations of man, and which no one thinks of questioning."[75] There would also be "a united body of moral authority, sufficient to extort acquiescence from the uninquiring, or uninformed majority."[76]

These passages were written in 1831, but Mill did not abandon the main themes and fundamental categories that he introduced in "Spirit of the Age."[77] He continued to regard his own time as having the features of what in 1831 he began calling a transitional age, and he continued to visualize ways in which a natural or organic state of society could super-

---

Rees, *John Stuart Mill's On Liberty*, 161. This shifting boundary between what is obligatory and what is only praiseworthy would seem to call for qualification of the statement, "There is a clear and simple line to be drawn between morality and prudence." Ryan, *Philosophy of John Stuart Mill*, 219.

[75] "Spirit of the Age," *CW*, 22, 244.

[76] Ibid., 304–5.

[77] See above, chapter 6, text at note 47. Cf. Ten: "The Mill of this period [when 'Spirit of the Age' was written] differed radically from the Mill of *On Liberty*." *Mill on Liberty*, 170.

sede the transitional state. This was evident in what he wrote about the kind of society recommended by Coleridge, in what he wrote about social statics and the conditions of stable political society, and in his anticipations of a future religion of humanity. Since many of these reflections immediately preceded or were contemporary to his composition of *On Liberty* or were republished at this time, it should be assumed that these ideas, including those about a religion of humanity, were not abandoned when *On Liberty* was written.[78] In varied places, including *On Liberty*, he invoked the image of a religion of humanity in ways that had implications for his views on the claims of liberty.

The problematic status of liberty in an organic state of society, including one with a religion of humanity, becomes particularly clear where Mill discusses the sociological conditions necessary for such a state of society to exist—what he called "the requisites of stable political union." Following Comte, he explained that to understand such requisites was the task of Social Statics, a science which explained how mankind could overcome the divisiveness caused by the powerful selfish tendencies in uncultivated human nature. Mill's inquiries into Social Statics allowed him to conclude that "social existence is only possible by a disciplining of those more powerful propensities [of selfishness], which consists in subordinating them to *a common system of opinions*" (emphasis added).[79]

This perspective is explained in greater detail in the well-known passages in *Logic* (and earlier in "Coleridge") in which Mill offered an explanation of the three conditions necessary for a stable—that is, an organic—state of society, such as would exist when a religion of humanity was in place. The first of these conditions, it will be recalled, was a system of education that provided a *"restraining discipline"* which would create the habit of subordinating personal impulses and aims to what were considered the ends of society.[80] Of course this was a description of education in the widest sense, as it called for socialization that led to subordination of the individual to society, and it seems to be the negation of the ideal of individuality put forth in chapter three of *On Liberty*. However, he could

---

[78] For consideration of why "Spirit of the Age" was not reprinted in *Dissertations and Discussions*, see below, chapter 9, text between notes 23 and 24. Gray acknowledges that the doctrine of liberty is weakened if the religion of humanity is regarded as part of Mill's perspective. *Mill On Liberty: A Defence* (1983), 123. Richard Vernon notes that Mill's religion of humanity does not allow for private life, and he asks whether "the real Mill is a more conservative and authoritarian figure than liberals would like to believe?" (Authoritarian, perhaps, but conservative?) "J. S. Mill and the Religion of Humanity," in *Religion, Secularization and Political Thought: Thomas Hobbes to J. S. Mill*, ed. James E. Crimmins (London: Routledge, 1984), 170–71; see also 175, 177.

[79] *Logic*, CW, 8, 920, 926.

[80] Ibid., 921; see above, chapter 6, text at notes 31–35, for a full statement.

not have believed *On Liberty* was incompatible with what he had written about the condition of stable political society, for he reprinted these passages as they had appeared in "Coleridge" (1840) in *Dissertations and Discussions*, which appeared in the same year as *On Liberty*; and this was deliberate, for there were other notable articles he did leave out and yet others he radically edited, leaving out some parts. The passages on stable political society, which were also included in *Logic* (1843), were similarly retained in the 1862 edition of *Logic*, which in other parts was radically altered. By deliberately retaining what could have been deleted, Mill testified to his sense of the compatibility between these critical passages and *On Liberty*.

The second proposition that identified a condition necessary for permanent political society held that there had to be a feeling of allegiance or loyalty to "*something* which is settled, something permanent, and not to be called in question." This one thing might be a God, a person, laws, or principles; and it was necessary in any and all forms of government. Thus there would be "some fixed point: something which people agreed in holding sacred," and even where freedom of discussion was an established principle, this shared belief generally "was in the common estimation placed beyond discussion."[81] In other words, while in theory anything could be discussed, in practice, certain matters were taboo. Here was an acknowledgment that however much liberty of discussion was necessary in a transitional state of society, less than full liberty of thought and discussion would exist in a post-transitional state, that is, in a future organic state of society.

The third proposition held that stability required an "active principle of cohesion" such as exists where there are shared feelings of mutual sympathy among those within national boundaries. This is evident where there is a feeling of being one people with common interests and a feeling that "evil to any of their fellow-countrymen is evil to themselves, and [they] do not desire selfishly to free themselves from their share of any common inconvenience by severing the connexion."[82] Since this feeling of cohesion and obligation would limit what an individual felt free to do, this condition also has implications for liberty.

How are these propositions about the conditions of stable political society to be reconciled with the argument of *On Liberty*? They clearly visualize a state of society with much less of the ample liberty Mill recommended in the early chapters of *On Liberty*.[83] A restraining discipline that

---

[81] Ibid., 922.
[82] Ibid., 923.
[83] George Grote was dismayed by these passages. He believed in the importance of freedom to hold any opinion before he read *On Liberty*, and when he did read it, he regarded

subordinates personal impulses to the ends of society is not compatible with a liberating individuality. Nor is the existence of something settled which is not expected to be called into question and which is regarded as sacred and beyond discussion, consistent with the full liberty of discussion advocated in *On Liberty*.[84]

The propositions in *Logic* are not consistent with *On Liberty*, at least not with the first three chapters where Mill presents his strongest arguments for liberty. In these chapters liberty is defended primarily for its usefulness in discarding error and discovering truth and for discrediting customs and creating openings for new practices and institutions. Liberty of thought and discussion was expected to contribute to the erosion of Christian belief; and freedom from custom and established expectations was supposed to liberate those with individuality so they could perform their functions, including that of criticizing the old and obsolete, but also to allow them to develop new doctrines and new institutions for a future age. In all these ways liberty was to serve a transitional era by permitting criticism, undermining, and delegitimizing—to hasten its disintegrating ethos, and create conditions that would permit the emergence of an organic state of society. It flourished under conditions fundamentally different from those that would exist in an organic type of society, including the conditions for a stable society described in *Logic*.

There is another part of the argument of *On Liberty*, however, which is not inconsistent with the propositions about the requirements for a

---

it as eloquent confirmation of his views. But the passages in *Logic*, especially the one about certain things being settled and not called into question, led him to question Mill's belief in liberty. He "never ceased [according to Bain] to convert this remark into an expression for the standing intolerance of society towards unpopular opinions." Bain, *Mill*, 57. Some of Mill's distinctive rhetoric in *On Liberty* is remarkably similar to language used by Grote in his enthusiastic account of Periclean Athens (in *History of Greece*) and quoted by Mill in "Grote's History of Greece [II]" (1853), *CW*, *11*, 320.

[84] Nicholas Capaldi denies that there is incompatibility but on the ground that the sacred doctrine, which was to be beyond discussion, would be a "belief in rational discussion." Mill did say that the sacred doctrine might be "the principles of individual freedom and political and social equality," and he also said, "this is the only shape in which the feeling [of] attachment is likely to exist hereafter." *Logic*, *CW*, 8, 922. While this statement by Mill gives a small measure of plausibility to Capaldi's argument, it leaves unexplained the apparent contradiction between Mill's definition of liberty and the first proposition, which called for restraining discipline; nor does it explain the passage in *On Liberty* about "the consolidation of opinion" (see text at notes 85–88); nor the relation of these passages to Mill's religion of humanity, nor the hypothesis that the passages in *Logic* describe a stage in historical development and therefore a state of society altogether different from the state of society in which the recommendations in *On Liberty* would be most valuable. See Nicholas Capaldi, "Censorship and Social Stability in J. S. Mill," *The Mill Newsletter* 9, no. 1 (fall 1973): 12–16. C. L. Ten offers a perspective similar to Capaldi's: see *Mill On Liberty* (Oxford: Clarendon, 1980), 92, 97, 162–3. And elsewhere, like Capaldi, Ten ignores the first of Mill's three propositions. "Mill's Place in Liberalism," *Political Science Reviewer* 24

stable political society in *Logic*. In this part Mill looks ahead to an organic state of society in which the conditions specified in those propositions would actually exist. He had this future state of society in mind in chapter four where he encouraged displays of distaste and contempt and the use of other kinds of social pressure meant to discourage the selfishness that prevented the emergence of a new altruistic age.

He also had this future organic state of society in mind when he made allusions to a future when there would be a reduced need for liberty of speech and discussion. "It is useful," he said, "that while mankind are imperfect there should be different opinions" (260), the implication being that once perfection is achieved, diversity, including the liberty that accompanies it, will be less useful. The same implication can be drawn from the statement, "in an imperfect state of the human mind, the interests of truth require a diversity of opinions" (257).[85] The assumption that there can and will be a future state with less diversity and less liberty is even more clearly evident in a passage that forecasts a "consolidation of opinion."

> As mankind improve, the number of doctrines which are no longer disputed or doubted will be constantly on the increase: and the well-being of mankind may almost be measured by the number and gravity of the truths which have reached the point of being uncontested. The cessation, on one question after another, of serious controversy, is one of the necessary incidents of *the consolidation of opinion*; a consolidation as salutary in the case of true opinions, as it is dangerous and noxious when the opinions are erroneous. (250; emphasis added)

This development was "inevitable and indispensable," but it was achieved at a cost, for with less diversity of opinion there would be a loss of discus-

---

(1995): 202. See also Hilail Gildin, "Mill's *On Liberty*," in *Ancients and Moderns*, ed. Joseph Cropsey (New York: Basic Books, 1964), 294–99.

[85] See also 252. Similar observations had appeared earlier: "Among the truths long recognized by Continental philosophers, but which very few Englishmen have yet arrived at, one is, the importance, in the present imperfect state of mental and social science, of antagonist modes of thought: which, it will one day be felt, are as necessary to one another in speculation, as mutually checking powers are in a political constitution. A clear insight, indeed, into this necessity is the only rational or enduring basis of philosophical tolerance; the only condition under which liberality in matters of opinion can be anything better than a polite synonym for indifference between one opinion and another." "Coleridge," *CW*, *10*, 122. This passage was included in the reprint of "Coleridge" that appeared in the same year as *On Liberty*. See *Dissertations and Discussions: Political, Philosophical, and Historical* (London, 1859), *1*, 399. See also Mill to John Sterling, 20–22 October 1831, *CW*, *12*, 77. Also, "The plan of instruction [of Manchester New College] was founded upon the principle which I have always most earnestly contended for as the only one on which a University suitable to an age of unsettled creeds can stand, namely, that of leaving each Professor unfettered as to his premises and conclusions." Mill to James Martineau, 21 May 1841, *CW*, *13*, 476.

sion as an aid to the "living apprehension of a truth." On balance, Mill decided that the sacrifice was justified. The loss, "though not sufficient to outweigh, is no trifling drawback from, the benefit of its [the truth's] universal recognition" (251). To make up for the loss of genuine discussion, Mill hoped some contrivance would be found to convey the grounds for believing the truth about which all agreed. Although he did not mention the device of a devil's advocate at this place, evidently this is what he had in mind.[86]

In the distant future with its consolidation of opinion there would be less disagreement, less conflict, and less diversity than in the present transitional state of society. This helps explain how Mill could hold two apparently incompatible views about public opinion which were in fact part of a single coherent perspective. In *On Liberty* he held that the norms endorsed by existing public opinion ought not be used as a standard for judging self-regarding conduct; whereas in "Utility of Religion" he made it clear that the influence of public opinion would be welcomed. Reflecting the first of these two views, Mill famously complained in *On Liberty* against "tyranny of the prevailing opinion and feeling" (220); and that "the public of *this age and country* improperly invests its own preferences with the character of moral laws" (284; emphasis added). This complaint was not directed against public opinion in all conceivable circumstances but against public opinion as it existed in his time, which he regarded as mediocre, mass opinion, reflecting "the present low state of the human mind" (268–69). In these circumstances diverse opinions were desirable, as diversity made it possible for those with elevated views to struggle against the others, and therefore consolidation would be "dangerous and noxious." But this was not a necessary condition. "The power of public opinion . . . is a source of strength inherent in any system of moral belief which is generally adopted,"[87] and so it would be when society was in an organic state, that is, when disparities between opinion of superior natures and public opinion would be greatly reduced and perhaps eliminated. In these circumstances the consolidation of opinion that accompanied an organic state of society would be "salutary." Meanwhile, during a transitional period, when public opinion reflected a depraved morality, those with individuality, since they were in advance of their time and could anticipate future developments, could legitimately act on their opin-

---

[86] The devil's advocate is mentioned at 232 and 245. This theme in *On Liberty* is consistent with the statement in "Spirit of the Age" that "the list of received doctrines is increasing as rapidly as the differences of opinion among the persons possessing moral influence will allow." "Spirit of the Age," *CW*, 22, 291. Yet it is a commonplace in the literature on Mill that he thought "that any attempt to homogenize the ethical or religious life of our society would be ethically and socially disastrous." Jeremy Waldron, *Liberal Rights*, 56.

[87] "Utility of Religion," *CW*, 10, 410.

ions and censure the depraved, for their opinions reflected the wholesome public opinion that would emerge in the future.[88]

His anticipation of a future consolidation of opinion did not mean he was indifferent to the survival of liberty once an organic state of society was in place. He even regarded it as especially valuable in such conditions, but he recognized that when a future organic state of society was established liberty and individuality would have an uncertain fate. He speculated about how a consolidation of opinion might develop and how liberty would fare.

> Some particular body of doctrine in time rallies the majority round it, organizes social institutions and modes of action conformably to itself, education impresses this new creed upon the new generations without the mental processes that have led to it, and by degrees it acquires the very same power of compression, so long exercised by the creeds of which it has taken the place. Whether this noxious power will be exercised depends on whether mankind have by that time become aware that it cannot be exercised without stunting and dwarfing human nature. It is then that the *Liberty* will have its greatest value.[89]

Failure to protect against this future threat to liberty during a new organic period made projects of reform such as Comte's, liberticide.[90]

Although Mill recognized the problem and hoped for a remedy, it cannot be said that he foresaw a clear resolution favorable to liberty. When he addressed the issue he asserted that liberty could coexist with a stable, cohesive society, but he did not explain how this would be achieved. Thus he looked ahead to that future society with its strong claims of morality "grounded on large and wise views of the good of the whole, neither sacrificing the individual to the aggregate nor the aggregate to the individual," and as "giving to duty on the one hand and to freedom and spontaneity on the other their proper province." The important question is, of course, how much of a claim would be made on behalf of the aggregate, that is, how large a province would there be for duty, and how would duties be enforced? There is an indication in this passage of how these questions should be answered; in fact, it is in the same sentence, for it is here that Mill refered to the inferior natures which would be subject to

---

[88] His benign judgment of public opinion as it could affect conduct was reflected in his conversation as recorded by Caroline Fox: "Discussed . . . dread of public opinion. This dread is a very useful whipper-in, it makes nine-tenths of those affected by it better than they would otherwise be . . . because [they] dare not act below the standard." Caroline Fox, *Memories*, 1, 201.

[89] *Autobiography*, CW, 1, 259–60. This theme is emphasized by Allan D. Megill, "J. S. Mill's Religion of Humanity and the Second Justification for the Writing of On Liberty," *Journal of Politics* 34 (1972): 616–27. The same observation is made by Semmel, *Mill and the Pursuit of Virtue*, 183.

[90] Mill to Harriet Taylor Mill, 15 January [1855], CW, 14, 294.

"the superadded force of shame."[91] Evidently Mill assumed there would be constraint of the inferiors.

In another look at the future status of liberty he asserted that liberty and individuality would survive, without, however, explaining how this would be accomplished.

> I looked forward . . . to a future which will unite the best qualities of the critical with the best of the organic periods; unchecked liberty of thought, perfect freedom of individual action in things not hurtful to others; but along with this, *firm convictions as to right and wrong, useful and pernicious, deeply engraven on the feelings by early education and general unanimity of sentiment.* (emphasis added)[92]

While Mill asserts the survival of freedom, one is bound to note the parallel between his reference here to "general unanimity of sentiment" and the second of his conditions for stable, permanent political society, which included provision for "some fixed point" that was "in the common estimation placed beyond discussion";[93] as well as the parallel between the first of those conditions, which included training the human being "in the habit . . . of subordinating his personal impulses and aims, to what were considered the ends of society,"[94] and what he says here about "firm convictions . . . deeply engraven on the feelings by early education." Once again, one wonders how experiments in living and an expansive and unpredictable individuality would thrive in such conditions.

It is evident that Mill was prepared to accept less liberty in a society with a religion of humanity than in a society in a transitional state, but this does not mean that *On Liberty*, with its strong advocacy of free expression for both speech and conduct, was incompatible with his project for moral reform, including his advocacy of a religion of humanity. Although *On Liberty* emphasized the permanent value of liberty and therefore its importance in an organic state of society, it also promoted the freedom necessary in a transitional period. Chapters one to three, the most prominent parts of the book, not only celebrated liberty but also justified the liberties that would hasten the demise of the obsolete beliefs and customs of existing society. This was not the entirety of Mill's argument, however, for in the last two chapters he provides justifications for intrusions and constraints on the selfish persons with miserable individuality who prevented the new organic state of society from emerging and whose conduct might have to be restrained even after the religion of humanity was established. One part of the book emphasized liberty, while

[91] "Utility of Religion," *CW, 10,* 421.
[92] Early Draft, *CW, 1,* 172.
[93] *Logic, CW, 8,* 922.
[94] Ibid., 921.

the other, without strong emphasis, provided for control. This is how he regarded it. When he planned the book, it will be recalled, he told Grote "he was cogitating an essay to point out what things society forbade that it ought not, and what things it left alone that it ought to control."[95] And this is why he could say that Comte, representing authority and control, had half the truth, while the liberal or revolutionary school, advocating liberty, had the other half.[96] And this is why in *On Liberty* he held that in the great practical concerns of life it was important to achieve "the reconciling and combining of opposites," such as sociality with individuality and discipline with liberty (254).[97]

Since he was so well aware of the need to combine liberty with sociality, discipline, cohesion, and authority, he became irritated by accusations that he was indifferent to the importance of authority. Thus after reading articles by James Fitzjames Stephen which anticipated *Liberty Equality Fraternity*, the book in which Stephen presented a defense of authority against what he assumed to be Mill's position, Mill reacted by saying Stephen "does not know what he is arguing against."[98]

A combination of liberty and control was necessary. Sometimes liberty would predominate over control; at others, control would come to the fore. It depended on many circumstances, above all on the stage of historical development. *On Liberty* appears inconsistent with the propositions about stable political society in *Logic* and other descriptions of post-transitional society, but the claim of inconsistency is sustained only if it is assumed that Mill's sole purpose was to establish a rationale for maximum liberty. The claim of inconsistency collapses if it is recognized that, in addition to defending liberty and individuality, Mill also intended to promote moral regeneration; and that *On Liberty* was only one of several works with which he promoted this goal; and that much of what he wrote, including *On Liberty*, rested on assumptions about future societal development derived from his theory of history. These considerations allow us to recognize that *On Liberty*, while proclaiming the inherent value of liberty, also includes a defense of liberties that would be especially useful in hastening the completion of the present transitional period. It also becomes evident that other writings, in which Mill argued for authority, cohesion, and subordination of self to society, far from contradicting, actually complement the most prominent theme of *On Liberty*. During

---

[95] Bain, *Mill*, 103.

[96] *Auguste Comte and Positivism*, CW, 10, 313.

[97] By combining opposites he would avoid making the error of profound thinkers (like Plato, Comte, Bentham), which "consisted of seeing only one half of the truth; and (as is also usual with such thinkers) the half which he [Plato] asserted, was that which he found neglected and left in the background by the institutions and customs of his country": "Grote's Plato," CW, 11, 436.

[98] Bain, *Mill*, 111.

transitional periods, when liberty would be cultivated to the maximum, there would be devices (as suggested in his chapter four) to allow for the constraints and penalties on selfishness and depravity that would encourage a move toward a morally regenerated society. During organic periods liberty would not disappear, but it would be modified sufficiently to allow moral authority, cohesion, duty, and altruism to coexist with it. In such a society there would be an accommodation between liberty and consolidated opinion and there would be an increasingly wide array of moral obligations.

Chapter Nine

MILL'S RHETORIC

> No writer, it is probable, was ever more read between the
> lines. . . . It seems hardly becoming in an author who has
> attained the highest rank of influence in the intellectual
> councils of his time, to write as if there were something
> behind which, as a veracious thinker on human life and
> morals, he would like to say, but which, under the piteable
> bigotry of society, must be reserved for an age that
> does not persecute its benefactors.
>
> (*James Martineau*)

THERE IS SOME IRONY in considering that *On Liberty*, a book
that pleads for candor and openness, is also a book in which Mill
disguises, conceals, equivocates, and seeks to mislead. He wrote
less as one seeking to present the truth than as a practitioner of rhetoric
seeking to shape beliefs. This dimension of Mill's writing was recognized
by R. P. Anschutz: "As war is sometimes said to be an extension of policy,
so philosophy for Mill was an extension of politics. If, then, he sometimes
failed to declare his whole mind on some speculative question, he was
merely practicing in philosophy the usual and necessary reticence of the
politician."[1] This meant that, in spite of his admiration for Socrates, Mill
avoided following the Socratic example of forthrightly stating doubts and
opinions about the most sensitive issues and sacred matters. Mill, instead,
was cautious and reticent.

There should be no surprise that he practiced this kind of rhetoric in
On Liberty and in other writings, for he was trained to it from an early
age. When composing his autobiography he recalled his father's comments on his written analyses of Greek and Roman orators, including
Demosthenes. Mill emphasized that his father especially "pointed out the
skill and art of the orator—how everything important to his purpose was

---

[1] R. P. Anschutz, *The Philosophy of J. S. Mill* (Oxford: Oxford University Press, 1953),
62. Anschutz thought Mill was mainly concerned with politics of the day, but his observation is also relevant to the cultural politics in which Mill also was engaged. Mill's practice
of rhetoric, including the concealing of some opinions, has also been noted by Justman,
though in his interpretation, what Mill played down was a committment to the ideals of
civic republicanism. *The Hidden Text of Mill's Liberty*, 9, 10, 27–28, 33, 62, 113, 118, 121,
144–45, 156. Janice Carlisle also recognizes the rhetorical dimension of *On Liberty*. She
suggests that he sought to conceal the sources of his own thought and his motives for writing

said exactly at the moment when he had brought the minds of his hearers into the state best fitted to receive it; how he made steal into their minds, gradually and by insinuation, thoughts which expressed directly would have roused their opposition." Although he was too young to fully appreciate such things, his father's lesson "left seed behind."[2] He also claimed that this lesson was reinforced by experiences at the East India Company where he was employed for most of his adult life. In deliberations about how to respond to dispatches from the government in India he often faced opposition, and from this, he said, "I was thus in a good position for finding out by practice the mode of putting a thought which gives it easiest admittance into minds not prepared for it by habit."[3]

There are abundant examples of his attempts to practice this art. His inquiry into the foundation of belief in *Logic* and his longstanding critique of intuitionism, still occupying him in *Examination of Sir William Hamilton's Philosophy* (1865), all cast doubt on the foundation of Christian belief without stating the conclusion Mill himself had drawn. This was another example of "a mere fetch," like the structuring of his argument for free discussion in chapter two of *On Liberty*, where he argued for unrestricted discussion without explaining or defending the expected outcome of such discussion.[4] Mill regarded this way of writing as prudent and unobjectionable.

While his practice of rhetoric on many occasions included concealing or disguising his opinions about religion, it was not confined to this subject. When considering in 1850 whether to write an article on the position of women, including divorce, for the *Westminster Review*, he decided against it. "My opinions on the whole subject are so totally opposed to the reigning notions, that it would probably be inexpedient to express all of them and I must consider whether the portion of them which the state of existing opinion would make it advisable to express, would be sufficient to make the undertaking a suitable or satisfactory one to me."[5] On many subjects he felt burdened by the need for caution and by a sense of constraint.

---

as they affected his thought. Thus she attributes to him a wish to manipulate: *John Stuart Mill and the Writing of Character*, 211–14.

[2] Early Draft, *CW, 1*, 22, 24.

[3] *Autobiography*, *CW, 1*, 87.

[4] *Hamilton, CW, 9*, 60; see above, chapter 5, text at notes 59–61. Mill made an exception to his practice of concealment in one undisguised statement included in this work: "I will call no being good, who is not what I mean when I apply that epithet to my fellow-creatures; and if such a being can sentence me to hell for not so calling him, to hell I will go." Ibid., 103. The imprudence of including this statement was demonstrated by the controversy it caused during the 1865 election. See Bruce Kinzer, Ann P. Robson, and John M. Robson, *A Moralist In and Out of Parliament: John Stuart Mill at Westminster 1865–1868* (Toronto: University of Toronto Press, 1992), 48–51.

[5] Mill to William E. Hickson, 19 March 1850, *CW, 14*, 48.

His use of rhetorical devices also was recommended to others. When George Henry Lewes sought his comments on an article on Shelley, which included a defense of Shelley's religious opinions, Mill found it deficient, for, he told Lewes, "you do not seem to me to have laid down for yourself with sufficient definiteness, what precise impression you wished to produce, and upon what class of readers. It was particularly needful to have a distinct view of this sort when writing on a subject on which there are so many rocks and shoals to be kept clear of."[6]

Along with his wish to avoid arousing religious enmities, Mill also constructed his rhetorical strategies to avoid being branded as too theoretical or too utopian. The English were practical and relied on experience, and consequently were suspicious of theory.

> Whoever, therefore, wishes to produce much immediate effect upon the English public, must bring forward every idea upon its own independent grounds, and must, I was going to say, take pains to conceal that it is connected with any ulterior views. If his readers or his audience suspected that it was part of a *system*, they would conclude that his support even of the specific proposition, was not founded on any opinion he had that it was good in itself, but solely on its being connected with utopian schemes, or at any rate with principles which they are "not prepared" (a truly English expression) to give their assent to.[7]

With this understanding of the English political temperament (and, of course, he was not the first to take note of it), Mill was bound to feel the need to suppress some of his thoughts. For he did have a systematic perspective, even a utopian scheme, and it included expectations about developments in morality, institutions, and even national character, that he regarded as being within the realm of possible achievement. His promotion of such changes constituted the agenda in much of his writing, especially in the many essays, including *On Liberty*, planned with his wife during the mid-1850s. But he faced obstacles, for his agenda involved

[6] Mill to George Henry Lewes, [probably late 1840], CW, 13, 448–49. He added, "an opinion on so difficult and delicate a matter, I would say that the idea of a *vindication* should be abandoned. Shelley can only be usefully vindicated from a point of view nearer that occupied by those to whom a vindication of him is still needed. I have seen very useful and effective vindications of him by religious persons." Lewes's article called Shelley's religious opinions merely speculative and sincere and benevolent; and it criticized the humanity and religion of those who persecuted him. "Percy Bysshe Shelley," *Westminster Review* 35 (April 1841): 305–6 and *passim*.

[7] "Comparison of the Tendencies of French and English Intellect," CW, 23, 445. Also, "Large ideas must be made to look like small ones *here*, or people will turn away from them. This is not a place for speculative men, except (at most) within the limits of ancient and traditional Christianity." Mill to Gustave d'Eichthal, 12 November 1839, CW, 13, 413. Also, "the very idea of beginning a reformation in men's minds by preaching to them a comprehensive doctrine, is a notion which never would enter into the head of any person who has lived long enough in England to know the people." Mill to Gustave d'Eichthal, 9 February 1830, CW, 12, 48.

changes most of his contemporaries would have regarded as alien and impractical, if not abhorrent. In spite of such feelings, he was confident he could anticipate the future—this made him an advanced thinker—but, given the present-minded, narrow focus of his contemporaries, he could not openly share his thoughts about the future. In one of his ruminations about rhetoric, entered in his diary at about the time he was planning *On Liberty*, he worried about the difficulties faced by those who were "in advance of their time" as they tried "to gain the ear of the public."[8] To gain their ear, he had to insinuate his ideas, and this led to gaps in the argument of *On Liberty*, as well as the apparent contradictions, the obscurity of his expectation that free discussion would lead to the undermining of Christian belief, the invisibility of his agenda regarding a religion of humanity, and the inconspicuousness of his advocacy of pressure and shaming for selfishness.

It seems evident, then, that in *On Liberty* Mill was less than forthright, and that the arguments, as presented, were not complete and detailed statements of his views. This might have been assumed, in light of his complaints in the book that an author faced prejudice and social censorship. But he did not even leave it to guesswork, for he gave a strong indication that the book offered less than what he had in mind when he said, "opinions contrary to those commonly received can only obtain a hearing by studied moderation of language, and the most cautious avoidance of unnecessary offense" (259).

Mill could have found approval for his rhetorical strategy in a work that is supposed to have been a source of inspiration for him—Wilhelm von Humboldt's *The Sphere and Duties of Government*. Humboldt recommended that in "remodelling of the present" one had to make sure that reform "proceed[ed] as much as possible from men's minds and thoughts."[9] This was accomplished, Humboldt explained, by insinuating one's ideas and not by confronting culture and institutions as they existed. Thus,

> without directly altering the existing condition of things, it is possible to work upon the human mind and character, and give them a direction no more correspondent with that condition; and this it is precisely which he who is wise will endeavour to do. Only in this way is it possible to reproduce the new system in reality, just as it has been conceived in idea.[10]

---

[8] Diary, 10 March [1854], *CW*, 27, 660.

[9] Wilhelm von Humboldt, *The Sphere and Duties of Government*, trans. Joseph Coulthard (London, 1854), 192, 195.

[10] Ibid., 194. See also J. B. Schneewind, Introduction, *Mill's Ethical Writings* (New York: Collier, 1965), 38. Mill's aim was "constructing a view that would introduce new ideas

While Mill drew the epigraph for *On Liberty* from Humboldt's book, this passage could have served as an epigraph for an account of his rhetorical strategy.

———————

Mill's rhetorical approach can be observed in the positions he took in *On Liberty* and other publications.

A few of Mill's more discerning contemporaries were aware of his lack of candor. James Martineau, as noted above, recognized that Mill engaged in self-censorship and suggested it made him less a philosopher than a "mystagogue."[11] James Fitzjames Stephen, himself critical of laws and customs that prevented freedom of religious discussion, also understood that Mill was holding back. George Grote, who concealed his own atheism and counseled like-minded persons to do the same, certainly knew of the discrepancy between what Mill published about religion and what he believed.[12] Bain also was aware of Mill's disguises and concealments.[13] Much more judgmental than any of these critics and friends, his step-daughter Helen Taylor was aware of his lack of forthrightness and condemned it. When she considered the discrepancy between his public equivocation and his beliefs, she criticized his attempts to conceal, to which she contrasted her own "ideas of plain speaking and precise truth."[14] But Mill knew better, identifying himself with those "speaking against the reigning sentiment" who were "driven to collateral argument, circumlocution, and more or less of manoeuvre."[15]

Examples of circumlocution and maneuvre will be recalled. His defense of fully free discussion in chapter two would have liberated freethinkers and atheists, and Mill expected their participation in debate about religion would lead to the erosion of Christian belief—something he would

———————

without offending old habits of thought." Because James Fitzjames Stephen adopted the opposite strategy, Mill said his early articles criticizing *On Liberty* were "more likely to repel than to attract people." Bain, *Mill*, 111.

[11] James Martineau, *Essays*, 3, 535.

[12] But Grote apparently did not understand Mill's rationale for controls and restraints, nor for his reversal on the ballot, nor for his enthusiasm about Comte, all of which he regarded as idiosyncratic. Bain reported that Grote "had always a certain misgiving as to his [Mill's] persistence in the true faith. He would say to me, 'Much as I admire John Mill, my admiration is always mixed with fear'; meaning that he never knew what unexpected turn Mill might take." Bain, *Mill*, 83.

[13] Ibid., 73, 103, 107, Bain to Mill, 14 March [1859]; National Library of Scotland; see above,chapter 4, text at note 16, re. throwing off the mask.

[14] Helen Taylor to Kate Amberley, 14 March 1867, Mill-Taylor Collection, vol. 19, fols. 30–31. British Library of Political and Economic Scienc. See above, chapter 4, text at note 18.

[15] "Grote's History of Greece" (1849), *CW*, *25*, 1128.

have welcomed, as he revealed elsewhere. It is difficult to avoid concluding that he designed the argument of chapter two with this end in mind. Circumlocution and maneuvre is also evident in Mill's observations about Jesus. They can be read as reflecting Christian sympathies, but analysis of what is said makes it clear that, while Jesus is portrayed as a moral exemplar, he is denied divine status and divine authority and is distanced from historical Christianity.

The rhetorical dimension of *On Liberty* was also evident in the way Mill presented his argument about the pressure of opinion. He argued eloquently and openly against the pressures and moral coercion of public opinion as it affected self-regarding conduct, giving the overwhelming impression that he was opposed to all such pressure, while, in fact, he regarded the pressure of opinion coming from superior natures with individuality as quite legitimate. Public opinion (during a transitional state) was not to intrude into self-regarding conduct; individual opinion from those in the speculative class could do so. He could have more clearly distinguished between the two types of opinion, but since he did not, one should consider whether this was a matter of circumlocution and maneuvre.

Mill's rhetoric also can be discerned in his contrasting views of public opinion. In *On Liberty* such opinion is described with disapproval for reflecting the prejudiced views of the masses. "Those whose opinions go by the name of public opinion . . . are always a mass, that is to say, collective mediocrity" (268). Thus he regretted the leveling that gave "ascendancy of public opinion in the State" and also the absence of social support for "opinions and tendencies at variance with those of the public" (275). But this hardly was a full account of how he visualized the role of public opinion, for in "Utility of Religion" he describes the great power of public opinion as a source of support for any system of moral belief, and far from disapproving of this, he shows how its strength can be harnessed to the moral beliefs incorporated into a religion of humanity.[16] Thus the great power of public opinion should be used to implant in each person's mind "an indissoluble association between his own happiness and the good of the whole."[17] This more benign evaluation of public opinion is at most only obscurely present in *On Liberty*, yet it is an important part of his moral and political thought.

His practice of rhetoric is also evident in his explanation of the distinction between self-regarding conduct and conduct (and dispositions) that harmed others. He conveys the impression that only the harmful conduct would be punished, yet in chapter four he inconspicuously acknowledges

[16] "Utility of Religion," *CW*, *10*, 410, 421.
[17] *Utilitarianism*, *CW*, *10*, 218.

that "a person may suffer very *severe penalties* at the hands of others, for faults which directly concern only himself" (278; emphasis added). This statement is not easily reconciled with most of his observations about self-regarding conduct, yet it was not included in the book from inadvertence or carelessness, and it is one of the ways Mill reveals but keeps inconspicuous his approval for control as well as liberty.

Another reflection of his rhetoric appears in the account of the way pressure might be brought to bear on those whose self-regarding conduct is objectionable. In *On Liberty* Mill indicates and emphasizes that one might suggest, try to persuade, exhort, avoid their company, but, in addition, he inconspicuously indicates that distaste or contempt should also be expressed. The former of these approaches appears noncoercive (except for avoidance, which is similar to ostracism); the latter constitutes pressure and is akin to coercion. But in *On Liberty* he is unwilling to acknowledge the coercive dimensions of his proposals for dealing with the self-regarding conduct that is also objectionable. Only in other works, notably in "Utility of Religion," does he call this shaming. There he gives a detailed description of the various forms it might take and welcomes "the fear of shame, the dread of ill repute, or of being disliked or hated" for its deterring effect.[18] In contrast to what he argues in *On Liberty*, here he defends the manipulation of such fears and dreads as a normal and accepted way of enforcing morality.

His use of rhetoric also was apparent in the false impression he gave in chapter five that fornication, gambling, idleness, and drunkenness were to be tolerated, whereas, in fact, these were examples of the self-indulgence that called for distaste or contempt from those who were morally superior. While he conspicuously exempted such conduct from legal punishment (and also from the moral coercion of the public opinion of existing society), he disguised his view that such conduct was to be subjected to the harsh judgments of those who decide what is distasteful and contemptible.

Mill's rhetoric was additionally evident in the obscurity of his statement attributing political functions to persons with individuality of character. This passage (267), which is rarely noticed, is surrounded by passages praising individuality for its intrinsic value, which are most usually noted and commented upon. Even the title of chapter three—"Of Individuality, as One of the Elements of Well-Being"—by suggesting that individuality is inherently valuable, obscures the crucial functions persons with this kind of character were to perform.

It was part of Mill's rhetorical strategy to make obscure the role persons with individuality would have in pressuring (through expressions of

---

[18] "Utility of Religion," *CW, 10*, 410–11.

distaste and contempt and shaming) the depraved and inferior. The persons with individuality were left unlabeled in chapter four of *On Liberty* but were clearly labeled in other writings as superior natures and members of the speculative class. These persons were also unidentified in chapter two, but since one of their functions was to point out what once might have been true but was true no longer, they would be the freethinkers and atheists engaged in the debate Mill envisaged about Christianity, once full liberty of thought and discussion was permitted. Thus those with individuality were to play important parts in the activities considered in chapters two and four, even though they were only covertly present there.

The rhetorical dimension of *On Liberty* becomes most evident by considering Mill's views of individuality. The effusive admiration in *On Liberty* strongly suggests not only that he was not unequivocal in his approval of individuality but also that he would place few limits on its expression. "In each person's own concerns, his individual spontaneity is entitled to free exercise" (277); "Their choice of pleasures . . . are their own concern" (298); and, "liberty consists in doing what one desires" (294). His discussion hardly suggests that there also was something called "miserable individuality," which he strongly condemned and which would be subject to penalties. This phrase, used in a contemporary work, was left out of *On Liberty*, and consequently Mill's wish to discourage and control the miserably individualistic was concealed. This could not have been inadvertent.[19]

Mill also wrote equivocally about spontaneity. He prominently linked it to individuality and appeared to praise it in complaining that "individual spontaneity is hardly recognized by the common modes of thinking as having any intrinsic worth" (261). Yet he also attributed its opposite—"the sternest self-control" (264)—to those with individuality of character and also noted that the strong impulses of such persons would be "under the government of a strong will" (264). And his clearest criticism of spontaneity appeared at the end of the posthumously published "Nature" (composed in 1853–54), where he held that "the doctrine that man . . . ought to make the spontaneous course of things the model of his voluntary actions, is equally irrational and immoral." It is irrational because useful action involves "improving the spontaneous course of nature"; and immoral because the spontaneous course of natural phenomena is "replete with everything which when committed by human beings is most

---

[19] Carlyle entirely missed this part of Mill's argument: "As if it were a sin to control, or coerce into better methods, human swine in any way;—as if the greater and the more universal the 'liberty' of human creatures of the *Swine* genus, the more fatal all-destructive and intolerable were not the 'slavery' the few human creatures of the *Man* genus are thereby thrown into, and kept groaning powerless under. *Ach Gott im Himmel!*" David Alec Wilson, *Carlyle to Threescore-and-Ten*, 342.

worthy of abhorrence."[20] These judgments indicate that spontaneity would often issue in conduct that would be condemned and controlled by Mill.

Another example of silence concerns the religion of humanity, which he strongly approved of during the years when *On Liberty* was planned and composed. Since he was concerned about the survival of liberty once the religion of humanity was established, certainly there was reason to include discussion of it in an essay about liberty. Yet it is not mentioned in *On Liberty*. His rationale was twofold. "[Comte's] religion is without a God. In saying this, we have done enough to induce nine-tenths of all readers, at least in our own country, to avert their faces and close their ears. To have no religion, though scandalous enough, is an idea they are partly used to: but to have no God, and to talk of religion, is to their feelings at once an absurdity and an impiety."[21] In addition, the subject was avoided, as it betrayed utopian goals which were unacceptable. Mill went beyond self-censorship, for he even went out of his way to suggest opposition to a religion of humanity, doing this by criticizing Comte in *On Liberty*. His criticisms were repeated in *Auguste Comte and Positivism* and in later editions of *Logic*.[22] In being so critical of Comte while in fact sharing many of his ideas and goals, Mill sought to mislead. In giving the impression of being opposed to a religion of humanity, he was deliberately concealing.[23]

His wish to avoid being associated with the idea of a religion of humanity is also made evident by comparing what he published with what he withheld from publication. With the exception of *Auguste Comte and Positivism*, in which the phrase "religion of humanity" is used in descriptions and criticisms of Comte, in the writing he published he did not use the phrase, reserving it for private correspondence and posthumous publication. The wish to conceal his hopes for a religion of humanity may additionally have influenced his decision not to reprint "Spirit of the Age" in *Dissertations and Discussions*, a collection of previously published essays that appeared the same year as *On Liberty*. "Spirit of the Age" revealed the historical framework for much of his thought. His long-range goals and expectations could have been inferred from it, and, as we know, Mill thought that revealing such things was rhetorically foolish. If "Spirit of the Age" and *On Liberty* were juxtaposed, it would have been evident

---

[20] "Nature," *CW*, *10*, 402.

[21] *Auguste Comte and Positivism*, *CW*, *10*, 332.

[22] Also in *Utilitarianism*, *CW*, *10*, 232; and *Autobiography*, *CW*, *1*, 219–21.

[23] Mill's consistent spurning of English positivists, all followers of Comte, who would have welcomed his cooperation, reflected more than his disapproval for their lack of concern about Comte's indifference to individual liberty. It also could have arisen from their candor regarding Christianity and the openness of their embrace of the religion of humanity.

that the liberty recommended in *On Liberty* was especially valued because it would hasten the undermining of old doctrines and institutions which occurred during transitional periods. Moreover, the account in "Spirit of the Age" of the natural state of society which was supposed to follow the transitional period, would have raised questions about how liberty would survive in a natural, organic type of society, which, of course, had close affinities with the religion of humanity.[24] His keeping "Spirit of the Age" out of *Dissertations and Discussions* reflected the same purpose he had in being silent about the religion of humanity in *On Liberty*.

Whereas in *On Liberty* some matters are de-emphasized, such as shaming, and some are not mentioned, such as miserable individuality and religion of humanity, in essays and books written contemporaneously with *On Liberty* they are introduced and made quite visible. This indicates that *On Liberty* should be interpreted in combination with those other writings, for their contents complement what Mill included in *On Liberty*. He recommended this procedure in the Preface to *Dissertations and Discussions*.

> Where what I had written appears a fair statement of part of the truth, but defective inasmuch as there exists another part respecting which nothing, or too little, is said, I leave the deficiency to be supplied by the reader's own thoughts; the rather, as he will, in many cases, find the balance restored in some other part of this collection.[25]

Such a procedure, whereby one combines what he wrote in different places, should also be applied to *On Liberty* in combination with other works.

This view—that Mill's goals and agendas were the same in *On Liberty* as in most of the other works that followed his disenchantment with Benthamism, including the Early Draft of his autobiography and the essays on religion held back for posthumous publication—is not compatible with the so-called "two Mills" thesis.[26] Especially challenging to that argument is the coexistence of similar positions in *On Liberty* and in the writings of the "other Mill"—such as descriptions of the attributes of "miserable individuality," accounts of the consolidation of opinion or the existence of common opinions in a post-transitional state of society, and

---

[24] For all these reasons, interpreters emphasizing Mill's libertarianism insist that Mill's perspective in "Spirit of the Age" was significantly different from what it was in *On Liberty*. For example, see C. L. Ten, *Mill on Liberty*, 169–70.

[25] *Dissertations and Discussions* (London, 1859), *1*, iv. See also J. B. Schneewind, Introduction, *Mill's Ethical Writings*, 16–17: "In putting his moral views before the public, he did not at first publish a systematic treatise. Instead he suggested his opinions in numerous essays . . . he outlined or defended an aspect or a part of them in a critical essay here or there."

[26] Himmelfarb, *On Liberty and Liberalism*, 3–139.

advocacy of shaming and other kinds of pressure as a way of shaping and controlling character and conduct. Mill's positions on these matters may be inconspicuous in *On Liberty*, but they are demonstrably present. One might suggest that there were indeed two Mill's, but they would be the Mill as he presented himself to his countrymen, as he appeared in rhetorical dress, incomplete, moderate, diluted; and the other, as he would have presented himself, if there had been no need for rhetoric, whose views were more radical and more utopian. The latter, I suggest, is the authentic portrait.

There are other features of Mill's argument—not so much his positions as his presentation of them—that raise questions about his straightforwardness. An example of his unnecessary and misleading use of the double negative has already been mentioned. His use of it obscured the statement which, shed of the double negative, held that the feelings of praise or disapproval with which a person is regarded ought to be affected by his self-regarding qualities or deficiencies, and that it was neither possible nor desirable that it be otherwise. In other words, distaste and contempt, as he explained subsequently, would and should be directed against the selfish.[27]

There are also examples of Mill reversing course, seeming to move his argument in opposite directions. An example is the title of chapter four and the first sentence of the chapter. The title: "Of the Limits to the Authority of Society over the Individual." The first sentence: "What, then, is the rightful limit to the sovereignty of the individual over himself?" The title points to limits on society and to protection of individual liberty; the first sentence points in the opposite direction.

In another example, he develops an argument that compression of a selfish person is justified; it develops "the social part of his nature, rendered possible by the restraint put upon the selfish part" (266). Yet Mill suddenly shifts gears and ends the paragraph with a paean to individuality and a tirade against despotism.

This feature of Mill's way of presenting his argument was noticed by the distinguished mathematician, philosopher, and economist W. Stanley Jevons, who concluded that "there is no certainty that in his writings the

---

[27] See above, chapter 8, text at note 11. Another example: "No argument, we may suppose, can now be needed, against permitting a legislature or an executive, not identified in interest with the people, to prescribe opinions to them, and determine what doctrines or what arguments they shall be allowed to hear" (228). By implication, a government identified in interest with the people might prescribe opinions to them. Another example: "What is requisite . . . is not that public opinion should not be, what it is and must be, the ruling power." "Tocqueville on Democracy in America," *CW, 18*, 198.

same line of thought is steadily maintained for two sentences in succession." Jevons's critique, which was mainly directed against the *Logic* but also at all of Mill's works, was relentless, and he added, Mill seemed "unconsciously to mix up two views of the same subject."[28] After a sustained analysis of certain arguments in the *Logic*, Jevons, bewildered by what he found in the work of one reputed to be a clearheaded logician, mused that Mill seemed to be "one of those persons who are said to think independently with the two halves of their brain." And he suggested that "Double-mindedness, the Law of Obliviscence [as in oblivious, or forgetting, or having forgotten]" ought to be invoked.[29]

Some other difficulties were less the result of Mill's developing two different lines of argument than his seeming to uphold contradictory positions. For example, discussing the person with self-regarding faults, Mill says "we may express our distaste, and we may stand aloof . . . but we shall not therefore feel called on to make his life uncomfortable" (279). But how can such a person's life be other than uncomfortable, since Mill on the previous page identified our distaste as a penalty for self-regarding faults? To take another example, in this passage Mill tells us we may express our distaste to the person with self-regarding faults "if he displeases us" (279). Yet he had already denied the propriety of attempting to restrain someone for reason of "mere displeasure" (266).[30]

A further illustration again involves the person with self-regarding faults. "It is not our part to inflict any suffering on him" (280). Yet such persons will suffer "the *natural* penalties which cannot be prevented from

---

[28] W. Stanley Jevons, "John Stuart Mill's Philosophy Tested," *Contemporary Review* 31 (December 1877): 168. Jevons extended his criticism to Mill's religious views as they appeared in *Three Essays on Religion* (1874). He found incompatible definitions of religion and incoherence when the three essays were considered together. Letter to the Editor, *Spectator*, 27 October 1877, p. 1332.

[29] Jevons, "John Stuart Mill's Philosophy Tested," Part II, *Contemporary Review* 31 (March 1878): 263. Jevons's articles were composed in 1868 but were delayed, as he encountered resistance from the editor of a leading journal. *Letters and Journal of W. Stanley Jevons* (London, 1886), 245, 329, 374. Alan Ryan claims Jevons was unfair; yet he also says that Mill can be saved from Jevons's criticisms only by escaping from the fire into the frying pan; that one of Mill's difficulties is fatal; that he "gives hostages, not to fortune but to Jevons." Alan Ryan, *The Philosophy of John Stuart Mill*, 79–80. Ryan in saying that Jevons was unfair claims support from Reginald Jackson, "Mill's Treatment of Geometry—A Reply to Jevons," *Mind*, n.s. 50 (1941): 22–42. Kubitz, however, says Jevons's analysis "is probably the best internal criticism of Mill's logical views from a strictly logical standpoint." Oskar Alfred Kubitz, *Development of John Stuart Mill's System of Logic* (Illinois Studies in the Social Sciences, Urbana, 1932), *18*, 306. Jevons was challenged by Croom Robertson, editor of *Mind*, among others. *Mind* 3 (1878): 141–44, 283–84, 287–89. Jevons countered with the charge that reading Mill leads to mystification: 287.

[30] Moreover, still considering the person with self-regarding faults, Mill says "we shall not treat him like an enemy of society: the worst we shall think ourselves justified in doing is leaving him to himself" (280). How much of a difference is there between these two penalties? Are they not both at least ostracism?

falling on those who incur the distaste or the contempt of those who know them" (282). Of course, Mill emphasizes that distaste and contempt will occur naturally, that is, involuntarily, without those passing judgment intending to cause suffering. But this does not remove the difficulty, unless one assumes that those expressing distaste and contempt cannot control their reactions. Since such persons were Mill's intellectual and moral heroes and were portrayed as disciplined, it is difficult to assume that Mill thought them so utterly lacking in self-control.

Examples similar to these did not escape Jevons's notice, for he remarked on Mill's "inextricable difficulties and self-contradictions,"[31] but whereas Jevons traced these lapses to incoherence, it seems more likely that Mill was deliberately obfuscating. Mill, after all, was capable of clarity and rigor, and, moreover, *On Liberty* was not carelessly written. "There was not a sentence of it that was not several times gone over by us together [he and Harriet Taylor Mill], turned over in many ways, and carefully weeded of any faults, either in thought or expression, that we detected in it."[32] He also recalled, "None of my writings have been either so carefully composed, or so sedulously corrected as this. After it had been written as usual twice over, we kept it by us, bringing it out from time to time and going through it *de novo*, reading, weighing and criticizing every sentence."[33] In light of these statements, it appears that the Double Mindedness Jevons noticed should be traced not to Mill's intellectual failings but to his rhetorical strategy.[34]

Mill's lack of candor was accompanied by an intense interest in the morality of deception. This was an occasional theme in his writing, though

[31] *Contemporary Review* 31, 182.

[32] *Autobiography*, CW, 1, 257, 259.

[33] Ibid., 249.

[34] Yet Mill enjoyed a reputation for great clarity. According to a correspondent (W. T. Malleson) in the *Spectator*, "it is very difficult to misunderstand Mr. Mill, so anxious was he always to be clear, to be just, to keep back nothing." *Spectator*, 20 October 1877, 1302. And in *On Liberty* he displayed "distinctness of conception and pellucid clearness of expression." *Spectator Supplement* 32 (12 February 1859), 189. Another commentator, while regarding Mill as a "model of lucidity," notes the contradictions only to attribute them to Mill's lapses from his usual high standard. Mill "could occasionally slip into an inept phrasing of his ideas. Where such is the case, many a critic has had an easy time of it by rendering Mill's argument in its most vulnerable terms. But Mill, as any other writer of his stature, should be given the benefit of literary doubt; if such a rendering seems egregiously out of line with his obvious intent, there is a prima facie case for challenging its pertinence—particularly where it is possible to construe his argument in terms more in keeping with his general outlook and level of intellectual sophistication." David Spitz, "Freedom and Individuality," in *On Liberty*, ed. David Spitz (New York: Norton, 1975), 211. By way of contrast, see F. E. Sparshott, who attributes to Mill "a dexterity that distracts the eye from the workings of a devious mind." Introduction, *Essays on Philosophy and the Classics*, CW, 11, lxxv.

nowhere did he address the question systematically. Of course, he disapproved of lying—it undermined the mutual trust that supported social well-being, and it was, moreover, cowardly. But he was quick to say that the principle could not be applied without considering circumstances. "Yet that even this rule, sacred as it is, admits of possible exceptions, is acknowledged by all moralists." He would not encourage the making of exceptions, but "if the principle of utility is good for anything, it must be good for weighing these conflicting utilities against one another."[35] Mill was aware of this issue from an early age, for in 1827, at age twenty-one, in an editorial comment in Bentham's *Rationale of Judicial Evidence*, he quoted William Paley—"a writer of undisputed piety, who, in a system of morals professing to be founded upon the will of God as its principle, makes no difficulty in giving a license to falsehood, in several of its necessary or allowable shapes."[36] And in his diary he wrote sympathetically about Machiavelli's view that "good men reserved their conscientiousness for the choice of ends, and thought that to be scrupulous about means was weakmindedness." And Mill added, "*Some* such arguing with themselves is incident to honest men in all ages—even in the present. The question what means are or are not immoral, always depends in part on the practice of the age; on what is done by other people."[37] In this passage he seems to be reserving a defense for his own practices, and he may have had in mind close friends, such as Carlyle and Grote, who certainly kept their religious opinions to themselves, as well as the many others who, he claimed, did the same.[38]

---

[35] *Utilitarianism*, CW, *10*, 223; "Bentham," CW, *10*, 112. The observation about cowardice appeared in "Bentham." On he hustings he said, "Lying as the vice of slaves, and they would never find slaves who were not liars." "The Westminster Election of 1865 [4]" (8 July 1865), CW, *28*, 35. He asked, "What ought to be the exceptions (for that there ought to be some, however few, exceptions seems to be admitted) to the general duty of truth?" He indicated how he would justify an exception by adding, "The effect which actions tend to produce on human happiness is what constitutes them right or wrong." Mill to Henry Sidgwick, 26 November 1867, CW, *32*, 185.

[36] *Miscellaneous Writings*, CW, *31*, 19.

[37] Diary, 4 February [1854], CW, *27*, 650.

[38] See also "Remarks on Bentham's Philosophy," CW, *10*, 7. Also, "A skillful advocate will never tell a lie, when suppressing the truth will answer his purpose; and if a lie must be told, he will rather, if he can, lie by insinuation than by direct assertion." "Brodie's History of the British Empire" (1824), CW, *6*, 5. Mill certainly had read Bacon's essay "Of Simulation and Dissimulation." On his attempt to reconcile equivocation with honesty, see above, chapter 4, text at note 20. In light of his caution, certain statements to his wife might be understood as Mill's attempts at irony, as when he referred to a public document as being "direct, uncompromising and to the point, without reservation, as if we had written it." On another occasion, referring to American feminists at a time before the Mills' opinions were widely known, he said they were, "like ourselves speaking out." Mill to Harriet Taylor Mill, 3 March [1854], [after 29 October 1850], CW, *14*, 175, 49. Cf. text between notes 4 and 5, above.

Mill enjoyed a reputation for honesty. His young friend John Morley, for example, insisted he was "absolutely truthful."[39] Mill must have thought of himself in the same way, but to arrive at this conclusion, he must have had, as he put it, to argue with himself. His quest for self-justification, especially evident in his brief discussion of equivocation, is reminiscent of the appendix on Lying and Equivocation in Newman's *Apologia*, where Newman identified four types of "verbal misleading." Drawing on both Catholic and Protestant writing and from contemporary debates, he examined possible justifications for each type—(1) lying, that is, saying a thing that is not; (2) a play on words, or equivocation; (3) evasion; and (4) silence.[40] Mill could have recognized his rhetorical devices as examples of three of Newman's types, though not as lying, in spite of his willingness, with regard to it, to take into account special, justifying circumstances.

Equivocation, or a play upon words, occurred, according to Newman, when ambiguous words were used "in a sense which they will not bear," as when "an equivocator uses them in a received sense, though there is another received sense."[41] The hearer or reader is misled if he attributes one meaning to the words, while the speaker's or author's true belief would be revealed only if the other meaning were used. As we saw, Mill justified equivocation and insisted that the practice of it did not make one a liar. And he did practice equivocation (in Newman's sense of the term) when he used the name of Jesus: while a secular hero and moral exemplar but not a divine figure for Mill, his readers, on seeing the name, might assume otherwise. On another occasion, when Holyoake asked the grounds on which Mill was able to take his oath as a Member of Parliament, which included the words "on the true faith of a Christian," Mill justified his equivocating: "I am as much entitled to call my own opinion about Christ the true faith of a Christian, as any other person is entitled to call his so."[42] In another example, he said, that if "issues wrong mandates

[39] Quoted in *John Stuart Mill: A Selection of His Works*, ed. John M. Robson (New York: Macmillan, 1966), vii, Also, "the careful truthfulness of Mr. Mill himself." *Spectator*, 10 November 1877, 1399. Also, "the honesty of Mill's mind." Berlin, *Four Essays*, 201.

[40] John Henry Newman, *Apologia Pro Vita Sua*, ed. David J. DeLaura (1864; New York: Norton, 1968), Note G, Lying and Equivocation, 259–69. For Mill on equivocation, see chapter 4, text at note 20, above. On the background to Note G, see Josef L. Altholz, "Truth and Equivocation: Liguori's Moral Theology and Newman's *Apologia*," *Church History* 44 (1975): 73–84.

[41] Newman, *Apologia*, 260, 265.

[42] This passage from a draft reply was not included by Mill in a letter to George Jacob Holyoake, 8 August 1869, CW, 17, 1631, n 4. The manuscript draft includes the following additional passage which ends before the sentence was completed: "It would not be so if I thought"; evidently Mill's arguing with himself did not lead him to a satisfactory conclusion. Manuscript draft in Mill-Taylor Collection, I, f. 322; British Library of Political and Economic Science.

instead of right, or any mandates at all in things with which ought not to meddle, it practices a social tyranny" (220). This sounds like a complaint against such tyranny, but he did not discuss, what the statement clearly allows, the propriety of society issuing not wrong but right mandates or the circumstances in which society ought to meddle. In yet another example, the idea of a sovereign individual was put forward, implying that he was free to do as he liked, provided harm was not done to others; but Mill also had in mind the consequences that would fall on such a person if their individuality was selfish and "miserable."

Evasion, another of Newman's types, occurs when the speaker diverts the attention of the hearer; or suggests an irrelevant fact or makes a remark that confuses him; or throws dust in his eyes; or states some truth, from which he is quite sure the hearer will draw an illogical or untrue conclusion. Newman noted that "the greatest school of evasion was the House of Commons or perhaps the hustings."[43] An example of Mill making a true statement that would mislead his audience occurred in 1868 when he was a candidate for a seat in Parliament; accused of being an atheist, he defied anyone to find an atheistic statement in any of his publications.[44] Earlier, in 1865, he challenged his critics by referring them to what he had "written and published," which, of course, did not include "Utility of Religion," "Nature," or letters such as some of those to Carlyle and Comte.[45]

Finally, there is the method of silence, of misleading by avoiding occasion to address an issue. Mill used this method when he avoided discussion of the consequences of fully free discussion for Christian belief; when he avoided mentioning the religion of humanity; and when he avoided acknowledging that the changes he proposed were but stepping stones to a large-scale, utopian transformation.[46]

---

[43] Newman, *Apologia*, 265.

[44] Ann P. Robson, "Mill's Second Prize in the Lottery of Life," in *A Cultivated Mind: Essays on J. S. Mill Presented to John M. Robson*, ed. Michael Laine (Toronto: University of Toronto Press, 1991), 232. See also Mill to Frederick Bates, 9 November 1868, *CW* 16, 1483.

[45] Mill to Charles Westerton, 21 June [1865], *CW*, 16, 1069. For other examples in which he refers to the deity in conditional statements or in the form of a question, see *Utilitarianism*, *CW*, 10, 222; *Inaugural Address*, 21, 254.

[46] Mill's wish to be silent helps explain why be turned down invitations to join the Metaphysical Society in 1869 and again in 1871. The Society included James Knowles (the Founder), Walter Bagehot, Frederic Harrison, R. H. Hutton, T. H. Huxley, Gladstone, Cardinal Manning, James Martineau, John Ruskin, Henry Sidgwick, J. F. Stephen, Leslie Stephen, Tennyson, Connop Thirlwall, and W. G. Ward—Anglicans, Catholics, Unitarians, agnostics, but no professed atheist. The Society was formed to promote candid discussion that would lead to common ground among those representing different opinions but not to the rejection of all religious belief. Since Mill, as a matter of policy, was not candid, had he joined the Society, he would have had to abandon his habitual rhetorical posture, but presumably this was unacceptable, for the membership did not include trusted friends,

If Mill had been interested in how Newman judged these methods, he might have been comforted to know that Newman had no difficulty with the method of silence, nor even with the method of evasion, which was acceptable, provided there was just cause (which, of course, was a condition Mill's project would not have met). Mill satisfied his own sense of right and wrong, however, not by consulting Newman but by "weighing . . . conflicting utilities against one another." Since in his equivocations, evasions and silences there was a more-or-less tortured avoidance of "saying the thing that is not," he sought justification by contemplating the happiness that would be experienced by his reaching his goal.

It might be asked why Mill included in *On Liberty*, even inconspicuously, the theme of constraint. He could have explained that harm to others would be punished, either through law or public opinion, but he need not have included the passages on the suffering that would be experienced by those with self-regarding faults, nor did he have to include the passages on distaste and contempt, nor the allusions to shaming and ostracism. All this could have been the subject of a separate work.

The inclusion of these matters had something to do with Mill's quest for intellectual honesty. He recognized that concealing one's opinions was questionable. He included "dissimulation and insincerity" among the dispositions which were immoral and subject to disapprobation (279). And in criticizing the secret ballot, he argued that it was important and valuable to reveal one's opinions. Yet he had a dilemma, for there might be consequences from such openness, and thus in his opposition to the secret ballot he also said, "The moral sentiment of mankind . . . has condemned concealment, unless when required by some overpowering motive."[47] The motive for Mill was to avoid speaking against the reigning sentiment, either to avoid what perhaps would have been disrepute for his atheism, or merely to avoid appearing out of step for writing unsympathetically about the self-indulgence that was widely practiced, or to avoid seeming

---

though it did include acquaintances. Had he joined, he could have engaged in open debate of the kind advocated in chapter two of *On Liberty*, but his adversaries would have included persons with strong convictions but not the thoughtless persons, ignorant of the grounds for their beliefs, such as the audience hypothesized in chapter two. Moreover, he could have expected that his public facade would be penetrated, especially as he would have faced James Martineau and J. F. Stephen, who knew he concealed his rejection of Christianity. There were also the positivists Harrison and Congreve, who might have identified his covert convictions about the religion of humanity. Others who declined invitations included Matthew Arnold, G. H. Lewes, Carlyle, Browning, Newman, Spencer, and Bain. See Brown, *Metaphysical Society*, 21–22, 165, 190; and Mill to W. G. Ward, 29 March 1869, *CW*, 17, 1583–84.

[47] *Representative Government*, *CW*, 19, 337.

to be an impractical utopian. In each case he would have become suspect and would have lost credibility and perhaps his audience. His father, with respect to religion, had faced the same dilemma, and chose to conceal, and Mill did the same, with regard to Christianity, the religion of humanity, and constraints upon the self-indulgent, selfish egotism that led to "miserable individuality."

While he chose to conceal, or at least to disguise, Mill also responded to the other side of the dilemma, which called for candor, and this was reflected in the inconspicuous presence of the constraint theme in *On Liberty*. The theme's inconspicuousness satisfied his wish to be prudent while its presence reflected his wish to avoid feeling he deserved to wear what, in another context, he called the badge of slavery.

His disguised disclosures included warnings that the exercise of liberty might have consequences. Thus in chapter one he says liberty requires "doing as we like, subject to such consequences as may follow" (226). Of course, while he identifies the consequences that will be faced if we harm others, he does not spell out the consequences for self-regarding faults that arise from self-indulgence and selfishness. These consequences were very briefly described in chapter four, but in this passage in chapter one he diverts attention from them: our liberty will be "without impediment from our fellow-creatures . . . even though they should think our conduct foolish, perverse, or wrong" (226). While there would be no impediment, the consequences —distaste or contempt—would discourage making the same choice on future occasions. There are repeated references to consequences without, however, explanations of what the consequences would be.[48] Also, in chapter five, entitled "Applications," where we might expect details, he tells us there will be only enough detail "to illuminate the principles, rather than to follow them out to their consequences" (292). These repeated references to consequences that might attend self-regarding conduct seem to point to the penalties referred to in Mill's statement that a person might "suffer very severe penalties" for self-regarding conduct. Emphasizing one part of his message while not being false to other parts and to all his purposes, Mill weighed his words, being cautious, seeking to reveal enough to avoid dishonesty or misrepresentation without disclosing the full extent of his approval for constraint.

The decision to include the constraint theme could also have been related to his health and that of Harriet. Since both of them had alarming symptoms of tuberculosis when *On Liberty* was being planned and written, neither expected to live very long. With such prospects, Mill felt great urgency to commit to paper his thoughts about Christianity, the religion of the future, ethics, ethology, and liberty—all subjects that were im-

---

[48] See above Chapter 8, text at notes 12 & 13.

portant in his plan for moral regeneration. Reflecting this sense of urgency, Mill told Harriet, "We must cram into it [the volume on liberty] as much as possible of what we wish not to leave unsaid."[49] Not knowing how long they would survive (Harriet died three years later), and eager to claim moral authority for those whose judgments were to be directed against the persons with self-regarding faults, the constraint theme found its way into the book. Since they used the pemican metaphor for the part of their thought that was to be recognized as valuable only in the distant future, this theme was introduced with the expectation that it would provide intellectual nourishment later on.

As he did include the constraint theme, it might be asked, why the title? Mill anticipated this question, and his response revealed a good deal about his rhetorical subtlety as well as his quest for intellectual integrity. At the time *On Liberty* was planned, he entered in his diary an observation about the relation of a book's contents to its title.

> Many books have been severely criticized for no better reason than that they did not satisfy the idea which the critic had formed from the title of what the book ought to contain; the critic seldom in these cases deigns to consider that all he says rather proves the title to be in the wrong than the book. *So if a history or a biography professes, though but by implication, to tell anything, and then does not do so, but purposely keeps anything back, the writer may justly be blamed, not however for what his book is, but for what it professes to be without being.* (emphasis added)[50]

The title (and much of the argument) of his book encourages the reader to assume that extensive liberty would be permitted; yet the inclusion of the constraint theme indicates that the title promises more than the author was prepared to allow. In this diary entry he is telling us to judge the contents—all of them—and not the title alone.

Mill would not have acknowledged, however, that his title was inappropriate. This is suggested in the same diary entry where he comments on Goethe's great care in choosing a title.

> Goethe avoided this snare [of promising more in a title than the book would deliver] by calling his autobiography, which tells just as much about himself as he liked to be known, "*Aus* meinem Leben Dichtung und Wahrheit." The *Aus* even without the *Dichtung* saves his veracity.[51]

Mill formulated his title with equal care: *On* [that is, about] *Liberty.* The title did not make a claim that the book was a defense of the view that

---

[49] Mill to Harriet Taylor Mill, 16 February [1855], *CW, 14,* 332.
[50] Diary, 19 February [1854], *CW, 27,* 655.
[51] *Ibid.*

liberty ought to override every other consideration. He merely left it to most of his readers to assume this was his position. Comparably to Goethe's *Aus*, the *On* saves his veracity.

Of course, Mill could have followed the more forthright example of John Austin. Coldly analyzing liberty, Austin concluded it was not preferable to restraint but should be judged in light of its consequences. Mill was familiar with Austin's argument, having read the volume in which it was published as well as having twice heard the lectures on which the book was based. According to Austin, "Political or civil liberty is not more worthy of eulogy than political or legal restraint. Political or civil liberty, like political or legal restraint, may be generally useful, or generally pernicious; and it is not as being liberty, but as conducing to the general good, that political or civil liberty is an object deserving applause."[52] But rather than Austin's forthrightness, Mill chose circumlocution and maneuvre.

By revealing the limitations he would place on liberty, Mill would have challenged a reigning sentiment. Austin had complained that "political or civil liberty has been erected into an idol, and extolled with extravagant praise by doting and fanatical worshippers."[53] Others also assumed that liberty was highly valued and widely praised. Matthew Arnold, while implicitly criticizing Mill, blamed the entire spirit of the age for being anarchic. He pointed to "our strong individualism, our hatred of all limits to the unrestrained swing of the individual's personality, our maxim of 'every man for himself.' " There was also, Arnold noted, "our national idea, that it is man's ideal right and felicity to do as he likes."[54] This tendency was noticed by the perceptive Harriet Grote who remarked on "the obvious impatience of restraints of all kinds, which characterize our epoch."[55] Macaulay also recognized the widespread taste for liberty and thought it was largely satisfied and that Mill had exaggerated the restrictions on liberty, and this led him to accuse Mill of crying fire in Noah's flood.[56] Another who thought liberty not in danger was William Maccall, whose work Mill acknowledged for anticipating some of his ideas. "We

---

[52] John Austin, *The Province of Jurisprudence Determined* (1832), in *Lectures on Jurisprudence or the Philosophy of Positive Law*, ed. Robert Campbell (London, 1873), 282.

[53] Ibid., 281–82.

[54] Matthew Arnold, *Culture and Anarchy*, ed. J. Dover Wilson (1869; Cambridge: Cambridge University Press, 1932), 49, 75; see also, 77. Mill used the phrase "doing as we like" (226); and he said, "liberty consists in doing what one desires" (294; see also 301).

[55] Harriet Grote to Joseph Parkes, 15 August 1859, *Posthumous Papers: Comprising Selections from Familiar Correspondence during half a century*, ed. Harriet Grote (London, 1874), 148.

[56] George Otto Trevelyan, *The Life and Letters of Lord Macaulay*, 2, 379–80.

are perishing from an excess of liberty," Maccall said.[57] Another indication that liberty was already highly valued came from reviewers who assumed that in *On Liberty* Mill was not challenging but rather reaffirming a well-established tradition. Mill himself, while complaining about intolerance regarding some matters, noted, as to others, "the strange respect for liberty" (304). And he acknowledged that, at least "to superficial observation, [liberty] did not seem to stand much in need of such a lesson" as provided by *On Liberty*.[58]

Mill was not about to make clear how much he would qualify the claim to the liberty that was so much a part of reigning sentiment. For his countrymen, a fond belief in the value of liberty was part of what he called "the furniture of the mind," and logic or philosophic argument was powerless to alter it.[59] Therefore, while Mill, in deference to intellectual honesty, did introduce his argument for the penalizing of self-regarding faults, in deference to the reality of the reigning sentiment, he made his position obscure. There is a cryptic passage in his diary, written when the essay on liberty was being planned, that seems to describe this part of his rhetorical strategy.

> Those who are in advance of their time need to gain the ear of the public by productions of inferior merit—*works grounded on the premises commonly received*—in order that what they may be able to write of first-rate value to mankind may have a chance of surviving until there are people capable of reading it. (emphasis added)[60]

Whether or not he wrote this with his plan for *On Liberty* in mind, it is a strategy compatible with his pemican metaphor, for by appealing to "the premises commonly received," that is, by suggesting to readers that he was enhancing the liberty to which they were already strongly attached, he hoped that the other, less palatable part of his book—the message of chapter four—would have "a chance of surviving" until a time when it would be more acceptable.

This strategy also was compatible with his belief that in writing for the English one "must write in the manner best calculated to make an

---

[57] *New Materialism*, 11, 18. Also, "When told to go and attack idiocy and indolence, you [English] raise a silly whine about interference with human liberty." William Maccall, "England and Science," a lecture, 8 January 1854, in *National Missions* (London, 1855), 232–33.

[58] *Autobiography*, CW, 1, 259. Also, "I am aware that there is not, in this country, any intolerance of differences of opinion on most of these topics" (254). The topics included democracy and aristocracy, property and equality, and luxury and abstinence.

[59] Diary, 2 February [1854], CW, 27, 649.

[60] Diary, 10 March [1854], CW, 27, 660. *If* this observation is applicable to *On Liberty*, clearly he only would have meant that it was a work of "inferior merit" in the sense of being less than a full account of all his opinions.

impression upon their minds"; and that "one must tell them only of the next step they have to take, keeping back all mention of any subsequent step."[61] The next step was to encourage liberty, for in 1859 it still had much to contribute, as it made possible the criticism of Christianity, customs, and institutions that upheld existing society, which were the obstacles to the emergence of altruism, equality, and socialism. Mill approved of those who possessed large scale theories that defined their distant goals but who also moderated their judgments so that "the choice of principles for present application is guided by a systematic appreciation of the state and exigencies of existing society."[62] The historical period that was to follow would have different circumstances, and it would require, in addition to liberty, greater emphasis on constraints. Mill regarded these two things—liberty and constraint—as complementary, but he recognized that others would only discern contradiction. Therefore, he played down the argument for constraint, which, in any case, he knew, was contrary to the spirit of the times. By emphasizing the role of liberty, Mill put forth only part of his overall position, which perhaps explains his characterization of *On Liberty* as "a kind of philosophic text-book of a single truth."[63]

---

[61] "Comparison of the Tendencies of French and English Intellect," *CW*, *23*, 446.
[62] Duveyrier's Political Views of French Affairs, *CW*, *20*, 313.
[63] *Autobiography*, *CW*, *1*, 259

Epilogue

MILL—especially the Mill of *On Liberty*—has always been linked to liberalism. Mill's essay was published as liberal ideas were gaining great influence, and it seemed to breathe the spirit and articulate the values of the emerging ethos. This association has continued to our time, and in recent commentary he is portrayed as the emblematic liberal by those upholding the traditional interpretation (Berlin, Ten); by the revisionists (Rees, Ryan); by those who suggest he developed a conception of positive liberty (Semmel); and by conservative critics, as well. Cowling, for example, calls him the godfather of modern liberalism. Even John Gray, writing from a postmodern perspective, labels Mill as "*the* paradigm liberal thinker."[1]

This study, however, casts doubt on the suitability of linking Mill so closely to liberalism. The liberal label is questionable whatever species of liberalism is considered, but, of course, the reasons for this conclusion will depend on the particular type of liberalism that is compared with Mill's position.

Mill's distance from liberalism is greatest and most evident when one considers whether he would agree with the liberal doctrine that defends a conception of negative liberty for largely autonomous individuals who are protected within a realm of privacy from intrusions by either government or society and who are free to make choices and develop within this private realm. This kind of liberalism attaches great importance to the public-private distinction, and it upholds the principle of moral pluralism and the related view that governments should be neutral with regard to the moral choices of citizens. Some of those adopting this perspective also attribute certain rights, which are equally distributed, to all individuals—minimally, civil and political rights, but others are sometimes added. Liberalism is most often defined in terms of this constellation of features, though, of course, not all spokesmen for this conception of liberalism agree about each of its attributes or on their relative importance. Although it has been widely criticized, this conception of liberalism dominates contemporary discourse, and one variant or another is attributed to Mill by representatives of several of the varied interpretations of his thought.

[1] John Gray, *Liberalism* (2nd ed.; Minneapolis: University of Minnesota Press, 1995), 87.

It is not difficult to find passages in *On Liberty* that lend credence to a belief that Mill was this kind of liberal, but there are many aspects of his position, in *On Liberty* and in other writings, that are incompatible with this belief. Most of these incompatible features originated in his turn to cultural politics after he became disappointed with the results of political reform. This meant that he looked for human improvement less in institutional change and more in reform of religion and morality as a way of reshaping character, values, and motives. This already points to goals beyond the boundary of the typical liberal agenda, which focuses on defining and expanding the role of citizens and the civil rights that accompany that role. By seeking to shape character, values, and motives, Mill reveals his wish to limit the choices made by citizens, and this is hardly compatible with the value pluralism often attributed both to Mill and to the liberal position.

Mill's wish to reshape moral character was evident in his pervasive and continuing critique of selfishness in its many forms and in his wish to improve moral character by reducing opportunities and even the desire to gratify selfish impulses. This led to his upholding altruism as a more worthy motivation and to his promoting a religion of humanity, which would socialize all persons to believe that altruism provided both utility and happiness. This view was incorporated into his revised utilitarianism: "The happiness which forms the utilitarian standard of what is right in conduct, is not the agent's own happiness, but that of all concerned." This he proposed to achieve by "establish[ing] in the mind of every individual an indissoluble association between his own happiness and the good of the whole"; and by creating in each individual "a direct impulse to promote the general good . . . [as] one of the habitual motives of action."[2] This position is perfectly compatible with a culture in which duty and altruism dominate. It is, however, incompatible with the individualism, the emphasis on self-determination, and the moral pluralism often attributed to Millian liberalism.

Mill's condemnation of selfishness was also evident in his use of the phrase "miserable individuality," a label he used for the kind of character that adopted the values of existing society but which were in polar opposition to his revised utilitarian standard. Such a character was "miserable" because it embodied selfishness, and Mill condemned its varied manifestations (self-conceit, wish to dominate, gross sensuality, hurtful self-indulgence, not living within moderate means, pursuit of animal pleasures at the expense of those of feeling and intellect). By harshly criticizing these things and by advocating penalties (including shaming and expressions of distaste and contempt) to deter such conduct, even though it was confined

---

[2] *Utilitarianism,* CW, 10, 218.

to a private realm and did not cause harm to others, he implicitly rejected the public-private distinction as a device for defining a private realm protected from intrusion, encroachment, or interference.

His provisions for subjecting persons to outside pressures also make it difficult to attribute to Mill a belief in autonomy as a fundamental right. Those subjected to pressures and penalties for self-regarding, "private" conduct would not be enjoying autonomy, nor would those whose choices had been programmed by a socialization process that made concern for others or the general good, however defined, one of the "habitual motives of action." The attribution of autonomy also is incompatible with Mill's assumption that what, at one time, one was free to do or not to do, would, at a later time, after moral improvement took place, become an enforceable obligation. It would then be outside the realm of autonomous choice.

The greatest difficulty with the claim that Mill's position can be easily assimilated to liberalism—whether the radically individualistic kind or any other type—is his defense of a kind of society in which liberty would in many ways be limited. It would be limited even during transitional periods when liberty would be most useful, for at such times, as a matter of moral education, it was necessary to penalize those with miserable individuality. Mill acknowledged this: "The spirit of improvement is not always a spirit of liberty, for it may aim at forcing improvements on an unwilling people" (272). But liberty was also to be circumscribed during an organic period with a religion of humanity in place, for then the educational system would instill a "restraining discipline" that would create the habit of subordinating personal impulses to the good of society; there would be a shared loyalty to "something which is settled, something permanent, and not to be called in question"; and there would be an "active principle of cohesion."[3] Reflecting these conditions, there would also be a "consolidation of opinion" (250), which would not allow for much of the free choice or diversity of opinion and conduct or the varied manifestations of individuality usually associated with Millian liberalism.

There is yet another part of Mill's arguments in *On Liberty* that has no place in liberalism. Mill made it clear that opinion was an appropriate sanction for disapproved conduct. He endorsed using "the moral coercion of public opinion" (223) as punishment for harm done to the interests of others, and such punishment would be instituted without any procedural safeguards to protect individuals from inequitable or unfair treatment. Given the ways such punishment would be determined and enforced, it is difficult to visualize how procedural safeguards and therefore a rule of law could be combined with them. There is a similar difficulty with the expressions of opinion in the form of displays of distaste or contempt or

[3] *Logic, CW,* 8, 921–23.

other ways of shaming, which he approved as ways of penalizing those with miserable individuality. He suggested no way of subjecting the determination and enforcement of such penalties to equitable principles, and he seemed unconcerned that such judgments would appear to be and probably would be arbitrary.

It is not surprising to discover these nonliberal and, in some respects, antiliberal features of Mill's position once one takes into account the diverse sources of his principal ideas. He drew many of these ideas from intellectual figures that have no place in the liberal tradition—among notable contemporaries, St. Simon, Coleridge, and Comte, and looking much further back, Plato. Of course Mill's perspective was not shaped only in the light cast by these figures—there were also Bentham, Mill's father, and Grote, and (though his point of view was hardly the same) Tocqueville. Mill of course was aware that he was heir to widely different intellectual traditions, and he even made the cultivation of such diversity part of his intellectual strategy, arguing that "many-sidedness" was valuable and that a mind that is "first-rate . . . varies and multiplies its points of view."[4] Thus he was eclectic, but he wanted no part of the kind of eclecticism that consisted of a quilt-like juxtaposition of unassimilated ideas. Instead, he sought to blend and make seamless the varied ideas that shaped his thought. His aspiration was announced in *Logic*: "to harmonize the true portions of discordant theories, by supplying the links of thought necessary to connect them, and by disentangling them from the errors with which they are always more or less interwoven."[5] He sought to reconcile and combine Bentham and Coleridge, progress and order, democracy and enlightened leadership, competition and cooperation. And to this list should be added liberalism and its opposite, which, however labeled, included provision for authority, obedience, cohesiveness, and stability. In undertaking these tasks he assumed that the incompatibility between the two sides was more apparent than real. As he said of Bentham and Coleridge, "These two sorts of men, who seem to be, and believe themselves to be, enemies, are in reality allies. The powers they wield are opposite poles of one great force in progression."[6]

The wish to synthesize ideologically opposed values and ideas affected the place of individual liberty in his overarching plan for moral reform. It was even evident in *On Liberty* where he acknowledged that "Truth, in the great practical concerns of life, is so much a question of the reconciling and combining of opposites" (254). Among his examples of such opposites, significantly, he included liberty and discipline and individuality

[4] Carrel, *CW*, *20*,188.
[5] *Logic*, *CW*, *7*, cxi (Preface to all editions).
[6] "Coleridge," *CW*, *10*, 146.

and sociality. If liberty and individuality were to be combined with and therefore moderated or restricted by, respectively, discipline and sociality, the magnitude of liberty and individuality would be significantly diminished.

His attempts to harmonize liberalism and its opposite should affect the way we assess his relationship to liberal thought. Since combining liberalism and its opposite required the disentangling of truth from error in each of these constellations of ideas, he developed mixed judgments—criticisms as well as appreciations—of both liberal and nonliberal positions. With regard to liberalism, along with the appreciation for which he is best known, there also were severe criticisms. He made this abundantly clear when he assessed liberalism—first, however, describing it, as it happens, in a way congenial to its late-twentieth-century defenders.

> [L]iberalism . . . is for making every man his own guide and sovereign master, and letting him think for himself and do exactly as he judges best for himself, giving other men leave to persuade him if they can by evidence, but forbidding him to give way to authority; and still less allowing them to constrain him more than the existence and tolerable security of every man's person and property renders indispensably necessary.[7]

Having said this, Mill proceeded to leave no doubt about how he assessed this kind of liberalism: "It is difficult to conceive a more thorough ignorance of man's nature, and of what is necessary for his happiness or what degree of happiness and virtue he is capable of attaining than this system implies."[8] He was only partially committed to liberal values and ideas.

An analogous mixture of judgments were also directed to ideas which he regarded as being in opposition to liberalism. They concerned the claims of society, order, duty, obligations to others, and authority, and sometimes he associated them with Coleridge, sometimes with Comte. In addition to the very prominent criticisms of them in *On Liberty* and *Autobiography*, he also indicated his appreciation by saying that Coleridge is "the natural means of rescuing from oblivion truths which Tories have forgotten, and which the prevailing schools of Liberalism never knew."[9]

Having offered mixed judgments of both liberalism and its opposite, Mill concluded that "the amount of truth in the two to be about the same." One side (now represented by Comte) had got hold of half the truth, and the so-called liberal or revolutionary school possessed the other half; each saw what the other did not, and seeing it exclusively, drew

---

[7] Mill to John Sterling, 20–22 October 1831, *CW*, *12*, 84.
[8] Ibid.
[9] Coleridge, *CW*, *10*, 163.

consequences from it which, to the other, appeared mischievously absurd.[10] Mill was convinced that on neither side would there be persons with "minds sufficiently capacious and impartial" (254) to combine these opposing but equally important perspectives.[11] He clearly was distancing himself from both sides—from that which defended organicism while being blind to the value of liberty and from that which asserted the importance of liberty to the exclusion of duty, obligation, and authority; indeed, which asserted liberty to the exclusion of the control required to assure the presence of these necessary attributes of a wholesome social order.

If Mill did not claim to be heir only to liberal ideas, it should be asked why so many spokesmen for late-twentieth-century liberalism (the kind that emphasizes negative liberty, radical individualism, the public-private distinction, value neutrality) regard Mill as the quintessential liberal, and why he is so easily, even though incorrectly, portrayed in this way. This claim in part originates in a present-mindedness which looks to Mill's essay as a source of arguments that can bolster a conception of liberty that has wide appeal today. An ideological affinity with Mill is claimed, and it is assumed that his agenda was the same as that of late-twentieth-century liberalism. Thus *On Liberty* is analyzed to establish definitions of the scope and limits of liberty and to find what are called (though Mill did not use these phrases) a principle of liberty and a harm principle. These principles are then attributed to him and are regarded as comprehensive statements of what Mill had to say about individual liberty.

For Mill, however, the arguments in *On Liberty* were much more than this. He thought about liberty in relation to its social and intellectual consequences, in the context of his theory of history, and, above all, with respect to how it would affect the implementation of his plan for cultural reform or, as he called it, moral regeneration. Accordingly, he thought about liberty as a source of religious skepticism, as a stimulus to doubts about the value of Christian morality, as a justification for rejecting and discrediting the customs of existing society, and as a means of putting an end to the prejudices and restrictions that prevented morally and intellectually superior persons from criticizing existing culture and visualizing a morally reconstructed society. By not seriously considering this part of Mill's position, which can be discerned in *On Liberty* but is abundantly evident in his other writings, including contemporary writings, those who look to *On Liberty* as a source of arguments bearing on late-twentieth-century liberal agendas tap into only a small and narrow segment of Mill's

[10] *Auguste Comte and Positivism, CW, 10,* 313.

[11] He had written of Carrel, that he "had an intellect capacious enough to appreciate and sympathize with whatever of truth and ultimate value to mankind there might be in all theories." "Armand Carrel," *CW, 20,* 174.

position, and in presenting it as the entirety, they misrepresent his position. Since liberty would be greatly affected by the way he proposed to achieve moral regeneration and by the kind of society in which it would be achieved, the failure to consider these aspects of his arguments leads to incomplete or false conclusions.

There is another kind of liberalism, quite different from the radically individualistic type and much closer to Mill's position, though hardly identical to it. This type of liberalism is somewhat "communitarian," though those who speak for it need not and usually do not adopt this label. With this type of liberalism liberty is exercised in a community setting in which character is shaped by a moral culture. It is assumed that there will be moral education that teaches virtues, and consequently choices will be freely made but by "situated selves" in a social setting in which custom, mores, and religion define the limits to what can and should be chosen. Liberty restrained in this way falls far short of the fully negative liberty defended by spokesmen for the radically individualistic kind of liberalism. Examples of this moderate liberalism can be found in works of communitarian liberalism (Sandel, Galston) and among Mill's contemporaries, in the thought of Tocqueville, Macaulay, or Bagehot or Acton. It is the kind of liberalism attributed to Mill by those who regard him as having a conception of positive liberty (Semmel) and by Himmelfarb in her characterization of the "other Mill," i.e., other than the Mill of *On Liberty*. Of course there are variations in the conception of liberty among these authors and (where offered) in their accounts of liberalism, but there are also broadly defined similarities. All such writers could agree that liberalism should reject the idea of an exclusively negative liberty and should repudiate the conceptions of the self and the assumptions about moral neutrality associated with the radically individualistic theory of liberalism.

Mill clearly shared with liberals of this kind a strong belief in the importance of liberty tempered by a morality which infiltrates law and custom and public opinion and which is perpetuated by a system of education broadly understood as the socialization process. Those who lived in a society with these features would have a shared respect for the goals and values of their community and would agree about the religion or the secular principles that explained and justified its values. They would, moreover, be restrained in their conduct and would acknowledge limitations on their liberties. Such a society would avoid the disorganization and "violent animosities" which are by-products of liberty directed to antisocial ends.[12] All this is amply explained in, among other places, Mill's account of the conditions for political society, and allusions to it appear in *On Liberty*—for example, where he indicates that it is necessary to balance liberty with discipline and individuality with sociality (254). By recognizing these themes in Mill, those who have defended liberty while also emphasizing the importance of forming character, teaching virtue, and avoiding license can claim that Mill is part of the same liberal tradition. Thus Mill would be associated with nineteenth-century contemporaries such as Tocqueville or Macaulay or Acton and with twentieth-century liberals critical of radical individualism.

In light of these affinities, one might go further in describing Mill's relationship to this kind of liberalism. If one recalls his observation about the liberal school and its opposite each having half the truth, one might consider the possibility that this kind of liberalism has managed to achieve "the reconciling and combining of opposites" (254) which Mill thought necessary. For it does seek to combine liberty with discipline and individuality with sociality.

Although this suggestion has an appearance of plausibility, there is a difficulty arising from the way Mill tilted the balance between liberty and restrictions. For one should recall his expansive definition of harm; his wish to punish even dispositions to do harm (270); his designation of the "moral coercion of public opinion" (223), including "moral reprobation" (279) and "social stigma" (304), as legitimate punishments; and his willingness to visualize a future "consolidation of opinion" (250) and a "general unanimity of sentiment."[13] It should also be recalled that he endorsed a campaign to morally improve those with miserable individuality; he advocated applying the "superadded force of shame" to such persons; and he recommended a general and intrusive censoriousness.[14] It is difficult to imagine Tocqueville or Macaulay or contemporary spokesmen for moderate liberalism being comfortable with the extent of surveillance, intrusion, and restriction proposed by Mill. The difference between Mill and them is revealed by noting that whereas liberals of this type would rely on virtue as a guide and restraint on choices made by free individuals, Mill, while he called for virtue, had no confidence that it would perform this function, and consequently he relied on surveillance, censure, and penalties that caused "*fear* of shame," "*dread* . . . of being disliked or hated," and "*painfulness*" of knowing that one is regarded in this way (emphases added).[15]

[12] "Coleridge," *CW*, *10*, 133–34.
[13] Early Draft, *CW*, *1*, 172.
[14] "Utility of Religion," *CW*, *10*, 421.
[15] "Utility of Religion," *CW*, *10*, 410–11.

The difference between Mill's position and this moderate, somewhat communitarian liberalism is also revealed by comparing his views with Tocqueville's, a contemporary whose understanding of the relation of liberty and social institutions is congenial to twentieth-century critics of the highly individualistic model of liberalism with its emphasis on moral pluralism and negative liberty. While in principle Mill, like Tocqueville, recognized the importance of the cultural and institutional setting in which character is formed, in practice he promoted undermining Christian belief, discrediting Christian morality, and the denial of the authority of custom. He sought, in other words, to do away with the cultural and institutional conditions that Tocqueville relies upon as the source of moral teaching and the moral constraints that were to accompany liberty and prevent it from becoming excessive or being misused. Whereas Mill looked forward to liberty in combination with newly modeled customs and morality and a new secular religion, it is not clear that liberty was more important to him than the elimination of existing custom and religion. This is suggested by his reaction to Tocqueville's *Democracy in America*. He appreciated the book, mainly for its analysis of democracy; but about Tocqueville's major argument that Christian belief was a crucial obstacle to the tyrannical use of democratic power, Mill in two long reviews was silent. In contrast to Tocqueville, for Mill, liberty did not require custom and Christianity for its survival—indeed, it was to be exercised to promote erosion of Christian belief (*On Liberty*, chapter two) and to criticize Christian morality and despotic custom (chapter three). Mill rejected Tocqueville's argument and distanced himself from the moderate liberal position that closely links liberty with custom and religion.

The reason for Mill's distance from this moderate kind of liberalism is to be found in his agenda, which included a reordering of class, property and family relations, the establishing of a new foundation for intellectual and moral authority, and the achievement of a moral regeneration that would subdue selfishness by reshaping human nature. He sought nothing less than a cultural tranformation, and this went far beyond anything visualized by moderate liberals. It was not that he disapproved of this kind of liberalism. In the context of Parliamentary politics in the 1860s, he associated himself with the Liberal party—the party of Gladstone and Acton—and spoke favorably about "advanced Liberalism," which, however, he defined vaguely as "a common allegiance to the spirit of improvement."[16] But while he sympathized with many of its policies, he did not share its underlying philosophy. In sharp contrast to the philosophical assumptions of mid-nineteenth-century liberals, Mill had an underlying

---

[16] W. E. Gladstone [1], *CW*, *28*, 97; he gave an account of how he thought it his duty "to come to the front in defense of advanced Liberalism" in Autobiography, *CW*, *1*, 276.

philosophy that was much more comprehensive. It included his theory of history, his views on the need for moral regeneration, and his assumption that moral authority had to be reinstitutionalized by means of a secular religion. All this fostered his ambition for vast cultural reform, and this made the program and policies of even advanced Liberalism seem piecemeal, unambitious, and deficient. His theories about history, society, and morality, in contrast, brought him to "far bolder aspirations and anticipations of the future."[17] From his more comprehensive perspective, liberalism was valuable but incomplete, and his commitment to liberal values was diminished by another, not obviously compatible belief in the need to subdue and control the inherent selfishness of human nature by imposing order and authority upon it. He upheld liberal values, but only as representing part of the truth, leading him to attempt to "combine and reconcile" liberal and other nonliberal truths. Consequently his position diverges considerably from even that of moderate liberalism. Liberals, even those of the anti-individualistic, somewhat communitarian sort, can regard Mill as congenial only if they ignore his underlying philosophy and all that it called for. If one focuses on all his goals and all that he quietly proposed for reaching them, it will be seen that his position, while it overlaps with that of liberalism, does not coincide with it and even is implicitly critical of it.

[17] "Armand Carrel," *CW*, 20, 184.

INDEX

Acton, Lord John, 79, 231–33
altruism, 103–4, 108, 131, 134–38, 142, 192, 226
Amberley, Lord John, 77, 169
Annan, Noel, 84
Anschutz, R. P., 203
Aristotle, 134
Arnold, Matthew, 222
art, distinguished from science, 27–28
Art of Life, 186–87
Ashley, W. J., 112
atheism: among Mill's circle, 66–67; concealment of (*see* concealment of religious views); impact of a liberated, 95; Mill's, 45, 51n47, 55–58
atheists: "genuinely religious," 147; liberty for, 88–91; persecution of, 76–81, 87–88; prosecution of, 71–75
Auguste Comte and Positivism, 125–28
Austin, John, 66, 222
Austin, Sarah, 68, 79

Bagehot, Walter, 79, 231
Bain, Alexander: the English, 163; equality, 142; Harriet's contribution, 27; penalties and punishment, 15, 188; religious views, 51, 62–64, 80–81, 90, 147–48; rhetoric, 207; self-regarding conduct, 177, 180
Balfour, A. J., 83
ballot, secret, 58, 92, 114, 173–74, 219
Bentham, 113–21
Bentham, Jeremy: Blackstone, 90; Coleridge, opposite of, 35, 37, 113–20; concealment of religious views, 60, 62–63; critique of, 113–15, 191; influence on Mill, 18, 46, 228; limitations of, xiv; religion, 44, 97; rulers, 22; secret ballot, 58; utilitarianism, 103, 108, 133
Berlin, Isaiah, 4
Blackstone, William, 71, 90–91
blasphemous libel, 71–75
Bonald, Louis-Gabriel-Ambroise de, 120
Bradlaugh, Charles, 69, 82, 93
Bridges, John Henry, 128
Brown, Alan, 83
Buckle, Henry, 69, 76, 78

Burke, Edmund, 33
Byron, Lord George, 68

Calvin, John, 137
Calvinism, 160
candor. *See* concealment of religious views
Carlile, Richard, 63, 66, 69, 72–73
Carlyle, Thomas, 45, 52, 55, 59, 68, 151, 156, 216
Carrel, Armand, 139
causation, historical, 32
censure. *See* shame and shaming
Chadwick, Owen, 53, 79
Chambers, Robert, 70
Chapman, John, 60, 77
character: English, 161–64; ethology, 23, 118, 136; faults, 13; impact of Macaulay's critique, 22–23; individuality (*see* individuality); moral transformation of, 20–22; passivity v. individuality, 159–61, 164–67; shaped by shaming, 171–80
Christianity: blasphemous libel, 71–75; Christian belief, 87–91, 95–97, 104–7; concealment of opinion regarding (*see* concealment of religious views); dead belief in, 98–99; free discussion of, 95–100; and intuitionism, critique of, 47; Jesus Christ in, 100–103; Mill's disbelief in (*see* atheism, Mill's); passivity, promotion of, 160–61; and the religion of humanity, 139–41; selfishness of, 43–44, 179; theism, critique of, 48–49; utility of, 97–98. *See also* religion
coercion. *See* moral coercion of public opinion; penalties and punishment
Cohen, Marshall, 8
Coleridge, 113–21
Coleridge, Samuel, xiv, 23, 35, 37–38, 114–21, 228–29
communitarianism, 231–34
competition, 143, 145
compromise, objection to, 33–35
Comte, Auguste: concealment rejected, 93; education, 137; English society, 60; equality and socialism, 142, 146; influence on Mill, xiv, 228–29; public authority of the